THE HOLLYWOOD RENAISSANCE

THE HOLLYWOOD RENAISSANCE

Revisiting American Cinema's Most Celebrated Era

Edited by Peter Krämer and Yannis Tzioumakis

BLOOMSBURY ACADEMIC
NEW YORK • LONDON • OXFORD • NEW DELHI • SYDNEY

BLOOMSBURY ACADEMIC
Bloomsbury Publishing Inc
1385 Broadway, New York, NY 10018, USA

BLOOMSBURY, BLOOMSBURY ACADEMIC and the Diana logo are
trademarks of Bloomsbury Publishing Plc

First published in the United States of America 2018

Cover design: Louise Dugdale
Cover image © Everett Collection/MaryEvans, *Easy Rider*, from left, cinematographer
Laszlo Kovacs, director and co-star Dennis Hopper, on location, 1969

A catalog record for this book is available from the Library of Congress.

ISBN: HB: 978-1-5013-3787-1
       PB: 978-1-5013-3788-8
       ePDF: 978-1-5013-3790-1
       eBook: 978-1-5013-3789-5

Typeset by RefineCatch Limited, Bungay, Suffolk
Printed and bound in the United States of America

To find out more about our authors and books visit www.bloomsbury.com
and sign up for our newsletters.

CONTENTS

LIST OF CONTRIBUTORS

Melis Behlil is an Associate Professor and Chair of Radio, Television and Cinema Department at Kadir Has University in Istanbul. Her book *Hollywood is Everywhere: Global Directors in the Blockbuster Era* came out from Amsterdam University Press in 2016. She also co-hosts a weekly radio show, and is a member of the Turkish Film Critics Association.

Warren Buckland is Reader in Film Studies at Oxford Brookes University. His publications include *Conversations with Christian Metz: Selected Interviews on Film Theory* (co-edited with Daniel Fairfax, 2017), *The Routledge Encyclopedia of Film Theory* (co-edited with Edward Branigan, 2014), *Hollywood Puzzle Films* (ed. 2014), *Film Theory: Rational Reconstructions* (2012) and *Directed by Steven Spielberg* (2006).

Philip Drake is Professor of Film, Media and Communications and Director of the Centre for Communication, Cultural and Media Studies (CCCMS) at Queen Margaret University, Edinburgh. He recently co-edited *Hollywood and the Law* (2015), and has published widely on Hollywood cinema, screen industries, creative industries policy and screen performance. He recently completed a project on Video-On Demand and independent film.

Oliver Gruner is a Lecturer at the University of Portsmouth. His research focuses on historical film, cultural memory and representations of the 1960s. His work has appeared in a number of journals including the *Historical Journal of Film, Radio and Television* and *Rethinking History* and in numerous collections. His book *Screening the Sixties: Hollywood Cinema and the Politics of Memory* was published by Palgrave in 2016.

Peter Krämer is a Senior Fellow in the School of Art, Media and American Studies at the University of East Anglia. He is the author and editor of eight academic books, including *The New Hollywood: From Bonnie and Clyde to Star Wars* (Wallflower, 2005).

A. T. McKenna is Senior Lecturer in Film and Television Studies at the University of Derby. He is the author of *Showman of the Screen: Joseph E. Levine and his Revolutions in Film Promotion* (2016), co-author of *The Man Who Got Carter: Michael Klinger, Independent Film Production and the British Film*

Industry (2013) and co-editor of *Beyond the Bottom Line: The Producer in Film and Television Studies* (2014).

Gary Needham is Senior Lecturer in film and media at the University of Liverpool. He is the author of *Brokeback Mountain* (EUP 2010) and the co-editor of *Asian Cinemas* (EUP 2006), *Queer TV* (Routledge 2009) and *Warhol in Ten Takes* (BFI 2013). He is the co-editor with Yannis Tzioumakis of the book series American Indies (EUP) and Hollywood Centenary (Routledge). He is currently working on a book on Andy Warhol, Edie Sedgwick and Factory filmmaking for Bloomsbury.

Charlene Regester is an Associate Professor in African, African American and Diaspora Studies and Affiliate Faculty with the Global Cinema Studies Minor at the University of North Carolina-Chapel Hill. She is the author of *African American Actresses: The Struggle for Visibility, 1900–1960* (Bloomington: Indiana University Press, 2010) and has written a number of articles on early black cinema.

R. Colin Tait is an Assistant Professor at Texas Christian University. In addition to his co-authored monograph entitled *The Cinema of Steven Soderbergh: Indie Sex, Corporate Lies and Digital Videotape*, he has written extensively on authorship, genre, masculinity and acting in television. He is currently writing the monograph *De Niro's Method: Acting, Authorship and Agency in the New Hollywood* (1967–1983) for the University of Texas Press.

Julie Turnock is Associate Professor of Media and Cinema Studies at the University of Illinois, Urbana/Champaign, in the College of Media. She is the author of *Plastic Reality: Special Effects, Technology, and the Emergence of 1970s Blockbuster Aesthetics,* from Columbia University Press, and has published on special effects, spectacle and technology of the silent and studio era, the 1970s and recent digital cinema in *Cinema Journal, Film History, Film Criticism* and *New Review of Film and Television Studies.*

Yannis Tzioumakis is Reader in Film and Media Industries at the University of Liverpool. He is the author of four books, most recently of *American Independent Cinema: An Introduction*, 2nd edition (Edinburgh University Press, 2017) and co-editor of four collections of essays, most recently of *The Routledge Companion to Cinema and Politics* (Routledge, 2017). He also co-edits the Routledge Hollywood Centenary and the Cinema and Youth Cultures book series (both for Routledge).

Frederick Wasser is Professor in Television and Radio at Brooklyn College CUNY. He has authored books on home video and Steven Spielberg. His articles and book chapters cover a range of topics in the field of media industries. He was a Hollywood sound editor in a previous life.

Justin Wyatt is Assistant Professor of Communication Studies and Film/Media in the Harrington School of Communication and Media at the University of Rhode Island. He is the author of *High Concept: Movies and Marketing in Hollywood* and the co-editor of *Contemporary American Independent Film: From the Margins to the Mainstream.*

ACKNOWLEDGEMENTS

The editors would like to thank Katie Gallof, Senior Commissioning Editor for Film and Media Studies at Bloomsbury Academic, for embracing enthusiastically the idea for this volume from the start and especially for being such a great pleasure to work with. We also would like to thank editorial assistants Susan Krogulski and Erin Duffy for all their support, with Erin in particular helping us significantly with the last details of the manuscript submission.

We would like also to express our gratitude to the contributors to this collection for sharing our vision and for producing some fantastic work as we revisited some of the films that left an indelible mark in American cinema and popular culture at large.

Peter Krämer would like to thank the friends with whom, as a teenager, he started going to late night shows at the local cinema in the mid-1970s, often watching American movies from the late 1960s and early 1970s which, he later realised, belonged to something called the 'Hollywood Renaissance'. They (the friends and the movies) changed his life.

Yannis would like to thank the School of the Arts at the University of Liverpool for a small grant that enabled him to visit the Margaret Herrick Library in Los Angeles in search of some primary sources on the film *Easy Rider* and Bill Osgerby and Oliver Gruner for reading and commenting on early drafts of his chapter. Like Peter, he discovered most of the films of the 'Hollywood Renaissance' period in after midnight double bills in legendary theatres in Thessaloniki, Greece (especially Esperos and Rivoli), which he often attended together with Rigas Goulimaris and Panayiotis Koutakis during their student years in the late 1980s and early 1990s. Alkisti Charsouli was there too as was Leonidas Tzioumakis from 1991 onwards. It was certainly an education! Yannis would like to dedicate this book to Siân and Roman.

INTRODUCTION

Peter Krämer and Yannis Tzioumakis

'The New Cinema: Violence ... Sex ... Art'. With this dramatic headline –
accompanied by publicity stills for *Bonnie and Clyde*, a hugely controversial
recent release – the cover of the *Time* magazine issue of 8 December 1967
declared the beginning of a new era in American film history. Inside the
magazine, the cover story, entitled 'The Shock of Freedom in Films', started with
descriptions of three scenes from movies released in 1967: two women kissing
in *The Fox* (directed by Mark Rydell), a case of severely disorienting editing in
Point Blank (John Boorman) and a bank robbery suddenly shifting from
comedy to graphic violence in *Bonnie and Clyde* (Arthur Penn). 'At first viewing,
these scenes would appear to be photomontages from an underground-film
festival', *Time* commented, but 'they are all from Hollywood', which 'enjoy[s] a
heady new freedom from formula, convention and censorship' and thus 'has at
long last become part of what the French film journal *Cahiers du cinéma* calls
"the furious springtime of world cinema"'.[1]

The *Time* article emphasized that the 'New Cinema' of the United States
happened at the (commercial) heart of the film industry, not just at its margins,
that the very mainstream of American film culture was undergoing a dramatic
transformation, which amounted to a 'renaissance'.[2] Importantly, *Time*
introduced this periodizing term in the context of a warning about the potential
downside of the transformation under way: 'innovation does not in itself
guarantee quality'; 'the relaxation of censorship' often leads to 'euphemistic
clichés' being replaced with 'crass clichés'; there will be 'ambitious failures' and
'cold, calculated imitations'.[3] While generally hopeful about the future of
American cinema, the magazine therefore concluded: 'For all the new talent,
new money and new freedom available, it is not certain that Hollywood can or
will sustain the *burden* of living in a renaissance'.[4]

As it turned out, in commercial terms, the years ahead were among the most
difficult in Hollywood history, with annual ticket sales dropping to record lows
in the early 1970s, probably because the daring, innovative 'New Cinema', with
its emphasis, as the *Time* cover put it, on violence, sex and art, alienated many
(potential) cinemagoers, so that they stopped going to the movies altogether,
with dramatically increasing ticket prices also bound to have played a role in
this decline (the average ticket cost almost 50 per cent more in 1973 than it had
in 1967).[5] At the same time, the major Hollywood studios (Columbia, Fox,
MGM, Paramount, United Artists, Universal and Warner) continued to release

about 150 films every year (except for 1968 which saw 177 releases); these had to compete for market share with well over 200 hundred (American-made and imported) films released by independent distributors annually.[6] Average production and marketing budgets were steadily increasing in the late 1960s and early 1970s across the film industry and especially for major studio releases (among them numerous superexpensive blockbusters).[7] As a result of all this, between 1969 and 1971 five of the seven major studios made a loss in at least one year, if not across the period as a whole.[8]

This grim financial picture contrasts sharply with the high esteem in which quite a few of the films released in the late 1960s and early 1970s have been held. Fifty years on from *Time* magazine's worries about 'crass clichés', 'ambitious failures' and 'cold, calculated imitations', the verdict of cinephiles, critics and scholars about the period would appear to be almost unanimous: the late 1960s and early 1970s *were* indeed a kind of golden age in American film history, with a wide range of formally and thematically challenging films made (and in many cases released with great success at the box office) during this period having stood the test of time. For example, in *Sight and Sound*'s 2012 survey of international critical opinion concerning 'The Greatest Films of All Time', the top 100 include six Hollywood productions from the years 1967 to 1974: *2001: A Space Odyssey* (MGM, Stanley Kubrick, 1968; at no. 6), *Once Upon a Time in the West* (Paramount, Sergio Leone, 1968; jointly at no. 78), *The Wild Bunch* (Warner, Sam Peckinpah, 1969; no. 84), *The Godfather* (Paramount, Francis Ford Coppola, 1972; no. 21), *The Godfather Part II* (Paramount, Coppola, 1974; no. 31) and *Chinatown* (Paramount, Roman Polanski, 1974; jointly at no. 78).[9]

These and other American films from the period, as well as the filmmakers most closely associated with it, have been the subject of an enormous amount of scholarly (and also of popular) writing, most of which takes a largely favourable view of their achievements.[10] While some of this writing, implicitly or explicitly referring back to the above quoted *Time* cover story, uses the label 'Hollywood Renaissance',[11] the majority employs other periodizing terms such as 'New Hollywood'[12] or 'American New Wave',[13] or even 'the Seventies' (whereby it is usually understood that this is not so much referring to the actual decade as to a series of developments that started in the late 1960s and continued into the 1970s).[14] Some of the most celebrated filmmakers of the late 1960s and 1970s are frequently grouped together in generational terms as 'whiz kids', 'movie brats' (a.k.a. the 'film generation' or 'film school generation') or even the 'sex-drugs-and-rock 'n' roll generation'.[15] Among the dozens of books (and countless journal essays and book chapters) about key films and filmmakers of the late 1960s and 1970s, there are many which signal already in their titles that they conceive of their object of study as a period of greatness (perhaps the last one in Hollywood history) and of dramatic, even revolutionary change, (temporarily) giving rise to a 'new' American cinema. This is perhaps best exemplified by Mark Harris's *Scenes from a Revolution: The Birth of the New*

Hollywood and the edited collection *The Last Great American Picture Show: New Hollywood Cinema in the 1970s.*[16]

Before outlining what the present collection has to add to this rich literature, it is worth briefly reflecting on what it means to declare that something is 'new' in Hollywood cinema, so new indeed that it amounts to a break in its history, a point at which a different kind of cinema comes into existence – in other words a moment of 'rebirth' (the literal translation of the French 'renaissance'). It is also useful to sketch what is usually said about this reborn cinema, notably about its particular qualities, its scope (as not all American films of the period are characterized by the newness observed by *Time* magazine) and its historical context (most importantly, the conditions which helped bring this new cinema into existence and later on brought it to an end).

To begin with, it is important to note that the *Time* cover story from 8 December 1967 was by no means the first press announcement about the emergence of a new cinema in the United States. Claims about there being something fundamentally new in American cinema had been made with astonishing regularity from the late 1940s onwards, with American critics variously writing about a 'new maturity', the 'New Movie', a 'new art of the movies', a 'new Hollywood', the 'New American Cinema' and 'America's "new wave"' – all this initially with regards to films made between the late 1940s and the early 1960s, whereby in most cases this newness was ascribed to Hollywood's output rather than to that of avant-garde or otherwise non-mainstream filmmakers in the United States.[17]

When discussing exactly which innovations had been introduced in prominent studio releases, writers at different times foregrounded an increased 'realism' with regards to both subject matter and film style (this realism drawing both on documentary filmmaking and on European art cinema); a more pronounced engagement with social reality, especially through quite topical and definitely serious subject matter (often with a left-liberal, progressive slant); the self-conscious foregrounding of form and style, inviting audiences to understand films as works of art (in turn to be understood in relation to the directors making them); protagonists (mostly male and young and often rebellious) who, due to their characterization and the actors' performance styles, could be at times unsympathetic and difficult to relate to; the loosening of the cause-and-effect chains of the stories being told (in favour, among other things, of self-contained spectacle or the foregrounding of artistic elements associated with a particular director) and also on occasion ambivalent endings, which might encourage audiences to actively interpret the film, looking for hidden meanings; and, last but not least, a more explicit depiction of sexuality and violence.[18]

It has to be emphasized that these were observations made by journalists and other commentators between the late 1940s and early 1960s about contemporary developments. They are surprisingly similar to the claims that were made by press reports like the *Time* cover story, and later on by film scholars, about the key characteristics of the films of the Hollywood Renaissance.[19] What is more, the explanations usually given for innovations in film form, style and content during the late 1960s and early 1970s are similar to those offered by earlier writers for filmic developments from the 1940s to the 1960s: the liberalization of (self-)censorship in mainstream American cinema; the impact of European art cinema and of developments in the other arts; the fundamental restructuring of the major Hollywood studios (referring to the dissection of fully vertically integrated companies into producer-distributors on the one hand and theatre chains on the other in the wake of anti-trust rulings in the late 1940s, whereas the Hollywood Renaissance is often said to be connected to the disruption brought about by conglomerate takeovers of film studios across the 1960s); the rise of independent filmmaking (with varying definitions of 'independence' being applied to the immediate post-war decades and to the late 1960s and 1970s); the overall decline in ticket sales and the increased importance of the youth audience (much commented on as the key demographic already in the 1940s and 1950s, and then again in the late 1960s); the influence of television (on cinema audiences and filmmakers in both the 1950s and the 1960s); the training and early careers of key filmmakers outside the studio system (a background in theatre being of particular importance from the 1940s to the 1960s, with television directors also making a huge impact from the 1950s onwards, whereas the careers of most film school graduates only got going in the 1970s).[20]

It would seem, then, that post-war Hollywood history is perhaps best understood in terms of an ongoing process of filmic innovation, driven by a fairly persistent set of contextual factors (liberalization, developments in other arts and media, film industrial reorganization, the increasing importance of youth in an ever-shrinking cinema audience, the decreasing importance of in-house training for studio filmmakers, etc.). This suggests that one has to be very cautious about making claims concerning fundamental breaks and turning points in American film history. It is possible that a systematic comparison of American cinema in the late 1940s and 1950s with that of the late 1960s and 1970s would reveal that in the latter case filmic innovations are more fundamental and comprehensive than in the former, and that the rate of change across the later period is higher than across the earlier one. But it is not easy to see how one would conduct such a comparison.[21] This also applies to familiar claims about the unprecedented rapidity and intensity of sociopolitical changes across the 1960s and into the 1970s (to do, for example, with the later phases of the Civil Rights movement, the sexual revolution, the Vietnam War, various assassinations, the counterculture and second wave feminism), which are understood to have influenced Hollywood. How could one determine whether these developments were indeed more profound than those associated with, for example, the Great Depression, the Second World War or post-war prosperity? It is advisable, then, not to overstate the unique qualities of the late 1960s and early 1970s in American (film) history.

Nevertheless, it is of course possible to study the group of innovative films associated with this period in their own right, without necessarily having to make grand claims about Hollywood history – although, quite understandably, we will always be inclined to do so to give our analyses more rhetorical weight. This rhetoric can be justified with reference to the fact that the films and filmmakers of the Hollywood Renaissance have, as previously mentioned, been the subject of an unusual amount of critical writing, which exceeds, it would seem, the amount of writing about the key films and filmmakers of other periods (if we exclude the exceptional cases of D. W. Griffith, Charles Chaplin, Alfred Hitchcock and Orson Welles).

These reflections raise the deceptively simple question of how to constitute our film corpus, that is the Hollywood Renaissance canon. Obviously, this canon does *not* include all the many hundreds of American films made and released during the period, but only a very small subset (although some writing about the Hollywood Renaissance might encourage readers to mistake the part for the whole). At this point in time, the most obvious approach to identifying the films in this subset would be to look at the existing scholarly literature about the 'Hollywood Renaissance' and create a list of the titles they cover (or perhaps of the titles regularly covered, thus leaving out highly idiosyncratic choices by some authors). One of the problems with this approach is the fact that, as mentioned earlier, writers often use other labels, most notably 'New Hollywood', to discuss the same phenomenon (that is, the prominence of formally and thematically challenging films in Hollywood cinema of the late 1960s and 1970s).

To further complicate matters, yet other authors employ 'New Hollywood' to refer not to a specific subset of films but to the American film industry and American film culture as a whole and, even more confusingly, they do so with regards to different periods. Thus, 'New Hollywood' might be understood as American cinema between the late 1960s and the mid-1970s, or *since* the mid-1970s, or indeed *both* periods combined.[22] In most writing the two periods are in fact contrasted with each other, with the mid-1970s serving as another historical turning point (closely associated with the release of *Jaws* [Steven Spielberg, 1975] and/or *Star Wars* [George Lucas, 1977]), separating the, by and large, more highly esteemed cinema of the late 1960s and early to mid-1970s from the cinema of later years. In his book *New Hollywood Cinema*, Geoff King marks the difference with the following chapter titles: 'New Hollywood, Version I: The Hollywood Renaissance' and 'New Hollywood, Version II: Blockbusters and Corporate Hollywood'.[23] There is thus considerable scope for misunderstandings when writing about the Hollywood Renaissance, the New Hollywood, etc., and using these labels should certainly always be accompanied by an explanation of what they are meant to refer to in a given context.

As mentioned earlier, for the purposes of this book 'Hollywood Renaissance' refers to a group of American films which were released from the late 1960s onwards and have widely been regarded (at the time of their release and later) as being particularly innovative or challenging. When examining the existing critical literature on this group of films, it is noticeable that 1967 is most often chosen as the starting point (with two of that year's releases – *Bonnie and Clyde* and *The Graduate* [Mike Nichols] – almost always, and the *Time* cover story sometimes, getting a mention), while there is usually no clearly defined end point. This has a lot to do with the fact that discussions are almost invariably organized in terms of directorial oeuvres, which in most cases span several decades. There are some exceptions to this focus on directors; most notably, *Easy Rider* (1969) is always mentioned, without necessarily highlighting the importance of its director Dennis Hopper and any other films he directed. But, by and large, the Hollywood Renaissance is defined in terms of films made by a certain group of directors from 1967 onwards, whereby the late 1960s and 1970s are regarded as a – perhaps *the* – highpoint of their careers. For each of these directors critics tend to identify a significant decline in the quality (and often also in the quantity) of their output at some point in the 1970s or even as late as the early 1980s, which is why there is no agreed upon, clear-cut ending of the Hollywood Renaissance. However, there does appear to be a general agreement that, as a group, the directors associated with the Hollywood Renaissance did most of their best work between 1967 and 1974, with overall decline setting in thereafter.

So as to get a sense of who these directors are, it is worth taking a closer look at David Cook's volume on the 1970s in Scribner's authoritative *History of American Cinema* series; about a fifth of this book is taken up by a chapter entitled 'The Auteur Cinema: Directors and Directions in the "Hollywood Renaissance"'.[24] Despite the fact that this is a volume about the 1970s, the chapter starts with comments on 1967 as an important turning point (*Bonnie and Clyde* and *The Graduate* being highlighted) and on various developments leading up to it. The chapter also discusses the importance of *Easy Rider* before moving on to an extensive discussion of the work of individual directors, which accounts for 85 of its 90 pages. What follows is a listing of these directors with the headings under which Cook groups them:

- 'Major Independents from the 1960s': Penn, Kubrick, Peckinpah, Robert Altman
- 'Auteurs *Manqué* and *Maudit*': Nichols, Peter Bogdanovich, William Friedkin, Bob Rafelson, Hal Ashby, Alan Pakula
- 'Niche Figures': Paul Mazursky, Bob Fosse, Woody Allen, Mel Brooks
- 'Eccentrics': John Cassavetes, Terrence Malick
- '"Film Generation" Auteurs, or the "Hollywood Brats"': Coppola, Lucas, Spielberg, Martin Scorsese, Brian De Palma, John Milius, Paul Schrader.

While other authors may exclude some of these names or include some names missing from this list, it *is* typical for the literature on the Hollywood Renaissance. This literature can therefore be said to deal almost exclusively with films made by white, male directors born between the early 1920s and the late 1940s (whereby many of these directors were in fact hyphenates, that is writer-directors, director-producers or writer-director-producers). What is more, the vast majority of the films in question focus on white, male protagonists, mostly in their twenties or thirties (whereas the directors tended to be in their thirties and forties when they made these films). Perhaps not surprisingly, most of the people writing about the Hollywood Renaissance have been white males as well – which is reflected in the composition of the team of contributors to this collection.

This rather extreme white male bias makes it especially important to point out that the Hollywood Renaissance canon constitutes only a small fraction of the output of the American film industry of the late 1960s and 1970s, a period during which African-American directors, for the first time, made inroads into Hollywood.[25] One could also point to isolated female directors starting their Hollywood careers in the 1970s, but it is perhaps more important to challenge the overwhelming emphasis on directors in the literature on the Hollywood Renaissance and indeed in much of Film Studies as a whole (despite all the critical and theoretical debates about, and challenges to, 'auteurism').[26] Of all film professions, directing has always been one of the *most* male-dominated (topped perhaps only by cinematography). Paying more attention to the work of, for example, writers, actors, editors, musicians, sound designers and producers immediately reveals the presence and important contributions of women (and also of some minorities), even in the Hollywood Renaissance canon. At the same time, shifting the focus away from directorial oeuvres opens up opportunities for contextualizing individual films in diverse and complex ways. Rather than concentrating on the continuities and differences between films made by the same director, one can instead aim to reconstruct the collaborative process of making a particular film and its specific film industrial, cultural and sociopolitical circumstances.

The present collection is designed to show how this can be done for a range of films from 1966 to 1974, with each chapter focused, more or less narrowly, on a particular title (with numerous other films being mentioned, and in some cases briefly analysed, as well). The selection includes both films securely positioned within the Hollywood Renaissance canon and films which were certainly innovative as far as studio filmmaking at the time was concerned but have rarely, if ever, been mentioned in critical debates about the period. *Who's Afraid of Virginia Woolf?* stands out because it was released before the watershed year of 1967. Yet, as Chapter 1 shows, it was the production and release of this film that brought about important changes in Hollywood's system of self-censorship, which in turn made it possible for major studio productions to deal with previously taboo subject matter and to do so in an unprecedentedly explicit and graphic manner.

Hollywood releases breaking long-standing taboos to do with sex, violence, race relations, religion, drugs, politics and much else, most of them also departing from the formal and stylistic conventions of classical Hollywood cinema, started to have a significant, in some cases huge, impact on critics and audiences from 1967 onwards, among them *Bonnie and Clyde*, *The Graduate*, *Easy Rider*, *Midnight Cowboy* (John Schlesinger, 1969), *Medium Cool* (Haskell Wexler, 1969), *Zabriskie Point* (Michelangelo Antonioni, 1970), *Harold and Maude* (Ashby, 1971), *Lady Sings the Blues* (Sidney J. Furie, 1972) and *Mean Streets* (Scorsese, 1973), all of which are the subject of individual chapters in this collection. *Funny Girl* (William Wyler, 1968) is included because it breaks one of the most fundamental rules of mainstream cinema, which demands that leading ladies are widely regarded as beautiful, while *2001: A Space Odyssey* is so unconventional that, in certain sequences, it is hardly recognizable as narrative filmmaking at all. *The Conversation* (Coppola, 1974), the subject of the book's final chapter, is enormously inventive in its sound design.

While the analysis of film form, style and content is central to some chapters, all case studies examine production histories and processes, with particular emphasis on the economic underpinnings and the collaborative nature of film production. Thus in addition to, or instead of, the usual focus on directors, this collection covers the operations of, and relationships between, the major studios and independent producers (and production companies), and the work of writers, editors, actors and special effects personnel. In doing so, individual chapters explore the connection between particular films and their sources in other media (notably publishing, music and the theatre) as well as developments both in Hollywood genres and in non-mainstream filmmaking (European art, exploitation, avant-garde and underground cinema). What unites all chapters is their emphasis on previously neglected or under-researched perspectives related to the films they discuss, and on the ways in which these perspectives can help us enhance our understanding of the Hollywood Renaissance as a whole.

Chapter 1 is concerned with the extent to which *Who's Afraid of Virginia Woolf?* can be seen as an American art film, which initiated a number of developments directly related to the Hollywood Renaissance. It did so especially by prompting what was in effect the suspension of the Production Code in 1966, when, in the wake of special arrangements made for the release of *Who's Afraid of Virginia Woolf?*, the Production Code Administration introduced the 'suggested for mature audiences' label which in turn led to the Code's replacement with a ratings system in 1968. Chapter 2 concentrates on editors and the ways in which they started transforming the syntax of film language in American cinema. The chapter focuses primarily on Dede Allen and her work on *Bonnie and Clyde*, while also referencing the groundbreaking work of Ralph Rosenblum on *The Pawnbroker* (Sidney Lumet) which preceded the Hollywood Renaissance in 1965 and of Sam O'Steen on *The Graduate*. *The Graduate* is the key film to be examined in Chapter 3, though the emphasis here is on its producer Joseph E. Levine and his company Embassy Pictures. The chapter considers how Levine used *The Graduate* to transform his small independent exploitation company into a mainstream studio that was taken over by the Avco corporation months after the film's release and great success at the box office, while also more broadly examining the corporate machinations that have impacted the period in question.

Chapter 4 explores the reasons why Columbia Pictures cast Barbra Streisand, a young, unconventionally looking performer with no prior movie experience, as the lead of its hugely expensive musical *Funny Girl*. The chapter considers her cross-media stardom and the enormous impact of film musicals at the US box office in the mid-1960s, and argues that, while the emphasis on youth and ethnicity in *Funny Girl* and Streisand's later films is perfectly in line with the Hollywood Renaissance canon, as a powerful woman working in female-oriented genres Streisand also was completely at odds with it. Chapter 5 focuses on another key film of the period that, like *Funny Girl*, sits uneasily in studies of the Hollywood Renaissance, the effects-laden science fiction epic *2001: A Space Odyssey*. Rather than offering yet another Kubrick-centred discussion of the film, the chapter focuses on the highly complex and innovative work of the special effects team that drew both on traditional Hollywood techniques and avant-garde filmmaking, and established a new ideal for the pictorial 'realism' of later science fiction, fantasy and action blockbusters.

With 1969 representing a peak year of sorts in the history of the counterculture and arguably the Hollywood Renaissance, the collection includes three chapters dealing with key films from that year. Chapter 6 examines *Medium Cool*, a film that has been considered by many as the epitome of a political Hollywood cinema, especially in the ways in which it mixes a fictional story with the real historical events of the 1968 Democratic Convention in Chicago. Through an examination of its production history and its reception, the chapter challenges this view by demonstrating the limitations of the film's political project and emphasizing instead its fashionable, exploitable elements. Chapter 7 undertakes a similar questioning of accounts that have seen *Easy Rider* as an independent production representing Hollywood at the peak of its openness, creativity and willingness to take chances. Finding contradictions in existing academic and popular accounts of the film's production and aiming to separate mythology from fact through recourse to a wide range of sources, the chapter argues that Columbia Pictures, the film's distributor, was much closer to the film from the start than has previously been suggested. The last film from 1969 to be considered in this collection is *Midnight Cowboy*. Here the emphasis is on the film's relationship to underground cinema, especially as this was represented by the films of Andy Warhol which were making a splash in the New York scene of the mid-1960s. Chapter 8 discusses the complex relationship of *Midnight Cowboy* with this kind of cinema and makes a broader argument about the need to explore the impact of underground cinema. This impact has been almost completely ignored in the existing literature on the Hollywood Renaissance which tends to privilege the influence of European art cinema instead.

Chapter 9 develops a related argument by examining Italian filmmaker Michelangelo Antonioni's *Zabriskie Point*. Placing Antonioni within the long history of European filmmakers working at some point in their career in the United States and exploring the production history, the form and content as well as the disappointing commercial performance and critical reception of *Zabriskie Point*, the chapter complicates the impact of art cinema on the Hollywood Renaissance by demonstrating that American cinema in turn influenced Antonioni and other art cinema directors. Chapter 10 focuses on Hal Ashby's *Harold and Maude* so as to explore the politics of intersectionality, which, it argues, makes for often disruptive ideas and representations, even by the standards of the newly permissive environment of the time. With *Harold and Maude* (and Ashby's earlier film *The Landlord* [1970]) failing to find an audience during their original release, the chapter then considers the extent to which the film's later success and its transformation into a cult object weakens its politics while at the same time contributing to the marginalization of Ashby as a Hollywood Renaissance auteur.

Chapter 11 picks up another film which is rarely considered in the history of the Hollywood Renaissance, *Lady Sings the Blues*. With African Americans almost completely excluded from most studies of the Hollywood Renaissance and histories of African-American contributions to American cinema often associating the early 1970s very narrowly with so-called 'blaxploitation' films, this chapter complicates existing accounts. Following a detailed production history of the film which highlights the involvement of African Americans, the chapter argues that *Lady Sings the Blues* is a film marked by contradictions, on the one hand making use of the new freedom in filmmaking to put the experiences of a black female character (blues legend Billie Holiday), especially her sexual experiences and drug addiction, at the centre of a crossover production, while, on the other hand, framing this story in problematic ways to do especially with male agency and racial politics.

Unlike Chapter 11, the next chapter discusses a very well-known and much discussed film of the period, *Mean Streets*. Rather than offering another auteur study on what is arguably the most discussed filmmaker in Hollywood cinema of the last fifty years, Martin Scorsese, Chapter 12 focuses on the contribution to this film of one of its stars, Robert De Niro, with a view to develop an approach that sees this and other productions in which De Niro and Scorsese collaborated as the product of a creative pair. Using archival material, the chapter shows the extent to which De Niro shaped *Mean Streets* and thus influenced the emerging identity of Scorsese as a filmmaker. The collection finishes with a chapter on *The Conversation*, which discusses the film in relation to its literary and filmic models, and to the work of Walter Murch for both Coppola and Lucas during the 1970s. Chapter 13 argues that Murch's sound design for *The Conversation* pulled back from some of his earlier experimentation, thus turning *The Conversation* into a transitional film which ultimately paved the way for the new sound aesthetic dominating Hollywood blockbusters, among them *Star Wars* and *Apocalypse Now* (Coppola, 1979), from the late 1970s onwards.

The chapters in this collection focus on the years 1966–74, but, as noted, they often point to later developments as well. To conclude this introduction, it is worth providing a brief overview of the American film industry's output and financial performance from the mid-1970s to the early 1980s. *The Conversation* was one of 129 films released by the major studios in 1974.[27] As mentioned earlier, with the exception of 1968 (177 titles) the studios had been releasing around 150 films from the mid-1960s to the early 1970s, but in the mid-1970s this figure was reduced drastically, with a low point of 78 in 1977 while in the surrounding years it was in the region of 100 (a third less than the previous average of 150).[28]

At the same time, attendance levels, which had been at their historical low point in the early 1970s (the absolute nadir being 1971, with 16 million tickets sold every week), made a dramatic recovery, with 20 million weekly ticket sales in 1975 (25 per cent more than in 1971); with the exception of 1976 (18 million), weekly sales stayed at or exceeded 20 million in subsequent years.[29] Annual box office revenues in the United States almost doubled between 1971 and 1975 (helped by the ongoing rise in ticket prices) and, with the exception of 1976 and 1980, continued to increase until the mid-1980s (the figure for 1984 was almost twice that for 1975).[30] While average production and marketing costs for studio releases also continued their long-term increase, the reduction in the number of films being released and the rapid growth of box office revenues in the United States (and also, probably, abroad) meant that income far exceeded expenditures and studio profits recovered from the crisis years of 1969–71, reaching record levels by the end of the 1970s.[31]

In the literature about the Hollywood Renaissance, the studios' financial turnaround across the 1970s is closely associated with the record-breaking box office success of films like *Jaws* and *Star Wars*, and with a perceived decline in the overall quality of American films, due to decreasing support for the work of the great auteurs. But we should perhaps be cautious with such general judgements. For example, the period 1975–80 does remarkably well in *Sight and Sound*'s 2012 survey of international critical opinion, with the following five films making it into the top 100: *Barry Lyndon* (Warner, Kubrick, 1975; at no. 59), *Nashville* (Paramount, Altman, 1975; no. 77), *Taxi Driver* (Columbia, Scorsese, 1976; no. 31), *Apocalypse Now* (United Artists, Coppola, 1979; no. 14) and *Raging Bull* (United Artists, Scorsese, 1980; no. 53).[32] While this is by no means proof of the overall quality of American filmmaking after 1974, it does at least suggest that the work of the Hollywood Renaissance auteurs could co-exist with the film industry's increased focus on, and success with, genre films such as *Jaws* and *Star Wars*.

What is more, these and most of the other big breakaway hits from the mid-1970s to the mid-1980s were the products of two filmmakers who are usually included (at least with their early films) in the roster of Hollywood Renaissance auteurs, namely Steven Spielberg and George Lucas.[33] This can serve as further confirmation of the claim that the filmmakers who rose to prominence, or got their start, in Hollywood in the late 1960s and early 1970s made a truly lasting impact, which helps to explain the continued engagement of critics and historians with this period. Yet, as many chapters in this book argue, it is high time to pay much more attention to people other than directors involved in the process of filmmaking during the Hollywood Renaissance, to consider their individual approaches to the tasks at hand and the collaborative relationships they enter and to examine the immediate production circumstances for their work, including contractual and financial arrangements as well as corporate strategies. Despite the enormous amount of existing writing about the Hollywood Renaissance, there is so much yet to be found out.

Notes

1   Stefan Kanfer, 'The Shock of Freedom in Films', *Time*, 8 December 1967, 66–76, reprinted in *The Movies: An American Idiom*, ed. Arthur F. McClure (Rutherford, NJ: Fairleigh Dickinson University Press, 1971), 322–33, here 322.

2   Kanfer, 'The Shock of Freedom in Films', 333.

3   Kanfer, 'The Shock of Freedom in Films', 333.

4   Kanfer, 'The Shock of Freedom in Films', 333. Emphasis added.

5   Joel W. Finler, *The Hollywood Story* (London: Octopus, 1988), 288.

6   Finler, *The Hollywood Story*, 280.

7   Alex Ben Block (ed.), *George Lucas's Blockbusting* (New York: itbooks, 2010), 415, 417. Due to ticket price inflation, total box office revenues in the United States were also increasing (despite falling ticket sales), but this increase would appear to have been smaller than that of production and marketing budgets; Finler, *The Hollywood Story*, 280.

8   Finler, *The Hollywood Story*, 286–7.

9   'The Top 100 Films', *Sight and Sound*, September 2012, 56. It is also remarkable that the 2007 edition of the American Film Institute's list of the '100 Greatest American Films of All Time', compiled by a jury of 1,500 film artists, critics and historians, includes seventeen titles released from 1967 to 1974 (http://www.afi.com/100years/movies10.aspx). As far as the opinion of film fans, rather than film professionals, is concerned, it is worth noting that the Internet Movie Database's users' chart places *The Godfather* and *The Godfather Part II* at numbers 2 and 3 (http://www.imdb.com/chart/top, last accessed 1 November 2017).

10 An important exception to the usual celebration of the Hollywood Renaissance is the sustained critique developed in James Bernardoni, *The New Hollywood: What the Movies Did with the New Freedom of the Seventies* (Jefferson, NC: McFarland, 1991).

11 See, for example, Diane Jacobs, *Hollywood Renaissance* (South Brunswick, NJ: Barnes, 1977); Glenn Man, *Radical Visions: American Film Renaissance, 1967–1976* (Westport, CT: Greenwood, 1994); Daniel Smith-Rowsey, *Star Actors in the Hollywood Renaissance: Representing Rough Rebels* (Basingstoke: Palgrave, 2013); Kevin Alexander, 'The Auteur Renaissance, 1968–1980', in *Screenwriting*, ed. Andrew

Horton and Julian Hoxter (New Brunswick, NJ: Rutgers University Press, 2014), 81–100; and Chapter 4 ('The Auteur Cinema: Directors and Directions in the "Hollywood Renaissance"') of David A. Cook, *Lost Illusions: American Cinema in the Shadow of Watergate and Vietnam* (New York: Scribner's, 2000), 67–157. The idea of a renaissance is also invoked in the title of James Morrison (ed.), *Hollywood Reborn: Movie Stars of the 1970s* (New Brunswick, NJ: Rutgers University Press, 2010). Confusingly, the following book about American cinema between the late 1930s and early 1960s also carries 'Hollywood Renaissance' in the title; Sam B. Girgus, *Hollywood Renaissance: The Cinema of Democracy in the Era of Ford, Capra, and Kazan* (Cambridge: Cambridge University Press, 1998).

12 Recent examples include Derek Nystrom, 'The New Hollywood', in Part IV ('1966–1975') of *The Wiley-Blackwell History of American Film Volume III: 1946–1975*, ed. Cynthia Lucia, Roy Grundmann and Art Simon (Malden, MA: Wiley-Blackwell, 2012), 409–34; Henrik Gustafsson, *Out of Site: Landscape and Cultural Reflexivity in New Hollywood Cinema 1969–1974* (Saarbrücken: AV Akademikerverlag, 2012); Tom Symmons, *The New Hollywood Historical Film, 1967–1978* (Basingstoke: Palgrave, 2016); Adam O'Brien, *Transactions with the World: Ecocriticism and the Environmental Sensibility of the New Hollywood* (Oxford: Berghahn, 2016); and Nicholas Godfrey, *The Limits of Auteurism: Case Studies in the Critically Constructed New Hollywood* (New Brunswick, NJ: Rutgers University Press, 2018).

13 For a recent example, see 'The American New Wave: A Retrospective', international conference at Bangor University, 4–6 July 2017.

14 See, for example, Peter Lev, *American Films of the 70s: Conflicting Visions* (Austin: University of Texas Press, 2000) and Jonathan Kirchner, *Hollywood's Last Golden Age: Politics, Society, and the Seventies Film in America* (Ithaca, NY: Cornell University Press, 2012). Similarly, books about the 1960s sometimes emphasize key developments which carried over from the late 1960s into the early 1970s, e.g. J. Hoberman, *The Dream Life: Movies, Media, and the Mythology of the Sixties* (New York: The New Press, 2003).

15 See, for example, Chapter 5 ('The Whiz Kids') of James Monaco, *American Film Now: The People, the Power, the Money, the Movies* (New York: New American Library, 1979), 139–84; Michael Pye and Lynda Myles, *The Movie Brats: How the Film Generation Took Over Hollywood* (New York: Holt, Rinehart and Winston, 1979); Chapter 14 ('The Film School Generation') of John Belton, *American Cinema/American Culture* (New York: McGraw-Hill, 1994), 298–321; and Peter Biskind, *Easy Riders, Raging Bulls: How the Sex-Drugs-and-Rock 'n' Roll Generation Saved Hollywood* (New York: Simon and Schuster, 1998). In addition, Robert Kolker has grouped some of the key filmmakers of the late 1960s and 1970s together without attaching a generational label in *A Cinema of Loneliness: Penn, Kubrick, Coppola, Scorsese, Altman* (Oxford: Oxford University Press, 1980). In the introduction to the book's second addition, he makes a point of using modernism as a periodizing term by referring to 'the brief modernist movement in commercial American cinema'; Robert Kolker, *A Cinema of Loneliness: Penn, Kubrick, Scorsese, Spielberg, Altman* (Oxford: Oxford University Press, 1988), xii.

16 Mark Harris, *Scenes from a Revolution: The Birth of the New Hollywood* (London: Canongate, 2008); and Thomas Elsaesser, Alexander Horwath and Noel King (ed.), *The Last Great American Picture Show: New Hollywood Cinema in the 1970s*

(Amsterdam: Amsterdam University Press, 2004). An interesting variant of this strong emphasis on dramatic change is the title of Elaine M. Bapis, *Camera and Action: American Film as Agent of Social Change, 1965–1975* (Jefferson, NC: McFarland, 2008).

17 Peter Krämer, 'Post-classical Hollywood', in *The Oxford Guide to Film Studies*, ed. John Hill and Pamela Church Gibson (Oxford: Oxford University Press, 1998), 291–6.

18 Krämer, 'Post-classical Hollywood', 291–6.

19 For more on the journalistic and scholarly debates of the late 1960s and 1970s, see Krämer, 'Post-classical Hollywood', 296–305. It is perhaps worth noting that there is comparatively little academic work which systematically explores the formal and stylistic characteristics of films associated with the Hollywood Renaissance. Important exceptions include David Bordwell, Janet Staiger and Kristin Thompson, *The Classical Hollywood Cinema: Film Style & Mode of Production to 1960* (London: Routledge & Kegan Paul, 1985), 367–77; numerous references to developments of the late 1960s and early 1970s in David Bordwell, *The Way Hollywood Tells It: Story and Style in Modern Movies* (Berkeley: University of California Press, 2006); and Todd Berliner, *Hollywood Incoherent: Narration in Seventies Cinema* (Austin: University of Texas Press, 2010). For detailed discussions of sound and of the presentation of violence and sex, see Jay Beck, *Designing Sound: Audiovisual Aesthetics in 1970s American Cinema* (New Brunswick, NJ: Rutgers University Press, 2016); Stephen Prince, *Savage Cinema: Sam Peckinpah and the Rise of Ultraviolent Movies* (London: Athlone, 1998); and Linda Williams, *Screening Sex* (Durham, NC: Duke University Press, 2008), 68–180.

20 Once again, see Krämer, 'Post-classical Hollywood', 291–305.

21 An important starting point could be David Bordwell's recent study of the innovations of Hollywood cinema between the late 1930s and early 1950s; if this were to be complemented by a similarly wide-ranging study of the late 1960s and 1970s, a direct comparison between periods would be possible; David Bordwell, *How 1940s Filmmakers Changed Movie Storytelling* (Chicago: University of Chicago Press, 2017). If one focuses only on Hollywood's biggest hits, rather than its overall output or its most innovative films, then it is actually quite easy to show that the period 1967–76 is very different from earlier and later historical eras; see Peter Krämer, *The New Hollywood: From Bonnie and Clyde to Star Wars* (London: Wallflower, 2005).

22 This is discussed in Krämer, 'Post-classical Hollywood', 301–5. Recent examples for expanded definitions of 'New Hollywood' include Krämer, *The New Hollywood*, and Geoff King, *New Hollywood Cinema: An Introduction* (London: I.B. Tauris, 2002). Importantly, surveys of American cinema between the mid-1960s and the mid-1970s do not *always* employ the term 'New Hollywood' – see, for example, Drew Casper, *Hollywood Film 1963–1976: Years of Revolution and Reaction* (Malden, MA: Wiley-Blackwell, 2011) – nor do books covering all of American cinema since the late 1960s; see, for example, Michael Allen, *Contemporary US Cinema* (London: Pearson Education, 2003) and Jon Lewis (ed.), *The New American Cinema* (Durham, NC: Duke University Press, 1998).

23 King, *New Hollywood Cinema*, table of contents.

24 Cook, *Lost Illusions*, 67–157.

25 See, for example, Novotny Lawrence and Gerald R. Butters, Jr. (ed.), *Beyond Blaxploitation* (Detroit: Wayne State University Press, 2016).

26 See Aaron Hunter, *Authoring Hal Ashby: The Myth of the New Hollywood Auteur* (New York: Bloomsbury Academic, 2016).

27 Finler, *The Hollywood Story*, 280.

28 Finler, *The Hollywood Story*, 280.

29 Finler, *The Hollywood Story*, 288.

30 Finler, *The Hollywood Story*, 288.

31 Finler, *The Hollywood Story*, 286–7; Block, *George Lucas's Blockbusting*, 415, 417.

32 'The Top 100 Films', 56.

33 Indeed, *American Graffiti* (1973, Lucas, at number 62), *Jaws* (no. 56), *Star Wars* (no. 13), *Raiders of the Lost Ark* (1981, directed by Spielberg and produced by Lucas, no. 66) and *E.T. The Extra-Terrestrial* (1982, Spielberg, no. 24) are all highly placed among the 'AFI's 100 Greatest American Films of All Time', as are many other films from the second half of the 1970s and the early 1980s. This suggests, first of all, that these Lucas and Spielberg films were not only huge box office hits but also have considerable critical standing today and, secondly, that the decade following the peak years of the Hollywood Renaissance (1967–74) saw the continued output of films that have stood the test of time. The IMDb users' chart confirms both points with regards to the judgement of film fans.

Chapter 1

BRIDGING COMMERCE AND CLASSIFICATION THROUGH THE AMERICAN ART FILM: THE CASE OF *WHO'S AFRAID OF VIRGINIA WOOLF?* (1966)

Justin Wyatt

Nominated for thirteen Academy Awards (one in every eligible category), Mike Nichols' adaptation of Edward Albee's *Who's Afraid of Virginia Woolf?* (1966) recalls the days when box office revenue and critical acclaim matched more often than not. The film was a cultural sensation creating a firestorm of press and public interest. More than fifty years on, the film retains its power as an effective drama of psychological and marital warfare. Expertly crafted with clever, though subtle and small, changes from the play, Nichols followed his theatrical source closely. Recognized by the National Film Registry in 2013 as culturally significant and worthy of preservation in the Library of Congress, *Virginia Woolf* continues to be well regarded and a classic example of post-studio era dramatic filmmaking. Beyond the public and critical acclaim, *Virginia Woolf* is perhaps even more significant for breaking down institutional barriers in Hollywood. The film heralded a new era of film classification and can be viewed as one of the first 'American art films' of the Hollywood Renaissance of the late 1960s through the mid-1970s. In this chapter, I explore the key factors which led *Virginia Woolf* to be this groundbreaking work for the Hollywood Renaissance. Following conventional Hollywood logic, most of these defining elements are motivated, first and foremost, by a commercial imperative. The regulatory and historical landmarks of the film are merely 'collateral damage' occurring in the quest for strong box office revenue and studio market share.

Hollywood and the shifting cultural landscape

Set up in 1934 as a means of industry self-censorship, the Production Code Administration (PCA) ensured that Hollywood films adhered to a set of guidelines limiting adult material, sex and criminality. Each film from a studio was submitted for the 'Seal of Approval', which was essentially the industry's mechanism to make sure that local and national forces would allow the exhibition of the film unfettered by censorship or controversy. Over the decades, the system worked well in securing a smooth flow of film for the national marketplace. Deviations from the Production Code were limited. In 1953, for instance, director Otto Preminger was denied a Seal for the romantic comedy *The Moon Is Blue* on the basis of the film's 'light and gay treatment of the subject of illicit sex and seduction.' United Artists (UA) chose to release the film without the Seal. Although it ended up as the fifteenth most financially successful film of the year, *The Moon Is Blue* nevertheless was targeted for its subject matter, with the states of Kansas, Ohio and Maryland banning the film. The success of the film in release without the Seal helped to signal that the Seal was not always needed to secure a solid national audience.[1]

By the start of the 1960s, films were increasingly attempting to deal with more adult subject matter. The results were illuminating for the increased flexibility of the Production Code. For instance, in 1961, *Splendor in the Grass* (Elia Kazan) was rejected by Geoffrey Shurlock of the PCA for 'overly vivid portrayal of sex in a number of sequences.'[2] Jack Warner negotiated the dubbing, cutting and re-cutting of the film until a Seal was finally approved in October 1961. Even by this point, the studios viewed skirting the Production Code Seal as a strategy to be avoided.

In parallel, the Legion of Decency, transformed into the National Catholic Office for Motion Pictures (NCOMP) in 1965, served a similar function. Unlike the PCA, the Catholic institution was not directly linked to the film industry. As a result, films were classified ex-post rather than analysed as early as the script level by the PCA. Operating since 1933, the Legion of Decency was designed to uphold 'moral standards' by alerting potential moviegoers about content that would be objectionable. Of particular significance were the most stringent categories: a Legion classification of 'B' meant that a film is morally objectionable, while a 'C' rating gave a film condemned status. The latter was feared for impacting box office revenue and limiting audience and publicity/promotion for a film. As with the PCA, by the early 1960s, the Legion was engaging with liminal films that somehow were spared the 'C' rating. Stanley Kubrick's *Lolita* (1962), for instance, was accepted by the Legion as 'morally unobjectionable' but for adults (over 18) only.[3] Much more explicit in theme and content than *Baby Doll* (Elia Kazan, 1956), condemned just five years earlier, Kubrick's film demonstrated just how flexible the Legion of Decency had become in dealing with the increasingly adult social content in film.

In addressing the landscape for movie censorship and classification, critic Richard Corliss sums up the impetus for much of the changes with the phrase, 'Blame it on the Europeans!'[4] Indeed, the influx of foreign films post-Second World War created not just a distinct market segment with its own theatres, marketing and distribution, but also the presentation of more adult content and themes. While these foreign films evidenced a strong aesthetic impact on the conventions of classical Hollywood storytelling, there was also a commercial impact of this new market. By the mid-1960s, independent distributors – from Cinema V to Audobon Films, Janus and New Yorker Films – started to feel some pressure from the studios. UA was the most aggressive in exploring the independent cinema terrain. Rather than risk tarnishing their own brand with potentially transgressive content, UA chose to release some of these films under the label of Lopert Films, their art house subsidiary. UA, for instance, pacted with Svensk Film-Industrie for global distribution of Ingmar Bergman films.[5] Other studios, such as MGM with Premier Productions, followed suit by releasing foreign films with adult content through subsidiaries. This method allowed the studios to observe their agreement with the PCA to release only films with the Seal of Approval.

Against the background of foreign films making small, but significant, inroads to the marketplace, the domestic studios were being challenged via several parameters. The post-war era brought a rise in independent production along with the major studios divesting their theatre chains in light of the Paramount Consent Decrees. The competition from television was fierce during this period as well. Television made huge strides during the 1950s; by the end of the decade, only 1 in 10 homes were without a TV set.[6] Meanwhile, film production costs were escalating and the studios were depending upon large-scale epics, often in a roadshow release pattern. While this pattern could be very lucrative (e.g. *The Sound of Music* [Robert Wise, 1965]), it could also lead to underwhelming results across a variety of genres (e.g. comedy, action-adventure, musical). In addition, these epics were inevitably accompanied by a larger production cost as well. Historian Drew Casper assesses this period as Hollywood mobilizing a 'big kill strategy', banking on large-scale projects above all else. Casper recounts the ultimate failure of this strategy: 'Specifically, "the big kill" strategy precipitated a deluge of high-priced items, mostly historical spectacles and musicals whose mythologies were being scrutinized and snubbed by the very portion of the public still in a movie frame of mind.'[7] The net result of all these factors was dire. David James describes the economics of Hollywood production in a downward spiral with average weekly movie theatre attendance dropping from an early Depression high of 90 million to just 40 million in 1960.[8]

James' argument on weekly attendance matches motion picture box office receipts data which show a year-to-year slide from 1959 to 1963 ($958 million to $903 million). Motion picture theatre receipts as a percentage of consumer expenditure show an even more precipitous decline from 0.31 per cent in 1959 to only 0.19 per cent in 1970.[9] This contraction was also evident in the number of films released, falling to 156 in 1966 from 272 just ten years earlier.[10] All these indicators join to create a more competitive environment for Hollywood production. The traditional 'rules' governing profit and loss in the studio system were long gone by the mid-1960s.

Considering the slippery relationship between the PCA and the studios over the more adult 1960s film content and the challenges facing Hollywood in terms of box office and attendance, it is hardly surprising that Hollywood would seek to present a different 'product' to appeal to a wider audience base. More interesting though is the route taken for this new product. Rather than returning to films of the past, the marketplace morphed the perceived constraints into a type of film that would, in fact, take advantage of the public interest in the aesthetics and thematics of the foreign film. This new product would also tackle the adult content of those liminal Hollywood and independent productions, such as *Baby Doll* and *Lolita*, head on. Consequently, both institutional and social forces aligned with the commercial imperative of Hollywood filmmaking. The result was the 'American art film'. The paradigm was Mike Nichols' cinematic adaptation of *Who's Afraid of Virginia Woolf?*

The perfect storm of commercial and artistic forces

The impact of *Virginia Woolf* depended on aesthetic and commercial forces joining together to produce a film capable of shifting the overall marketplace for production and distribution of American film. *Virginia Woolf* benefited from a rare combination of popular and critical acclaim. Both were required to make an intervention into mainstream studio moviemaking. In terms of aesthetics, through this film, the art film shifted from its European roots.

The most significant precursor to *Virginia Woolf* in terms of social impact was Sidney Lumet's 1965 drama *The Pawnbroker*. The story of a Nazi concentration camp survivor creating a new life for himself as a small-time pawnbroker in Harlem, the film featured nudity and frank adult situations and themes. The main scene in question matched a prostitute baring her breasts with a flashback of the pawnbroker's wife forced into prostitution in the concentration camp (see also Chapter 2). While the Legion of Decency condemned the film given the nudity, the PCA requested minimal cuts, still allowing the nudity to be included in the final cut.[11] Working from a low budget of $500,000 and released by independent Allied Artists, the film was ultimately too small-scale to create great attention for its impact on the PCA. *The Pawnbroker* was important, however, for presenting other factors: serious themes (the Holocaust, post-war survival), acting (Rod Steiger's Oscar nominated lead performance) and realistic psychological investigation. All these factors could align to create the circumstances to 'break' the rules of the Code. The film suggested that the Code was especially susceptible to those films with a serious purpose or intent whose 'objectionable' subject matter was necessary for the storytelling. *Virginia Woolf*, on the other hand, was a game changer, representing the perfect combination of commercial and aesthetic qualities needed to change the structure of the industry. Unlike *The Pawnbroker*, Nichols' film had such strong credentials and higher visibility so that the issues with adult content could not be dismissed as an isolated incident. *Virginia Woolf* served as the archetype for future studio releases and led the way for the institution of the Motion Picture Association of America (MPAA) ratings system in 1968.

Virginia Woolf surpassed *The Pawnbroker* for both dramatic and marketing/commercial impact. In terms of credentials, the Edward Albee play source material could not be more stellar: the play won both the 1963 Tony Award for Best Play and the 1962–3 New York Drama Critics' Circle Award for Best Play.[12] Told over three hours in three acts, the play considers two couples: George, a middle aged, deceptively milquetoast college History professor, and Martha, his brazen wife, hosting a late night after party, with Nick and Honey, a new-to-campus younger Biology professor and his even more youthful and gullible wife. Ugly verbal battles, skirmishes and mind games between George and Martha lead to a series of revelations about both couples. The night ends with illusions and fabrications made visible, particularly with the hope of a new beginning for George and Martha. Touching a nerve of realism, both psychological and interpersonal, the play combined, to borrow from Leonard Leff and J. L. Simmons, 'the realism of Arthur Miller, the poetry of Tennessee Williams, and the symbolism of Eugene O'Neill.'[13] The result was a property of the highest cultural significance, just waiting for a transition to the silver screen.

Albee's play inspired a range of critical reactions and interpretations, including a few that angered the playwright. Some critics considered the play to be a veiled representation of a gay couple warring and enacting elaborate mind games. Much of this reading seems located in playwright Edward Albee as a gay man. Albee has vehemently denied the gay reading of the play.[14] Nevertheless, some evidence does suggest that Albee was, at some point, conceiving of the play in a different way: director Dov Fahrer claims that Albee told him he changed the characters after being told that audiences would not want to see a play about homosexuals.[15] Over the decades, debate has continued on the impact of sexuality, gender roles and stereotypes in the presentation of the play.[16]

The play's protagonists are described by Albee as 'Martha: a large boisterous woman, 52, looking somewhat younger; ample, but not fleshy' and 'George: Her husband, 46; Thin, hair going grey.'[17] Albee has stated that Bette Davis and James Mason would have been the ideal duo for a screen adaptation of his play.[18] The casting of Elizabeth Taylor (aged 34) and Richard Burton (41) failed to match Albee's description – with Taylor almost two decades too young for the role! Nevertheless, it would be hard to overestimate the value of the Taylor-Burton team to the film's presence in the marketplace. Both were among the Top Ten Stars of 1965 and 1966 in the annual poll of exhibitors by Quigley Publications.[19] This external validation does not adequately convey the fascination of Taylor-Burton as a romantic and professional duo.

Taylor and Burton were initially paired in Joseph L. Mankiewicz' historical epic *Cleopatra* (1963). Their roles in *Cleopatra* were framed by the enormous publicity surrounding their affair (both were married at the time) and Taylor's unprecedented $1 million salary for the film.[20] The paparazzi were overwhelmed by the pair's glamour, volatility and open displays of love, anger and unhinged emotion.[21]

While Burton was concerned about the publicity negatively impacting his career, his salary for their follow-up film *The V.I.P.s* (Anthony Asquith, 1963) actually doubled.[22] Burton more than gained in 'stardom' what he may have lost as a 'serious artist'. He was also vaulted into the category of romantic leading man, a somewhat unexpected trajectory for one of England's 'angry young men'.[23] As Alexander Doty notes, the post-*Cleopatra* Taylor-Burton films were designed to reap the financial rewards of the pair's notoriety. They also maintained a vestige of 'prestige' separating their films from routine Hollywood fare.[24] *The V.I.P.s* concerns a mix of unlikely strangers, from a pompous filmmaker to a penniless Duchess, stranded at London Airport due to fog, along with the personal and professional consequences of the delay. Written by the acclaimed British playwright Terence Rattigan, the film featured Taylor and Burton as a wealthy couple on the verge of a break-up due to infidelity. The parallels to their own relationship were obvious. The fancy cars, expensive jewellery, high fashion and suggestions of both passion and pain echoed the real Taylor-Burton liaison to a tee.

While *The V.I.P.s* could be justified as a high-class melodrama, the next pairing, *The Sandpiper* (Vincente Minnelli, 1965) was heavier on the side of soap opera and lighter on the serious drama. *The Sandpiper* was a melodrama, set in Big Sur, about a free-spirited artist in love with a married clergyman. It was financially successful (the seventh highest grossing film of 1965)[25] but received dim critical notices. As Taylor commented about the film, 'We never thought it would be an artistic masterpiece. We did it for the money.'[26]

Virginia Woolf as a project played beautifully into the desired dual goal of 'popular' and 'prestige' sought by Taylor and Burton. Apart from the critical acclaim of Albee's play, the roles of George and Martha dovetailed marvellously with the public/private images of Taylor and Burton. As Taylor commented about her romance with Burton, 'We adore fighting.'[27] The play offered roles that presented a sparring couple, and also reflected so many of the larger issues with the public fascination of the couple. George and Martha's endless games of truth vs illusion seemed to be just another variant of what's true and what's false in the gossip columns about Taylor-Burton. By playing a character older, more jaded and more openly sexually suggestive, Taylor made the parallel between the real and fictional couples even more lurid and provocative. Of course, this only enhanced the ability to market and promote the film.

The other element that solidified both the commercial and artistic aspects of the film was the choice of director Mike Nichols. Suggested by Elizabeth Taylor, Nichols had never directed a feature film. He had achieved considerable success as a theatre director, winning an impressive three Tony Awards from 1963 to 1965. He did, however, also possess another background that added a useful filter to the play and its adaptation. As half of the improvisational duo Nichols and May, Nichols helped to establish the insightful form of observational comedy built on understanding character, social situations and ideology. Sometimes the Nichols and May routines would revolve directly around the difference between truth and illusion. In this way, the art of a Nichols and May routine anticipated the verbal

Figure 1.1 *Who's Afraid of Virginia Woolf?*: Fighting on and off-screen. Copyright Warner Bros.

and psychological gamesmanship in *Virginia Woolf*. Albee was apparently a fan of Nichols and May. As Nichols recounts, Albee suggested that their routines should end with a 'grey out' rather than a punch. That way, the routine would mimic closer the experience of everyday living.[28] The director's affinity for word play and his investigations of social and cultural manners fit perfectly with the main themes of *Virginia Woolf*. Having made the leap triumphantly from comedy performance to stage directing, Nichols was poised for his next career transition with a project that matched his sensibility and background.

Warner Bros. had originally set a budget of $3 million for the film. With Taylor ($1.2 million) and Burton ($750,000) co-starring and director Nichols' insistence on a lengthy rehearsal period and production, partly on location at Smith College in Massachusetts, the budget eventually grew to $7.5 million.[29] The cost was unprecedented, with *Life* magazine referring to *Virginia Woolf* as 'the most expensive black-and-white, non-spectacle production ever'.[30] Warner Bros. originally considered making the film as a 'theatrofilm'. Richard Burton's Broadway production of *Hamlet* (1964), directed by John Gielgud, was the prototype of the theatrofilm. *Hamlet* was recorded in live performance from seventeen camera angles and edited into a film that was shown as a special event for two days in nearly 1,000 movie houses across the country. The rough quality of the filming (inconsistent lighting, flat perspective) made for a film that was affordable but second-rate in quality. For this reason, Jack Warner moved on to thinking about *Virginia Woolf* as a large-scale production instead.[31]

Virginia Woolf proved to be an expensive proposition for Warner Bros. The larger budget made the film more of a focus than an independent, small budgeted item like *The Pawnbroker*. Studio chief Jack Warner was intent on realizing a profit from the project that he first purchased after seeing the play in 1963. With a large financial investment and solid marketing and publicity angles at hand, the film was set to become both a critical and commercial success. Warner needed to ensure that the film entered the marketplace in as strong a position as possible given this investment. Realizing that the film's strong content would garner attention from the 'censorship' arms (PCA, NCOMP), Warner Bros. was primed to seek a solution to any roadblocks – even if the challenge meant remaking the model for film classification and censorship overall.

The institutional impact of *Virginia Woolf* should not be separated from its aesthetic impact. The coarse language and abusive dialogue are, after all, in aid of the viewer building a true emotional connection with George and Martha. Nichols created a film of shocking intimacy. In this regard, Nichols was helped considerably by cinematographer Haskell Wexler. Wexler adopted a cinema-verite approach to the film, favouring often harsh close ups and realistic free-flowing coverage of the action. To the amazement of some of the other crew, Wexler also used a hand-held camera for several scenes; as Wexler commented on his approach, 'all the old-timers would walk away, and there would be a lot of snickering'.[32] Wexler used dimmers and umbrellas on single source lights to soften the intensity at times, but the overall effect was to draw the audience to a sometimes uncomfortable closeness with the actors.[33]

Nichols structured the film to build the intimacy further through his use of space. Ernest Lehman's adaptation of the Albee play opened the action to a minor degree, including an outside scene in the backyard and a trip to a nearby roadhouse. The dialogue and course of action are transposed from the Albee play like a blueprint, however. Rather than use the extra locations to give a sense of freedom for the action, Nichols, in fact, makes the film even more claustrophobic. The interior scenes at the home are intricately choreographed with the hand-held camera playing a central role at times (e.g. Honey dancing until she gets sick). When Nichols takes the action to the garden, instead of freeing the action, it is composed of more static shots of George and Nick. The stillness of the outside design is even more impressive given the freedom of Wexler's interior shooting. The effect is to forge a closer emotional bond with the characters. The boldness of Albee's text and the 'shocking' language are merely part of the larger picture: to create a psychological realism for character and dramatic situation.

Inspiring institutional change

Virginia Woolf was screened for NCOMP, with eighty-one volunteers from the Church attending and reporting to the head of the office, Monsignor Thomas F.

Little. The NCOMP board was composed of two bodies: the International Federation of Catholic Alumnae (IFCA), charged with 'traditional standards of morality upon which the sanctification of the individual, the sacredness of the home and ethical foundations of civilization necessarily depend' and 'Consultants', a group of film teachers and scholars, business people and writers. The latter group was more liberal in demeanour and more aware of the changing nature of American society. The Consultants voted for the less restrictive A–4 rating (61 per cent), whereas the IFCA voted in favour of the Condemned rating (58 per cent).[34] With the ratio of Consultants to IFCA as 3:1, NCOMP ruled in favour of approving the film. The general feeling was that a Condemned rating would not reflect the quality and significance of the film; as one rater described their reaction, 'I feel very strongly that at this time an arbitrary pronouncement regarding language by the Church would do nothing but assure its critics of a general lack of perception on the Church's part of the values of the film.'[35]

NCOMP therefore assigned the film an A–4 rating: 'morally unobjectionable for adults, with reservations'. The precise wording of the rating indicates just how sensitive their designation could be in that an A–4 film 'requires caution and explanation as a protection to the uninformed against wrong interpretations and false conclusions'.[36] This particular classification had been used for films of serious purpose containing adult content, such as *Suddenly, Last Summer* (Joseph L. Mankiewicz, 1959).

Monsignor Little commented: 'We put *Virginia Woolf* in what we call our "think film" category. This is the category we used for *Darling*, *8½* and *La dolce vita*.'[37] Accordingly, *Virginia Woolf* was saved not just from the 'C' rating (condemned), but also from the 'B' rating (morally objectionable in part for all). The Catholic office 'passing' *Virginia Woolf*, despite the strong and suggestive language, placed some pressure on the PCA to find a means of accommodating the film for a national release.

On seeing the completed film, Production Code censor Geoffrey Shurlock had proclaimed that *Virginia Woolf* could not be given a Seal of Approval due to the coarse language. Shurlock suggested to Jack Warner that he appeal that decision to the newly appointed President of the MPAA, Jack Valenti. Jack Warner, in particular, was faced with a difficult predicament. As Nichols had shot no 'protection footage' (scenes without the coarse language), Warner was faced with two options if no deal could be reached: either cut the offensive language or resign from the MPAA.[38] Another solution was brokered, however, in a conference with Jack Warner, his sales manager Ben Kalmenson, lawyer Louis Nizer and Valenti. As Valenti recounts, the meeting was, in some sense, productive: 'For some three hours in Warner's baronial office at the Warner Bros. studio, Jack [Warner], Ben, Louis and I talked about how to handle the Nichols film. At the end of the meeting, Jack and I had agreed that we would leave in "hump the hostess" but take out three instances of "screw you" and leave one intact.'[39] While Valenti thought that negotiating over a few swear words made little sense, the team was motivated to find a solution that would work for the release of the film. Warner Bros. wanted to protect their sizeable investment, and the MPAA hoped to offer guidance to moviegoers rather than censorship. The latter goal was especially the case since *Virginia Woolf* was treated as 'an artistic work of the highest order'. In that regard, Valenti claimed that the film caused him to do some 'lonely soul searching', to create a means to allow the public to see a film with such redeeming social value.[40]

With the suggestion from NCOMP, the agreement was made to release the film with an 'adults only policy'.[41] This would prohibit those under 18s from attending without parent or adult guardian. In this way, the policing of content was shifted away from the studios and producers to the exhibitors. Crucially, the deal was designed for Nichols' film and would not be applied to films of a lesser quality. So, *Virginia Woolf* was released for audiences 'no one under 18'. Through this classification, freer expression within motion pictures could exist.[42]

The MPAA Review Board met in New York on 10 June 1966 to screen the film and make a final decision. Warner Bros. advertising executive Richard Lederer, acting on behalf of Jack Warner, summarized the argument asking for an exemption for the film:

1. *Virginia Woolf* was a 'superior picture'
2. Warner Brothers' classification assured the MPAA that the picture would be shown to mature audiences
3. 'In the interests of the industry', Warner Brothers had honoured the MPAA's request to delete two words ('screw you' and 'frigging')
4. Exemption would apply only to *Virginia Woolf*, not films of lesser quality
5. NCOMP gave the film an A–4 rating.[43]

With those arguments in place, the Board decided to grant *Virginia Woolf* a Code Seal. Valenti noted that the decision was based on the quality of the film and the studio's agreement to prevent attendance of children. The latter proved to be short lived. Interestingly, by the time of *Virginia Woolf*'s second run, the tag had shifted to 'not recommended for children' instead of the exclusionary age restriction. At some of the drive-in engagements, the label was dropped entirely, with others even offering 'Children Under 12 Free' in their advertising.[44] The film proved to be strong both critically and in terms of attendance, placing it as the third highest grossing film of 1966.[45]

Very soon after *Virginia Woolf*, Valenti was confronted with another 'prestige' film flaunting the limits of the Production Code, Michelangelo Antonioni's *Blow-Up* (1966).[46] A mystery, loosely defined, set against the world of swinging 60s London photography, the film featured about 15 seconds of nudity of two female models cavorting with photographer David Hemmings. Condemned by the Catholic Church and refused a Seal of Approval by the Production Code, MGM chose to release the film under a subsidiary, Premier Productions, rather than break their agreement with the MPAA not to release a film without the Seal.[47] With the mark of the Italian auteur Antonioni, the film was released quickly to qualify for Oscar competition. Producer Carlo Ponti was apparently pleased with the issues from NCOMP and the PCA since the controversy created a large amount of free publicity for the film. Behind the scenes, even after the release, MGM actually cut a scene still hoping for a Seal of Approval. This process was halted when the film, in its uncut version, was doing strong box office.[48] With no Seal, *Blow-Up* grossed $6 million domestically and $20 million worldwide in its initial release – a very impressive figure for an art house film budgeted at $1.8 million.[49] The lesson to Hollywood was clear: forfeiting the Seal was fine for most moviegoers if there were enough reasons to watch the film. In that way, *Blow-Up* suggested another perspective: playing without the Seal might result in commercial success, but the possibility of obscenity and censorship also loomed in the background.

Between *Virginia Woolf*'s release and *Blow-Up*'s opening in December 1966, Valenti initiated an interim measure to allow for more adult content in filmmaking. In October 1966, the MPAA revised the Code to allow for the label 'Suggested for Mature Audiences' (SMA). This tag was designed to tell moviegoers that the film was not suitable for children. As Richard S. Randall describes it, the label was offered purely in marketing: 'For those films affected, it appeared only in first-run advertising, and there was no arrangement at the exhibition level to give it effect at the box office.'[50] Newspaper advertising after the institution of the SMA tag reveals a wide range of labels used by distributors beyond the SMA one. *Alfie* (Lewis Gilbert, 1966) and *Blow-Up* were labelled in newspaper ads as 'Recommended for Mature Audiences', and *I, A Woman* (Mac Ahlberg, 1965) as 'Recommended for the Mature Adult'. Age restrictions were also self-imposed in some cases: *James Joyce's Ulysses* (Joseph Strick, 1966) was tagged as 'Admittance will be denied to all those under 18 years of age', and *In Cold Blood* (Richard Brooks, 1967) as 'Positively no one under 16 admitted unless accompanied by a parent or guardian'. Many other prominent films did, in fact, utilize the 'Suggested for Mature Audiences' label, or the shorter 'SMA' tag: *Georgy Girl* (Silvio Narizzano, 1966), *A Funny Thing Happened on the Way to the Forum* (Richard Lester, 1966), *Two for the Road* (Stanley Donen, 1967), *Point Blank* (John Boorman, 1967), *Valley of the Dolls* (Mark Robson, 1967), *The Comedians* (Peter Glenville, 1967) and *Bedazzled* (Stanley Donen, 1967).[51] The SMA tag offered a useful stopgap measure to allow for more adult content in light of the issues raised by *Virginia Woolf* and *Blow-Up*. Valenti was, however, working on a more comprehensive ratings system that would involve restriction by age for some films.

In this period, certain films that would undoubtedly be rejected by the Production Code were released using the SMA tag as a warning label. John Huston's *Reflections in a Golden Eye* (1967), adapted from the Carson McCullers novel, clearly fell into this category. The film concerns Major Penderton (Marlon Brando) and his wife Leonora (Elizabeth Taylor) at an army base in the

Deep South. A veritable melting pot of lurid Southern Gothic content, the film contains adultery, naked horseback riding, gay voyeurism and an army wife who mutilates her nipples with garden shears. The Warner Bros. tagline spoke volumes, 'Leave the Children Home', and dovetails nicely with the SMA tag. While the film was released with the SMA label, NCOMP issued a Condemned rating for the male and female nudity, as well as 'almost no human insight'.[52] The flexibility offered by the SMA tag allowed the content to be presented on screen by the major studios without violating their promise to release only Code films.[53]

Although the SMA tag alerted moviegoers to the adult content, there were no age restrictions set against these films and enforced by exhibitors. While SMA allowed for more permissive content, Jack Valenti was also considering the impact of local classification boards appearing in different cities. In a Supreme Court case, the local Dallas classification board was ruled against because the guidelines were too vague.[54] The Supreme Court had no issues with the premise of local film classification per se. Valenti knew that a nationwide classification system with enforcement by age at the exhibition level would be a strong means to solve the skirmishes over adult content on the local and regional levels.[55]

Eager to replace the Hays Code with a comprehensive system that was responsive to the changing times, Valenti met with the creative guilds, craft unions, producers, religious organizations and film critics to refine his alternative. Legal counsel Louis Nizer advocated strongly for a classification plan, fearing that otherwise free speech would be curtailed: 'So we concluded that self-restraint by our own companies was necessary, or censorship boards, goaded by religious organizations, would multiply like viruses in a conducive environment.'[56] Valenti's plan rested largely on the theatre owners who would be the ones enforcing the new ratings system.[57] Valenti strategized with Sumner Redstone, then head of the Theater Owners of America, who approved of a plan that would allow for broader content and less interference from outside forces.

Once the exhibitors agreed to the plan, Valenti and the MPAA launched the new voluntary ratings system (G/M/R/X) for all films released after 1 November 1968. The 'X' rating barred those under 16 without qualification, while 'R' allowed for a parent or adult guardian to accompany those under 16. Valenti stressed that the plan was not designed to be 'an agent of social change', but rather just a guide for parents in deciding on content for their children.[58] Of course, the plan also created a new system of self-regulation at a time when Hollywood was increasingly out of step with the more adult content and issues playing out through the nation at that time.

Although Valenti stressed the need for a system that responded to the current times, it should not be discounted that the MPAA ratings system also had an economic imperative. Remember that the cratering losses and failed big budget production plans plagued the major studios throughout the 1960s. As Jon Lewis suggests, the MPAA ratings system was, among other aspects, a business proposition: 'studios needed to update their product line and the ratings system was a means to that end.'[59] The regime of big budget, family oriented spectacles placated any censorship challenges, but increasingly failed to engage audiences. The battles over civil rights, the Vietnam War and the 'generation gap' were pushing America into a mood for greater contemplation and weightier issues. The MPAA ratings system allowed for a more diverse set of films.

Hollywood took advantage of this opportunity immediately. In the initial set of films rated, 'M' and 'R' dominated.[60] In 1969, almost a third of films were classified as either 'R' or 'X', meaning that viewing was restricted by age. By 1970, 'R' became the most frequently applied rating (41 per cent of all films classified). Over the next ten years, 'R' ratings would remain at strong levels, accounting between 36 per cent and 47 per cent of total ratings each year.[61] Whereas an 'X' rating limited attendance by age absolutely, an 'R' rating allowed underage patrons to attend with a parent or an adult guardian. As a result, the 'R' rating became the 'preferred' rating to connote adult, but not pornographic.[62] Although it is difficult to prove the impact of a rating, by itself, on box office, Bruce Austin's statistical analysis demonstrates that initially ratings had an impact on attendance (the limitations on the audience posed by both 'R' and 'X' impacted the box office success according to Austin's model).[63] Austin also notes that enforcement of the age restriction at the theatre level became increasingly lax (he estimates that an unaccompanied minor had at least a 50 per cent chance of being admitted to an 'R' film).[64] A market for more adult content was created and realized, even if the functioning of age restrictions was flawed.[65]

Virginia Woolf *and the Hollywood Renaissance*

Looking at just the first five years of the MPAA ratings system, the impact on content and free expression was immediate and drastic. *Virginia Woolf* truly paved the way for the Hollywood Renaissance of the late 1960s through mid-1970s. Suddenly, adult content could be engaged with in a meaningful way through both 'R' and 'X' rated content. As David Andrews describes it, this era also usurped the commercial power of the foreign film: 'This change ushered in the New Hollywood, an art cinema that challenged the assumptions of the traditional usage of "foreign films".'[66] The importance of *Virginia Woolf* as a 'leading indicator' for this approach is evident. Consider just three landmarks of the Hollywood Renaissance: *Midnight Cowboy* (John Schlesinger, 1969), *The Last Picture Show* (Peter Bogdanovich, 1971) and *Last Tango in Paris* (Bernardo Bertolucci, 1972). All three utilize a strategy, approach or subject from *Virginia Woolf* only with the security and freedom of the MPAA ratings board – and, even better, the non-interference of the defunct Production Code.

Virginia Woolf's verbal battles between husband and wife left much 'between the lines', including the possibility that playwright Edward Albee was actually portraying a gay male couple rather than a straight one. A year after the MPAA ratings system was set in place, John Schlesinger's *Midnight Cowboy*, rated 'X' on initial release, won the Oscar for Best Picture. *Midnight Cowboy* shows the very unlikely friendship between potential hustler Joe Buck and street con man 'Ratso' Rizzo against the ultra-gritty world of New York City. Whereas the gay content of *Virginia Woolf* remained only a possible interpretation in both play and film, *Midnight Cowboy* sets its squabbling pair in a world of gay hustling with flashbacks to an implied gang rape of both Joe and his teenage girlfriend. *Cowboy's* other salient elements – psychedelic parties, oral sex in a movie theatre and beating a trick to near death in a seedy hotel room – all seemed to exist in a world far apart from the one where 'screw you' was a determinant of adult content in *Virginia Woolf* just three years earlier (see also Chapter 8).

While *Midnight Cowboy* revels in the new-found freedom to show moments of sex, violence and the unsavoury side of life, Peter Bogdanovich's 'R'-rated *The Last Picture Show* demonstrates how *Virginia Woolf's* genre – the melodrama – could be enriched through more frank treatment of sexuality.

Picturing a small Texas town in 1961, *The Last Picture Show* takes the sanitized family melodrama of *Peyton Place* (Mark Robson, 1957) and replaces it with an emotionally and sexually intimate portrayal of the town's residents. While the film portrays scenes of sexual contact, it does so with awkwardness and tenderness rather than an erotic sensibility. Bogdanovich matches this with scenes of emotional vulnerability and realism. The frank sex scenes add immeasurably to the overall depiction of the characters. The freedom allowed through the ratings

Figure 1.2 *The Last Picture Show*: New realism possible in the melodrama. Copyright Columbia Pictures Industries, Inc.

system lets the director paint a more nuanced view of his ensemble and allows the viewers to connect on a deeper level emotionally and intellectually.

Finally, recall that *Virginia Woolf*'s marketability was based on potent star power set against the prestige source material. With the classification system in place, this equation could be realized on an even grander scale. Bernardo Bertolucci's *Last Tango in Paris* placed one of Hollywood's long-term stars, Marlon Brando, in a tale of a depressed middle-aged American having an anonymous sexual liaison with a French teenager, played by Maria Schneider. Rated 'X', the film was released by UA to acclaim, controversy and strong box office. Pauline Kael, writing for *The New Yorker*, praised the film with a rapturous review: 'Bernardo Bertolucci's *Last Tango in Paris* was presented for the first time on the closing night of the New York Film Festival, October 14, 1972: that date should become a landmark in movie history comparable to May 29, 1913—the night *Le Sacre du Printemps* was first performed—in music history.'[67] Like *Virginia Woolf*, *Last Tango* placed a major star, renewed by the popularity *of The Godfather* (Francis Ford Coppola, 1972), in a role that mirrored his star image and the public fascination surrounding the reclusive figure. With *Virginia Woolf*, audience members could be fascinated by the potential parallels between the volatile Taylor-Burton duo and their fictional counterparts in the Albee drama. Now audience members were presented with a legendary star playing out scenarios of simulated sex with a beautiful young actress. Acclaimed director Bernardo Bertolucci added a layer of prestige, as did the locations, the Gato Barbieri jazz score and the supporting cast (including Jean-Pierre Léaud of François Truffaut's Antoine Doinel series).

The MPAA ratings system grew from the challenges provided by, among others, *Virginia Woolf* and *Blow-Up*. *Last Tango in Paris*, only six years after *Virginia Woolf*, represents the marriage of both of these tendencies: the American prestige film and the European art film. Like *Virginia Woolf*, *Last Tango* is driven commercially by star power and, to an even greater extent, notoriety. Like *Blow-Up*, it is also directed by a European master and guided by a strong authorial voice rather than the realism and transparency of classical Hollywood. Although the film follows a loose psychological investigation of Brando's character, the importance of sex as a form of communication and as a means of both domination and submission is explored in depth by Bertolucci. Despite Valenti's claim to the contrary, we must see the MPAA ratings system as a way to allow film artists to portray these very adult and serious treatments of sexuality.

Conclusion

Who's Afraid of Virginia Woolf?'s place in film history comes, first and foremost, through its facilitation of the classification system. The proverbial straw that broke the camel's back, the film possessed sufficient gravitas, both commercial and critical, to make Hollywood shift to a new form of classification allowing for more adult content and the exploration of serious, socially relevant themes. This classification system also allowed Hollywood to produce films that spoke to audiences in a more meaningful way through greater realism in character, psychology and situation. Filmmakers would also be engaged with new ways of storytelling, challenging and provoking viewers in the ways of the art cinema. The Hollywood Renaissance was amazingly short lived due to the ascendancy of marketing friendly, easily digestible films in the late 1970s. We have *Virginia Woolf* to thank as the catalyst for this fertile period of American film history. Just as the quest for box office motivated this realignment of the American film industry, it would also be inspired by the new revenue thresholds broken by high concept blockbusters such as *Jaws* (Steven Spielberg, 1975) and *Star Wars* (George Lucas, 1977). The balance between art and commerce in American film would be tilted permanently toward the dollar side of the spectrum from that point on.

Notes

1   Paul Monaco, *The Sixties: 1960–1969* (Berkeley: University of California Press, 2001), 56.
2   Marsmoonlight, 'Film Friday "Splendor in the Grass"' in Back to Golden Days Blog, 24 July 2015, http://back-to-golden-days.blogspot.com/2015/07/film-friday-splendor-in-grass–1961.html
3   Leonard Leff and J. L. Simmons, *The Dame in the Kimono: Hollywood, Censorship and the Production Code* (Lexington: University Press of Kentucky, 2013), 286.
4   Richard Corliss, 'Berating Ratings', *Film Comment* (September-October 1990): 3+.
5   'UA Pair from Ingmar Bergman; Indie Importers See Major's Move Into More "Art" Film "Takeover"', *Variety*, 11 January 1967, 5.
6   'Number of TV Households in America', in *TV History*, http://www.tvhistory.tv/Annual_TV_Households_50-78.JPG
7   Drew Casper, *Hollywood Film 1963–1976* (Malden, MA: Wiley-Blackwell, 2011), 48.
8   David E. James, *Allegories of Cinema: American Film in the Sixties* (Princeton, NJ: Princeton University Press, 1989), 26.
9   Monaco, *The Sixties*, 271.
10 Cobbett Steinberg, *Reel Facts,* (New York: Vintage Books, 1978), 369.
11 Richard Corliss, 'The Legion of Decency', *Film Comment*, 4, no. 4 (Summer 1968): 54.
12 Jennifer Schuessler, 'When George and Martha Met Tony', *The New York Times*, 6 June 2013, AR8.
13 Leff and Simmons, *The Dame in the Kimono*, 242.
14 Michael Ehrhardt, 'On the Return of Virginia Woolf', *The Gay & Lesbian Review* (January-February 2013): 28–31.
15 'Albee Seeking to Close an All-Male "Woolf"', *The New York Times*, 3 August 1984.
16 See, for example, Parisa Shams and Farideh Pourgiv, 'Gender Trouble in *Who's Afraid of Virginia Woolf?*', *Journal of Research in Gender Studies*, 3, no. 2 (2013): 85–100.

17 Edward Albee, *Who's Afraid of Virginia Woolf?* (New York: New American Library, 1962), Foreword.

18 William Hughes, 'R.I.P. Edward Albee, playwright of *Who's Afraid Of Virginia Woolf?*', *A.V. Club*, 17 September 2016, http://www.avclub.com/article/rip-edward-albee-playwright-whos-afraid-virginia-w-242757

19 Steinberg, *Reel Facts*, 407.

20 Alexander Doty, 'Elizabeth Taylor: The Biggest Star in the World', in *New Constellations: Movies Stars of the 1960s*, ed. Pamela Robertson Wojcik (New Brunswick, NJ: Rutgers University Press, 2012), 54.

21 Suzanne Leonard, 'True Love of Taylor and Burton', in *Reclaiming the Archive: Feminism and Film History*, ed. Vicki Callahan (Detroit: Wayne State University Press, 2010), 77–84.

22 Sam Kashner, 'A First Class Affair', *Vanity Fair*, July 2003, http://www.vanityfair.com/news/2003/07/elizabeth-taylor-affair-200307

23 Richard Burton discusses the impact of his films on his potential salary in a revealing portion of his diaries; *The Richard Burton Diaries*, ed. Chris Williams (New Haven: Yale University Press, 2012), 498–9.

24 Doty, 'Elizabeth Taylor', 52.

25 Steinberg, *Reel Facts*, 350.

26 Michael Koresky, 'Driftwood', *Reverse Shot*, 7 September 2011, http://reverseshot.org/archive/entry/968/sandpiper

27 Leonard, 'True Love of Taylor and Burton', 89.

28 Mel Gussow, *Edward Albee: A Singular Journey* (New York: Applause Books, 2000), 235.

29 Bob Thomas, *Clown Price of Hollywood: The Antic Life and Times of Jack L. Warner* (New York: McGraw-Hill, 1990), 268.

30 Thomas Thompson, 'Raw Dialogue Challenges All the Censors', *Life*, 10 June 1966, 92.

31 Leff and Simmons, *The Dame in the Kimono*, 251.

32 Ronald Bergan, 'Haskell Wexler obituary', *The Guardian*, 27 December 2015, http://www.theguardian.com/film/2015/dec/27/haskell-wexler

33 Ernest Callenbach and Albert Johnson, 'The Danger Is Seduction: An Interview with Haskell Wexler', *Film Quarterly*, 21, no. 3 (Spring 1968): 3–14.

34 Leonard Leff, 'A Test of American Film Censorship: *Who's Afraid of Virginia Woolf?*', *Cinema Journal*, 19, no. 2 (Spring 1980): 49.

35 Thompson, 'Raw Dialogue', 96.

36 Richard Corliss, 'The Legion of Decency', *Film Comment*, 4, no. 4 (Summer 1968): 49.

37 Thompson, 'Raw Dialogue', 96.

38 Leonard J. Leff, 'Play Into Film: Warner Brothers' *Who's Afraid of Virginia Woolf?*', *Theatre Journal*, 33, no. 4, (December 1981): 463–5.

39 Jack Valenti, *This Time, This Place: My Life in War, the White House and Hollywood* (New York: Three Rivers Press, 2007), 303.

40 Leff, 'A Test of American Film Censorship', 50.

41 Leff, 'A Test of American Film Censorship', 49.

42 Leff and Simmons, *The Dame in the Kimono*, 263.

43 Leff, 'A Test of American Film Censorship', 50.

44 Leff and Simmons, *The Dame in the Kimono*, 265–71.

45 Steinberg, *Reel Facts*, 350.

46 Bosley Crowther, 'In the Eye of the Beholder', *The New York Times*, 8 January 1967.

47 Robert Hofler, *Sexplosion: From Andy Warhol to A Clockwork Orange – How a Generation of Pop Rebels Broke All the Taboos* (New York: HarperCollins, 2014), xiv.

48 Peter Lev, *The Euro-American Cinema* (Austin: University of Texas Press, 1993), 96.

49 Steinberg, *Reel Facts*, 351; Richard Corliss, 'When Antonioni Blew Up the Movies', *Time*, 5 August 2007, http://content.time.com/time/arts/article/0,8599,1649984,00.html

50 Richard S. Randall, 'Censorship from *The Miracle* to *Deep Throat*', in *The American Film Industry*, expanded edition, ed. Tino Balio (Madison: University of Wisconsin Press, 1985), 525.

51 Film advertising images, *The New York Times*, 9 April 1967; 17 September 1967; 30 December 1967; 28 January 1968; 18 February 1968.

52 Vincent Canby, 'Filmmakers Show Less Fear of Catholic Office', *The New York Times*, 13 October 1967.

53 For an overview of the immediate period leading to the institution of the MPAA Ratings System in 1968, see Thomas Doherty, 'Sex, Violence, and Adult Themes: The MPAA and the Birth of the Film Ratings System', *Cineaste*, 42, no. 4 (Fall 2017): 10–15.

54 Robert Windeler, 'As Nation's Standards Change, So Do Movies', *The New York Times*, 8 October 1968, 75.

55 Vincent Canby, 'Ratings to Bar Some Films to Children', *The New York Times*, 8 October 1968, 49.

56 Louis Nizer, *Reflections without Mirrors* (New York: Doubleday, 1978), 428.

57 Valenti, *This Time*, 304.

58 Valenti, *This Time*, 305.

59 Jon Lewis, *Hollywood v. Hard Core: How the Struggle over Censorship Saved the Modern Film Industry* (New York: NYU Press, 2000), 135.

60 Of the first 43 films rated, 3 were rated General, 12 Mature, 14 Restricted and 3 'X' rated. All three of the 'X' rated films were imported. For more information on the early days of the ratings system, consult Vincent Canby, 'For Better or Worse, Film Industry Begins Ratings', *The New York Times*, 1 November 1968.

61 Bruce A. Austin, Mark J. Nicolich and Thomas Simonet, 'M.P.A.A. Ratings and the Box Office: Some Tantalizing Statistics', *Film Quarterly*, 35, no. 2 (Winter 1981): 28–30.

62 Justin Wyatt, 'Selling "Atrocious Sexual Behavior": Revising Sexualities in the Marketplace for Adult Film of the 1960s', in *Swinging Single: Representing Sexuality in the 1960s*, ed. Hilary Radner and Moya Luckett (Minneapolis: University of Minnesota Press, 1999), 111.

63 Austin, Nicolich and Simonet, 'M.P.A.A. Ratings', 28.

64 Bruce A. Austin, *Immediate Seating: A Look at Movie Audiences* (Belmont, CA: Wadsworth Publishing Company, 1989), 115.

65 An interesting analysis of the inner functioning of the ratings board and some early key cinematic ratings cases appears in Julian C. Burroughs, Jr., 'X Plus 2: The MPAA Classification System During Its First Two Years', *Journal of the University Film Association*, 23, no. 2 (1971): 44–53.

66 David Andrews, *Theorizing Art Cinemas: Foreign, Cult, Avant-Garde and Beyond* (Austin: University of Texas Press, 2013), 63.

67 Pauline Kael, 'Tango', in *Reeling: Film Writings 1972 to 1975* (London: Marion Boyars, 2012), 27–8.

Chapter 2

THE FILM EDITORS WHO INVENTED THE HOLLYWOOD RENAISSANCE: RALPH ROSENBLUM, SAM O'STEEN AND DEDE ALLEN'S *BONNIE AND CLYDE* (1967)

Warren Buckland

> Editing is directing the film for the second time. To gauge the psychological moment – to know exactly where to cut – requires the same intuitive skill as that needed by a director.
>
> — Kevin Brownlow[1]

The standard film histories that chart the transition from Classical Hollywood to the Hollywood Renaissance privilege directors and marginalize other creative personnel. In this chapter I examine the creative innovations of film editors who worked on Hollywood Renaissance (or proto-Hollywood Renaissance) films, and who continued to work in the industry after its demise. I briefly consider Ralph Rosenblum's editing of *The Pawnbroker* (1965) and Sam O'Steen's editing of *The Graduate* (1967) before focusing on Dede Allen's editing of *Bonnie and Clyde* (1967). The following discussion, limited to technical and stylistic innovations, attempts to 'reverse engineer' the films' editing choices, but in an idealized form, for it is usually impossible to write about what choices were actually made, at least on a moment-by-moment basis. Nonetheless, several potential sources of information exist to guide such a study: memoirs and interviews, editing manuals, the screenplay (the shooting script), film reviews (especially those written on a film's initial release) and the films themselves. In this chapter I analyse the films primarily through memoirs and editing manuals, an unusual mix of the informal and anecdotal on the one hand, and overtly technical and stylistic on the other.

Yet, memoirs and editing manuals are invaluable, for in different ways they represent 'filmic sensibility', the expert knowledge and procedures that filmmakers possess. Pauline Kael spells out what constitutes filmic sensibility and argues that, in his first film *She's Gotta Have It* (1986), Spike Lee has it while John Sayles does not:

> Lee himself is endowed with something more than training and imagination: he has for want of a better term is called 'a film sense'. It's an instinct for how to make a movie move – for how much motion there should be in a shot, for how fast to cut the shots, for how to make them flow into each other rhythmically. [...] (John Sayles has many gifts, but not a film sense – he doesn't gain anything as an artist by using film.)[2]

Acquiring filmic sensibility goes beyond merely knowing in abstract terms how to make a film; it also involves a very specific, practical skill – knowing how and when to implement that knowledge. In his discussion of camera movement, Stefan Sharff similarly notes that 'to know *when*, for *how long*, and most importantly *where* to move the camera [...] requires much skill and good cinema sense'.[3] The same principles apply to all filmic techniques. It is not simply a matter of whether to use a technique or not, but when, for how long and where.

Yet, filmic sensibility is not a fixed, transcendental quality. The Hollywood Renaissance inaugurated a fundamental shift in filmic sensibility in the 1960s, a shift away from the stylistic and production practices standardized in the Hollywood studios during its classical period.[4] The Hollywood Renaissance filmmakers challenged these standard rules and conventions. For example, on *Bonnie and Clyde*, newcomers and outsiders clashed with classical Hollywood veterans. Robert Benton and David Newman, writers for *Esquire* magazine, set themselves up as screenwriters, writing the treatment and then the screenplay for *Bonnie and Clyde*, influenced by the French New Wave films of Godard and Truffaut and deliberately flouting societal norms regarding violence and sex (as formalized in the Motion Picture Production Code). Director Arthur Penn notes that 'it wasn't just that we were sick of the [Hollywood] system. At that point [the early 1960s], the system was sick of itself'.[5] Actor and producer Warren Beatty worked in front of and behind the camera in order to get his career back on track after a number of failures (*All Fall Down* [John Frankenheimer, 1962] and *Lilith* [Robert Rossen, 1964]) following his commercial and critically successful debut with *Splendor in the Grass* (Elia Kazan, 1961). But the veteran cinematographer Burnett Guffey, who had been working in Hollywood since 1923, clashed with Arthur Penn over the style of *Bonnie and Clyde* – its low-level interior lighting, loose New Wave framing and lens flare. And Jack Warner, whose studio funded the film, disliked it intensely.

All the editors I have selected to discuss in this chapter were experts who knew the conventions of editing but broke them in distinctive and innovative ways – regarding flashbacks (Rosenblum) plus continuity editing and screen direction (O'Steen, Allen). They contributed to the Hollywood Renaissance by instigating an internal renewal of film style, which established alternative forms of perception and knowing. These processes of renewal can be detected in the films, but also in reviews, memoirs and interviews with practitioners. Yet, we need to be cautious when using memoirs and interviews because filmmakers do tend to exaggerate their own influence in the production of a successful film. At the same time, memoirs and interviews can be invaluable because they offer first-hand experience from an insider's perspective.

Ralph Rosenblum's The Pawnbroker

Ralph Rosenblum is renowned for introducing the subliminal flash cuts into *The Pawnbroker* (Sidney Lumet, made in 1963, released in 1965) and for editing Woody Allen's films in the 1970s. In his memoir *When the Shooting Stops . . . the Cutting Begins*[6] Rosenblum also explains how he re-edited and saved films such as *A Thousand Clowns* (Fred Coe, 1965), *The Night They Raided Minsky's* (William Friedkin, 1968) and *Annie Hall* (Woody Allen, 1977). He presents in written form his filmic sensibility, expert knowledge that solves editing problems and guides his ability to choose editing solutions at the right time, plus his awareness of the implicit assumptions about what does and what does not follow from choosing one particular solution (assumptions he spells out in the book). *A Thousand Clowns* was shot as a traditional drama with set bound dialogue scenes. In collaboration with the film's screenwriter Herb Gardner, Rosenblum was desperate to break up the film's lifeless, static theatrical space, by cutting scenes to music (the opening sequence of commuters going to work is cut to the sound of marching bands), or by keeping a dialogue between two characters continuous while the characters shift locations. The continuity derives from the music and dialogue, not the editing: 'This was a different sort of film action, one in which the real continuity was on the sound track, while the visuals offered a kaleidoscopic view of the world of Murray Burns [the main protagonist, played by Jason Robards]. It was a style arrived at by desperation and repair.'[7] The techniques Rosenblum introduced in *A Thousand Clowns* are familiar to today's film audiences, but were innovative in the 1960s for they challenged the conventions of classical Hollywood filmmaking.

Rosenblum also writes about his experimental editing in *The Pawnbroker*. The key to the film is a series of flashbacks representing the memories of Holocaust survivor Sol Nazerman (Rod Steiger). Rosenblum realized that the conventions of Hollywood editing of flashbacks (slow, laborious track-in to faces, slow dissolve to flashback, etc.), had become by the 1960s an artificial cliché. Rosenblum was influenced by Henri Colpi's innovative editing of the flashbacks in *Hiroshima Mon Amour* (Alain Resnais, 1959): sudden flashbacks that give the impression that the past and present are closely associated with one another, and flash cuts, or brief flashbacks lasting fractions of a second.

Rosenblum and director Sidney Lumet experimented by introducing sudden and subliminal flashbacks. Yet, both director and editor were uncertain whether the experiment would work, so Rosenblum edited the flashbacks conventionally as backup. He and Lumet were also unclear how many frames to use. In his memoir he writes: 'Back and forth we went from eight frames to six frames to four frames to eight frames. [. . .] Only the initial screening convinced [Lumet] that the experiment had worked'.[8] These subliminal flashbacks were edited into an otherwise conventionally constructed film in regards to editing and storytelling. The next example is more extreme.

Sam O'Steen's The Graduate

Sam O'Steen's memoir, *Cut to the Chase*, is based on interviews with his wife Bobbie O'Steen.[9] O'Steen is renowned for editing most of Mike Nichols' films, including *Who's Afraid of Virginia Woolf?* (1966) and *The Graduate,* plus Roman Polanski's *Rosemary's Baby* (1968) and *Chinatown* (1974). He began as an assistant editor at Warner Bros. in the 1950s, and assisted on films such as Hitchcock's *The Wrong Man* (1956). He moved from assistant editor to editor in 1964, beginning with *Youngblood Hawke,* the penultimate film of classical Hollywood stalwart director Delmer Daves. Fortunately, O'Steen began working with the Hollywood Renaissance directors, including Mike Nichols and Roman Polanski. At Warner Bros., Nichols chose to work with Sam O'Steen because O'Steen said he was willing to edit overlapping dialogue on *Who's Afraid of Virginia Woolf?*, whereas the veteran editors at Warner Bros. refused to break this convention.[10]

The most successful collaboration between O'Steen and Nichols was *The Graduate* an independent production Mike Nichols had set up with Joseph Levine's Embassy Pictures before filming *Who's Afraid of Virginia Woolf?* (see Chapter 3). Sam O'Steen decided to leave his lucrative job at Warner Bros. to work with Nichols. I shall briefly consider two well-known scenes. In the first, Mrs Robinson presents herself naked to Benjamin. O'Steen expresses Benjamin's surprise, not by selecting the single best take of him turning around and seeing the naked Mrs Robinson, but by editing together three separate takes of Benjamin as he turns around. The three consecutive takes prolong or slow down this moment of revelation. The resulting dialogue was initially edited conventionally, as shot/reverse shot: close ups of Mrs Robinson's face cut with close ups of Benjamin's face, intercut with close ups of Mrs Robinson's body from Benjamin's perspective. O'Steen informs us that, after he assembled the scene in this way, he and Nichols agreed that this conventional editing did not work.[11] O'Steen therefore chose an outtake, a shot of Benjamin from over the shoulder of Mrs Robinson, and decided to delete all of the close ups of faces. We only see Mrs Robinson's face once, in medium shot when she begins to talk, and we only see Benjamin's face from behind Mrs Robinson's shoulder

Figure 2.1 *The Graduate.* Copyright MGM.

(see Figure 2.1). For the rest of the scene, her speech is off screen (or acousmatic). O'Steen also experimented with subliminal editing; he acknowledges Rosenblum's work on *The Pawnbroker* and followed his example, by limiting the close ups of Mrs Robinson's body in three frames.

The resulting scene is therefore edited unconventionally:

- Three similar takes of Benjamin turning around are edited together
- The director and editor rejected the standard shot/reverse shot editing of the characters talking, and replaced it with a shot structured around foreground/background (Benjamin in the background with Mrs Robinson's shoulder in the foreground)
- Subliminal close ups of Mrs Robinson's body, and
- A reduction of synchronized voice in favour of an off-screen acousmatic voice.

The scene works because it focuses almost exclusively on Benjamin's panicked reaction and sense of entrapment. The off-screen sound of Mr Robinson returning home only increases Benjamin's anxiety and tension within the scene. In addition, the *mise-en-scène* technique of foreground/background was used previously in the scenes where Benjamin and Mrs Robinson talk; it is therefore consistent with those previous scenes. This example demonstrates how a filmic sensibility can integrate disparate techniques such as camera position and angle, framing and composition, dialogue, off-screen sound, as well as editing into a unified scene that conveys a character's emotional state of mind.

The second example is the famous montage sequence showing the progression of the affair between Benjamin and Mrs Robinson. The conventions of continuity editing, codified in Karel Reisz's chapters of *The Technique of Film Editing*, are designed to create a smooth homogeneous space in the same scene. But in *The Graduate*, they are employed to edit together separate spaces:

Benjamin's home and the hotel. The conventions are: match on action cuts, directional continuity and analytic cut-ins. Reisz points out that the match on action cut 'keep[s] the action and movement shown in consecutive shots accurately continuous';[12] that is, 'the actions of two consecutive shots of a single scene should match'.[13] Directional continuity preserves a sense of screen direction by placing the viewer on the same side of the action.[14] Reisz points out that directional continuity and the match on action cut frequently work together to preserve the consistency and direction of an action across a cut. The purpose of an analytic cut-in is to show a portion of space in the previous shot.

The function of all three continuity techniques is to create simultaneity of space and consecutiveness of time across successive shots in the same scene. However, O'Steen used these continuity techniques to create a smooth continuous link between *two different spaces*. Match on action cuts and directional continuity create the impression that Benjamin walks back and forth from his parents' house and the hotel room. For example, he walks out of his parents' swimming pool, puts on a white shirt and then walks inside the house. As he goes inside, the next shot shows Benjamin walking out of the hotel bathroom. The two shots are linked by a match on Benjamin's actions (opening a door) and directional continuity (he moves in the same direction). Benjamin is also filmed in long shot in bed, accompanied by Mrs Robinson undressing him; an analytic cut then shows him in close up in bed. Yet, the cut-in to a close up is not in the same space or time, for there is a change in location, which is not evident when the cut takes place, due to the similarity of Benjamin's body position and his expression and the similarity of the décor. The change in location from hotel room to home across the cut is evident only when the analytic cut-in continues and we see Benjamin get up from the bed and go to the open door, where his parents are located. The scene disrupts the presumption that the match on action cut, directional continuity and the analytic cut-in preserve the unity of a singular space and time.

This technique of using the conventions of continuity editing in an unconventional manner culminates in the famous cut from Benjamin in the pool jumping onto the raft to Benjamin in the hotel room jumping onto the bed where Mrs Robinson is located. These two separate events are linked by a match on action cut and by the preservation of directional continuity. Moreover, the match on action between the two disparate spaces works because the speed Benjamin is moving in both shots is the same. This disparity of space is heightened when we hear the voice of Benjamin's father while seeing the shot of Benjamin and Mrs Robinson in bed: Benjamin in the hotel room looks up and off screen when his father's voice is heard on the soundtrack. The next shot shows Benjamin's father outside looking down and off screen. The eye line match links the two shots whereas the difference in location (interior/exterior) creates disjunction. This example also demonstrates a creative use of dialogue editing – more specifically, the J-edit, or pre-lapping of voice (the off-screen voice is heard; cut to the source of the voice).[15] In the J-edit the sound of the off-screen voice motivates the cut to the source of the voice.[16] But this example in *The Graduate* is creative and subversive because the voice appears to derive from a different location. The resulting humour – the impression that Benjamin's father is observing his son and Mrs Robinson in the hotel room – is created by the unconventional use of the J-edit (in combination with the eye line match, the match on action cut, the matching of the speed of the action across the cut and directional continuity).

Dede Allen's Bonnie and Clyde

Dede Allen is renowned for editing six of Arthur Penn's films, most famously *Bonnie and Clyde* and *Night Moves* (1975), and for editing other accomplished films such as *Dog Day Afternoon* (Sidney Lumet, 1975), *Reds* (Warren Beatty, 1981)*, The Breakfast Club* (John Hughes, 1985) and *Wonder Boys* (Curtis Hanson, 2000). Although Allen did not write a memoir, she has been interviewed several times. In an interview with Ric Gentry she states that her contribution to a film as an editor is guided primarily by the characters: 'It's how I'm going to work on the characters. You have to know who the characters are, what they're going to do, how they're going to react. The director of course guides you in this and with how he shoots it, at least much of the time.'[17] An actor's performance dictated Allen's decision-making process, specifically the need to keep the point of focus on a character's eyes in each shot and on eye lines across shots. She emphasized performance and eyes by editing the shots without listening to the dialogue, although as Vincent LoBrutto points out, she memorized the dialogue before she began cutting:

> [S]he learned to memorize the dialogue of a scene and cut it without the track. Later, the assistant editor would add the sound. This technique, also employed by Jerry Greenberg and Walter Murch, allows the editor to concentrate on the performance by watching the emotions and action without listening to the sound that has already been absorbed. The sound is finalized later during the sound-editing and mixing phase of moviemaking.[18]

Allen contributed to shaping an actor's performance in the films she edited. Mark Harris explains that Allen had to edit Faye Dunaway's performance carefully in *Bonnie and Clyde*: '[Dunaway's] performance as Bonnie was full of brilliant, quicksilver flashes that had to be selected carefully from takes in which her nerves got the better of her'.[19] Allen's editing complemented Arthur Penn's actor-driven directing. Penn emphasized the actor's physical performance, the rhythm of their gestures and their body movement in general. In an interview he noted that '[Dede Allen] understands what an actor is doing, so my whole theory about rhythm is a theory that she shares'.[20]

Penn kept asking Allen to cut *Bonnie and Clyde* faster, to make the scenes more economical: 'Arthur really wanted to give it all this energy. He kept saying, "Look at the film again. Make it go faster."'[21] In general, this meant increasing the film's cutting rate, or average shot length. Barry Salt has calculated that the average shot length for American films from 1964 to 1969 is 7.7 seconds,[22] and that *Bonnie and Clyde*'s average shot length is twice as fast, at 3.78 seconds.[23] In

Figure 2.2 End of Shot 1 of *Bonnie and Clyde*. Copyright Warner Bros.

Figure 2.3 Beginning of Shot 2 of *Bonnie and Clyde*. Copyright Warner Bros.

terms of an actor's performance, Dede Allen frequently reduced their actions and gestures to their most expressive moments, paring them down by leaving out some actions.

We can see this economical cutting in the opening few shots. The credit sequence begins with a series of still photographs interspersed between the credits. After the director's credit, Bonnie (Faye Dunaway) and Clyde (Warren Beatty) are introduced separately, in still photographs with a short biography.

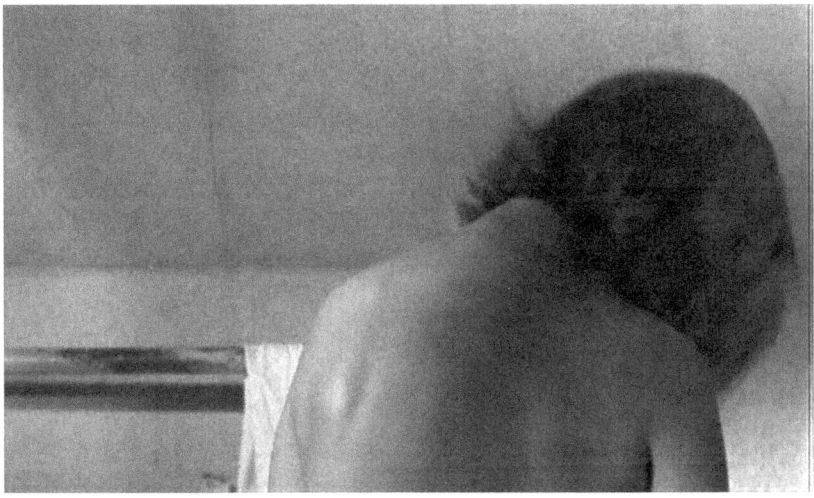

Figure 2.4 End of Shot 2 of *Bonnie and Clyde*. Copyright Warner Bros.

Figure 2.5 Beginning of Shot 3 of *Bonnie and Clyde*. Copyright Warner Bros.

The end of the credit sequence, the photograph of Clyde, dissolves into an extreme close up of Bonnie's lips as she puts on lipstick. The extreme close up becomes a close up as she turns screen right to look at herself in the mirror. The first cut occurs as soon as she begins to stand up (see Figure 2.2: End of Shot 1). In the second shot (medium close up) she has already stood up and is facing screen left (see Figure 2.3: Beginning of Shot 2); the middle part of her movement has been deleted, leading to a jump in the action. The second cut occurs as she drops to the bed; the cut takes place as soon as her downward movement begins (see Figure 2.4: End of Shot 2); at the beginning of the next shot the movement is almost complete (see Figure 2.5: Beginning of Shot 3). As with the first cut, in the second cut the middle part of the action is deleted, creating a jump in the action. As the shot continues, Bonnie hits the metal frame of the bed with her hand several times. She then sits up, and the camera tracks in to an extreme close up of her eyes.

Allen's choice of shots from the coverage Arthur Penn supplied is instructive, as are her cutting points (the moment she introduces a cut). The first cut is analytic: it takes place on the same axis or the same angle (the camera is pointing in the same direction in the shots but the shot scale changes [Figures 2.2 and 2.3]). The second cut is the opposite, for the camera position changes 180 degrees but maintains the same shot scale: as Bonnie begins to fall to the bed (Figure 2.4) the camera is focused on the back of her head and her naked back; the cut to the next shot (Figure 2.5) focuses on Bonnie's face at the other end of the bed. Although the 180 degree cut sounds jarring, it brings the spectator back to Bonnie's face and especially her eyes, thereby following Allen's key reason to cut. Moreover, shots 1 and 3 are symmetrical: shot 1 begins as an extreme close up of Bonnie's lips before changing to a close up of her face (framed in a mirror). Shot 3 begins as a close up of Bonnie's face (framed by the bars of the bed frame) before changing to an extreme close up of her eyes. Shots 1 and 3 therefore emphasize her lips and eyes, while shot 2 emphasizes her bare back. Although the symmetry makes the shots sound classical, the lack of a smooth match on action across the cuts (due to the deletion of the middle part of the action) makes it post-classical, as does the close framing and sudden camera movements as the camera closely follows Bonnie's frantic movements. Allen's selection of shots also shows Bonnie from all angles: facing the camera, in profile, from the back. There is no dialogue, but the soundtrack is rich with the sounds of birdsong and the rhythmic sound of machinery harvesting cotton. These sounds, together with the three shots that Allen has chosen to edit together, convey Bonnie's sense of entrapment, her frustration, restlessness and boredom.

But within a few minutes of meeting Clyde, Bonnie's mood changes from boredom to excitement. Both stand on a street corner drinking Coca Cola. Clyde shows Bonnie his gun and then heads into a grocery store to rob it. The drinking scene lasts 70 seconds and consists of 18 shots: 13 close ups of Bonnie and Clyde's faces edited together in a shot/reverse shot pattern, interspersed with 3 medium shots of them standing together in a two-shot, and 2 close ups of the gun. Allen's editing of the scene is fairly fast (3.8 seconds), matching the rest of the film. During the shot/reverse shot editing, Bonnie's eyes and expression are clearly visible. She continually looks off screen at Clyde, whereas for most of the scene Clyde has his eyes closed, looks down, or glances into the distance. The only time Bonnie looks away is when she thinks Clyde is bluffing regarding his criminal record. When he pulls out his gun, he looks into the distance while Bonnie looks at his gun and his face.

The shot/reverse shot editing is unconventional not only because it is cut twice as fast as the average for an American film of the late 1960s, but also because the shots are filmed with a long telephoto lens, making the space very tight and claustrophobic. Emphasis is also placed on Bonnie's lips as she drinks the Coca Cola, and on Clyde's shiny metallic gun. The tight claustrophobic framing comes to an end only when we see Clyde in a very long shot walking across the street to rob the store. The scene's master (or establishing) shot is therefore delayed by over a minute. The soundtrack remains quiet and the camera remains outside with Bonnie. The silence is broken when Clyde fires a warning shot in the air, an extremely loud hard sound made more startling by the silence that preceded it.

Allen also increased the film's pace via unusual scene transitions, by combining a fade with a straight cut:

> I broke many of my hard and fast rules about story, character, and how a scene plays. I think a lot of people at the time thought it wasn't good editing. The first time Jack Warner saw a cut, he couldn't believe that we were going to fade out at the end of a scene and then cut in with the next, or vice versa. He thought it was crazy. The way that started was when I tried a fade on one side and the other side wasn't ready yet. We looked at it that way and Arthur liked it and we began using it. It moved faster. It whooshed you in to the next scene, which Arthur thought was so important. A full fade has that black in the middle which stops.[24]

The first combination of a fade (a fade out) and a cut occurs 20 minutes into the film, in the transition from the scene where Clyde attempts to steal food from another grocery store to the beginning of the scene when Bonnie and Clyde first meet C. W. Moss (Michael J. Pollard). And the reverse combination is used around 46 minutes into the film: after the Barrow gang escapes from a police ambush, a cut is followed by a fade in.

Pauline Kael wrote a famous review of *Bonnie and Clyde* on its initial release – although she discussed the film's editing in just one paragraph near the end of her 7,000-word article. The paragraph begins: 'The editing of this movie is [...] the best editing in an American movie in a long time, and one may assume that Penn deserves credit for it along with the editor, Dede Allen.'[25]

Kael then mentions a number of scenes where the editing is 'inventive' (her term):

- The bank robberies
- The 'comedy sequence of Blanche running through the police barricades with her kitchen spatula in her hand'[26]
- In the final scene, showing the 'panic of Bonnie and Clyde looking at each other's face for the last time'.[27]

The most successful bank robbery takes place in Missouri (after the Barrow gang humiliates Texas ranger Frank Hamer [Denver Pyle], who was following them). The scene in the bank lasts 63 seconds, and consists of 41 shots taken from 8 different camera set ups in the bank and a further 2 outside. All the cuts observe the rules of continuity (match on action, directional continuity, eye line matches, analytic cut-ins, plus two inserts of C.W. Moss and Blanche [Estelle Parsons] outside the bank) but the cutting rate increases to 1.5 seconds as the scene shifts from 8 different points of interest, continually revealing and juxtaposing new areas of off-screen space.

The famous final sequence, the shooting of Bonnie and Clyde in an ambush, was filmed with multiple cameras with different focal length lenses running at different speeds. There were six takes in total. The sequence therefore had to be constructed from an enormous amount of footage in the editing room. Arthur Penn mentions that the final sequence was a collaborative effort between him and Dede Allen, together with her assistant editor Jerry Greenberg (who went on to edit *The French Connection* [William Friedkin, 1971], the helicopter attack sequence in *Apocalypse Now* [Francis Ford Coppola, 1979] and *Heaven's Gate* [Michael Cimino, 1980]). The finished sequence is dominated by:

- Rapid editing fracturing space
- Slow-motion shots combined with standard speed shots
- Overlapping action (especially of Clyde falling to the ground)
- Sudden hard sounds (birds, gunfire) breaking moments of silence
- Rapid camera movements, plus
- Restricted narration (although spectators know an ambush is being planned, they do not know the specific details – when and how it will take place).

These techniques (with the possible exception of slow motion) are not arbitrary or gratuitous, but are motivated. The rapid editing is motivated by shifting attention between several points of interest, with shots linked together or motivated by an eye line match (with most matches forming part of a point of view sequence). The hard sounds appear at the same time as a cut, making the shot transition more dramatic and startling than a J-edit. The restricted narration aligns the film spectator with Bonnie and Clyde (in terms of narrative information, not necessarily spatial position). Nonetheless, the accumulation of small details (Ivan Moss [Dub Taylor] jumping under his truck, the startled birds, the close ups of Bonnie and Clyde looking at each other) creates a moment of anticipation before the shooting begins. These techniques in turn maintain screen direction, and follow the drama and emotion of the sequence: a dramatic shift in tone and pacing from a relaxed to a tense atmosphere.

What is innovative in the scene of the shooting is Dede Allen's fast editing of the slow-motion shots – some of the action is slowed down but the cutting is quick (just over one cut a second). In addition, Allen adds to the mix normal motion shots of the action. The slow motion adds lyricism to the deaths of Bonnie and Clyde, and also extends the spectator's emotional reaction. Roger Crittenden argues in his *Manual of Film Editing* that, in *Bonnie and Clyde*, 'slow motion and other devices artificially extend the moment of high drama',[28] but Karen Pearlman argues in *Cutting Rhythms* that 'Penn and the editor Dede Allen use a rapid-fire mix of slow and faster shot speeds to convey the confusion, panic, and depths of feeling of the characters'.[29]

The visual and aural style of *Bonnie and Clyde* is reminiscent of Jean-Luc Godard's *Breathless* (1959), analysed by Gavin Millar in *The Technique of Film Editing*,[30] in which a police motorcyclist chases Michel (Jean-Paul Belmondo) but is later shot. Millar identifies Godard's innovations:

- The use of short shots (rapid editing) and their alternation with longer shots
- The sound of the gun (click of the gun being cocked, gunfire)
- Restricted narration (Millar says there is 'no omniscience'[31])
- Jump cuts
- Breaking screen direction.

In Millar's view, 'all these things, at first sight, [...] are obstacles to conventional smoothness and logic. Yet they are perfectly efficient in the sense that they create an impression of confusion, flight, fear, restrained violence, imminent danger, etc., [...]'.[32] The editing in *Bonnie and Clyde* moments before the two protagonists are gunned down creates the exact same effects, but without breaking screen direction or using jump cuts. However, whereas the killing of the policeman in *Breathless* barely appears on screen (Millar mentions that, when he is shot, we see the policeman on screen for 10 frames, or less than half a second[33]), in *Bonnie and Clyde* the killing is presented graphically on screen in slow and standard motion for almost 30 seconds. But Robert Benton and David Newman's screenplay says 'at no point do we see BONNIE and CLYDE in motion ... We never see BONNIE and CLYDE dead'.[34] This is the type of ending we see two years later in *Butch Cassidy and the Sundance Kid* (George Roy Hill, 1969), which ends on a freeze frame of the two titular protagonists while the gunfire continues on the soundtrack. Arthur Penn disregarded Benton and Newman's screenplay and designed the final scene.

Conclusion

The editors' memoirs and interviews are invaluable sources of information that reveal the collaborative relations as well as the demarcation of creative roles between editors and directors – who is contractually responsible for what aspect of a film. Editors require footage that has been filmed with editing in mind (shots that follow the conventions of screen direction, that match action and décor, angles and scale of shots that cut together) as well as sufficient coverage to enable the editor to experiment with different editing choices. Editors also require freedom from interference, for a proficient editor understands the requirements of an edited scene more than the director or producer. Whereas the director is the centre of the production process (with the producer standing close behind), the editor (or editorial team) is ultimately responsible for creating the technical and stylistic aspects of the answer print – not only its editing, but also the dialogue and the sound mix, plus grading the print's density and colour.[35] Guided by editing manuals, my analysis of a select number of key scenes from films edited by Ralph Rosenblum, Sam O'Steen and especially Dede Allen reveal that editors did not just splice together the inventive shots made by Hollywood Renaissance directors and cinematographers, but made significant and innovative contributions to the visual design of Hollywood Renaissance films.

Notes

1   Kevin Brownlow, quoted in Roger Crittenden, *The Thames and Hudson Manual of Film Editing* (London: Thames and Hudson, 1981), 74.

2   Pauline Kael, 'The Current Cinema: Bodies', *The New Yorker*, 6 October 1986, 127.

3   Stefan Sharff, *The Elements of Cinema: Towards a Theory of Cinesthetic Impact* (New York: Columbia University Press, 1982), 141–2.

4   See David Bordwell, Janet Staiger and Kristin Thompson, *The Classical Hollywood Cinema: Film Style and Mode of Production to 1960* (London: Routledge, 1985). However, in chapter 30, the authors maintain that the Hollywood mode of production and film style persisted after 1960: 'Just as the Hollywood mode of production continues, the classical style remains the dominant model for feature filmmaking' (Bordwell et al. *Classical Hollywood*, 370). Todd Berliner is more perceptive in his identification of narrational innovations in a number of key films from the Hollywood Renaissance (including *The French Connection* [Friedkin, 1971], *The Godfather* [Coppola, 1972] and *Taxi Driver* [Scorsese, 1976]): 'Such films [...] use the Hollywood paradigm as a point of departure, mining it for ideological incongruities, logical and characterological inconsistencies, and other unconventional and unsettling narrative perversities that seventies cinema made more common. Although seventies modes of narration became less pervasive after 1977, seventies filmmakers, by pushing against the limits of classical narration, discovered narrative options previously unexplored in Hollywood, options that quickly became part of Hollywood's regular repertoire of narrative strategies'. Todd

Berliner, *Hollywood Incoherent: Narration in Seventies Cinema* (Austin: University of Texas Press, 2010), 218–19.

5   Arthur Penn, quoted in Mark Harris, *Scenes From a Revolution: The Birth of the New Hollywood* (London: Cannon Gate, 2008), 9.

6   Ralph Rosenblum, with Robert Karen, *When the Shooting Stops . . . the Cutting Begins: A Film Editor's Story*, new edition (Cambridge, MA: Da Capo Press, 1986).

7   Rosenblum, *When the Shooting*, 183.

8   Rosenblum, *When the Shooting*, 153.

9   Sam O'Steen, as told by Bobbie O'Steen, *Cut to the Chase: Forty-Five Years of Editing America's Favorite Movies* (Studio City, CA: Michael Wiese Productions, 2001).

10 O'Steen, *Cut to the Chase*, 43–4.

11 O'Steen, *Cut to the Chase*, ix–x, 63.

12 Karel Reisz and Gavin Millar, *The Technique of Film Editing*, 2nd enlarged edition (London and New York: Focal Press, 1968), 217. (Reisz wrote the first part of this book [13–272] and Gavin Millar wrote the second part [279–387]).

13 Reisz and Millar, *Technique of Film Editing*, 216.

14 Reisz and Millar, *Technique of Film Editing*, 222.

15 Barry Salt, 'Reaction Time: How to Edit Movies', *New Review of Film and Television Studies*, 9.3 (2011): 343; Lori Jane Coleman and Diana Friedberg, *Jump Cut: How to Jump Start Your Career as a Film Editor* (New York: Routledge, 2017), 73–5.

16 Barry Salt notes that the opposite type of edit is called the 'L-edit', where the voice of the speaker on screen carries over to the next shot (Salt, 'Reaction Time', 343). Coleman and Friedberg call it 'post-lapping' (Coleman and Friedberg, *Jump Cut*, 73–5).

17 Dede Allen, in Ric Gentry, 'Dede Allen: An Interview', *Post Script: Essays in Film and the Humanities*, 19.3 (Summer 2000): 9.

18 Vincent LoBrutto, *The Art of Motion Picture Editing: An Essential Guide to Methods, Principles, Processes, and Terminology* (New York: Allworth Press, 2012), 82.

19 Harris, *Scenes From a Revolution*, 287.

20 Arthur Penn, quoted in Nat Segaloff, *Arthur Penn: American Director* (Lexington: The University Press of Kentucky, 2011), 157.

21 Dede Allen quoting Arthur Penn, in Gentry, 'Dede Allen', 23.

22 Barry Salt, *Film Style and Technology: History and Analysis*, 3rd edition (London: Starword, 2009), 302.

23 Barry Salt, 'Barry Salt's Database', *Cinemetrics* website, http://www.cinemetrics.lv/satltdb.php (n.d.).

24 Dede Allen, in Gentry, 'Dede Allen', 23.

25 Pauline Kael, '*Bonnie and Clyde*', in *Raising Kane and Other Essays* (London and New York: Marion Boyars, 1996), 123.

26 Kael, '*Bonnie and Clyde*', 123.

27 Kael, '*Bonnie and Clyde*', 123.

28 Crittenden, *Manual of Film Editing*, 87.

29 Karen Pearlman, *Cutting Rhythms: Shaping the Film Edit* (Oxford: Focal Press, 2009), 210.

30 Reisz and Millar, *Technique of Film Editing*, 346–53.

31 Reisz and Millar, *Technique of Film Editing*, 350–1.

32 Reisz and Millar, *Technique of Film Editing*, 351.

33 Reisz and Millar, *Technique of Film Editing*, 352.

34 Robert Benton and David Newman, *Bonnie and Clyde* screenplay, quoted in Harris, *Scenes From a Revolution*, 255.

35 Dede Allen mentions in her interview with Gentry that cinematographers usually work with the lab on grading a print, but in practice it is the editor who gets involved: 'On *Bonnie and Clyde*, (cinematographer) Bernie Guffey couldn't come to the lab, and the timing on that was very involved. In fact, *Bonnie and Clyde* was the first one where I became heavily involved in the color timing because Arthur [Penn] hated what they had done with the picture the first time he saw it. The color was saturated and very heavy. He wanted more of a Japanese look and discovered that none of those guys had seen anything like that' (Dede Allen, in Gentry, 'Dede Allen', 17).

Chapter 3

'I SMELL MONEY!': CLASS PRODUCT, *THE GRADUATE* (1967) AND THE CORPORATIZATION OF EMBASSY

A. T. McKenna

Introduction

The Graduate was released in December 1967 to critical acclaim and enormous commercial success. Its initial release came a week or so following the publication of the article 'The Shock of Freedom in Films',[1] *Time* magazine's account of a new, frank, European-influenced Hollywood; and just a few months after the surprise success of *Bonnie and Clyde* (Arthur Penn, 1967), a film that was seen as a watershed moment in American cinema, as was *The Graduate*: 'After months of prattle about the "new" American film (mostly occasioned by the overrated *Bonnie and Clyde*)', wrote Stanley Kauffman in the *New Republic*, '*The Graduate* gives some substance to the contention that American films are coming of age – of our age.'[2]

The Graduate's place in cinema history seemed to be sealed even before it completed its initial run. Having retained its evergreen lustre, film historians use its themes of intergenerational conflict and anti-materialism, as well as its supposedly bargain-basement origins, to romantically position its success as a triumph of youthful grass-roots idealism over the cynical, outdated and crumbling studio system. For J. W. Whitehead, *The Graduate* was 'the little film that could;'[3] and for Peter Biskind, '*Bonnie and Clyde* was a movement movie; like *The Graduate*, young audiences recognised it as "theirs".'[4] Such views are not without merit. One simply cannot discount the notion that the huge success of *The Graduate* represented a groundswell embrace from its youthful baby-boomer audience. But the romanticization of *The Graduate* and its commercial success overlooks the industrial and corporate manoeuvrings happening in Hollywood in the mid-to-late 1960s, manoeuvrings into which *The Graduate* was intricately woven.

The Graduate was financed and distributed in the United States by Embassy,[5] whose president, Joseph E. Levine, was famous as a master self-publicist, and as

America's foremost purveyor of exploitation films, glossy censor-baiting blockbusters, arthouse fare and 'weirdies'. Levine's involvement with *The Graduate* tends to be overlooked or disparaged by film historians (and, indeed, some of the film's makers), arguably because he represents the artless, commercially-minded cynicism to which the Hollywood Renaissance was supposedly a movement against. But Levine and Embassy were hugely influential in 1960s American cinema, and a closer engagement with them in a case study of *The Graduate* can provide a valuable vantage point to investigate the industrial tides of the period, which were peculiarly conducive to its production. Indeed, Levine's experience and versatility as a producer and promoter left him ideally positioned to sell *The Graduate* to the baby-boomer audience.

This chapter is split into three sections. The first section details Levine's importance in the film industry prior to the Hollywood Renaissance, but also shows how a series of misjudgements, along with changing audience tastes, led to the financial problems at Embassy for which *The Graduate* provided the solution. The second section concerns a massive policy overhaul at Embassy, and Levine's decision to concentrate on expensive English language productions. This section provides an analysis of the cultural climate Levine was responding to when he decided to associate himself with only 'class' product, and how he carefully promoted *The Graduate* to a discerning young audience. The third section analyses industrial forces and how, having returned to profitability with the success of *The Graduate*, Embassy became a takeover target in the speculative bubble of Hollywood conglomeration. Levine sold Embassy for $40 million, and joined Avco Embassy as president, before embarking on the quietest period of his career as Hollywood entered a recession.

The business machinations that occurred during the Hollywood Renaissance have not received the attention they deserve, and this chapter acts as a corrective. Beneath the freewheeling aesthetics of the Hollywood Renaissance ran undercurrents of industrial manoeuvrings, marketing innovations and creeping conglomerations. *The Graduate*, in its wider context, is a model example of these themes, and it enabled Levine to perform an audaciously executed reversal of fortune. Levine used its financial success, and its cultural cache, to demonstrate his business acumen, acquire the cultural capital he lacked, and sell his company for a fortune, amid one of the most turbulent times in Hollywood history.

Joseph E. Levine and Embassy's diminishing returns

Immaculate in appearance, and coarse in manner, Joseph E. Levine was Embassy's portly, irascible, motor-mouth president. Born into an immigrant family in the slums of Boston in 1905, Levine had been an exhibitor and film distributor in New England, before achieving fame with his blunderbuss saturation promotion of *Hercules* (Pietro Francisci, 1958) in America in 1959, which he released through a distribution deal with Warner Bros. Breaking the record for the number of prints in simultaneous circulation in the United States, 635 prints of *Hercules* toured the country, preceded by a national marketing campaign and localized media blitzes announcing its arrival in various territories, laying the groundwork for future summer blockbusters such as *Jaws* (Steven Spielberg, 1975). *Hercules* was a huge financial success, and made Levine a national celebrity.

It is unusual, to say the least, for a film promoter to become famous, yet that is exactly what Levine was. He was famous in the true sense of the word, in that his name was known by the man in the street. The huge *Hercules* promotional campaign was not just about promoting the film, it was about promoting Joseph E. Levine. 'We're reminding everybody that this is a circus business,'[6] he said, as he positioned himself as circus ringmaster. Following *Hercules*'s success, Levine was profiled in *Time*,[7] *Esquire*,[8] *Life*,[9] *Fortune*,[10] the *New Yorker*,[11] and lampooned as Joe LeVenal in *Mad* magazine.[12]

Levine adopted a populist pose and sought to antagonize members of America's cultural elite, or 'eggheads' as he called them, who were more than willing to be antagonized. Following the success of *Hercules*, Levine began importing and promoting European art films, notably *Two Women* (Vittorio de Sica, 1960) and *8½* (Federico Fellini, 1963), further upsetting those who were already critical of Levine's vulgar showman shtick. Dwight Macdonald, one of America's foremost intellectuals, worried, 'Mr. Levine aspires to more than just profits; he wants to make the art scene too. His ambitions . . . are now flowering like some exotic plant, say the Venus Fly Trap.'[13] Macdonald implies that Levine craved the cultural capital associated with art cinema, but it was not true. Levine revelled in his multifariousness as he continued to deal in low budget weirdies alongside prestigious arthouse films, and delighted in the consternation he caused with such indecorous cross-pollination, playfully prefiguring Pierre Bourdieu's contention, 'The most intolerable thing for those who regard themselves as the possessors of legitimate culture is the sacrilegious reuniting of tastes which taste dictates shall be separated.'[14] In keeping with his populist manner, Levine was often fiercely defensive of the audience for films such as *Hercules*, but would mischievously ridicule the 'eggheads' who enjoyed his arthouse films such as *8½*: 'That's a picture people talk about at cocktail parties. Nobody understood it. They just talked about it.'[15]

Levine enjoyed enormous success for much of the 1960s promoting films from all over the world and all across the cultural spectrum. In addition to low budget children's films such as *Morgan, the Pirate* (André de Toth and Primo Zeglio, 1961) and *Santa Claus Conquers the Martians* (Nicholas Webster, 1964), and Oscar-winning prestige product such as *Yesterday, Today and Tomorrow* (Vittorio de Sica, 1963) and *Darling* (John Schlesinger, 1964), Levine also worked as an independent producer for Paramount, producing spectacular tales of derring-do such as *Zulu* (Cy Endfield, 1964), alongside a string of sexy censor-baiting properties such as *The Carpetbaggers* (Edward Dmytryk, 1964),

A House is not a Home (Russell Rouse, 1964) and *Harlow* (Gordon Douglas, 1965). These latter films kept Levine in the critics' firing line as he was portrayed as a bad influence on American cinema in certain sections of the media.[16] High profile and controversial films, as well as Levine's tireless courting of the press, ensured that he remained a prominent figure in America and beyond.

Levine scored a massive success with his production of *The Carpetbaggers*, which became Paramount's highest ever grossing non-roadshow film. Subsequently, however, his investments began to bring forth diminishing returns, and other Paramount films such as *Where Love Has Gone* (Edward Dmytryk, 1964) and *Harlow* were, although money makers, not as financially successful as hoped or hyped. Such setbacks, while frustrating, should not have caused any significant financial problems for Embassy. By the mid-1960s Embassy was deeply embedded in the American film industry, and had developed its own idiosyncratic methods of operation. Levine was, first and foremost, a showman-promoter, but Embassy had a strong production record and distribution network, and many organizations were keen to work and be associated with Levine and Embassy. But, during the 1960s, Levine and Embassy embarked on countless production, co-production, distribution and investment deals, creating a truly byzantine web of partnerships and associations.[17] Many investments were made, and many losses incurred.

In August 1965 Levine told the *Hollywood Reporter* of his intention to expand operations at Embassy: 'We're going to produce and distribute with a greater intensity ... we're going to produce and distribute every conceivable type of picture ... American and foreign ... high budget and low budget.'[18] Levine splurged on low budget films: family films such as *The Daydreamer* (Jules Bass, 1966) and *Mad Monster Party* (Jules Bass, 1967), spaghetti western imports such as *A Pistol for Ringo* (Duccio Tessari, 1965), horror-western hybrids such as *Billy the Kid vs Dracula* (William Beaudine, 1966) and dozens more cheap curios. It was a gamble that did not pay off. In 1966, less than a year on from his announcement, Levine called a halt to the low budgeters, and announced a dramatic reversal of policy at Embassy, declaring that Embassy would now concentrate on 'nothing but "big" English language films'.[19]

This was a remarkable change of tack for Levine, whose filmic inventory was the most variegated in American cinema, distinguished by high-low culture clashes and odd juxtapositions. But the market he sought for his low budget offerings was simply not there. In interviews, Levine observed a changing market: 'Of course, that kind of promotion, that kind of picture,' he said of *Hercules* in 1966, 'you couldn't sell it now. People have become very skilful at smelling out what's good and what's lousy.'[20] Elsewhere he complained, 'We spent the last eighteen months making family films which no family saw. My son went to see *Blow-Up* [Antonioni, 1966].'[21]

Levine's comments are instructive. He had made a fortune from catering to young audiences with films such as *Hercules*, but the tactic of massively hyping a low rent movie was no longer working. It is also worth noting that Levine's showman contemporaries were also changing direction. William Castle, the febrile mind behind so many horror-movie gimmicks, had responded to his own diminishing audience by turning his attention to more prestigious fare by producing *Rosemary's Baby* (Roman Polanski, 1968), and Sam Arkoff of American International Pictures responded to the generation gap by making fewer beach and bikini movies and more biker and counterculture movies.[22]

Perhaps the American youth of the late 1960s was failing to detect and appreciate the irony inherent in the explosive promotional campaigns of *Hercules* and the like, or perhaps they had grown weary of the tactics that attracted them as children, and were looking for greater sophistication. But a feeling that was general in American cinema at the time was that movie-going habits had changed. Levine's observation, 'People don't go to the movies, they go to *a* movie,'[23] were echoed six months later by Paramount's Head of Production, Robert Evans: 'Today, people go to see a movie; they no longer go to the movies,' he told *Time*, 'We can't depend on habit anymore. We have to make "I've got to see that" pictures.'[24] And that was precisely the kind of picture Levine was looking to make when he set out to make, release and promote, *The Graduate*.

Expensive and in English

Having announced a change of direction in Embassy's production schedule in 1966, *Variety* reported on an even more remarkable change of policy: 'It is noted that the now celebrated line JOSEPH E. LEVINE PRESENTS ... has been absent from [Embassy's] low budget entries, and those close to Levine have made it clear that, at this stage in his career, the boss is anxious to have his name associated with "class" product only.'[25] Levine gloried in his low brow pedigree, loved the juxtapositions in his output, and would, hitherto, have tried to slap his name on any and every film that came into his orbit; but now he was, very uncharacteristically, attempting to acquire some cultural capital – courting rather than confounding the 'eggheads'.

Levine was no stranger to cultural capital; as noted, he distributed and funded many critically acclaimed films. But he was a great oppositionist who loved to skewer the pretentions of the high-minded and undermine the very notion of cultural distinction. Even as Embassy was releasing low budget efforts without Levine's name on, he was bragging to Dick Griffin that he was considering producing an adaptation of Christopher Marlowe's *Doctor Faustus* with Elizabeth Taylor and Richard Burton, and then contriving to mention his production of *Santa Claus Conquers the Martians* in the same sentence.[26] The ostentatious clashing of cultural forms was such a feature of Levine's output that it seems amazing that he would seek to associate himself with only 'class product', but that was the way it was to be, for a while at least; and *Variety* reported on the kind of class product Levine had in mind: *Runaway Train*, to be directed by Akira Kurosawa,[27] and *The Graduate*.[28]

The Graduate, a novel by Charles Webb, was published in 1963. Lawrence Turman, a young producer whose credits included *I Could Go On Singing* (Ronald Neame, 1963) and *The Best Man* (Franklin Schaffner, 1964), read it and felt inspired (the book 'haunted me' he said later).[29] He bought the rights for $1,000, teamed up with director Mike Nichols, and set about finding funding, which eventually came from Levine and Embassy. The film of *The Graduate* was announced in *Variety* in October 1964,[30] and the project took its place within Embassy's scattershot schedule. Levine's version of how the project began is:

> I met Mike Nichols ... when he was doing *The Knack* in a theatre I owned off-Broadway. I watched him rehearse. He was a genius of Broadway then and still is. I said, 'Why don't you make a movie?' The next day he brought in the book *The Graduate* by Charles Webb, and I read it. He asked, 'How'd you like it?' I said it was the worst thing I'd ever read in my life. 'Then you won't make it?' I said, 'I'll make it if *you* want to make it.'[31]

Nichols, however, remembered things differently, and said that approaching Levine for funding was, 'in every possible sense ... scraping the bottom of the barrel'; similarly, for Turman, Levine and Embassy represented 'the last stop on the line'.[32]

With such conflicting stories, it is difficult to know the truth. With Levine's anecdotes one should always read against the grain and assume a certain amount of embellishment; but it is also the case that both Nichols and Turman exaggerate the penny-ante status of Embassy. Levine's company had achieved Oscar acclaim for its arthouse imports, and Embassy was, at this time, in partnership with Paramount. So Turman's deal was not just with Levine's little company, it could have, potentially, led to major studio involvement: 'as usual' read *Variety*'s report about *The Graduate*, '[Levine has] allowed room for Paramount to enter the deal at a later date'.[33] Indeed, Paramount provided office space to Turman and Nichols during pre-production. But Levine mentioning *The Knack* is worth investigating. Levine was an investor-producer for this 1964 production of Ann Jellicoe's play, which Nichols directed, and nowhere in histories about *The Graduate* is this connection between Nichols and Levine mentioned, while disparaging assessments of Levine's supposed philistinism are commonplace.

The Knack was produced by The Establishment Theatre Company, a UK-based venture Levine had invested in, whose members included Peter Cook, Ivor David Balding and Sybil Burton. When the company was looking to set up a base in New York, Sybil Burton (recently divorced from the actor Richard Burton) approached Levine for funding through their mutual friend, Stanley Baker. Levine agreed and built up ties with the Establishment, and Burton praised him in *Variety*: 'he calls the group "Reservoir of Talent" and I think that is Levine's greatest quality. He recognizes and uses talent.'[34] Once again, some reading against the grain is necessary. Aside from the scepticism that should be afforded to any trade article in which a writer praises her benefactor, it should be noted that this article appeared in a gigantic eighty-three-page feature/advertisement for Levine, Embassy and its wares. Nonetheless, Levine's status as an investor in the Establishment provided him with a connection to Nichols, and Levine had a strong record of working with or nurturing talented artists and performers.

According to Turman, Levine was keen to fund *The Graduate* in order 'to be associated with Mike Nichols, who was already hot stuff in the N Y world of chic … *The Graduate* was his entrée into a classier world of film than he was used to.'[35] This is perhaps an overly cynical view, but it does chime with Levine's distancing himself from some of his lower-end productions in the mid–1960s. However, despite his schlockmeister reputation, Levine was drawn to gifted directors. He invested in most of Vittorio de Sica's 1960s output, and worked with other Euro-art directors such as Jean-Luc Godard[36] and Federico Fellini. In the mid–1960s he sought to make films with established talents such as Akira Kurosawa (the aforementioned *Runaway Train*) and John Huston (the unrealized *Will Adams*), and new talents such as Richard Attenborough (*Gandhi*, which was eventually released in 1983 without Levine's involvement). Levine was also, in 1964, complaining in the pages of *Variety* about the lack of young directing talent in Hollywood.[37] So, working with and nurturing directing talent was high on Levine's agenda at this time, though the cultural capital that Mike Nichols brought with him via his theatre successes was certainly another attraction.

In the three years between *The Graduate*'s announcement and its release, Nichols's cultural stock continued to rise. Nichols followed his success with *The Knack* with two successful Broadway productions: Murray Schisgal's *Luv* in 1964, and Neil Simon's *The Odd Couple* in 1965. This was followed by his feature film directorial debut, *Who's Afraid of Virginia Woolf?* (1966) which was controversial, critically acclaimed, financially successful and earned Nichols a Best Director nomination at the 1966 Academy Awards (see Chapter 1 of this collection).

As Nichols's stock rose, so did *The Graduate*'s budget. One thing that made the project attractive to Levine, according to Turman, was its low budget: 'I told him I could make it for a million bucks, which was my honest hope/intention at the time.'[38] But following the unwise investments in a large number of low budget family and exploitation films, Embassy was seeking to make fewer, but more expensive, films, as Levine told Calvin Tomkins in 1966:

> We won't be doing as many things as we've done in the past, but they'll all be big budget pictures. Like this picture Mike Nichols is doing for us now – *The Graduate*. Mike is a genius, and we may really have ourselves something there. It all depends on how things break of course.[39]

Although Aniko Bodroghkozy has suggested that Embassy 'jump[ed] on the rebellious youth bandwagon',[40] preparations for *The Graduate* had begun before the rebellious youth cycle of the 1960s; and the others of Levine's expensive English language films (*Runaway Train, Will Adams, Gandhi*) were prestige productions and not directed at the youth market. But Levine probably knew that something was changing in youth culture – after all, his son had been to see *Blow-Up*. This film, swinging London seen through a Euro-art lens, was successful in America, particularly among the young which, as Robert Sklar argues, was developing increasingly sophisticated tastes in cinema:

> Oriented to visual media as no previous generation had been ... when members of this new generation began to encounter classic European and Hollywood movies through college courses many were astounded by the wonders of past movies ... in comparison with television shows.[41]

Against a backdrop of youthful sophistication, films such as *Blow-Up, Tom Jones* (Tony Richardson, 1963), *Alfie* (Lewis Gilbert, 1966), *Morgan: A Suitable Case For Treatment* (Karel Reisz, 1966) and Embassy's *Darling*, became popular with young audiences. These films represented a new generation of European art films, from Britain, whose popularity with audiences was aided, in no small part, by the fact that they were in English, as well as their smart and savvy treatment of 'adult' themes. Moreover, opportune as *The Graduate* was, Levine was capitalizing on conditions he helped to create with his arthouse hits and British imports such as *Darling*. Indeed, Turman and Nichols paid homage to the European arthouse in *The Graduate* by casting Eddra Gale as Woman on Bus, having discovered that she had appeared in *8½*.[42]

J. W. Whitehead identifies *The Graduate* as an 'art-house film for the masses'.[43] Levine had probably done more to popularize art cinema than any of his contemporaries, and one of the reasons for his antagonistic relationship with critics was that he felt they had an undue influence on the success or otherwise of an arthouse film. 'I think my company brought more art house films here than any other company', he told the *Film Daily* in June 1967, 'You don't bring them here and be at the mercy of a couple of critics in New York. If they don't like an art film you're dead. If a commercial film is panned by the critics nobody pays any attention.'[44] One feature of the British films mentioned earlier is that they achieved box office success in America despite being critically divisive. These films were aimed at the youth market – not a demographic known for basing their consumption choices on critical opinion. With *The Graduate*, Levine had a chance to make what he had wanted to make for much of the 1960s – an art film that could circumvent critical influence.

According to Nichols, during production, 'Levine was never around; he gave us $3 million and then left us alone. If there were objections once we started filming, I never heard them.'[45] This rings true. As a producer, Levine often functioned as a participant investor rather than a hands-on producer, and he rarely claimed any credit for any specific production decisions made on *The Graduate*.[46] What he did do, however, is ascribe all the credit for the film's artistic success to Mike Nichols and, thereby, tangentially to himself for having 'discovered' Nichols. Following the success of *The Graduate*, Levine talked about the film and Mike Nichols often in interviews, but he never mentioned its producer and driving force, Lawrence Turman: 'once the film became a big hit he did everything he could to obliterate me' recalled Turman in 2006, 'including at our celebratory party attempting to seat me a mile away from himself with Mike Nichols and cast members. Mike had to intervene on my behalf.'[47]

Levine was a showman, and though he may not have contributed much beyond money to the production itself, he excelled in selling the film. Again, there are conflicting stories. Mark Harris's book, *Pictures at a Revolution*, contains speculation from both the author and the film's star, Dustin Hoffman, that Levine was dissatisfied with the finished film, unhappy at the lack of sexual content, and unsure of how to market the film.[48] Mike Nichols, however, recalled, 'When we showed Levine the finished movie, he said, [in a singsong voice] "I smell mo-ney!" I was very moved by that remark';[49] and Turman recalls that, on seeing the final edit, 'Joe loved it, as well he should have, considering the junky films he was used to putting out.'[50] Turman, who has no reason to say positive things about Levine, also says that, 'Joe Levine was a high-powered kick-ass salesman and he sure sold the hell out of *The Graduate*.'[51]

Mark Harris suggests that Levine was unsure of how to handle the finished product,[52] while both J. W. Whitehead and Andrew Sarris argue that *The Graduate*'s success came organically, with audiences attracted by word of mouth (for Whitehead), and *zeitgeist* curiosity (for Sarris). According to Whitehead:

Audiences [spoke] loudly in the film's favour with their cold hard cash. *The Graduate* immediately attracted a repeat word-of-mouth clientele that created serpentine lines around the city blocks at the two theatres where it was playing in Manhattan during its initial run ... *The Graduate* was the little film that could.[53]

According to Andrew Sarris:

The kids kept standing on line for a) Dustin Hoffman and b) Simon and Garfunkel. Then the adults stood on line to find out why the kids stood on line. Then the deep thinkers on the prestige publications stood on line to find out why the adults stood on line.[54]

Much of the writing about *The Graduate*'s initial success conforms to Hollywood Renaissance mythology: the young audience defining the screen agenda and creating a 'movement' which attracted the intellectual curiosity of cultural chroniclers. However, while *The Graduate* was still in production, and more than six months before its release, *Variety* hinted at how Levine planned to guide it to success: 'The film will open at Christmas with the usual Levine exploitation', ran the article, 'He may play it hard ticket in smaller theatres ...

"Word of mouth" says Levine, "is still the best publicity".'[55] Having made his name with saturation promotion, Levine opted for a less blunderbuss approach with *The Graduate*.

Word of mouth, the supposedly self-generating authentic voice of the grass roots, had been a strategy from the beginning. Levine had sought to make *The Graduate* what Robert Evans described as an 'I've got to see that' picture for a generation who were, as Justin Wyatt argues, unresponsive to the entreaties of roadshow extravaganzas.[56] Following the film's initial release, when the home-for-holidays target audience returned to their college campuses, Levine created more buzz by sending Nichols and Hoffman on a tour of college campuses to promote and discuss the film.[57] By the middle of 1968, with the film still playing in many cinemas, Jacob Brackman, in observations reminiscent of Levine's 'cocktail picture' assessment of *8½*, called *The Graduate* 'a nearly mandatory movie experience, which can be discussed at gatherings that cross boundaries of age and class.'[58]

Of course, Levine cannot be ascribed all the credit for the phenomenal success of *The Graduate*, but he can be ascribed credit for the thoughtful promotion – something that has been largely overlooked by film historians and scholars keen to embrace a romantic interpretation of a Hollywood Renaissance led by the grass roots. That said, having agreed to fund *The Graduate* in 1964, for it to come to fruition in 1967 was remarkably fortuitous.

Cashing in on The Graduate

In 1966 a wave of buyouts and conglomerations began rolling through Hollywood, beginning with Gulf & Western's takeover of the troubled Paramount. Following Paramount's takeover, Seven Arts bought Warner Bros. and, in 1967, Transamerica acquired United Artists. In 1969, Seven Arts sold Warner Bros. to Kinney National Services and, also in 1969, MGM sold out to real estate magnate Kirk Kerkorian. In the feeding frenzy atmosphere, it was natural that Embassy should attract attention. In May 1968, Levine sold Embassy to the Avco Corporation for $40 million, becoming president of Avco Embassy on a salary of $200,000 per year.

Speculative conglomerates were attracted by the undervaluation of studio stock, and asset stripping conglomerates were attracted by the valuable real estate owned by the studios; and everyone was interested in capitalizing on the studios' film libraries, which could be sold to television. Embassy was privately owned, so stock undervaluation did not apply in its case. Nor did the enticements of valuable real estate – Embassy owned no such property. What Embassy did have was a vast library of movies that could find a home on television. Embassy also had Levine, the most recognizable movie showman in America. Levine and Embassy had just released *The Graduate*, a film that was not only critically and financially successful, but also pointed toward fertile creative and commercial grounds for American cinema as the Hollywood Renaissance began to take shape. In addition, *The Graduate*'s director, Mike Nichols, had emerged as one of the most exciting talents in this new Hollywood, and Levine had a contract with him for two more films. All of these factors made Embassy an attractive proposition for Avco, a highly diversified corporation involved in everything from insurance and banking to the manufacture of farm equipment and weaponry, but no interests in films or entertainment.

Immediately prior to *The Graduate*, many of Levine's projects had been unsuccessful, and much of Embassy's back catalogue was unsuited to profitable television sales.[59] But in the gold rush atmosphere, and the urgency of competition as Embassy investigated other offers,[60] the very current and very dazzling success of *The Graduate* may well have overshadowed some or many failures on Embassy's books. But Embassy was more than just a movie vault. It was a notable success in the precarious world of distribution, and was a company that many other organizations were keen to collaborate with, both in terms of production, with Paramount being the most notable example, and distribution – two of Levine's most infamous successes, *Hercules* and *8½*, had been distributed by Warner Bros. and Columbia respectively. Moreover, even the casual observer would have noticed that movie-going habits were changing, and the market fragmenting. Levine was the most versatile promoter in the business, and had spent his career catering to niches.

Levine had made his fair share of misjudgements in the mid-1960s, but he was by no means a spent force. His profile was still high. In the trade and popular press, from *Variety* to *Women's Wear Daily*, he would appear to deliver idiosyncratic one-liners and spout pronouncements on the state of Hollywood and what should be done about it. Recent failures aside, Levine's successes in the film industry had been many and varied, his influence on the industry in the previous ten years had been extraordinary, and he was the most recognizable executive in American cinema. As Avco's president, James Kerr wrote in *Variety*:

> The question has been asked: would Avco have been interested in Embassy without *The Graduate*? The answer is an unqualified *yes* ... The remarkable success of the film did, on the other hand, affect the eventual financial arrangement. But we also had some knowledge of what Levine had up his sleeve in the way of projects and forthcoming releases.[61]

Once again, some reading against the grain in necessary here. Kerr's words come from an eighty-eight-page feature-advertisement in *Variety* for Avco Embassy, featuring pro-Levine tributes from influential people from the worlds of Hollywood and politics, and a plethora of advertisements which gave Avco Embassy a chance to promote its upcoming cinematic endeavours. But Kerr's words were not empty.

As for what Levine 'had up his sleeve', Embassy had released *The Producers* (Mel Brooks, 1967) shortly before the Avco deal was finalized, and released *The*

Lion in Winter (Anthony Harvey, 1968) shortly after; both were critically and commercially successful. The Avco Embassy spread in *Variety* also provided a glimpse of a varied slate of future releases from the new enterprise, including a couple of Harold Robbins adaptations, an adaptation of Ken Kesey's novel, *One Flew Over the Cuckoo's Nest*, to star Kirk Douglas,[62] and lower budget efforts such as *Macho Callahan* (Bernard L. Kowalski, 1970) and *The Man Who Had Power Over Women* (John Krish, 1970). Pride of place in the *Variety* feature, however, was *MN2*, standing for 'Mike Nichols 2', an as yet untitled project that would be Mike Nichols's second film for Embassy. 'Mike Nichols,' ran the blurb, 'Academy Award winning director of *The Graduate* will make his next film for Avco Embassy. ENOUGH SAID!'

The spectacular success of *The Graduate* was an important factor in Avco's acquisition of Embassy: 'Levine's company' wrote Kerr in *Variety*, 'provides Avco with an enhanced public image',[63] and *The Graduate* was key to that image-enhancement. Levine's involvement with *The Graduate* had seen a good deal of cultural capital bestowed upon him and his company, which could now be transferred to Avco. *The Graduate* was more than just a successful film; it was youthful, fashionable, intelligent and *a la mode*. It was a film about the generation gap that symbolized a break from the old studio-bound Hollywood to a more modern, artistic and freewheeling style of American filmmaking. It was directed by a *wunderkind* genius who had conquered Broadway, kick-started the Hollywood Renaissance, and was under contract to Levine for two more films. Having been nominated for the Best Director Oscar for his first feature, *Who's Afraid of Virginia Woolf?*, Nichols won the award for *The Graduate* in April 1968, a month before Avco's acquisition of Embassy. It would be impossible to put a price on such a combination of prestige and hip, but Avco had acquired it, and more besides, for $40 million.

If the release of *The Graduate* in 1967 had been fortuitous in allowing Levine to take advantage of a speculative bubble, then the sale of Embassy to Avco in 1968 had been doubly fortuitous. By the time of Avco's offer, *The Graduate*'s success had yet to make a dent in Embassy's sorry finances; its financial situation was dire, and Levine was in ill health. According to Tony Klinger, a filmmaker who was close with Levine at the time,

> Joe was literally having heart surgery when that deal came along to save his ass money wise. He thought the gig was up, he owed a fortune, with no prospect of payback. He was being wheeled to the operating theatre when the call with the deal came from Avco and he took the call before he was anaesthetised. He thought it was going to be to close his company down and he was, as ever, ready to fight, when he realised it was an offer way beyond his wildest dreams, to buy Embassy. He told us he couldn't fucking believe it![64]

Avco's millions had plugged the hole in Embassy's finances, and its billions provided an ideal capital base for future production. But, as Avco Embassy looked forward to a bright future, Hollywood entered recession. Ironically, *The Graduate* can be seen as a harbinger of that recession. The failure of Hollywood's family blockbuster strategies in the mid to late 1960s had led to the aggressive pursuit of other markets, which then proved unstable. As Thomas Schatz argues, 'Hollywood's cultivation of the youth market and penchant for innovation in the late 1960s and early 1970s scarcely indicated a favourable market climate. On the contrary, they reflected the studios' uncertainty and growing desperation.'[65]

Television, a driving force behind many of the conglomerate takeovers of the time, including the Avco Embassy merger, also proved to be unreliable. By 1969 the television bubble had burst. As Tino Balio observes, by 1968 television networks had acquired enough films to last them until 1972; and with movies on television every night of the week, an explosion in made-for-television films further contributed to 'a glut on the market that proved nearly catastrophic'.[66] As the recession took hold, Levine embarked on the quietest period of his career.

The staggering success of *The Graduate* had enticed Avco into a big money deal with Embassy, and Levine's relationship with Nichols had been trumpeted on the pages of *Variety*, but the relationship was not as fruitful as hoped. Nichols followed *The Graduate* with *Catch 22* (1970), which he made for Paramount, but he made his next two films for Avco Embassy: the well-regarded chamber piece, *Carnal Knowledge* (1971), and the widely ridiculed thriller about talking dolphins, *The Day of the Dolphin* (1973). Relations had soured between the two projects; *Carnal Knowledge* was announced with some fanfare, but Nichols made *The Day of the Dolphin*, according to a 1999 interview, 'because I needed to find something to get out of my contract with Joe Levine'.[67]

Levine's years at Avco Embassy were productive but, *Carnal Knowledge* aside, lacking in any significant successes (*The Producers* had been completed, and *The Lion in Winter* in production, before the Avco deal was signed). Throughout his years at Avco Embassy, Levine was less of a feature in the trades, and more likely to be found in the society pages of the popular press as he set about spending his vast wealth on art and other sundry items.

Having profited hugely from *The Graduate* and the industrial ructions that ran concurrent to the Hollywood Renaissance, Levine took a back seat and allowed the recession and his contract to play out. There is little doubt that he was miserable and frustrated during the Avco years, evidenced by the energy and enthusiasm he devoted to promotion and production once he had left Avco and set up once again as an independent with a new company, Joseph E. Levine Presents, with films such as *The Night Porter* (Liliana Cavani, 1974) and *A Bridge Too Far* (Richard Attenborough, 1977). *The Graduate* was the biggest hit of Levine's career. It also redefined his company, reinvigorated his reputation and allowed him to capitalize on a speculative bubble in an astonishing way. As he told Donna Rosenthal of the *LA Times* shortly before his death, the sale of Embassy to Avco was a 'horrible mistake, which made me rich'.[68]

Conclusion

At 9.00 pm EST on 8 November 1973, after *The Waltons*, *The Graduate* received its American television premiere on CBS. Its sale to CBS by Avco brought a lawsuit from its producer, Lawrence Turman. *The Graduate* had been sold as part of a package, and Turman accused Avco Embassy of overvaluing the other films in the package, and proportionally undervaluing *The Graduate*, thus diminishing the royalties due to Turman and Nichols, who had a three-way profit split with Embassy for the film. Turman was awarded $999,000 in 1980 after a lengthy dispute.[69]

It is a little ironic that Levine should be involved in block-booking, given that it was the Paramount Decree of 1948 (*United States* v. *Paramount Pictures, Inc.*, 334 US 131) which outlawed the practice, and provided opportunities for independent showman-entrepreneurs such as Levine to gain a foothold in the movie business; but it is not surprising. Levine was an opportunist and a gambler. His gambler's instincts had brought him huge success, but also led him to many unwise investments which nearly ruined him. Certainly, the industrial ructions of the late 1960s worked in his favour, yet this should not overshadow the fact that he was nimble and courageous enough to spot his mistakes and conduct a massive policy overhaul at Embassy. Indeed, in 1967 *Variety* called his new policy of making only expensive English language films 'the biggest gamble of his career'.[70]

The phenomenal success of *The Graduate* is something nobody could have predicted. The project had been rejected by, in Turman's words, 'every single studio',[71] but Levine had the instinct to invest, and this is something that should not be overlooked, or as disparaged as it has been, in histories of the Hollywood Renaissance. Moreover, Levine had spent his career hyping, amongst other things, exploitation films, arthouse fare and risqué Hollywood productions. From a showman's point of view, *The Graduate* can be understood as a combination of these three types, featuring the exploitable taboo of intergenerational adultery, an intelligent and stylized arthouse approach, and a glossy Hollywood treatment of sex.

Levine spent his career crossing cultural boundaries, which he began by hyping exploitation films such as *How to Undress in Front of Your Husband* (Dwain Esper, 1937), and sex-hygiene pictures such as *The Body Beautiful* (unknown director, c. 1938). Later, he applied exploitationist eventism on a national scale with films such as *Hercules*, targeting a burgeoning youth demographic. He then took his aggressive selling techniques to the arthouse, turning 8½ into a 'cocktail picture', and concurrently bothering censors with racy Hollywood product such as *The Carpetbaggers*. Levine's versatility, then, left him ideally positioned to sell *The Graduate*. He responded to a new audience's demands with sexy adult themes, intellectual interventions on college campuses and a genius auteur director. Restoring Levine to his proper place in the story of *The Graduate*, then, not only facilitates a fuller understanding of the industrial manoeuvrings of which *The Graduate* was such a part, but also highlights the all too often overlooked importance of exploitation and promotion in this most romanticized of periods in American cinema history, the Hollywood Renaissance.

Notes

1 Stefan Kanfer, 'The Shock of Freedom in Films', *Time*, 8 December 1967, http://www.time.com/time/magazine/article/0,9171,844256,00.html

2 Stanley Kaufman, 'Stanley Kaufman on Films', *The New Republic*, 23 December 1967, 22.

3 J. W. Whitehead, *Appraising The Graduate: The Mike Nichols Classic and its Impact in Hollywood* (Jefferson, NC: McFarland and Company, 2011), 28.

4 Peter Biskind, *Easy Riders, Raging Bulls: How the Sex 'n' Drugs 'n' Rock 'n' Roll Generation Saved Hollywood* (London: Bloomsbury, 1999), 49.

5 Following Embassy's merger with Avco in 1968, *The Graduate* was distributed by Avco Embassy in the United States; United Artists handled distribution in most overseas territories.

6 'Joe Unchained', *Time*, 24 February 1961, from Joseph E. Levine clipping file (hereafter JEL file), held in the Margaret Herrick Library, Academy of Motion Picture Arts and Sciences, Beverly Hills, California (hereafter MHL AMPAS)

7 'Joe Unchained', *Time*.

8 Gay Talese, 'Joe Levine Unchained: A Candid Portrait of a Spectacular Showman', *Esquire*, January 1961, 64–8.

9 Paul O'Neil, 'The Super Salesman of Super Colossals', *Life*, 27 July 1962, 76–82.

10 Katherine Hamill, 'The Super Colossal – Well, Pretty Good – World of Joe Levine', *Fortune*, March 1964, 130–2, 178–80 and 185.

11 Calvin Tomkins, 'The Very Rich Hours of Joe Levine', *The New Yorker*, 16 September 1967, 55–136.

12 Mort Drucker (artist) and Larry Siegal (writer), '*Mad* Visits Joe LeVenal: Hollywood's Latest Producing Genius', *Mad*, No. 66, October 1961, 21–4.

13 Dwight Macdonald, 'Mr Goldwyn and Mr Levine', in *On Movies* (New York: De Capo Press, 1981), 130–1.

14 Pierre Bourdieu, *Distinction: A Social Critique of the Judgement of Taste* (Cambridge, MA: Harvard University Press, 2002), 56–7.

15 Peter Dunn, 'The Last Movie Mogul', *Sunday Times*, 5 February 1978.

16 For further discussion of Levine's antagonistic relationship with critics at this time, see A. T. McKenna, *Showman of the Screen: Joseph E. Levine and his Revolutions in Film Promotion* (Lexington, KY: University Press of Kentucky, 2016), 111–29.

17 Levine and Embassy's dealings can be bafflingly complex. For a filmography of Levine and Embassy's outputs, with information on co-producers and distribution arrangements see McKenna, *Showman*, 209–18.

18 'Embassy Expanding Operations; Levine Will Give More Time to Production', *Hollywood Reporter*, 2 August 1965, JEL file, MHL AMPAS.

19 'Levine Budgets 8 Embassy Pix at $18 Mil in Next 6 Months', *Variety*, 10 August 1966, JEL file, MHL AMPAS.

20 Tomkins, 'Very Rich Hours', 119.
21 William Tusher, 'Levine's Nix To Family Pix', *The Film Daily*, 30 June 1967, JEL file, MHL AMPAS.
22 In his autobiography, Arkoff says that he changed his strategy following the success of *The Wild Angels* (1966). Sam Arkoff with Richard Trubo, *Flying Through Hollywood by the Seat of My Pants: From the Man Who Brought You I Was a Teenage Werewolf and Muscle Beach Party* (New York: Birch Lane Press, 1992), 166–7.
23 Charles Champlin, 'Levine, Maestro of Hoopla, Hope', *Los Angeles Times*, 2 June 1967, D10.
24 Kanfer, 'The Shock'.
25 'Levine Budgets', *Variety*.
26 Dick Griffin, 'Levine: Huckster with a Heart', *Los Angeles Times*, 21 June 1966, C9.
27 *Runaway Train* was eventually made in 1985 without Levine's involvement, directed by Andrei Konchalovsky and based on Kurosawa's script.
28 'Levine Budgets', *Variety*.
29 Lawrence Turman, *So You Want to be a Producer?* (New York: Three Rivers Press, 2005), 193.
30 'Turman to Film *Grad* For Levine; Ends Millar Tie', *Variety*, 6 October 1964, JEL file, MHL AMPAS.
31 'The Producer: Joseph E. Levine', in *Filmmakers on Filmmaking: The American Film Institute Seminars on Motion Pictures and Television*, ed. Joseph McBride (Los Angeles: J. P. Tarcher, 1983), 30.
32 Mark Harris, *Pictures at a Revolution: Five Movies and the Birth of the New Hollywood* (London: Penguin Books, 2009), 71.
33 'Turman to Film', *Variety*.
34 Sybil Burton, 'Euripides and The Establishment: Film Producer Puts His Money Where His (Legit) Enthusiasm Is', *Variety*, 22 April 1964, 15.
35 Lawrence Turman to the author, personal correspondence, 8 March 2006.
36 Levine's relationship with Godard on their production of *Le mépris* (1963) was, however, somewhat rancorous. See McKenna, *Showman*, 86–98.
37 'Shortage of Directors Deplored by Levine; CEO. Sidney Stays Mute', *Variety*, 11 November 1964, JEL file, MHL AMPAS.
38 Turman to author.
39 Tomkins, 'Very Rich Hours', 135.
40 Aniko Bodroghkozy, 'Reel Revolutionaries: An Examination of Hollywood's Cycle of 1960s Youth Rebellion Films', *Cinema Journal*, 41, no. 3, (Spring 2002): 39.
41 Robert Sklar, *Movie-Made America* (New York: Vintage Books, 1994), 300–1.
42 Turman to author.
43 Whitehead, *Appraising The Graduate*, 20
44 Tusher, 'Levine's Nix'.
45 David Fear, 'Mike Nichols on *The Graduate*', *Time Out*, 9 April 2012, https://www.timeout.com/newyork/film/mike-nichols-on-the-graduate
46 Levine did, however, sometimes try to claim credit for the casting of Dustin Hoffman as Benjamin. One tale he was fond of telling, which is almost certainly untrue, is: 'Nichols wanted a guy who didn't look like a movie star . . . Dustin Hoffman worked for me off Broadway as a stage manager . . . He was bothering me every day for a chance to act. So I told Nichols I didn't know if he could act his way

out of a paper bag, but he sure didn't look like a movie star.' 'Joe Levine: Still Adapting – and Cashing In', *Pittsburgh Post-Gazette*, 17 November 1978, 1.

47 Turman to author.
48 Harris, *Pictures at a Revolution*, 361–2.
49 Fear, 'Mike Nichols on *The Graduate*'.
50 Turman, *So You Want*, 206.
51 Turman, *So You Want*, 210.
52 Harris, *Pictures at a Revolution*, 362.
53 Harris, *Pictures at a Revolution*, 28.
54 Andrew Sarris, 'Review of *The Graduate*', *Village Voice*, 20 December 1973, *The Graduate* clippings file, MHL AMPAS.
55 'Embassy May Merge/Go Public', *Hollywood Reporter*, 31 May 1967, 1.
56 Justin Wyatt, 'From Roadshowing to Saturation Release: Majors, Independents, and Marketing/Distribution Innovations', in *The New American Cinema*, ed. Jon Lewis (Durham, NC: Duke University Press, 1999), 66–7.
57 Whitehead, *Appraising The Graduate*, 38; Sam Kashner, 'Here's to You, Mr Nichols: The Making of *The Graduate*', *Vanity Fair*, 25 February 2008, http://www.vanityfair.com/news/2008/03/graduate200803
58 Quoted in Whitehead, *Appraising The Graduate*, 30.
59 Most of Embassy's back catalogue was not suitable for evening screenings of 'big' movies by the major networks. Also, as Charles Champlin observed at the time, television audiences were largely unresponsive to foreign language films. Charles Champlin, 'TV Off and Running in High-Paying Movie Stakes', *LA Times*, 5 September 1965, B10.
60 'Levine Has "No-Comment" on Mad Sq. Merger, Plenty on Other Topics', *Variety*, 29 March 1967, JEL file, MHL AMPAS.
61 James R. Kerr, 'Billions Make a Nice Cushion Or, AVCO Goes To Embassy Movies', *Variety*, 13 November 1968, JEL file, MHL AMPAS.
62 Avco Embassy did not make this film. United Artists released an adaptation of *One Flew Over the Cuckoo's Nest* in 1975, starring Jack Nicholson, and produced by Michael Douglas – Kirk Douglas's son.
63 Kerr, 'Billions Make a Nice Cushion.'
64 Tony Klinger to the author, personal correspondence, 13 August 2015.
65 Thomas Schatz, 'The New Hollywood', in *Movie Blockbusters*, ed. Julian Stringer (London: Routledge, 2003), 22.
66 Tino Balio, 'Retrenchment, Reappraisal, and Reorganisation, 1948–', in *The American Film Industry*, expanded edition, ed. Tino Balio (Madison: University of Wisconsin Press, 1985), 437–8.
67 Gavin Smith, 'Interview with Mike Nichols', *Film Comment* (May 1999): 10.
68 Donna Rosenthal, 'Self-Made Mogul Hangs On: Joseph E. Levine, 82, Is Still Wheeling and Dealing', *New York Times*, 5 July 1987, K23.
69 Aljean Harmetz, 'Producer of *Graduate* Wins Ruling on Sales; CBS Says It Had to Buy Package', *New York Times*, 19 April 1980, 13; Turman, *So You Want*, 215–16.
70 'Levine Has "No Comment"', *Variety*.
71 Turman, *So You Want*, 195.

Chapter 4

'A TRIUMPH OF AURA OVER APPEARANCE': BARBRA STREISAND, *FUNNY GIRL* (1968) AND THE HOLLYWOOD RENAISSANCE

Peter Krämer

Barbra Streisand represents a triumph of aura over appearance. Her nose is too long, her bosom too small, her hips too wide. Yet when she steps in front of a microphone she transcends generations and cultures. [. . .] As soon as she became a superstar two years ago, her exotic, thriftshop clothes became the thing to wear. [. . .] It became 'in' to look Jewish. Today Barbra Streisand is 23 years old, real, thoughtful, still nervous and somewhat annoyed by the burdens of stardom.

— *Newsweek*, 28 March 1966[1]

When *Time* magazine, in December 1967, declared that there was a 'renaissance' in mainstream American cinema, it foregrounded dramatic departures in recent major studio releases from Hollywood's long-standing stylistic, formal and thematic conventions, the massive influx of new personnel into the film industry and the by industry standards relatively young age of many studio executives and filmmakers.[2] This emphasis on youth, new talent and filmic innovation has characterized much of the writing about the Hollywood Renaissance ever since. But such writing has rarely, if ever, addressed one of the most surprising cinematic developments, to do with innovations by young, new talent, of the late 1960s. Hollywood was willing to invest a large sum of money into the big screen debut of a young female performer whose looks were widely discussed as a radical break with the norms of female beauty in American society and most especially in Hollywood. What is more, instead of filmmakers and marketers trying to draw attention away from her unconventional looks, they were the very subject of her first movie.

Barbra Streisand was only twenty-three years old when, late in 1965, it was announced that she would make her movie debut in Columbia Pictures' big-budget adaptation of the stage musical *Funny Girl* in which she had

been starring – in the role of legendary Jewish comedienne Fanny Brice –
since March 1964. The musical told the story of Brice succeeding on Broadway
(and finding love) despite her unconventional looks, which, according to
numerous press reports, was also the life story of the actress playing her.
With explicit references to her large nose and her Jewishness, the press
emphasized that, like Brice, Streisand had made it on the New York stage against
all the odds.

There was some concern whether she would be able to do the same in
Hollywood. After all, norms of female beauty, especially with regards to facial
features, were, if anything, *more* rigorously enforced for leading ladies in the
film industry than for those in the theatre (due to the prevalence of close-ups of
faces being projected onto large screens). More generally, there was considerable
doubt about Broadway stardom easily translating into movie stardom. Indeed
Hollywood had a tendency of replacing stage performers with established film
stars in big-budget musical adaptations, most notably by giving Audrey
Hepburn the role made famous on stage by Julie Andrews in *My Fair Lady*
(George Cukor, 1964), with Julie Andrews then being cast in the Disney musical
Mary Poppins (Robert Stevenson, 1964, a film *not* based on a theatrical
production), which established her as a major Hollywood star who in turn was
chosen to replace Mary Martin in the 1965 screen version of the Broadway hit
The Sound of Music (Robert Wise, 1965).

So a major studio casting Streisand in *Funny Girl*, and other studios signing
her to star in two additional blockbuster productions – *Hello, Dolly!* (Gene
Kelly, 1969) and *On a Clear Day You Can See Forever* (Vincente Minnelli, 1970)
– *before* the release of *Funny Girl* in 1968 could confirm her viability as a movie
star, was the kind of bold move that has come to be associated with the
Hollywood Renaissance. It meant taking a chance on a young talent who was
completely untested, at least as far as Hollywood was concerned, and inextricably
linked to, indeed closely identified with, a break with one of most fundamental
conventions of mainstream American cinema.

In this chapter I first outline the pre-history of Columbia's production of
Funny Girl, with particular reference to the career of Fanny Brice and the multi-
media operations of the producer Ray Stark as well as the public debate about
Streisand's unusual looks during her early career. The second section maps the
tremendous scope of Streisand's pre-cinematic success, not only on the stage
but also on records and television, which, together with the dominance of
Hollywood musicals at the American box office in the mid-1960s, helps to
explain why the major studios were willing to take a gamble on her. In the third
section, I discuss *Funny Girl*'s huge success as well as Streisand's career in the
remainder of the 1960s and across the 1970s, exploring her exceptional status
as a successful woman in an industry which at that historical moment was
arguably more male dominated than ever before or since. Thus, this chapter
maps the first two decades in the career of the era's biggest cross-media star
whose films were complexly related to major trends in American cinema

(including the Hollywood Renaissance), insofar as they were completely at odds with some of these trends and perfectly in tune with others.

Fanny Brice, Ray Stark and Barbra Streisand

Funny Girl tells the story of a stage struck teenage Jewish girl who, after initially being rejected for her odd looks and behaviour, is a surprise success with audiences as a comedienne and singer. Even more surprisingly, soon after her breakthrough she becomes the star attraction of the *Ziegfeld Follies*, Broadway's leading musical revue. Parallel to her show business career, she falls in love with and marries a gambler who eventually has to go to jail for fraud; upon his release, the couple separate for good.

This story is based, not always very closely, on the life of Fanny Brice (born, in New York, in 1891) between *c.* 1910 and 1927, especially her stage career and her relationship with Nick Arnstein (who was, in fact, her second husband, not the first as in *Funny Girl*). Brice adopted an explicitly Jewish stage persona by frequently injecting Yiddish into her speech and by playing up her unconventional looks. Her cosmetic surgery in 1923 attracted a lot of press attention and led Dorothy Parker to quip: 'Fanny Brice cut off her nose to spite her race.'[3] Yet, performing in revues, musical comedies and vaudeville shows, making records and appearing on radio and in two films, Brice continued to play Jewish characters, before she became most closely associated with the hugely popular and no longer ethnically marked infantile persona of 'Baby Snooks' on radio from the 1930s onwards.[4]

Brice's fame was such that, already in 1939, her relationship with Arnstein was the (thoroughly fictionalized) subject of a Hollywood movie entitled *Rose of Washington Square* (Gregory Ratoff). In the years before her untimely death in 1951, she worked on an (unpublished) autobiography, which her son-in-law Ray Stark, a Hollywood agent and producer, then developed into a screenplay that focused on her relationship with Arnstein. When Stark failed to get this production financed, he asked Isobel Lennart to rework her screenplay into a script for a stage musical.[5]

By the early 1960s, Stark, working with leading – and frequently changing – Broadway personnel (including the producer David Merrick, the composer Jule Styne, the lyricists Stephen Sondheim and Bob Merrill as well as the directors Jerome Robbins and Garson Kanin), was ready to go into production. Many performers were considered for the all-important lead role, before relative newcomer Barbra Streisand was finally cast in June 1963, not least because her life and meteoric early career had many parallels to Brice's and *Funny Girl's* story, and her distinctly Jewish looks were perfect for the part.[6]

As early as 1961, in a review of one of Streisand's nightclub performances *Variety* commented on her talent and great potential as a singer, yet also pointed out that, 'if intent about her professional ambitions, perhaps a little corrective schnoz bob might be an element to be considered'; without cosmetic surgery, the paper suggested, she was more likely to succeed in comedy, like other large-nosed Jewish performers such as Jimmy Durante and Fanny Brice.[7]

When the *New York Journal-American* reviewed *I Can Get It for You Wholesale*, the first Broadway show Streisand appeared in (from March to December 1962), her performance in a supporting role was singled out for praise, and she was described as 'an amiable ant-eater'.[8] Reviewers tended to agree that she was in fact the show's main attraction and predicted great things for this 'shriek-voiced new comedienne who probably won't be out of work for the next eight years'.[9] She was nominated for one of Broadway's prestigious Antoinette Perry (Tony) awards and won the New York Drama Critics' award for 'Best Supporting Actress' as well as the National Association of Gag Writers' 'Fanny Brice Award' for 'Best Comedienne'.[10]

From 1961 to 1963, Streisand regularly appeared on late night talk shows and primetime variety programmes on television, being interviewed, doing sketches and singing, and from spring 1962 onwards, she also established herself as a major recording artist, by no means confining herself to comic songs.[11] Yet the size of her nose continued to be foregrounded in a cruelly comical fashion. When her debut album as a solo artist, *The Barbra Streisand Album*, was released in February 1963, syndicated columnist Robert Ruark wrote that '[h]er nose is more evocative of moose than muse', yet also compared her to some of the greatest female singers of the twentieth century: 'She is the hottest thing to hit the entertainment field since Lena Horne erupted, and she will be around 50 years from now if good songs are still written to be sung by good singers'.[12] Thus, already at this early stage, Streisand's career was expected to last as long as that of Fanny Brice. This, together with her comic skills and her large nose, did indeed make her a good choice for the lead in the musical about Brice's life.

Around the time that rehearsals for *Funny Girl* began in December 1963, David Merrick withdrew from the production, selling his shares to Stark, who remained as the show's sole producer, for a reported $100,000.[13] As Streisand's *Funny Girl* contract had been with Merrick, Stark had to re-negotiate the deal, which now specifically included provisions for four Streisand films that Stark would produce, the first one being an adaptation of the stage show.[14] Streisand's contract was non-exclusive, which meant that she would also be able to star in films that Stark was not involved in. In early March 1964, a few weeks before *Funny Girl*'s official Broadway premiere, newspaper columnist Dorothy Kilgallen described it as 'one of the biggest deals ever given an actress for her first film role'.[15]

Of course, Stark had yet to find a Hollywood studio for the movie version of *Funny Girl*. At this point in his long and varied career, Stark operated both as an independent (stage and film) producer and as one of the chief executives of Seven Arts.[16] This rapidly expanding Canadian company had acquired a vast movie library (including Warner Bros.' pre-1950 releases) which it sold to television broadcasters around the world, and it was also increasingly involved in producing films for theatrical release by the major Hollywood studios as well as financing the occasional Broadway show.[17] In fact, money for the stage production of *Funny Girl* had come both from Seven Arts and from Stark's own pockets.[18] For the film version he and Seven Arts would need a deal with one of the majors.[19]

Stark's confidence in his ability to interest the majors in *Funny Girl* partly derived from Streisand's success as a stage performer and recording artist across 1962 and 1963, and also from the fact that, due to extensive publicity and advertising, most of which centred on the star, advance ticket sales for *Funny Girl* had almost reached the $1 million mark, a sum far exceeding the production costs the show had accumulated up to this point.[20] The reviews of the official premiere on 26 March 1964 confirmed that Streisand was considered to be the show's main attraction and chiefly responsible for its huge commercial success.[21]

Nevertheless it took some time to convince the powers-that-be in Hollywood that, despite her unconventional looks and lack of movie experience, Streisand was viable as the lead for a big-budget movie. It was only on 17 December 1965, nine days before Streisand finally completed her twenty-one months run in *Funny Girl* on Broadway that Columbia Pictures announced that she would star in the movie.[22] By this time, Stark had begun to remove himself from Seven Arts (which was growing so big that by 1967 it would be in a position to take over Warner Bros.), so as to focus on his operations as an independent producer (with his own company Rastar Productions).[23]

A press report from June 1966 described the film version of *Funny Girl* as 'Mr. Stark's first completely independent project', independent, that is, from Seven Arts, but, at the same time, wholly dependent on his financing-and-distribution deal with Columbia Pictures.[24] The studio was going to invest in the region of $10 million at a time when the average Hollywood movie cost just over $1.5 million.[25] With the *Funny Girl* deal Stark seemed to be positioning himself for a longer-term involvement with the studio, and he would indeed soon become its most important producer, especially with four more Streisand films released from 1970 to 1975.[26]

While *Funny Girl* was being shot in the spring and summer of 1967, 20th Century Fox announced that Streisand was to take over the lead role (played by Carol Channing on stage) in its adaptation of the Broadway hit musical *Hello, Dolly!*, which was bound to become an even more expensive production than Columbia Pictures' *Funny Girl*.[27] Not long thereafter, Paramount signed Streisand to star in the movie version of *On a Clear Day You Can See Forever*, a musical which had not been particularly successful on Broadway but would nevertheless cost a lot of money to turn into a movie.[28]

With the release of *Funny Girl* still a year in the future, in September 1967 *Life* magazine pointed out how utterly unusual and unprecedented this situation was: The budget of Streisand's first three films 'will come to $30 million,[29] an almost unbelievable amount to risk on any novice except perhaps Barbra.'[30] The article also reminded readers, rather delicately, that Streisand simply did *not* look like a movie star: 'Her familiar face [...] still shimmers between great beauty and a parody of it.' Why, then, was Hollywood so eager to invest in this odd looking and, in movie terms, wholly unproven performer?

Hollywood musicals and Streisand's pre-cinematic stardom

When, in December 1965, Columbia Pictures announced the signing of Streisand as the lead in the movie version of *Funny Girl*, Hollywood was caught up in a musical box office bonanza that took everyone by surprise. Looking back in January 1966 on the financial performance of hit movies during the previous year and their impact on the all-time chart of top-grossing movies in the United States, *Variety* noted that '[t]he most remarkable changes in the all-time top grossers list during 1965' had been 'the advent of the James Bond films' and 'the unexpectedly big business done by' three musicals: *The Sound of Music* (released by Fox in March 1965), *My Fair Lady* (Warner Bros., October 1964) and *Mary Poppins* (Disney, August 1964).[31] These films were ranked eighth, eleventh and fourth in the all-time chart, and were expected to rise higher because they were still performing well at the end of 1965.[32]

Indeed, by the time of *Variety*'s next annual review in January 1967, *My Fair Lady* was at number six in the all-time chart (with domestic rentals, that is the share of ticket sales which the distributor receives from cinemas in the United States, of $30 million; all rental figures in this chapter relate only to the domestic market), *Mary Poppins* at number five ($31 million) and *The Sound of Music* at number one, having overtaken *Gone With the Wind* (1939) with rentals of $43 million, a record sum to which, *Variety* predicted, millions would be added in 1967.[33] (By the end of 1967, the rentals for *The Sound of Music* were going to add up to $66 million.)[34] These three musicals easily outperformed all other films released between 1960 and 1966 (only *Doctor Zhivago*, released in December 1965, would eventually match their earnings), and it was therefore tempting for Hollywood's decision makers to see them as a reliable model for exceptional success at the box office.

Two of the three hit musicals were based on Broadway shows and all three centred on female performers and were set in the past. It is not so surprising, then, that from 1965 onwards the major studios invested heavily in musicals, especially in adaptations of Broadway shows with a female lead and a historical setting.[35] And this certainly helps to explain why Columbia Pictures, Fox and Paramount were willing to bet so much money on *Funny Girl*, *Hello, Dolly!* and *On a Clear Day You Can See Forever*, respectively, because all of them were female-centred Broadway adaptations with historical settings (whereby the story of the last title switches back and forth between the contemporary period and the past).

But, as previously noted, the studios were usually quite reluctant to feature female Broadway stars in their big-budget adaptations, if these stars had not yet proven themselves in the movies. So why were they prepared not only to feature Streisand in the adaptation of the hit musical she had starred in on Broadway, but also to sign her up – *before*, it has to be reiterated, *Funny Girl* had even been released – in movie versions of stage musicals she had no prior association with (whereby the lead role in *Hello, Dolly!* was in fact meant for a much older actress)? The answer to this question must have a lot to do with the extraordinary level of success she achieved in her pre-cinematic show business career.

By the time Streisand was signed in December 1965 to appear in the movie *Funny Girl*, she had been, as mentioned above, the undisputed star of the stage version for twenty-one months, among other things being nominated for a Tony award.[36] She had also been, for over eight months in 1962, the award-winning main attraction of *I Can Get It for You Wholesale*. Before her Broadway debut Streisand had been performing, since 1960, as a singer at exclusive nightclubs across the United States. In 1963 she had a four-week and then a two-week engagement in Las Vegas and also gave numerous concerts around the country. She sang for President Kennedy at the annual White House press correspondents dinner in May 1963 (and for President Johnson at his inaugural eve gala in January 1965). On the basis of her success as a live performer and recording artist, in December 1963 *Cue* magazine named her 'Entertainer of the Year'.

Her debut records had been the original Broadway cast recording of *I Can Get it For You Wholesale* and a promotional single featuring songs from the show, including Streisand's signature song 'Miss Marmelstein' (both released in April 1962). She also performed several songs on *Pins and Needles*, a compilation of Harold Rome compositions released in May 1962. Yet her recording career did not take off until after she had signed an extremely favourable deal with Columbia Records (a company *not* connected with Columbia Pictures) in October 1962, which granted her creative control.[37]

From 1963 to 1965, Columbia Records released *six* Streisand albums, *all* of which were certified 'gold' (that is, each generated at least $1 million in wholesale revenues) and made it into the top ten of the weekly *Billboard* sales chart, most of them reaching number one or two, which was also the case for the seventh album she appeared on during these years, Angel's original Broadway cast recording of *Funny Girl*. The first two Streisand albums from 1963 still sold so well during the following year that they joined her third album in the top ten of the *end-of-year* chart for 1964. This means that she accounted for three of the ten top-selling albums of 1964, the year of the so-called British invasion (the Beatles had only one album among the year's ten top-sellers).[38]

In 1964 and 1965, Streisand also released seven singles, which did not, however, chart very highly, apart from 'People', a song from *Funny Girl* that was released in January 1964 and reached number five in the weekly *Billboard* chart. The National Association of Record Merchandisers (NARM) identified

Streisand as the 'Best Selling Female Vocalist' of 1963, 1964 and 1965. She received numerous nominations for the record industry's most important awards, the Grammys. Her wins included 'Album of the Year' for 1963, and 'Best Vocal Performance, Female' for 1963, 1964 and 1965; in addition, *Funny Girl* won the Grammy for 'Best Broadway Cast Album'.

In April 1965, her first television special *My Name Is Barbra* was broadcast on CBS. This was an hour-long one-woman show (highly unusually, there were no guest stars), which achieved a 35.6 per cent audience share, that is, more than one-third of all people watching television that evening were tuned in to the Streisand special. The programme won several Emmys, the television industry's most important awards, including 'Outstanding Program Achievement' and 'Outstanding Individual Achievement'. It also won a prestigious Peabody Award 'for Distinguished Achievement in Television'. In June that year, Streisand signed a $5 million ten-year contract with CBS for further TV specials; like her deal with Columbia Records (which was in fact owned by CBS), the CBS contract granted her creative control.

This overview reveals that by signing up Streisand for *Funny Girl* (probably with a view of working with Stark on further Streisand vehicles if the first one was a hit) in December 1965, Columbia Pictures was following the lead of CBS/Columbia Records, making a multi-million-dollar investment in what was arguably the single biggest attraction in American show business at the time. As it turned out, Streisand's unprecedented success continued across 1966 and 1967, albeit at a slightly less exalted level.

She starred in the sold-out London production of *Funny Girl* from April to July 1966. She also released four albums in 1966 and 1967, all of them achieving high rankings in *Billboard*'s weekly sales chart, with *Color Me Barbra*, the soundtrack for her second TV special from March 1966 (the third one, *The Belle of 14th Street*, was to follow in October 1967), being certified 'gold' and becoming the ninth biggest selling album of 1966. She contributed to an album featuring songs written by Harold Arlen, and released five singles in 1966, with more to follow in 1967. NARM identified her as the 'Best Selling Female Vocalist' of 1966. Finally, following on from a brief American concert tour in the summer of 1966, in June 1967 Streisand gave a free concert in front of 135,000 people in New York's Central Park (which was recorded for her fourth TV special *Barbra Streisand: A Happening in Central Park* to be broadcast in 1968). This was reportedly the largest crowd ever assembled for a single performer.[39]

It is against the background of Streisand's ongoing cross-media success story and of the astonishing, recent box office performance of movie musicals, that in the summer of 1967 Fox and Paramount decided that there was no need to wait for the release of Streisand's debut movie and instead signed her up straightaway for their big-budget adaptations of *Hello, Dolly!* and *On a Clear Day You Can See Forever*. These signings confirmed her status as the biggest star in American show business, which made it particularly appropriate that her first song in the movie version of *Funny Girl*, performed while she is impersonating a teenage Fanny Brice, who has just been thrown out of the chorus of a show she was rehearsing for, is 'I'm the Greatest Star' (originally written for the stage show, long before Streisand was cast).

The song preceding this in the film (once again taken from the stage show) also relates to both Brice and Streisand. Entitled 'If a Girl Isn't Pretty', it serves to underline the magnitude of Streisand's achievement by foregrounding what was perhaps the biggest obstacle she had had to overcome in her rise to stardom. 'Is a nose with deviation / such a crime against the nation?', Fanny's mother sings in response to her friends' negative comments about her daughter's looks and her vanishingly small chance ever to make it in show business.

Throughout her early career, Streisand had encountered critical remarks about her looks, especially her facial features, and yet, like the character she plays in *Funny Girl*, instead of downplaying her oddness, she had always amplified it (through her clothes, her accent, her choice of words, her quirky behaviour) so as to turn it into a (comic) spectacle. At the same time, her singing voice, while occasionally employed for comic effect (as it is at the beginning of the 'I'm the Greatest Star' number), was widely regarded as one of the most richly modulated and most dramatically expressive vocal instruments in American music – as is perfectly demonstrated by the rousing finale of 'I'm the Greatest Star'. The first two numbers of *Funny Girl*, then, set up the whole film as a retelling of, and a meditation on, the unlikely success story of Barbra Streisand, the Jewish superstar whose magnificent 'aura' triumphed over her unconventional 'appearance', as *Newsweek* put it in March 1966.[40]

Barbra Streisand and American cinema of the late 1960s and the 1970s

The premiere of Columbia Pictures' *Funny Girl* on 18 September 1968, was preceded by the broadcast of the star's fourth TV special *Barbra Streisand: A Happening in Central Park* on 15 September, and the concurrent release of the live album *A Happening in Central Park*. Both the TV show and the album included 'People', the best-known song from the stage version of *Funny Girl*, which was also featured prominently in the movie. The single 'Funny Girl' had come out in July 1968 and the *Funny Girl* soundtrack album in August. The latter rose high in *Billboard*'s weekly chart, was certified 'gold' by the end of 1968, and continued to sell so well the following year that it was ranked seventh in the end-of-year chart for 1969.[41]

Like most big-budget Hollywood releases up to the late 1960s, *Funny Girl* was a roadshow presentation, which meant that it was initially shown in only a few especially large and luxurious cinemas, with all the trappings of a night out at the legitimate (musical) theatre: bookable seats, expensive tickets, an orchestral overture and an intermission, long runs (often for months, even years, during which the film would also go on general release in regular cinemas at regular prices). From the outset, the film was a spectacular success, having already earned, by the end of 1968, almost $4 million in rentals from the small number of theatres in which it was shown in the United States.[42]

Looking back at the film industry's overall box office performance in 1968, *Variety* observed in January 1969: 'The biggest new name during the entire year [...] was "instant star" Barbra Streisand'.[43] The paper noted that the success of *Funny Girl* 'has made a lot of people breathe easier', because '[s]eldom in the history of films have so many millions of dollars been invested in or committed to one "untried" talent'.[44] In addition to the already completed, 'huge-budgeted' *Hello, Dolly!*, *On a Clear Day You Can See Forever* was about to start filming in January 1969, and Streisand had also recently been signed, by Columbia Pictures, for her first non-musical picture, the romantic comedy *The Owl and the Pussycat*.[45] The success of *Funny Girl* was particularly noteworthy because, as *Variety* noted, '[t]he year just ended was a bumpy one for tunepix', with big-budget roadshow musicals like *Doctor Dolittle* (Richard Fleischer), *Camelot* (Joshua Logan) and *The Happiest Millionaire* (Norman Tokar) (all originally released late in 1967) and *Half a Sixpence* (George Sidney, February 1968) performing disappointingly at the box office and being bound to incur losses.[46]

At the same time, *Variety*'s review of the year noted, the most impressive commercial performance belonged to a comedy starring one of the genuine '[u]nknowns', namely actor Dustin Hoffman, whose huge success with *The Graduate* (Mike Nichols) – released late in 1967, it had earned $39 million in rentals by the end of 1968, which meant that it was ranked fourth in the *all-time* domestic rentals chart – had established him as 'the New Big Demand Screen Personality of the Year'.[47] Referring to 'the "generation gap" question' (best to be addressed, the paper recommended, from the perspective of youth rather than old folks), the surprise success of *The Fox* (Mark Rydell, 1968) – 'a look at the lesbian hangup (and, apparently, only the beginning of a sex aberration film cycle)' – the impressive box office performance of *Bonnie and Clyde* (Arthur Penn, 1967) during its second year of release, and the very mixed results for films featuring established female stars Elizabeth Taylor and Doris Day, *Variety* was hinting at important changes under way in Hollywood.[48]

As it turned out, the next few years brought disappointing, in places catastrophic, box office results for many big-budget musicals and also for expensive roadshow releases in other genres (notably historical epics), which, together with the ongoing decline in cinema attendance levels, affected the overall finances of the major studios so badly that several of them made huge losses between 1969 and 1971; as a consequence Hollywood abandoned the roadshow release format altogether and drastically reduced its output of traditional musicals and epics.[49]

At the same time, following in the wake of the success of *The Graduate* and *Bonnie and Clyde*, several medium and low-budget films starring young(ish) performers and breaking long-established film industry taboos were doing surprisingly well at the box office, most notably the sex-drugs-and-rock 'n' roll road movie *Easy Rider* (Dennis Hopper, 1969; eventually earning rentals of $19 million), the X-rated homoerotic buddy movie (and Dustin Hoffman vehicle) *Midnight Cowboy* (John Schlesinger, 1969; $21 million) and the graphic black Korean War comedy *M*A*S*H* (Robert Altman, 1970; $37 million).[50]

What all of this amounted to was a fundamental reorientation in Hollywood's production and marketing strategies, a shift away from the major studios' long-standing emphasis on catering first and foremost to all-inclusive family audiences, in particular to women, and towards a strong focus on films appealing especially, even exclusively, to youth, in particular to young men (whereby the films usually associated with the Hollywood Renaissance mostly belong to this latter category).[51] One of the consequences of this reorientation was the widespread marginalization of female characters in Hollywood's output – as evidenced, for example, by *Easy Rider*, *Midnight Cowboy* and *M*A*S*H* – and the much reduced importance of female stars.

In its annual survey of film exhibitors in the United States, first conducted in 1932, Quigley Publications asked which stars they considered to be the top box office attractions (whereby the answers often depended on the performance of films released during the previous calendar year). Quigley's annual list of the ten top stars had been dominated by male stars ever since the 1940s (insofar as there were more men than women on it and the former were usually ranked higher than the latter), yet, quite remarkably, from 1960 to 1967 the top spot was, with the exception of 1965, awarded to a woman: Doris Day in 1960 and 1962–4, Elizabeth Taylor in 1961 and Julie Andrews in 1966–7.[52] During this period, there were on average three women in the annual top ten. In the decade after 1967, this figure was halved (in 1968–9, 1972 and 1977 there were two women in the annual top ten, in 1970–1 and 1973–6 there was only one), and female stars never took the top spot; indeed in most years they did not even come close.

Against this backdrop, Barbra Streisand's success in her new career as a movie star was truly remarkable. By the end of 1969, *Funny Girl* had generated rentals of $17 million, which meant that it had now earned more money than any other film released in 1968, and was placed at number twenty-nine in *Variety*'s all-time chart, the paper (correctly) predicting that it would continue to perform well the following year.[53] On the basis of *Funny Girl*'s performance, Streisand was ranked tenth in Quigley's top ten in 1969, and, due to the commercial success of her subsequent films, she was ranked ninth in 1970, fifth in 1972, sixth in 1973, fourth in 1974 and second in both 1975 and 1977 (she would also make the top ten in 1978 and 1979, by which time the number of women in the annual top ten had gone back up to three). From 1973 to 1975, she was the only woman in the top ten.

Streisand, then, was, by a very wide margin, the most successful female star of the decade 1968–77. What is more, the commercial performance of her films could not be matched by many, if any, *male* stars either, certainly not in terms of consistency. Following the success of her debut movie, Streisand appeared in nine films released between December 1969 and December 1976, only one of which (the highly unconventional drama *Up the Sandbox* [Irvin Kershner; released by National General in 1972]) was an outright flop at the box office. If we consider annual charts which take into account the lifetime earnings of films, rather than only the rentals they generated in the first year of their release, we find the following rental figures and chart rankings for Streisand's hit movies:

- *Funny Girl* (no. 1 for 1968, with total rentals of $26 million)
- *Hello, Dolly!* (no. 5 for 1969, $15 million)
- *On a Clear Day You Can See Forever* (no. 27 for 1970, $5 million)
- *The Owl and the Pussycat* (Herbert Ross; no. 10 for 1970, $12 million)
- *What's Up, Doc?* (Peter Bogdanovich; a romantic comedy released by Warner Bros.; no. 3 for 1972, $28 million)
- *The Way We Were* (Sydney Pollack; a Columbia Pictures romantic drama; no. 5 for 1973, $22 million)
- *For Pete's Sake* (Peter Yates; a Columbia Pictures comedy; no. 20 for 1974, $11 million)
- *Funny Lady* (Herbert Ross; Columbia Pictures' sequel to *Funny Girl*; no. 8 for 1975, $19 million) and
- *A Star is Born* (Frank Pierson; a Warner Bros. rock and pop musical; no. 2 for 1976, $37 million).[54]

The $3.5 million earned by *Up the Sandbox* meant that it barely made it into the top forty for 1972 and has to be considered a flop. By contrast, Streisand's top hits did not only do well in the annual charts but also in the list of 'All-Time Film Rental Champs', with four of them ranked in the top fifty of *Variety*'s January 1978 update (the highest being *A Star is Born* at number twenty-one).[55]

This overview strongly suggests that Streisand was *a*, if not *the*, crucial Hollywood star of the decade lasting from her movie debut in 1968 to 1977, the year in which *A Star Is Born* made most of its money. The case for her importance can easily be strengthened by examining a wider range of success indicators, with regards to both her movies and other media.[56] For example, Streisand was nominated for a Best Actress Oscar for *The Way We Were* and won that award for *Funny Girl* (for which she also won a Golden Globe as she did for her role in *A Star Is Born*). In addition, both 'The Way We Were' and 'Evergreen (Love Theme from *A Star Is Born*)' won the Oscar for Best Song (the latter was co-written by Streisand and also won a Golden Globe).

The Hollywood Foreign Press Association declared her to be the 'World Film Favorite, Female' of 1969, 1970, 1974 and 1977, and she won the People's Choice Award for 'Favorite Motion Picture Actress' in 1975 (when she also won the award for 'Favorite Female Singer') and 1977. The National Association of Theater Owners declared her to be Hollywood's 'Star of the Year' for 1968 and the 'Star of the Decade' for the 1970s. When, in 1970, the *Los Angeles Times* surveyed readers and also film industry insiders about the greatest achievements of Hollywood cinema in the 1960s, Streisand won with *Funny Girl* in the 'Best Female Comedy Performance' category in both the readers' and the industry poll. A survey among college students in 1978 revealed that Streisand was their favourite movie star.

Furthermore, the exclusive theatrical Friars Club honoured her as 'Entertainer of the Year' in May 1969, and soon thereafter she received a special Tony as Broadway's 'Star of the Decade'. *Cue* magazine and the American Guild of Variety Artists also named her 'Entertainer of the Year' in 1970, and the latter declared her to be the 'Singing Star of the Year' in 1972 and 1977. In addition to live concerts and television appearances, Streisand performed on a total of nineteen albums between 1968 and 1977, most of them solo albums or film soundtracks (seven of her ten films during this period had a soundtrack album). Many of these rose, like the *Funny Girl* soundtrack, very high in the weekly *Billboard* charts and were certified 'gold', with the soundtrack for *A Star Is Born* becoming the third biggest selling album of 1977 in the United States. Streisand also released dozens of singles, with 'The Way We Were' becoming the top selling single of 1974, and 'Evergreen' being ranked fourth in the end-of-year chart for 1977. 'Evergreen' also won two Grammys ('Best Vocal Performance, Female' and 'Song of the Year'). NARM identified Streisand as the 'Best Selling Female Vocalist' of 1976 and 1977, and in a *US* magazine readers' poll she was voted 'Top Female Vocalist' of the 1970s.

From 1968 to 1977 Streisand thus was just as powerful, even dominant, a force in American popular culture as she had been in the mid-1960s, with continuing outstanding success as a recording artist, a reduced, but still quite prominent presence as a performer on television and on the (concert) stage, and an almost unbroken string of hit movies.

Conclusion

Barbra Streisand's movie success with stories that revolved first and foremost around female characters in three genres – the musical, romantic comedy and romantic drama – which, according to audience surveys, suited female movie preferences much better than those of males, was at odds with the most important trends at the American box office in the late 1960s and early to mid-1970s, and also with the films (including box office hits as well as flops) usually associated with the Hollywood Renaissance.[57]

At the same time, her film career echoed some of the central preoccupations of the films and filmmakers of the Hollywood Renaissance. Her upfront Jewishness fitted in well with the emphasis on ethnicity (mostly Italian-American or Jewish-American) in the work of several key writers and directors such as Francis Ford Coppola, Martin Scorsese and Woody Allen, and of actors such as Dustin Hoffman, Al Pacino and Robert De Niro.

There is also a shared emphasis on youth (here mainly referring to people in their twenties and thirties) with regards to the age both of the people making movies and of the characters in those movies. In fact, of all the major artists and industry players in Hollywood of the late 1960s and 1970s, Streisand was among the very youngest. Born in April 1942, upon the release of *Funny Girl* she was still only twenty-five years old, whereas most of the people associated with the Hollywood Renaissance had been born in the 1920s and 1930s (notable exceptions include Pacino, Scorsese and De Niro). If the Hollywood Renaissance was, among other things, centrally concerned with ethnicity and youth, then it is worth noting that hardly any important person in Hollywood was more ethnic and youthful than Barbra Streisand.

Finally, there is the fact that, like so many directorial 'auteurs' of the Hollywood Renaissance, Streisand was, from the very beginning of her film career, trying to assert an unusually high level of creative control – as she had previously been contractually guaranteed, with regards to her records and television specials, by Columbia Records and CBS, respectively, and as she had also exerted during the production and long run of *Funny Girl* on stage.[58] For this purpose, Streisand joined forces with other leading movie stars (initially Sidney Poitier and Paul Newman, later also Steve McQueen and Dustin Hoffman) in a new production company called First Artists, which was formed in June 1969.[59] Together with Streisand's very own company, Barwood, First Artists was behind *Up the Sandbox* and *A Star Is Born*.

But Streisand did not need a separate company to exert influence over her productions; she could simply wield her star power, that is, the power which derived from these productions being designed as vehicles for, and thus completely dependent on, her. She could use this power to assert herself not only against the studios financing her films but also against producers and directors, and she did so even before her first movie had demonstrated that her audience appeal extended to cinemagoers.

During the production of *Funny Girl*, she frequently argued with the Hollywood veterans surrounding her (most notably the American film industry's most commercially successful and most celebrated director up to this point, William Wyler), often getting her way.[60] An article in *New York* magazine about the making of the film featured what would turn into an oft repeated quip: 'Willie shouldn't be so hard on her. After all, this is the first picture she's ever directed'; indeed, the article was entitled 'Barbra's Directing Her First Movie'.[61]

While such reports were often intended to malign the actress, portraying her as a kind of 'monster', they also, together with much more positive reminiscences of her collaborators, underline her ability to shape not only her own performances but also other aspects of the films she starred in. Could we say, then, that Barbra Streisand was, in fact, a Hollywood Renaissance filmmaker – young, self-consciously ethnic, controlling as well as both willing and able to offer an alternative to (at least one of) the basic conventions of traditional Hollywood cinema?

Notes

1 'Barbra', *Newsweek*, 28 March 1966, 92.

2 Stefan Kanfer, 'The Shock of Freedom in Films', *Time*, 8 December 1967, 66–76, reprinted in *The Movies: An American Idiom*, ed. Arthur F. McClure (Rutherford, NJ: Fairleigh Dickinson University Press, 1971), 322–33.

3 J. Hoberman and Jeffrey Shandler, 'Fanny Brice', in *Entertaining America: Jews, Movies, and Broadcasting*, ed. J. Hoberman and Jeffrey Shandler (Princeton, NJ: Princeton University Press, 2003), 154–5.

4 Arthur Frank Wertheim, *Radio Comedy* (New York: Oxford University Press, 1979), 369–76.

5 William J. Mann, *Hello, Gorgeous: Becoming Barbra Streisand* (Boston: Mariner Books, 2013), 235–6.

6 Mann, *Hello, Gorgeous*, 344.

7 *Variety*, 22 November 1961, quoted in Mann, *Hello, Gorgeous*, 166.

8 *New York Journal-American*, 23 March 1962, quoted in Mann, *Hello, Gorgeous*, 208.

9 *New York Morning Telegraph*, 23 March 1962, quoted in Ernest Cunningham, *The Ultimate Barbra* (Los Angeles: Renaissance Books, 1998), 93.

10 Cunningham, *The Ultimate Barbra*, 49, 209.

11 Cunningham, *The Ultimate Barbra*, 105–6, 127–30.

12 Ruark column, 26 February 1963, quoted in Cunningham, *The Ultimate Barbra*, 3.

13 Mann, *Hello, Gorgeous*, 414.

14 Mann, *Hello, Gorgeous*, 414–15, 463.

15 Kilgallen column, 5 March 1964, quoted in Mann, *Hello, Gorgeous*, 463.

16 Bernard F. Dick, 'The History of Columbia, 1920–1991: From the Brothers Cohn to Sony Corp.', in *Columbia Pictures: Portrait of a Studio*, ed. Bernard F. Dick (Lexington: University Press of Kentucky, 1992), 26–7.

17 See, for example, Seven Arts Productions Limited, 'Annual Report Year Ended January 31, 1962', published in July 1963, file 1693 Seven Arts, John Huston Papers, Margaret Herrick Library, Academy of Motion Picture Arts and Sciences (AMPAS), Beverly Hills; and the company's annual report for the following year, published in August 1964, file 3994 Seven Arts Productions, Hedda Hopper Papers, AMPAS.

18 And also from Capitol Records, according to Sam Zolotow, 'Merrick is out as Show Sponsor', *New York Times*, 13 December 1963, unpaginated clipping in 'Stark, Ray' clippings file, Performing Arts Research Center (PARC), New York Public Library.

19 Lewis Funke, '*Funny Girl* Producer Plans for Future', *New York Times*, 5 April 1964, 'Stark, Ray' clippings file, PARC.

20 Mann, *Hello, Gorgeous*, 462.

21 Mann, *Hello, Gorgeous*, 472–3.

22 Christopher Andersen, *Barbra: The Way She Is* (London: Aurum, 2007), 147.

23 'Report Par Buying Out 7 Arts' Share in Ray Stark Pix', *Variety*, 28 April 1965, 1 and 72.

24 'Stark Will Produce Plays and Movies Independently', *New York Times*, 29 June 1966, 'Stark, Ray' clippings file, PARC.

25 The original budget for *Funny Girl* was just under $9 million, but in the end it cost $14 million to make. See James Spada, *Streisand: Her Life* (New York: Crown, 1995), 190; Anne Edwards, *Streisand* (London: Orion, 1997), 242; and Matthew Kennedy,

Roadshow! The Fall of Film Musicals in the 1960s (Oxford: Oxford University Press, 2014), 149. For the average budget of Hollywood movies in the late 1960s, see Cobbett Steinberg, *Film Facts* (New York: Facts on File, 1980), 50.

26 Dick, 'The History of Columbia', 27–9.

27 Kennedy, *Roadshow!*, 62.

28 Kennedy, *Roadshow!*, 174.

29 This turned out to underestimate the actual cost of the three films which was almost $50 million: $14 million for *Funny Girl*, around $25 million for *Hello, Dolly!* and $10 million for *On a Clear Day You Can See Forever*. See Kennedy, *Roadshow!*, 149, 178 and 204; and Sheldon Hall and Steve Neale, *Epics, Spectaculars and Blockbusters: A Hollywood History* (Detroit: Wayne State University Press, 2010), 195.

30 John Hallowell, 'Barbra Switches from Stage to Studio and Starts at the Top', *Life*, 29 September 1967, 139.

31 Robert B. Frederick, '*Sound of Music*, 007 Pix, Streak Into All-Timers', *Variety*, 5 January 1966, 6.

32 'All-Time Top Grossers', *Variety*, 5 January 1966, 6; 'Big Rental Pictures of 1965', *Variety*, 5 January 1966, 6 and 36.

33 'All-Time Boxoffice Champs', *Variety*, 4 January 1967, 9; Robert B. Frederick, '*Sound* Blows *Wind* Off No. 1', *Variety*, 4 January 1967, 9.

34 'All-Time Boxoffice Champs', *Variety*, 3 January 1968, 21.

35 Kennedy, *Roadshow!*, passim.

36 Most of the information on awards has been taken from Cunningham, *The Ultimate Barbra*, 205–11. There are detailed listings of all kinds of other facts and figures concerning Streisand's career in Cunningham's book and also in David Bret, *Barbra Streisand* (London: Unanimous, 2000). The following paragraphs are largely based on these two sources.

37 Andersen, *Barbra*, 95.

38 *2001 People Entertainment Almanac* (New York: Cader Books, 2001), 223.

39 Spada, *Streisand*, 197.

40 'Barbra', *Newsweek*, 28 March 1966, 92.

41 Once again, information is taken from Cunningham, *The Ultimate Barbra*, and Bret, *Barbra Streisand*; also see *2001 People Entertainment Almanac*, 224.

42 Robert B. Frederick, '"Unknowns" in Dead-Heat with Stars', *Variety*, 8 January 1968, 18.

43 Frederick, '"Unknowns,"' 18.

44 Frederick, '"Unknowns,"' 18.

45 Frederick, '"Unknowns,"' 18.

46 Frederick, '"Unknowns,"' 18 and 'Tunepix: High Risk', *Variety*, 8 January 1969, 15.

47 Frederick, '"Unknowns,"' 15; 'All-Time Boxoffice Champs', *Variety*, 8 January 1969, 14.

48 Frederick, '"Unknowns,"' 15 and 18.

49 Kennedy, *Roadshow!*, passim; Hall and Neale, *Epics, Spectacles and Blockbusters*, 181–212; Peter Krämer, *The New Hollywood: From Bonnie and Clyde to Star Wars* (London: Wallflower, 2005), 40–7; Joel Finler, *The Hollywood Story* (London: Octopus, 1990), 286–7.

50 Krämer, *The New Hollywood*, 47–58.

51 Krämer, *The New Hollywood*, 38–66, and Peter Krämer, 'A Powerful Cinema-going Force? Hollywood and Female Audiences since the 1960s', in *Identifying Hollywood's*

Audiences: Cultural Identity and the Movies, ed. Melvyn Stokes and Richard Maltby (London: BFI, 1999), 95–8.

52 Steinberg, *Film Facts*, 57–60.

53 'All-Time Boxoffice Champs', *Variety*, 7 January 1970, 25.

54 This is based on unpublished annual charts compiled by Sheldon Hall from Lawrence Cohn, 'All-Time Film Rental Champs', *Variety*, 10 May 1993, C76–108; see also Krämer, *The New Hollywood*, 107–9.

55 'All-Time Film Rental Champs', *Variety*, 4 January 1978, 25.

56 Once again, information is taken from Cunningham, *The Ultimate Barbra*, and Bret, *Barbra Streisand*; also see *2001 People Entertainment Almanac*, 220 and 224, and Steinberg, *Film Facts*, 147 and 182.

57 Krämer, 'A Powerful Cinema-going Force?', 94–7; Krämer, *The New Hollywood*, 6–66.

58 Streisand's influence on the Broadway version of *Funny Girl* is documented in Mann, *Hello, Gorgeous*, 399–468.

59 Spada, *Streisand*, 290.

60 Spada, *Streisand*, 201–9.

61 Joyce Haber, 'Barbra's Directing Her First Movie', *New York*, 15 April 1968, 50–1; quoted in Cunningham, *The Ultimate Barbra*, 253.

Chapter 5

THE AUTEURIST SPECIAL EFFECTS FILM: KUBRICK'S *2001: A SPACE ODYSSEY* (1968) AND THE 'SINGLE-GENERATION LOOK'

Julie Turnock

A film technician watching *2001* cannot help but be impressed by the fact that the complex effects scenes have an unusually sharp, crisp and grain-free appearance – a clean 'single-generation look' to coin a phrase. [...] The circumstance is not accidental, but rather the result of a deliberate effort on Kubrick's part to have each scene look as much like 'original' footage as possible.

— Herb Lightman[1]

The term Hollywood Renaissance typically distinguishes the production of auteurist US filmmaking circa 1967–74 from both the studio-based big-budget productions of the early 1960s and the late 1970s science fiction blockbusters. Not only are special effects-heavy films rarely associated with the Hollywood Renaissance, effects-heavy films of the 1970s and 1980s such as *Star Wars* (George Lucas, 1977) or *Top Gun* (Tony Scott, 1986) are most frequently mentioned as reactionary counter-movements to the late 1960s and early 1970s period under exploration in this volume. In this way, Stanley Kubrick's *2001: A Space Odyssey* (1968) is a contradiction: among the most auteurist by any definition of Hollywood films of the era *and* a roadshow-style super-production funded with a nearly unlimited budget from American studio MGM.

Annette Michelson's brilliant essay on *2001* argues for what she calls the film's ability to make the elaborate effects program seem to 'disappear' in the viewer's experience, provoking a powerful visceral experience unmoored from traditional cinematic bodily orientations.[2] While granting Michelson's claim (and Scott Bukatman's expansions of Michelson's essay),[3] this chapter makes the effects, and likewise their technologies and the process of their labour, vividly visible to those who are *not* technicians. Doing so reveals, instead of erases, a production process whose many modes and uses of technologies were anything but seamless, smooth or natural. As I will argue, the film juxtaposes three defined diegetic segments – the Dawn of Man, the Space Missions and the Star Gate – with, broadly speaking, three distinct effects approaches: front projection, contact optical printing and avant-garde animation. The filmmakers create a homogenized visual field out of the three phases through a consistent approach to the effects' aesthetic. This 'single-generation look', as Lightman coined in the opening quote, is the desire to make the effects look as if captured unmanipulated in a single shot by a 70mm movie camera, however the effect was actually achieved.

The remarkably coherent 'disappearing' look of *2001*'s overall effects makes it difficult to see the radically different technologies and approaches to how the aesthetics were achieved. While the specific effects technologies Kubrick and his team used are complicated, providing detailed descriptions of their working process demonstrates the extraordinary effort that the very effective illusion of transparent realism entailed, and the labour that produced the thickness of every second onscreen. Consequently, approaching *2001* through its effects provides a model for considering a film's technical aesthetic program and the labour used to produce it, specifically here as it appears as a coherent whole. It is an approach that does not reduce the finished film's effects to merely supporting the overall narrative thematics or as a byproduct of the problem/solution model, but instead proposes that the effects and the processes and technologies that produced them potentially provide their own discursive import on and beyond the particulars of the film they appear in. Analysing primary source documentation, including material from the Stanley Kubrick Archive in London, both personally conducted and previously published interviews with crew from the shoot, as well as trade, specialist and fan publications, I will demonstrate the importance and centrality of effects work to *2001*'s entire endeavour, and the working methods that made up *2001*'s effects program.

The film's effects program produces its discourse by programmatically juxtaposing these varied approaches in the three main sections of the movie – the distant past, the near future and an atemporal potential. *2001* demonstrates in extreme form, through the years of effects labour that went into making its effects appear natural, direct and inevitable, how the vaunted 1960s and 1970s 'non-aesthetic' naturalism should be understood not as 'more real' than that of other eras, but as a very specifically stylized aesthetic, even when extensive effects were not involved. Attention to this labour history in effects production not only makes visible what Kubrick and his team tried to keep invisible; demonstrating the effects team's artistic initiative also provides an alternative discourse to the way characterizations of the Hollywood Renaissance overemphasize the role of the auteur and 'his' mastery of all aspects of the production to the exclusion of other creative forces.

2001's effects program: The single generation look

First, however, what does it mean to identify a film's or Kubrick's 'effects program'? In the first instance, the film's effects program is the sum total of the design aesthetics, technology and labour that results in the effects producing a legible and decipherable discursive outcome. Secondly, the specific actors in creating these aesthetics, including the director, cinematographer, production designer and effects artists, certainly play an important role, but their statements are analysed *as* discourse. It is a model that does not only rely on a thematic reading of technology as a *topos* but instead incorporates the production history and technical specificity as well as an analysis of the historical technologies chosen.

As I have argued elsewhere, *2001*'s effects program provided an important precedent and model for subsequent (self-styled) auteurist filmmakers using extensive effects to realize their visions, both in the 1970s but also in more recent digital era effects filmmaking, most notably directors such as David Fincher, Christopher Nolan or Darren Aronofsky.[4] Analysing the film's approach also provides a way to historicize and denaturalize the prevalent style of 'crisp', 'sharp' photorealism that *2001* has inspired, and that we still associate with the ideal, most conventionally realistic effects style.[5] Therefore, rather than uncritically accepting the unspecific, transhistorical and teleological statement 'Kubrick wanted the effects to look more realistic than ever before', we can specifically describe the very exacting and novel *style* of realism he and his collaborators designed and executed for the single generation look.

American Cinematographer correspondent Herb Lightman's observations are relevant largely because he published the only set report and interview with Kubrick and his crew conducted during the production of the *2001*.[6] His coinage of the single generation look, with, 'unusually sharp, crisp and grain-free appearance', is also a terminology that focuses us directly not only on the technical specifications of the photographed image, but also on its aesthetic contours. It is instructive that Lightman (who was a trained cameraman) did not choose the term 'first generation look', but instead chose 'single-generation look', a term that emphasizes the look of *one* profilmic camera pass, rather than the first of many. The filmstrip's first generation is directly recorded profilmic action in front of the camera, or what is generally considered 'straight' or 'normal' shooting. If that developed filmstrip is duplicated and printed again (as was typically the case with all pre-digital composite technology) this is the image's second generation. Every generation's duplication and reprinting, typically required several times for multi-element compositing of the kind used in *2001*, means visual information and density is lost, resulting in the thinning (or diminishing) of the first generation image. In effects terms, this usually meant loss of sharpness in the image, as well as a fading of colours, most especially blacks and whites. In other words, Lightman is saying that even though it was impossible to actually film space directly, Kubrick still wanted the look of the highest definition unduplicated cinematic image. In constructing a very specific look of futuristic 'science fact', Kubrick and his effects team carefully combed through the existing effects possibilities, some of which had been largely defunct for decades.[7]

This description of the single generation look probably does not seem strange or unusual as an effects approach, but it certainly was for a big-budget colour film in the mid-1960s. Due to various technical difficulties with reproducing colour values, crispness and sharpness of the kind designed for *2001* were more associated with black and white still photojournalism.[8] In popular print culture, still photography in colour tended towards softer focus as well as 'softer' subjects, such as fashion, celebrity, travel and slice of life. Televisions in people's homes in the mid-1960s were still mostly black and white.[9] Moreover, a 'sharp, crisp look' was not the style of colour cinematography practiced by either the studio blockbusters or the ascendant filmmakers associated with the Hollywood Renaissance. The former preferred colour film in a more expressive style using filters and/or Technicolor saturation, appropriate to musicals, melodramas and historical adventures. The latter auteurist group tended towards the colour cinema *verité* look of desaturated colours and 'available' bounced lighting. In other words, the quasi-photojournalistic colour single generation look was a quite radically different visual style, and at odds with its cinematic contemporaries.

Moreover, it is important to note that there was nothing 'naturally' more realistic to this look, however it may seem in retrospect. More specifically than science fact, Kubrick conceived of the single generation look as what might be called 'NASA aspirational', that is, as if shot by the ideal version of a Super Panavision 65mm camera and film, through the finest ground lenses and with the illusion of a single bright point light source.[10] Despite the impossibility of obtaining such footage, and the lack of actually existing examples, Kubrick nevertheless wanted the look of the highest resolution moving colour image of space possible. This meant having the sharpness and clarity of *imaginary* documentary NASA colour moving camera footage, in order to visualize a believable future for viewers to contemplate the interrelation of humans and technology.[11] Genuine NASA footage from space at the time was actually grainy, low definition and in black and white, looking nothing like the convincingly futuristic footage produced for *2001* we can see in the spacecraft waltzing to Strauss example described below.

The single generation look was remarkable to Lightman and needed new terminology because it was not a style that had been used previously, particularly in science fiction films. By contrast, the most influential look for space effects in the previous generation of Hollywood effects filmmaking was created by matte paintings, where background artwork was composited into live action backgrounds or simply served as establishing shots. Bob Rehak in his essay on the varied career of Chesley Bonestell, illustrator as well as frequent matte artist on many 1950s science fiction films, discusses how the 'astrofuturist' space effects of the era, no matter how well researched and carefully rendered, contain an element of the fanciful.[12] Bonestell's space illustration work, which appeared in *Scientific American* and other popular publications, provides an example for the mid-century approach to speculative science illustrations, combining a popular science look with Technicolor fantasy where strict photorealism is not the goal.[13] Likewise, matte paintings for effects work, rather than imitate the camera lens' focus and definition, must be looser and almost impressionistic in order to be 'read' by the camera as a realistic backdrop.[14] Matte painting's fuzzy definition and heightened colour fields suggest an aesthetic associated with publishing and illustration.

More specifically, for Hollywood's highest budget science fiction realism in the 1950s, we can look to director (and former Warner Bros. effects head) Byron Haskin's work for Paramount on *Conquest of Space* (1955, also directed by Haskin) (Figure 5.1). Unlike, say, *Forbidden Planet* (Fred M. Wilcox, 1956), *Conquest* was meant to be a minimally fanciful exploration of scientific possibility, and Paramount promoted it as such, with taglines like 'See how it will happen in your lifetime!' The effects strove for an imaginative kind of scientific realism, much like in Bonestell's illustration work (he also worked on *Conquest* as a matte painter). It was not the crisp, late 1960s photorealism of *2001*, but a mid-1950s popular illustrated scientific realism, which suited the soft edges of Technicolor saturation as well as the exaggerated contours and shallow spatiality of popular science graphics.

Importantly, this meant that *2001* in both its live action footage and its effects footage would deploy neither the cinematographic styles associated with recent high budget science fiction, nor the style that was becoming associated with the late 1960s auteur movement as practiced (or soon to be practiced) by

Figure 5.1 *Conquest of Space*. Copyright Paramount.

directors Sidney Lumet, Robert Altman and Monte Hellman and by cinematographers such as László Kovács, Néstor Almendros and Gordon Willis. Instead, *2001*'s single generation realist aesthetic meant the sharpness, clarity and immediacy of an as yet impossible and imaginary high definition future.

2001: *The Effects Production*

I can say that it was necessary to conceive, design, and engineer completely new techniques in order to produce the special effects. This took 18 months and $6.5 million out of a $10.5 million budget. [...] But I felt it was necessary to make this film in such a way that every special effects shot in it would be completely convincing—something that had never been accomplished by a motion picture.

Stanley Kubrick[15]

You had to be *enormously* patient; because if you were not, or if you couldn't take criticism, then forget it—you couldn't work for Kubrick.

Tony Masters[16]

Kubrick's collaborators attest that he had less of a specific idea in mind for the film's realist aesthetics than he had a particular aesthetic ideal.[17] In other words, he did not necessarily know what the spaceships should look like, or precisely how to accomplish the Star Gate. Instead, he would know it when he saw it. And he kept his team designing and working until that happened, providing the effects team with a great deal of individual initiative. The ramifications of Kubrick's slow (laborious, time consuming, perfectionist) effects practice prompts the question, why go to all the considerable time, trouble and expense to produce the single generation aesthetic in what then seemed an outrageously ambitious 200-plus effects shots?[18] What did hewing to that particular look *mean*? And how did the push to achieve that look prompt the team to choose particular techniques?

Kubrick's production company reported in their submission for Academy Awards effects consideration in 1969 ways in which the production did and did not conform to expected effects techniques. The award form listed five categories: Full-sized Mechanical Effects, Matte Paintings, Miniatures, Opticals and Transparency Projection Process. The submission explicitly stated that the production used no matte paintings, no optical traveling mattes and no conventional rear projection, three of the five expected categories. Instead, it described the unconventionally large full-sized mechanical and physical effects, the large scale and highly detailed 'miniature' spacecraft, the composites that were completed by contact printing, the unusual use of front projection and the technical specification of Douglas Trumbull and his team's Slit Scan rig used on the Star Gate.[19] In other words, the awards form was used to stress how *un*conventional the effects production was.

Again, taken in the order the movie presents events to us, *2001* displays a juxtaposition of three diegetic spaces and three experiences of time: the prehistoric Africa of the 'Dawn of Man'; near-future outer Space Missions; and a Star Gate 'beyond infinity'. Moreover, each section creates a distinct discourse about cinematic realism, made in temporal terms: a plausible distant past 'could have been', then a credible speculative future 'could be' and finally an atemporal post-human potentiality beyond our grammar. The aesthetic of the single generation look transforms these imaginary, speculative conditional tenses into something cinematically immediate and actual.

The three segments also further the movie's discourse on technology. A match cut transitions literally and metaphorically from bone to satellite between the first two segments. In doing so, it leaps from the representation of the pre-technological past to imagined but plausible technologies that could have evolved out of it. Then in the film's final part, the plausible future dissolves into as yet incomprehensible visioning systems, exposing human inadequacies and limitations to interpreting these images.

In cinematically manifesting this discourse, each section also deploys very different effects approaches: front projection composites for the first part, contact printing optical composites for the central section and avant-garde animation for the last. The final Star Gate section importantly divorces the single generation look from a necessary relation to realism as conventional naturalism. These three sections, although produced very differently, nevertheless coalesce into a coherent tripartite whole.

In these ways, the film's discourse on technology and realism can be, and is, related via the special effects program. While neither the effects techniques used nor the film's production schedule map precisely on this abstracted chronology, this three-part schematization does help organize the complex ways we as viewers are meant to take in and interpret the effects in different parts of the film. I will now elaborate on these issues by discussing each part of the film separately.

The Dawn of Man

An incredibly bright image on a huge screen lends tremendous scope to a limitless subject and adds an extra dimension to the art of filmmaking.

Herb Lightman[20]

When Lightman paid a visit to the *2001* set, the effects method that most intrigued him was the use of the composite technique front projection, most prominently in the opening Dawn of Man sequence.[21] This sequence depicts the Earth's pre-human first encounter with a monolith, touching off a mysterious effect on the humanoids that eventually leads to their adoption of technology. Much like the ape-men's adoption of bones as tools and as weapons, the section takes advantage of a version of conventional mid-1960s composite filmmaking, but also makes incrementally innovative use of those pre-existing technologies. Lightman perceived the future of effects through the improved scope, dimensionality and brightness of front projection. By comparison, front and rear projection composites, the conventional effects processes of the 1960s present, discursively constitute the film's past, or more specifically, its outmoded pre-history.

Although both rear projection and front projection use pre-filmed background plates that were projected and filmed on-set at the same time as the live action principal photography, front projection differs from the more established practice of rear projection in a few significant ways. Instead of projecting onto a screen set up *behind* the actors, front projection, as its name suggests, projects its pre-filmed images via the camera side, from the front. More specifically, the combination of powerful lights, the precise alignment of an angled mirror and intense light-bouncing screens 'trick' the camera (specifically the latitude of the film) into registering front projected material and live action material as part of the same space.[22] The *2001* front projection team, led by Tom Howard, boosted the traditional front projection set up by using unusually large 8x10 format still images (known as transparencies) for what Kubrick called their 'surplus of resolution'.[23]

Although the *mise en scène* was composited using film shot at different times, these enhancements of conventional rear projection combine to create a front projected single generation look of a pre-human African landscape. Practically speaking, the outsized projected images, the larger background reflective screens and more powerful lights mean the background colour values are less distorted than in conventional rear projection, and the screen brightness boosted the resolution of the front projected plates' picture quality. This results in a production method that was seen as an upgraded version of the most conventional effects practice in mid-century Hollywood where the composite was made on-set during principal photography.

In a still from the Dawn of Man segment (Figure 5.2), the humanoid ape man, having just discovered the power of technology, throws his new bone tool in the air. As in most of the sequence, the still demonstrates the carefully constructed, lit and framed composition of the composite work in this section. While the foreground and middle ground planes were shot on a soundstage, the extreme background is a large format still transparency image, shot on location in South Africa and projected onto reflective screens, creating a very convincing illusion of an integrated time and space environment.[24]

In the majority of the shots in the Dawn of Man segment, the filmmakers compose the composites in a fairly conventional mid-1960s manner. The middle ground, made up of large rock outcroppings, is lit a brighter brown, with the distant peaks of background and sky luminously bright. As was usual, the

Figure 5.2 Dawn of Man. Copyright MGM.

action in the foreground is emphasized through figure movement so that the viewer does not focus closely on the background elements. However, the sequence also departs from traditional practices. Instead of the typical defined and sculpted foreground lighting in projection methods, the *2001* proto-humans in the foreground are unusually illuminated to softly blend with the sandy, rocky, dun-coloured foreground elements. They are barely distinguishable from the setting. For most of the segment, they are generally lit indistinctly, more as shapes than individuals, in soft, even, magic-hour light.

However, this pattern is broken at the ambivalent moment of evolutionary breakthrough, when the extreme brightness of the projected background plays a role. The ape man is monumentalized nearly in silhouette, his dark fur sharp against the brighter immediate and deep background. This makes a composition where the humanoid stands in contrast to all three distinct foreground, middle ground and background planes, breaking free of his context, metaphorically reaching to distances beyond. At this moment, temporalities of past, present and future are layered over the ape man, a gesture reinforced by the front projection technologies that likewise superimpose projected elements shot at different production instances. Thanks to the influence of the sharply defined monolith, the humanoids begin their evolution to human individuality.

While today considered a moribund and 'dated' effects process, front projection methods, as Lightman's assessment suggests, were very much the 'now' of effects techniques in the mid-1960s, and the composition of the ape man's defiant gesture brings him up to that 'now'. However, projection composites in the 'pre-human' Dawn of Man sequence contrast sharply with the subsequent Space Missions section of the film. This creates the implication that such methods are the past and will not serve us in the future as technology evolves. Discursively, the Dawn of Man section's approach to a conventional, on-set registration of composites will no longer be sufficient for the kinds of imagery needed to depict the near future of space travel. And projection composites were indeed on the way out. It was instead the next section's effects approach that proved influential for the near future of effects technologies.

The Space Missions

> Often [...] several elements would be photographed onto held-takes photographed several months apart. [...] Also, since the elements were being photographed onto the same strip of original negative, it was essential that all exposure matched precisely. If one of them was off, there would be no way to correct it without throwing the others off. [...] But even with all these precautions there was a high failure rate and many of the scenes had to be redone.
>
> Stanley Kubrick[25]

After the humanoid throws the bone in the air and the film cuts to a satellite above the Earth (thereby skipping from 1968's distant past to the nearish future), a satellite, backlit by the Earth, waltzes to music by Strauss as it orbits. The detailed satellite miniature, with its ridges, fans and tail on a starfield background, revolves around the radiantly bright Earth surface as the 'camera' tracks into (and almost through) a revolving, circular double-wheeled space station. The point of view approaches close enough to distinguish windows, struts and surface detail. Finally, a shuttle with a Pan Am logo glides into view from the right side of frame, and the film then cuts to the inside of the shuttle to our first human character, Dr Heywood Floyd, being ferried from the Earth to the space station. The sequence, compositing three separate miniature spacecraft, flat colour artwork of the Earth, an animated sun and a starfield background, is staged as if shot from the point of view of a movie viewfinder (Figure 5.3). It is actually one of the less elaborate of the film's middle Space Missions scenes, since others include composites of figures in windows and screen displays, among other complications. Nevertheless, the long, two minute sequence's slow waltz-time pace, implying peaceful, awe-inspiring progress, provides time for the spectator to contemplate the 'evolution' from the raucous, aggressive humanoid Dawn of Man section of the film. It also allows the viewer's eyes to linger on the photorealistic, high definition colour environments.

Likewise, the film's effects approach also cuts from an on-set, 'real time' projection composite approach to one that radically fragments the *mise en scène* as well as the production timeline. Rather than what one might call a

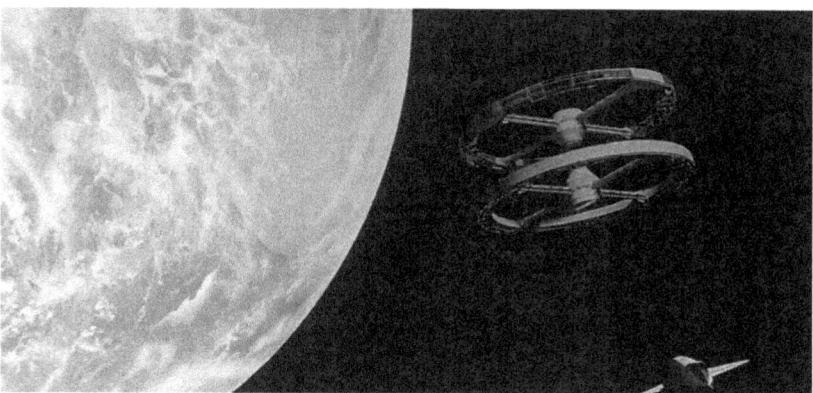

Figure 5.3 Space Missions. Copyright MGM.

'primitive' *mise en scène*, that is, one that is shot in the conventional 1960s manner, the middle part of the film represents the effects sequences of a plausible (and it turns out, actual) near future. Instead of compositing on the principal photography set like projection methods, it is a *mise en scène* built up piece by piece, layer by layer, over extended periods of time. Here, the single generation look is much more intensively artificial, with shots of spacecraft consisting of as many as ten separately shot elements (a great deal for the time) to be merged into a credible whole by optical compositing. While the Dawn of Man's single generation look models conventional mid-1960s aesthetics as much as possible, with its low-contrast colour palette, diffused natural looking lighting and softer focus, the film's middle section imagines the near future through a new, sharper focus and high contrast aesthetic. The voyaging spacecraft here are strongly contrasting black and white or robustly coloured, in pin-sharp focus and lit from a strong single source light. Instead of looking to cinematic aesthetics of the 'present', the Space Missions section models its look on what was in the mid-1960s imaginary high definition NASA space photography, as if shot from by a 65mm Panavision camera, on colour film in space. In this way, the look is not only NASA aspirational, but also human aspirational, or how humans might experience space if we could look at a film shot from an ideal vantage point. The juxtaposition of these first two segments suggests that the distant past and its ways of thinking are still superimposed over the future, the bone in the satellite.

In deciding upon the effects approach to this segment, Kubrick rejected conventional blue screen travelling mattes from the outset. Instead, to produce a 'sharp, crisp and grain-free appearance' while still using optical composite technologies, Kubrick went further back to the past. Lightman quotes Kubrick at length:

We purposely did all of our duping with black and white three-colour separation masters. There were no colour inter-positives used for combining the shots, and I think this is principally responsible for the lack of grain and the high degree of photographic quality we were able to maintain. *More than half the shots in the picture are dupes, but I don't think the average viewer would know it.* Our separations were made, of course, from the original colour negative and we then used a number of bi-pack camera-printers for combining the material. A piece of colour negative ran through the gate while, contact printed onto it, actually in the camera, were the colour separations, each of which was run through in turn. [. . .] It was literally just a method of contact printing.[26]

What this complex quote explains is that to achieve the 'high degree of photographic quality', it would be necessary to eliminate the telltale signs of blue screen composites: matte lines (where the seams between the composited elements show), colour fading due to multiple re-copying of composite elements and image wobble in the elements caused by inconsistent printing methods.

The production would use three major techniques to maintain image quality despite duplication in multi-element composite shots: colour separation reprinting, contact printing and, as several technicians reported, constant re-does. Despite Kubrick's claims, the *2001* team invented none of these techniques, and in fact they are all decades-old practices, although some were novel in effects work. Colour separation reprinting in effects work derives from three-strip Technicolor's technique to build its colour palette by printing the separately filtered cyan/magenta/yellow filmstrips into one combined, full colour strip. The effects process adapts this by the procedure Kubrick described above, where the element is shot in colour, then filtered into three black and white filmstrips, and eventually recombined so that the image is restored to its full colour, sharpness and definition. Contact printing is amongst the oldest forms of composite work, where one takes a master negative and lines up and prints in subsequent positive elements frame by frame with a step printer, so that elements are not duplicated in reprinting, but each element remains at first generation quality.[27] This technique means any mistake in every printing step risks ruining the original element. And for the *2001* production, this is why the constant re-does were necessary. Not only did effects artists on the film such as Douglas Trumbull, Wally Gentleman and others attest to the 'endless trial and error', to get the composites exactly right by Kubrick's standards,[28] but one can see the stacks of notebooks in artist Con Pederson's handwriting including page after page of trial reports, neatly entered, covering the entire date range of the production at the Kubrick archive.[29] The composite process makes visible and accentuates the invisible labour that it took to create the illusion of image fullness and the thickness of time and reality Kubrick required.

This section's effects also deployed other kinds of non-standard temporality that went beyond the *mise en scène* elements having been shot months or even years apart. Effects miniatures must also be shot at higher or lower frame rates than the standard 24 frames per second in order to be 'read' as commensurate with their weight and size. Therefore, the (often very large) miniatures had to be shot at extremely slow frame rates to keep them in the desired sharp focus, so that they would look like full-sized vehicles and not miniatures. As Lightman put it: 'The obvious solution of using more light was not feasible because it was necessary to maintain the illusion of a single bright point light source.'[30] Kubrick elaborated: 'It was like watching the hour hand of a clock. We shot most of these scenes using slow exposures of four seconds per frame, and if you were standing on the stage you would not see anything moving.'[31]

The effects artists not only radically fragmented what appears to be conventional shooting time by extending it far beyond the usual 24 frames per second. Demonstrating the result of the constant re-does and temporal back and forth of the production process also granulates the effects artists' most miniscule effort. Cross-sectioning these frames and examining the layers exposes the hidden labour in every frame, every visual layer and in every fragment of the film's running time.

As already discussed above, the composites required the effects team's careful environmental matching, multiple element compositing using contact printing with emulsion to emulsion line up to the original negative, long lag times between shooting and compositing, as well as constant testing and repetition until Kubrick's idea of perfection was reached. The team atomized all possible aspects of the conventional filmmaking process (frame rate, *mise en scène*, production temporality, etc.) and then recombined the pieces into what would read on screen as the single generation look. This suggests that the filmmaking of the near future would be able to create a composite *mise en scène* where the filmmaker could manipulate every element, down to a granular level. And still they could maintain the illusion of having shot conventionally with a single camera and a single light source, a prediction for the year 2001 that came even more true than Kubrick could have imagined. The next generation of filmmakers making science fiction films such as George Lucas, Steven Spielberg and James Cameron took up and adapted the aesthetic of Kubrick's Space Missions for their influential and popular effects films, setting the look for photorealism that has persisted though the digital age.

The Star Gate

Kubrick had said that he wanted the camera to 'go through something' but nobody knew quite what or how.

Douglas Trumbull[32]

Slit scan [...] can take something that is essentially flat, dull and static and turn it into something dimensional with movement and depth and colour.

Douglas Trumbull[33]

If for the Space Missions, as effects crew member Bryan Loftus put it, 'Kubrick's priority [was] to make it as real as human knowledge could make it', the final section of the film, known popularly as 'the Star Gate' challenges and overturns the approaches of the first two sections.[34] Previously, the effects created a composite *mise en scène* to resemble a primeval Africa or space ships docking on space stations, physical objects and environments that the eye could reality test. Instead, the Star Gate effects generate and visualize impossible images that abstract the film's most ambitious ideas. By twisting and ultimately dismantling the carefully constructed photorealism of the Space Missions segment, the effects in the final section of the film push the single generation aesthetic to the limit, while at the same time making it feel like an extension of the previous segment. Although the Star Gate frequently contains non-figurative imagery that would be difficult to describe as 'realistic', the sequence plays out as a hyper-subjective 'trip' undergone by both Dave Bowman and the viewer.[35] In other words, the effects team designed and executed a sequence that is both visually abstract *and* plausibly representative of Dave's experience.

At the beginning of the Star Gate sequence, as Dave 'enters' the 'gate', much of the sequence's impact comes from the more-extensive-than-usual use of what is presented as Dave's point of view. What he appears to be withstanding is organized visually as material that recedes rapidly into the deep z-axis, appearing to come at Dave and the viewer. Moreover, in realizing Kubrick's directive of making the camera 'go through something', the effects artists had a great deal of leeway as to what that would mean. What is astonishing is not only that the effects team was charged with the daunting task of visually demonstrating the limits of human reason and understanding, but how effectively they achieved it.[36]

The team used an effects approach which was entirely different from the 'primitive' projection techniques of the Dawn of Man and the 'near future' optical compositing of the Space Missions to realize this goal. The Star Gate sequence approached effects imagery in a way that both indicated an un-visualizable future state of humanity and used techniques outside of conventional effects production. Appropriately, it was one that was more associated with 1960s avant-garde practice. As Trumbull said, his approach to the Star Gate material was inspired in part by experimental animator (and commercial motion graphic artist) John Whitney Sr, who 'had done some incredible things in combining completely abstract optical effects with computerized graphics'.[37]

A major innovation in how this sequence was conceived was by using effects and animation techniques to create a sense of movement and volume through painstaking manipulation of the z-axis, and by rendering movement and depth through the way film registers light, movement and colour. In other words, to paraphrase Trumbull, it meant turning something flat, dull and static into something dimensional with movement, depth and colour or, to put it differently, animating shapes and colours to make visible Dave's experience of the Star Gate. The intensely composited and manipulated effects work in the final sequence of the film consists of a collection of techniques that might be called photo-animated sequences, in that they combine some aspects of traditional effects photography and some aspects of traditional animation, as well as aspects of 1960s experimental animation. In generating non-figurative but intellectually comprehensible imagery, the Star Gate team managed to eliminate nearly every aspect of conventional profilmic shooting.

As Trumbull explained, the challenge his team had was to 'produce a photographic image of something that does not actually exist'.[38] To craft movement through light, Trumbull developed the famous slit scan rig to create the sense of 'moving through' something by adapting the procedure of streak photography to move in depth, 'in *space*, so to speak'.[39] Slit scan, simply put, is a kind of animated streak photography or, as Trumbull put it more complicatedly, 'extended time exposures of stratoscopic sequence multiple exposures to show changes in shape, direction, or velocity by exposing an entire movement onto a single film plate'.[40] Slit scan creates the effect of motion by having either the camera move in relation to what is being photographed or vice versa, with the coordination of the movement during the exposure creating the distortion effect. These light distortions, carefully plotted on a grid, are built up frame by frame to suggest movement into depth. Also, paralleling the labour that produced it, the resultant images create the effect of distending time and space.[41] The Star Gate segment therefore forms a tangible, explorable *mise en scène* out of cinema's most basic abstracted elements: light, movement and colour.

As the sequence progresses, the team generated moving shapes through backlit artwork of various existing designs, including printed circuits, op-art style patterns and photos of molecular structures. However, the effects team then defamiliarized these shapes further by exposing them to multiple colour filters. For example, during the initial stages of 'entering' the Star Gate, softly striated streaks in shades of ruby, scarlet, cherry tomato and fuchsia, with spots of jade, tangerine, teal, gold and white on a black background pulsate and emanate swiftly from a central vertical slit of one-point perspective in the centre to the periphery of the frame (Figure 5.4a). While totally non-figurative, these abstracted shapes, colours and light intensities suggest being pulled through a corridor. Although disconcerting, the hues suggest wonder more than danger, despite the frequent cuts to Dave's anguished face. Organizing the colour compositions, the 'slit' also created a kind of split or bisecting line in the visual frame, in which the forward movement collapses into the centre line at variable rates of speed.

How, then, does the slit scan and other techniques in the sequence suggest irrationality, or moving into a space beyond human rationality? The Star Gate

Figure 5.4a Star Gate. Copyright MGM.

sequence defamiliarizes a number of visual tropes associated with scientific rationality and cinematic orientation, especially those related to visual epistemology, namely the horizon, one-point perspective and the mirror. As Annette Michelson argued, the film does this elsewhere, especially in the Space Missions sequences, using the body untethered from gravity to disorient our already unstable sense of cinematic positioning that the classical Hollywood continuity system has long reinforced.[42] The Star Gate even more radically dismantles this stable sense of viewership by cuing the way sentient beings orient themselves to the natural world, a horizon, and transforming it into a site of uncertainty rather than reassurance. In the Dawn of Man, the horizon provided a familiar point of certainty for the pre-humans. Here, in the post-human, the horizon is a false one, its verticality dislocating or inverting 'natural' perspective and distance perception. Likewise, one-point perspective, a reproduction strategy associated with Renaissance and Cartesian space, is not used to make the reproduced world 'through a lens' readable or meaningful. Instead, here it disorganizes space, rather than structuring it. The slitted false horizon also creates a kind of mirror reflection effect. The mirror, a longstanding cinematic metaphor, also seems to malfunction, only intermittently reflecting the other side, and mostly creating asymmetry. In other words, the usual ways of knowing and gleaning meaning from the natural world, the reproduced world and metaphoric language all fail us.

After 'passing through' the gate, the imagery diversifies, ranging from astronomical galaxy-like images and diaphanous cloud-like wisps to quasi-zoological jellyfish blobs and human reproduction imagery suggesting embryos, sperm and ovum. These are intercut with human eyes (Figure 5.4b) and 'flyover'

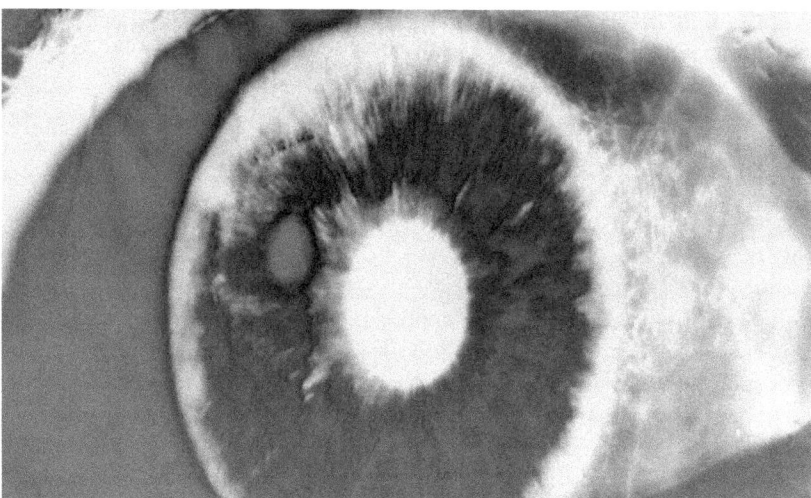

Figure 5.4b Star Gate. Copyright MGM.

landscape imagery. With the exception of what is assumed to be Dave's eye, these images are also camera mobile, and suggest moving through, past and over. Nevertheless, even as imagery becomes more figurative, and identifiable, colour filtering distorts the expected colours and replaces them with combinations that, for traditional aesthetics, seem clashing and 'wrong'. For example, one of the blinking eye close ups combines amethyst purple with cerulean blue, both equally intense. Effects artist Bryan Loftus said that Kubrick rejected their early colorations as too expected. Instead, he said they threw darts at a color wheel to get 'weird' combinations their conventional brains would not think of.[43]

A malfunctioning mirror, the creation of a new landscape and an unnatural, false horizon combine for an anti-rationalist, anti-epistemological cinematic space. And once we have gone 'through something' totally abstract, and the photography returns to figurative 'actors on a set', we as viewers feel our own metaphors have mixed: we have gone over a new horizon through the looking glass and experienced the big bang of an alternative universe. And through the point-of-view vantage point, the effects generate out of photo-animation a wholly irrational single generation look that the viewer nevertheless undergoes as direct experience. Although the description of the single generation look of this section seems like it should result in an aesthetic effect very different from the first two sections, the Star Gate sequence nevertheless feels a part of the realism effect of those two sections. Despite its abstract and disorienting qualities, the effects team, through avant-garde animation techniques, bent the photorealism of the Space Missions out of shape. They managed to materialize and make physical Dave's, and the viewer's, voyage 'through something' into the infinite. And they have indeed even remade the viewer's perception into something post-human.

Conclusion

Despite the radically different technologies and approaches used to achieve it, the resultant single generation look over the course of *2001* homogenizes for the viewer into a remarkably consistent whole. Nevertheless, the sum total of the design aesthetics, technology and approach over the three sections results in the effects producing a legible and decipherable discourse around how the specific technology used makes vividly real our experience of the interconnectedness of human knowledge, evolution and their limitations. Aesthetically, the film's chronology skips from the production of classical studio era effects, past its present day to cinema's future in intensified composite *mise en scène* and the elongated post-production timelines of later decades, and eventually into near abstraction.

Similar to the film's famous match cut from the prehistoric humanoid's bone to the near-future orbiting satellite, *2001* bypasses the filmmaking norms of its own time to present possible future aesthetics. And in fact, by presenting the aesthetic for a plausible near future, the film established a new aesthetic for cinematic photorealism that not only influenced the science fiction filmmakers of the 1970s and 1980s such as Lucas, Spielberg and Ridley Scott, but is still being practiced in the effects of blockbuster filmmaking today.[44] Moreover, *2001* provides a paradigmatic example of the 1960s American auteur's focus, fixation and perfectionism through, not in spite of, extensive effects work. Likewise, attention to the effects artists' considerable contributions to the meaning of the film add a layer of critical discourse that challenges the Hollywood Renaissance auteur as the single, dominating creative force.

Author's Note: Thanks to Amanda Ciafone and Anita Say Chan for their extremely helpful comments on this chapter.

Notes

1   Herb Lightman, 'Filming 2001: *A Space Odyssey*', *American Cinematographer* (June 1968): 442.
2   Annette Michelson, 'Bodies in Space: Film as "Carnal Knowledge"', *Artforum* 8, no. 6 (1969): 54–63.
3   Scott Bukatman, *Matters of Gravity* (Durham, NC: Duke University Press, 2003).
4   Julie Turnock, *Plastic Reality Special Effects, Technology, and the Emergence of 1970s Blockbuster Aesthetics*, (New York: Columbia University Press, 2015), 263–74.

5 Julie Turnock, 'The ILM Version: Recent Digital Effects and the Aesthetics of 1970s Cinematography', *Film History* 24, no. 2 (2012): 158–68.

6 Lightman's account is historically important because, as he claimed in a 2011 interview, '[*2001*] was the film that I scooped the world on. Stanley didn't give any other information out about *2001* while it was in production. [. . .] He called me from London and the result of that were two massive articles that I published in *American Cinematographer* magazine when I was the editor there. He held nothing back from me.' Lightman was interviewed by Justin Bozung by telephone in 2011. The interview was published online, on 1 May 2014, after Lightman's death (http://blog.tvstoreonline.com/search?q=lightman).

7 Lightman, 'Filming *2001*', 412.

8 This style does not especially match Kubrick's own photojournalistic work for *Look* magazine which is often more expressive and moody rather than hard edged. See Turnock, *Plastic Reality*, 70–5.

9 Erik Barnouw, *Tube of Plenty: The Evolution of American Television*, 2nd edition (Oxford: Oxford University Press, 1990), 149.

10 Lightman, 'Filming *2001*', 444. For a more extensive discussion of historical styles of photorealism in effects work, see Turnock, *Plastic Reality*.

11 Lightman, 'Filming *2001*', 412–13.

12 Bob Rehak, 'Shooting Stars: Chesley Bonestell and the Special Effects Of Outer Space', in *Special Effects: New Histories, Theories, Contexts*, ed. Dan North, Bob Rehak and Michael Duffy (Basingstoke: Palgrave Macmillan, 2015), 207.

13 For examples of Bonestell's space art see http://www.bonestell.org/

14 Mark C. Vaz and Craig Barron, *The Invisible Art* (San Francisco: Chronicle Books, 2002), 22.

15 Eric Nordern, 'Playboy Interview: Stanley Kubrick', in *Stanley Kubrick: Interviews*, ed. Gene Phillips (Jackson: University of Mississippi Press, 2001), 72.

16 *2001* Production Designer Tony Masters, quoted in Don Shay and Jody Duncan, '*2001*: A Time Capsule', *Cinefex* 85 (April 2001): 81.

17 This information aggregates material available at the Stanley Kubrick Archive (SKA) at the University of the Arts, London. I would like to thank Sara Mahurter, Jessica Womack, Richard Daniels and Wendy Russell for their assistance.

18 Lightman, 'Filming *2001*', 412.

19 Stanley Kubrick, 'Notes on Special Effects for *2001: A Space Odyssey*', 9 January 1969, SKA.

20 Herb Lightman, 'Front Projection for *2001*', *American Cinematographer* (June 1968): 420.

21 Lightman, 'Filming *2001*', 444. Front projection was also used for scenes of astronauts walking on the lunar surface.

22 In front projection, the background image superimposes the foreground set. The foreground set lights, in tandem with the extreme reflectiveness of the 3M material screens, are powerful enough to make the front projected image invisible in the foreground and visible only in the background. Those on the set can see the front projected image, but the film does not register the front projection, creating a latent image layering the foreground image.

23 Lightman, 'Front Projection', 420.

24 Kubrick sent a small photographic unit to a remote location in South Africa to take large format stills to be used as backdrops for the Dawn of Man.

25 Kubrick, quoted in Lightman, 'Filming *2001*', 443.

26 Kubrick, quoted in Lightman, 'Filming *2001*', 442 – emphasis added by the author.

27 For a description of conventional contact printing, see Raymond Fielding, *The Technique of Special Effects Cinematography* (New York: Hastings House Publishers, 1968), 107–8. Contact printing stopped being a common practice in the 1910s and 1920s.

28 Lightman, 'Filming *2001*', 444.

29 Con Pederson's ledgers can be found at the SKA.

30 Lightman, 'Filming *2001*', 443–4.

31 Kubrick, quoted in Lightman, 'Filming *2001*', 444.

32 Douglas Trumbull, 'The Slit Scan Process as used in *2001*', *American Cinematographer* (October 1969): 998.

33 Trumbull, 'The Slit Scan Process as used in *2001*', 1026.

34 Bryan Loftus (UK cinematographer and optical printer operator on *2001*); personal interview with the author, London, UK, 25 October 2007.

35 According to Trumbull, the drug trip associations of the section were purportedly not intentional. Douglas Trumbull, 'Creating Special Effects for *2001*', *American Cinematographer* (June 1968): 452.

36 Despite Kubrick's attempt to take credit for all the effects, it is important to stress that the effects team, in particular the group headed by Trumbull, conceived of all the visual material of this section, even if their ideas were approved or nixed by Kubrick.

37 Trumbull, 'The Slit Scan Process', 998. Here computerized means computer assisted, not computer generated. Whitney and his brother James were known for programming decommissioned military computers to make experimental films such as *Lapis* (1966) and *Permutations* (1968).

38 Trumbull, 'The Slit Scan Process', 1012.

39 As Trumbull explained further: 'An almost infinite plane may be created by moving an illuminated image behind a very narrow, long slit opening, while the entire mechanism moves toward the camera—we call this the slit scan.' Trumbull, 'The Slit Scan Process', 1012 – emphasis in the main text was added by the author.

40 Trumbull, 'The Slit Scan Process', 1000.

41 The device also has to repeat itself exactly for each frame, requiring the camera rig to be on a kind of precisely controlled incrementally repositioned 'worm gear', a forerunner to what would become in the next decade computer-assisted motion control.

42 Michelson, 'Bodies in Space', 57–8

43 Loftus, personal interview.

44 Turnock, *Plastic Reality,* 270–4.

Chapter 6

'ABOUT AS BRUTAL, RELEVANT AND EXPLOITABLE AS THEY COME': *MEDIUM COOL* (1969) AND POLITICAL FILMMAKING

Oliver Gruner

Her face illuminated by the television's glare, Eileen (Verna Bloom) looks on transfixed as Martin Luther King delivers what will turn out to be his final public speech: 'I don't know what will happen now. We've got some difficult days ahead.' By this stage in *Medium Cool* (Haskell Wexler, 1969), an account of events surrounding the Chicago Democratic National Convention of 1968, the civil rights leader is already dead. Replayed as part of a media retrospective, his words appear as a grim prophecy of both his own assassination and the social upheaval following in its wake. A quick cut instigates a change in tone. From Eileen's awe-struck eyes we jump to her companion John Cassellis (Robert Forster). Stood in the doorway, hands in his pockets, he appears as cynical foil to her sadness. 'You see, the media's got a script,' Cassellis growls. 'Flags at half-mast. Trips cancelled.' The list of journalistic clichés goes on: 'Then the funeral procession . . . A lot of experts say how sick our society is, how sick we all are . . . and when the script is finished, everybody goes pretty much back to normal.' As a storm brews outside, Cassellis' anti-media invective reaches its climax. So too does the homage to King. With the crash of thunder as accompaniment, we flashback to 1963 and his famous 'I have a dream' speech: 'free at last, free at last, thank God almighty we are free at last.'

A collage of emotional juxtapositions, temporal shifts and political commentary, this scene exemplifies *Medium Cool*'s complex approach to its themes. Produced as a response to issues bedevilling America through 1968, the film swings between intense vitality – being *there* on the streets with history in the making – and jaded cynicism about the nation's recent past and immediate future. Critics have noted the film's formal innovation, its ideological prescience and indebtedness to European art cinema (in particular, to the films of Jean-Luc Godard).[1] Some go so far as to contend *Medium Cool* is the closest 1960s Hollywood came to capturing, as Jonathan Kirshner puts it, 'the spirit of May '68'.[2] Certainly, its portrayal of the confrontations igniting American city streets – as they were in Paris, Prague, Tokyo and elsewhere around the world – was but one of a small cluster of studio releases to focus on the New Left and its concerns.[3] This chapter situates *Medium Cool* within broader public debates of the 1960s. Examining the film's production history, I discuss the ways in which it was shaped and reshaped in line with events and discourses pertaining to class, race, gender, the Vietnam War and, more generally, the commercial operations of Hollywood cinema. As a political drama distributed by a major studio, *Medium Cool* exemplifies how creative and economic exigencies of the period were engaged and negotiated. While popular and scholarly criticism often touts the film as representative of the Hollywood Renaissance at its most political (radical, even), a focus on production suggests a more contradictory text, where certain issues were emphasized and developed, while others were curtailed and/or modified as it travelled from concept to script to screen. I conclude with an overview of *Medium Cool*'s critical reception. It is notable the extent to which many contemporaneous arbiters celebrated the film's formal qualities, while simultaneously highlighting its limitations as a political text. In these diverse readings, *Medium Cool* appeared to differing degrees 'as brutal, relevant and exploitable as they come'.[4]

To the barricades: Making Medium Cool

Medium Cool emerged out of a film industry in the throes of significant transformation. With regard to its financing, formal and stylistic qualities and distribution the film epitomized what Yannis Tzioumakis has termed 'a new marriage' between independent film production and Hollywood's major studios.[5] Haskell Wexler was first offered the chance to direct his own feature in late 1967.[6] Having received an Academy Award earlier that year for his cinematography on *Who's Afraid of Virginia Woolf?* (Mike Nichols, 1966) – and having just completed work on *In the Heat of the Night* (Norman Jewison, 1967) – he was riding a wave of success. But moving from cinematographer to director in Hollywood still required support and resources. That came in the form of Peter Bart, then assistant to Robert Evans, head of production at Paramount. Aged thirty-four, Bart was previously employed as a correspondent for the *New York Times*. In August 1966, he had written a feature about a new generation of young, innovative producers. The thirty-six-year-old Evans received top billing.[7] This article – at least according to Evans – changed 'the entire course of [his] life and career'.[8] Within two days, Evans had been hired by Paramount, and by November was promoted to head of production. He promptly hired Bart as his assistant.[9] Their rise intersected with broader developments within Hollywood. Throughout the 1960s, all but three studios were taken over by larger corporations (Paramount itself was bought by Gulf + Western in 1966).[10]

CEOs with little understanding of the film business were tempted by young filmmakers and producers because they were adaptable, relatively inexperienced (and thus could be hired for less), were presumed to have a greater understanding of the important youth market and, as David Cook puts it, 'knew more . . . about the production and marketing of motion pictures than the nonfilm executives'.[11]

Announcing a new stable of writers at Paramount, Evans informed *Variety* in early 1968 that his studio would not only be 'relying on the supposedly "safe" experienced writers who have already established their reputations'. Rather, he and Bart used their new-found power to court lesser-known entities and/or those of a countercultural sensibility: Elaine May (*A New Leaf*, 1971; also directed by May), Buck Henry (*Catch 22* [Mike Nichols, 1970]), Arnold Schulman (*Goodbye, Columbus* [Larry Peerce, 1969]) and, indeed, Haskell Wexler, to name but a few.[12] At a time of financial crisis within the industry – which reached its apex during the recession of 1969–71 – the majors were willing to take a gamble on low-budget youth-oriented pictures, which already by 1967 were proving unexpected successes, most famously *Bonnie and Clyde* (Arthur Penn, 1967) and *The Graduate* (Mike Nichols, 1967).[13] What Paramount were not prepared to offer, at least in advance, was any upfront financial contribution. Instead, the studio agreed to purchase *Medium Cool* as a 'negative pickup'. Wexler would produce the film with his own funds and Paramount would buy the finished article.[14] Whether all of the upfront cash (estimated to be eight hundred thousand dollars) came from Wexler's personal fortune or loans is unclear. It is notable, however, that his brother Jerrold is credited as co-producer. As director of Jupiter Corporation – a large Chicago-based company with interests in real estate and oil – Jerrold would certainly have been able to guarantee any loans, should they be required.[15] Either way, the deal offered Wexler the opportunity to develop independently his own project and to see it through to fruition.

Forty-seven years old, Wexler could hardly be included amongst the youthful 'film generation' often discussed as central to Hollywood of the late 1960s and early 1970s.[16] However, he shared similarities in terms of experience and outlook with another group of creatives then rising to prominence. The 'television generation', as Peter Krämer terms it, encompassed a group of filmmakers born between the early 1920s and mid-1930s (Mike Nichols and Arthur Penn are two prominent examples). Many, though not all, started their careers on the small screen and/or in theatre, tended to be more liberal in their politics than their older Hollywood peers, 'placed a higher value on the realistic depiction of contemporary American society and understood themselves to be social commentators and artists as well as entertainers'.[17] Wexler's career actually stretched back to the late 1940s. As David Talbot and Barbara Zheutlin note, he began as a documentary maker for a host of left-wing causes. Many of his films of the late 1940s were supported by labour unions and progressive organizations: *Deadline for Action* (Carl Marzani, 1946), funded by the United Electrical,

Radio and Machine workers union and *Half Century with Cotton* (Haskell Wexler, 1948), a film about an Alabama textile mill, for example. Like many leftists of his generation, he struggled to maintain political projects with the rise of McCarthyism and the House Un-American Activities Committee (HUAC).[18] Through the early 1950s he worked on television commercials as well as documentaries, including an Academy Award-nominated short about urban renewal, *The Living City* (Haskell Wexler, 1953).[19] He moved to Hollywood in 1956, but struggled to break into the cinematographers union for several years, so worked on low-budget pictures such as *Stakeout on Dope Street* (Irvin Kershner, 1958). Not until the 1960s did Wexler's stock in Hollywood begin to rise. His extensive experience in documentary was attractive to filmmakers seeking an 'authentic' look to their productions. Concurrently, the growing prominence of the New Left opened up the space for Wexler to return to his political roots. In features such as *The Best Man* (Franklin J. Schaffner, 1964) – his first union assignment – and *Who's Afraid of Virginia Woolf?*, he developed a distinctive gritty aesthetic, while in documentaries such the civil rights-themed *The Bus* (Haskell Wexler, 1965) he pursued his interests in social justice.

By 1967 Wexler was fast building a reputation as a highly-skilled cinematographer and one of Hollywood's most outspoken political voices. Interviewed after *In the Heat of the Night*'s release, he lamented this production's 'fake sociological script, with little understanding of today's South'.[20] In the same interview, he praised documentary-maker Frederick Wiseman's first film *Titicut Follies* (1967), a controversial exposé of conditions in a Massachusetts correction facility.[21] Wiseman was but the latest of several documentary and experimental filmmakers active throughout the 1960s that had provided inspiration for the Hollywood Renaissance. Improvised scenes, an 'observational' style, gritty aesthetics and hand-held camerawork defined the work of luminaries such as John Cassavetes, Shirley Clarke, D. A. Pennebaker and Robert Frank.[22] Wexler's interest in such techniques, coupled with his political views, and experience of working in contemporary Hollywood would find an outlet in *Medium Cool*. But before he could begin writing, some negotiation was required. If Wexler had Chicago in his sights, Paramount had another 'Concrete Wilderness' in mind.

Jack Couffer's novel *The Concrete Wilderness* (1967) chronicled the relationship between a wildlife photographer and a teenage boy in New York City. Couffer also had a background in cinematography. In fact, both he and Wexler had worked on a film that, to some degree, anticipated *Medium Cool*. Weaving a fictional voiceover around documentary footage of Los Angeles, *The Savage Eye* (Ben Maddow, Sidney Meyers and Joseph Strick, 1959) followed a woman's journey through the darker side of city life. Due to this shared history – coupled with Couffer's vivid descriptions of New York City – Peter Bart suggested to Wexler that here was a 'cameraman's film' and offered him the project.[23] *Concrete Wilderness* is usually seen as more a digression on the road to *Medium Cool* than a serious influence. Wexler initially kept the title and wrote into his script a similar relationship between a cameraman and a country boy living in a big city.[24] There was, however, one key theme that appears in *Concrete Wilderness* and is radically developed in *Medium Cool*. Both novel and film devote much space to the city as a prominent 'character' within their narratives. 'The wake of a ship down on the river made silver ripples as lights were reflected on the moving mirrors of wave and trough,' Couffer writes at one point, describing a vista of the Hudson. 'From the distance it was difficult to imagine the water as it really was ... a vile polluted sewer.'[25] Throughout *The Concrete Wilderness*, there are contrasting images of the incandescent Manhattan skyscrapers and unpleasant detritus that blight the city's less auspicious enclaves.

Wexler, too, is concerned with digging beneath his city's glossy exterior. But the environmentalist theme of *The Concrete Wilderness* (and the New York setting) was quickly discarded in favour of a socio-political approach to Chicago. 'I felt it wasn't the sort of film I could make in good conscience,' he said referring to the novel *The Concrete Wilderness*, 'with all these momentous events going on.'[26] Before 1968 had even begun in earnest, various arbiters were laying the groundwork for what would certainly prove a 'momentous' year in American politics. At the time of *Medium Cool*'s release, much was made of Wexler's prophetic screenplay. Written through early 1968, the first draft already included scenes of violence outside the Democratic National Convention, which did not take place until August.[27] Yet, as Wexler himself noted at the time, his ability to 'anticipate' events in Chicago was hardly unique: 'there were actually many indications that there would be a confrontation between police and the antiwar demonstrators.'[28] In fact, one might say that the script for Chicago '68 was – in the words and deeds of many a politician and activist – being preordained. In October 1967 Mayor Richard J. Daley secured the convention. Alongside the prestige and extra income that came with its hosting, it would be an opportunity for Chicago to promote its own success at a time when grim tales of decline surrounded America's cities. In the view of many commentators, the nation's metropolises were in the throes of an 'urban crisis'.[29] From New York and Detroit to Los Angeles and Oakland, articles about 'crime in the streets, filthy sidewalks, bombed-out slums, drugs, moral decline, overcrowding, traffic jams, racial tension, pollution, labor unrest, and political corruption' abounded.[30] At this stage, Daley promoted his city on the basis that, unlike many others, Chicago had not yet erupted with widespread racial violence.[31]

From early in its production, *Medium Cool* was intended to counter Daley's rose-tinted view of Chicago. This was going to be a film about poverty and conflict ignored, or brushed under the carpet, by government officials. Exemplifying what Lawrence Webb has termed the 'cinema of urban crisis', it was one of many late 1960s and 1970s productions intent on providing a stark portrayal of cities on the brink of implosion.[32] Wexler would take his camera into Chicago's slums; the impoverished Appalachian and black communities that Daley and his colleagues avoided in their battle for prestige. Paul Cronin's documentary *Look Out Haskell, It's Real: The Making of Medium Cool* (2001) reveals that radio presenter and Chicago historian Studs Terkel was involved early in the film's production.[33] Terkel's book of oral histories *Division Street America* was first published in 1966 and offered a kaleidoscopic overview of the class, race and ideological tensions brewing in the windy city, and might be viewed as much a 'source' text for *Medium Cool* as *The Concrete Wilderness*.[34] It was Terkel's extensive contact list that provided access to persons and neighbourhoods that might otherwise have been suspicious of a Hollywood invasion. For example, Wexler was introduced to Peggy Terry, an organizer in the Uptown area. Originally from Kentucky, Terry moved to Chicago in the mid-1950s. She had been active with the Congress for Racial Equality (CORE) and Students Nonviolent Coordinating Committee (SNCC) and was now spearheading a campaign for the city's poor to receive a guaranteed income: Jobs or Income Now (JOIN).

Wexler shot scenes of Terry explaining JOIN to Eileen. 'If they can't give us a job, then give us an income,' she says. Another scene has Terry discussing the killing of a black man in the city, and encouraging Eileen to join the Poor People's Campaign. Both attend a rally that features a speech from civil rights activist Jesse Jackson.[35] This material combined provides various political threads that did not remain in the finished film. The removal of this footage had a triple effect. Firstly, it reduced its female protagonist's agency. Eileen does not experience a political awakening, nor does Terry serve as her mentor. Rather, it is left to Cassellis to guide her through the firestorm of Chicago 1968. As has been argued with many Hollywood films of the late 1960s and early 1970s, for all their formal and thematic experimentation, the roles offered to women remained strangely regressive. Secondly, it tempers what might have been an engagement with white working-class struggles at a time when much political rhetoric was attempting to draw a dividing line between them and the 'noisy' middle-class student protestors. According to David Farber, large numbers of the white working class of the late 1960s were angered by political elites *and* by left-wing protestors, who they considered equally disrespectful of ordinary people. The rhetoric of Richard Nixon and George Wallace stoked the fires of division, claiming political activists to be against (white) working men and women.[36] Had Wexler maintained the above material in *Medium Cool*, it would have offered a rare union of the white working classes and activists that Nixon, Wallace and others endeavoured to keep apart. Thirdly, and on a similar note, the deleted scenes also suggested a political coalition of working-class whites and African American civil rights activists. Terry and Elaine are not just fighting for their own interests; they attend larger civil rights speeches and demonstrations. Ultimately, these erasures would cut any sense of a politically engaged Appalachian community. Victims of political circumstances, yes, but active agents in a wider movement they are not. Editor of the film Paul Golding explained in an interview that the changes were simply the result of time constraints and the need to shorten the narrative.[37] Yet, when one considers them within these specific historical circumstances, the decision to cut these particular aspects of the narrative impacted upon the film's political address.

The above issues are discussed in further detail below. But if *Medium Cool* erased this content, it certainly responded to many other key issues circulating through 1968. Working with hand-held cameras and a small crew, Wexler could bring a news-like immediacy to events unravelling often at breakneck speed. And there was more than enough to cover. While Mayor Daley went on celebrating 'the city that works' to any politician and journalist who would listen, a gathering storm of political ferment was about to thrust Chicago, and indeed *Medium Cool*, in unexpected directions. 'Tet. King. Kennedy. Chicago. Nixon. Nineteen sixty-eight was a bad year,' begins Kirshner in his assessment of the film culture to emerge out of what several commentators have termed America's '*annus horribilis*'.[38] This roll-call of traumatic events – lethal wartime conflicts, assassinations, failed progressive campaigns – are so ingrained into 1960s lore as to virtually define '68 in the popular imagination. Histories of the 1960s often cite the year as springboard for a national implosion.[39] And while a large body of academic work has since sought to challenge this interpretation, observing how charting downfall as of 1968 ignores the burgeoning women's liberation movement, gay rights movement, continued civil rights struggle and counterculture's expansion to far wider reaches of the American public through the 1970s, the year is nevertheless rightly noted for its fraught political landscape.[40]

Looming at the centre of this storm was the Democratic Convention. Anyone involved in protest movements circa 1968 knew that something was going to happen in Chicago. Formed in late 1967, the Yippies (official title The Youth International Party) began their existence with an eye on the Convention. The brainchild of several New York politicos and artists – most famously Jerry Rubin and Abbie Hoffman – the Yippies were an attempt to combine free-wheeling elements of the hippie counterculture with the commitment of the New Left. As Farber puts it: 'They meant to make Yippie! a cry, a myth, a party, a reality that would explode at the 1968 Democratic National Convention in Chicago.'[41] Both Hoffman and Rubin had been involved in civil rights activism in the South. Both also believed in the power of the image as a political weapon. The Yippies planned a publicity-grabbing 'Festival of Life' in Chicago, featuring music, street theatre, the faux nomination of a real pig, Pigasus for President and, notoriously, a threat to dose the city's water supply with LSD. In a sense, they, like Wexler, were already imagining Chicago in August 1968 to be the perfect site for a visual extravaganza. While the Yippies planned their convention hijinks, the National Mobilizing Committee to End the War in Vietnam (the Mobe) was preparing its own large-scale protest. The organization had just helped to bring seventy thousand people to the Pentagon in one of the 1960s' largest anti-war rallies. In the weeks following this success, they began to turn their eyes on Chicago.[42] It would certainly seem that the city's political elite decided the threat of protest serious enough to require some pre-convention research. In August 1968, deputy mayor David Stahl confronted Yippie Paul Krassner on his organization's plans. 'Didn't you see *Wild in the Streets*?' replied Krassner, referring to the hippie exploitation movie that had just arrived in cinemas and featured counterculture guru Max Frost (Christopher Jones) and his followers poisoning the capital city's water supply with LSD. Stahl's reply: 'We've seen *Battle of Algiers*,' Gillo Pontecorvo's fiercely political drama about the struggle for Algerian independence. As J. Hoberman notes, 'where the Yippies threatened to dose reservoirs with LSD, Chicago officials anticipated a scenario in which urban guerillas blew up ice cream parlors'.[43] Yippie, New Left activist and politician alike, it seems, was conceiving of Chicago in visual terms. And against this backdrop of angry, aesthetic anticipation, Wexler and his crew took their cameras into the breach.

Now it's on to Chicago: Images of '68

A dense assemblage of social commentary, intertextuality and visual puns, *Medium Cool* exemplifies many traits associated with Hollywood Renaissance filmmaking. Shot through the summer of 1968, it offers an intense confrontation with unfolding events. From racial discord to anti-war protests and urban decline, Wexler takes a scalpel to the tensions besetting Chicago throughout a year of upheavals. In its continuous allusions to European art cinema, reference (in title if not always in content) to Marshall McLuhan, its self-reflexivity and scathing view of consumers of mainstream media, *Medium Cool* also brims with the kind of 'hip' detachment prominent in countercultural discourses of the period. The film's narrative focuses on cameraman John Cassellis and his relationship with Appalachian migrants Eileen and her son Harold (Harold Blankenship). But *Medium Cool* uses this story as a vehicle through which to explore Wexler's interests in politics and the nature of the image. As Jay Beck puts it, 'the result is an intimate film that fractures many assumptions of narrative stability to force the viewer into a critical relationship with the fictional material on both the image and sound tracks'.[44]

After a title credit announcing 'Chicago 1968', we cut to a rear-view mirror. In its reflection, we see Cassellis and his sound operator Gus (Peter Bonerz). The camera refocuses and the car's cracked windscreen comes into view. As the men scope the vehicle, they encounter a woman lying sprawled outside the driver's side door. Paying little heed to her plight, they go on filming the wreckage. With its bloodied victims, smashed-up vehicles and apparently unconcerned protagonists, the scene shares an affinity with the extended car wreck scenes in *Weekend* (1967), Jean-Luc Godard's surreal meditation on French politics and society of the 1960s.[45] And whether taking explicit form – the poster of frequent Godard collaborator Jean-Paul Belmondo on Cassellis' bedroom wall (see Figure 6.1), the pastiche of *Le Mepris* (Jean-Luc Godard, 1963) appearing in *Medium Cool*'s final scene – or, more general nods to

Figure 6.1 Allusions to the French New Wave: Cassellis and Belmondo. Copyright Paramount.

European New Waves (breaking of the fourth wall, jump cuts and detached anti-heroes), this is a film that wears its influences on its sleeve. One might also note this scene's similarity to one of the Hollywood Renaissance's most famed productions, *Bonnie and Clyde*. This tale of 1930s outlaws ends with the camera lingering on a cracked car windscreen, shattered in the hail of bullets that have destroyed its protagonists. By offering a similar shot at the beginning (as opposed to the end) of *Medium Cool*, one could say that Wexler was commenting on his own film's cultural immediacy. This is no hark back to criminals of yore, but a direct engagement with America *now*. Hip bank robbers Bonnie and Clyde have morphed into the cold-hearted newsmen Cassellis and Gus, potent symbols of a society immune to, or accepting of, violence as just another spectacular entertainment.

With knowledge of the film's conclusion this scene is also, of course, a premonition of Cassellis' own untimely demise. If not a flash-forward in the true sense of the term, it shares with other films of 1969 – *Easy Rider* (Dennis Hopper), *They Shoot Horses, Don't They?* (Sidney Pollack), for example – a desire to communicate in advance, through visual and/or aural means, its protagonists' tragic fate. *Medium Cool* does contain an actual flash-forward. Right at the film's end, seconds before Cassellis and Eileen hurtle into a tree, a radio announcement refers to their car crash and the latter's death. One could argue that the ominous nature of political discourse circa 1968 (discussed above) was symbolically embedded in the very language of cinema by way of this formal technique. And eerie premonitions appear throughout *Medium Cool*. Fake tear gas sprayed early on anticipates the real tear gas used on protestors (and Wexler) in Chicago; camera set-ups in Washington D.C. for Robert Kennedy's funeral are similar in appearance to that in the film's final shot; comic brawls during a roller derby scene prepare us for the battles in Grant Park. As Wexler's script predicted events outside the convention so, too, is *Medium Cool* intent on prophesizing its own narrative denouement.

The film unravels as a series of stark confrontations. As often noted, *Medium Cool* is about violence: the violence of war, the violence on television, the violence ingrained into America's social fabric.[46] Right after Cassellis has taken his car crash footage, he immediately passes the tape container to an anonymous motorcyclist. The scene is imbued with criminal overtones as a precious and dangerous cargo changes hands. Beck notes the driving soundtrack and stylized visuals of this sequence are in striking contrast to the 'minimal sound and visual information' of the previous scene.[47] It is the first of many stylistic-juxtapositions to pervade *Medium Cool.* On one level, this moment introduces visually a key aspect to Cassellis' character: the way he is quick to divest himself of any responsibility toward his subjects. Shoot from the hip and run – this is the mantra by which he lives. On another, the association of news footage with a criminal enterprise alludes to the representation of the media throughout the film. Television is presented as narcotic. 'I've made films on all kinds of social problems,' announces one journalist during an early scene. Concluding with the stereotypical image of a docile consumer, he notes: 'they'd rather see thirty seconds of someone getting his skull cracked, turn off the TV and say "let me have another beer."' Soporific newscasts made by cynical reporters for quasi-comatose audiences – *Medium Cool* is certainly unremitting in its assault on news practices of the 1960s. Cassellis' reference to a media 'script' (noted in the introduction), is but one of many contrivances with which this film associates the fourth estate.

There is a certain irony in the film's first ten minutes. Indulging in an afternoon Martini, news reporters congregate to discuss their respective brushes with danger. 'It is a risk of the profession,' says one. 'We deal with the violence' agrees Cassellis. Stories of journalists attacked and killed in the line of duty ensue. A reporter recalls covering civil rights protests and the fear of police brutality. Another remembers being threatened by men 'yelling Black Power'. These accounts sit uncomfortably with the following scene. A sudden cut takes us into what seems initially to be a battlefield. A man stands beside a jeep clutching a rifle. On the windscreen, we see 'Press' written large. As the words 'shoot em' are heard another man suddenly jumps out and prepares to take a photograph. There is here the obvious connection between the gun and the camera. If the reporters of the previous scene conceived themselves as detached outsiders targeted by state and/or political operatives, this moment appears to reconceive the media as directly contributing towards a culture of violence.

As the scene unfolds, however, its representation becomes ambiguous. We discover that this is not a real battle, but a National Guard training exercise. Soldiers literally play at being protestors, goading their colleagues and making anti-war speeches. Whether intended or not, the National Guard take a certain jubilation in imitating the Movement (see Figure 6.2). As Penny W. Lewis points

Figure 6.2 War games with the National Guard. Copyright Paramount.

out, the National Guard at the time was not necessarily a cradle of hawkish sentiment. She cites African American Guardsmen staging a demonstration at Fort Hood, Texas, in the run up to the convention: 'the cherry-picked troops who were eventually sent from Texas to Chicago were not actually deployed at the protests because it was not clear which side they would fight on.'[48] Revelling amongst pretend fights, sarcastically-delivered speeches and fake tear gas, Cassellis is presented as both cynical toward, and strangely naïve about, the reality of political conflict. Subsequent scenes of him running down drab, anonymous looking corridors visually position him as part of a Kafkaesque nightmare; more victim than observer of the state's sinister machinations. Toward the end of the National Guard sequence, Wexler appears to transcend the film's diegesis and to turn the camera on himself. One of the first moments of a self-reflexivity that pervades *Medium Cool*, soldiers break the fourth wall as they announce 'let's get the guys with the cameras'. Is this Cassellis or Wexler under the microscope; upon whom does the final judgement fall?

Objectivity vs involvement, observation vs activism, cynicism vs positive social change – these opening scenes pose the conflicts with which *Medium Cool* grapples throughout. In their wake, we are introduced to a series of real political events. Cassellis and Gus film young Robert Kennedy supporters in Chicago, then visit Washington D.C. to take footage of the Poor People's Campaign and its demonstration against economic inequality, 'Resurrection City'. Interestingly, they have gone all the way to D.C. to find the campaign's 'Appalachian' contingent. As Cassellis will shortly discover, the poverty blighting this community could be found on his own Chicago doorstep. The protestors' rendition of gospel song 'This May Be the Last Time' is couched in a bitter irony with a cut to the Ambassador Hotel, site of Robert F. Kennedy's assassination. Back to D.C. and Cassellis appears ambivalent to events of recent months.

When asked by a taxi driver whether he is in the city to cover Kennedy's funeral, he ignores the question, turning instead to Gus to discuss the previous evening's revelries. Only after he begins a relationship with Eileen and Harold does Cassellis begin to re-conceptualize his detached outlook toward the world around him.

In a film that references so many conflicts of 1968, there are two omissions. While civil rights activists and anti-war protestors receive coverage (discussed below), white working-class activism and women's liberation are largely absent. Peggy Terry (noted earlier) was just one figure to find her contributions to Chicago's political life under-represented by the time *Medium Cool* reached the big screen. Another Kentuckian and local organizer, Charles Geary, has a brief role in the film as Harold's father. Though Geary was heavily involved in Chicago politics there is little suggestion of this in *Medium Cool*.[49] Instead, his brief role in the drama sees him teach his son how to fire a gun and dispense a lecture on women. 'A man has got to be boss of his home,' he explains. 'Because there ain't no two bosses in the family.' Such sentiments are echoed throughout a film that employs the swaggering machismo so common in New Left circles of the late 1960s. When Cassellis' colleague Gus refers to there being 'four-and-a-half women' to every man in Washington D.C. an accompanying burst of fetishized portraits visually convey this statistic. Female characters like Ruth (Mariana Hill) and the blonde who joins the reporters on one drive around the city are seemingly courted and discarded on Cassellis' whim. Nor does Wexler bequeath Eileen much in the way of individual agency. Rather, she becomes a channel through which Cassellis begins to rethink his attitudes. She is the 'authentic' story that he has been looking for.

Regarding these points, however, one might say that the film does seek to problematize its own perspective. Indeed, the extent to which *Medium Cool*'s ideas are constantly undercut through self-reflexive devices would suggest that Wexler is critiquing his own practices as much as those of Cassellis. In one of the film's most politically powerful episodes, the reporter visits a black taxi driver, Frank Baker (Sid McCoy) to conduct an interview. As he attempts to leave the apartment he is accosted by several of the young black men and women at the house 'You came down here with fifteen minutes of a black sensibility,' says one. These comments lead to a series of speeches made directly to the camera (see Figure 6.3). Here, perhaps, Wexler is reflecting on his own role as a (white) documentary maker and the activities of filmmakers more generally. Is *Medium Cool* a genuine attempt to deal with the issues of the day, or a more exploitative appropriation of a black 'human interest story' intended to assuage white guilt and give the impression of a democratic media? 'You can't expect to walk in here out of your arrogance,' says one of the black men, 'and expect things to be like they are … you are the exploiters.' In its expansive, scattered series of political vignettes, we may have reference to Martin Luther King, the Poor People's Campaign and a racist media. But there is something equally disconcerting about the ways in which issues disappear from the film as

Figure 6.3 'You are the exploiters': Breaking the fourth wall in *Medium Cool*. Copyright Paramount.

it moves on to its next hot topic. The very fact that *Medium Cool* does *not* return in any meaningful way to the subject of racial conflict after this sequence, imbues these speeches with an eerie prophetic nature. Speaking to the *New York Times* just after *Medium Cool*'s release, Wexler argued it to be very much a self-critique. 'When people are into their own thing, there is a socially acceptable rationalization for not getting involved,' he observed. 'Photography is a way of being there and not being there.'[50] An image might capture a moment, but reveals little about the commitment of the person behind the camera.

The film is riddled with this kind of introspection, which reaches its apex in one of its most familiar lines: 'Look out, Haskell, it's real.' The line is spoken during a confrontation between protestors and police (real documentary footage), though was not recorded at the time. Rather, it was added during post-production, and thus embodies *Medium Cool*'s ongoing dialogue between 'realism' and fiction. As Beck notes, *Medium Cool* undermines its 'realism' in order to 'question the ontological veracity of the *cinéma vérité*-style sounds and images'.[51] The fact that the words were added as an afterthought raises the question as to whether they compromise the film's documentary approach or simply add magnitude to events transpiring. This is a subject explored throughout, where real events and the fictional narrative come to their respective climaxes. Harold has gone missing and Eileen heads downtown in search of him. The next twenty minutes weaves together scenes inside the Democratic Convention, where Cassellis is shooting the candidates, and carnage on the streets outside. The first musical accompaniment for this extended sequence is the Mothers of Invention's 'Mom and Dad', its bleak foretelling of cops shooting 'girls and boys' anticipating the violence soon to erupt. Armies of police congregate as demonstrators mill around brandishing

Figure 6.4 Carnage at the Democratic National Convention. Copyright Paramount.

anti-war posters. As the Mothers of Invention song winds down a quick cut to chanting crowds ups the ante: 'hell no, we won't go.'

Wearing a visually striking yellow dress, Eileen's attire emphasizes her symbolic isolation from police and protestors. Cassellis too is portrayed as disconnected from the protests; inside the convention hall he watches the pageantry and theatre of America's political establishment reach its denouement. Of course, the 'real' theatre is raging outside. The twee orchestral number 'Happy Days are Here Again' provides a soundtrack as the film jumps between scenes in the convention and bloodied, beaten protestors (see Figure 6.4). Back and forth we go, from the convention, to the streets, to Grant Park where police are embarked on a full-fledged riot. The film's remainder follows Eileen through the carnage until she finally reconnects with Cassellis. As they make their escape, Cassellis loses control of his car. The wreckage brings us full circle. Just as Cassellis had casually filmed the car crash at the beginning, so too do tourists slow down to snap his grisly fate. A final zoom disappears down the lens of a camera operated by Haskell Wexler himself. Is this another moment of self-critique – Wexler turning his camera on Wexler – or a call for the film's audience to recognize their own complicity in what has transpired? Either way, it offers a climactic moment for a film that has maintained a dialogue with its viewers throughout. And with *Medium Cool* now complete, a host of political and cultural arbiters were waiting to continue this dialogue.

Conclusion: The medium or the message?

One year on and the ashes of Chicago still glowed hot. *Medium Cool* reached cinemas in August 1969, entering a public sphere where commentators continued to reflect on the convention's political and visual legacy. While it received many positive reviews, assessments of *Medium Cool*'s politics were less uniform than one might expect. Vociferous advocates declared it to be the exciting offspring of a new and improved Hollywood. Placing *Medium Cool* upon the pantheon of recent classics – *The Graduate* and *Easy Rider*, for example – Roger Ebert, critic at the *Chicago Sun-Times*, praised the film's complex characterizations and self-consciousness. About the latter, Ebert noted that Wexler 'evokes our memories of the hundreds of other movies we've seen to imply things about his story that he never explains on the screen.'[52] Ebert revisited *Medium Cool* in a second review two months later. Here he provided a riposte to the film's detractors, suggesting that criticisms were based on a misreading of its narrative. 'The audience for *Medium Cool* has to make its connections,' he wrote. 'It has to decide what these strange, juxtaposed, maybe unconnected events mean.'[53] In the *Saturday Review*, Hollis Alpert was similarly impressed by its formal innovation, describing it as 'one of the most visually exciting films ever made.'[54] Both Ebert and Alpert viewed *Medium Cool* as a cerebral production; a rare film to demand work on the part of its viewers. Neither, however, said a great deal about its political content, something addressed in diverse ways by other commentators.

Charles Champlin of the *Los Angeles Times* was particularly fulsome in his praise of the film's 'provocative' subject matter. Comparing it favourably to other 1969 releases *Easy Rider* and *Midnight Cowboy* (John Schlesinger) Champlin lauded *Medium Cool*'s engagement with contemporaneous issues, describing it as 'the most provocative and important yet of the new American statement films.'[55] Ebert's counterpart at the *Chicago Tribune* Gene Siskel praised the film's 'sensitivity and insight', and, like many critics of the time, paid homage to the scene set in Chicago's black neighbourhood.[56] Interestingly, however, he describes the footage set outside the Chicago convention – scenes that have become iconic in discussions of *Medium Cool* – as 'weak'.[57] Other critics joined Siskel in suggesting that the film's violent denouement lacked visceral punch. 'You find yourself admiring the enterprise of the cameras and the tempo of the editing, as though watching some enactment of the Battle of Solferino,' wrote Robert Hatch in *The Nation*.[58] The *New York Times* critic Vincent Canby concurred, suggesting that 'clever editing and beautiful color can diminish the horror'. Though praising its visual impact, Canby was less convinced that *Medium Cool* had managed to 'surpass the devastating live show that television … presented as the Chicago riots were taking place.'[59] The proximity to these past events, and the fact that they had been broadcast live a year earlier, appears to have tempered *Medium Cool*'s power in some reviewers' eyes.

Writing for *The New Yorker*, Penelope Gilliatt conceded that *Medium Cool* had 'its heart in the right place', but she was wary of its 'fashionable' critique of the news media as offering 'an ersatz form of truth'.[60] She also drew connections between *Medium Cool* and other recent films (here noting similarities to *Blow-Up* [Michelangelo Antonioni, 1966]). But the comparisons were negative, suggesting that the former was hardly treading new territory. Gilliatt argued that the final scene undercuts any 'shock' present in the convention riots, concluding archly: 'Medium Cool ends as a slashing indictment of car driving.'[61] And if Gilliatt's comments were particularly blunt, she was not alone in viewing the fictional elements of Medium Cool as serving more to obscure than to enrich its documentary realism.[62] While in retrospect the blending of fact and fiction is one of the film's most praised qualities, this technique was not always viewed favourably at the time. As Canby put it, 'Wexler's fictional story and the facts never mix with any sense of conviction.'[63] In an extremely scathing attack, Andrew Sarris declared that 'Medium Cool parades its innocence, clumsiness and simplemindedness as civic virtues'. Sarris lambasted Wexler for exploiting 'Chicago more than he explores or even exhumes it.'[64] Comparing events in Chicago to the Republican Party's convention in Miami that had also taken place in August 1968, Sarris noted that seven African Americans had been killed in clashes surrounding the latter. 'But there were no photographers present,' he remarked. 'No upper-middle-class demonstrators, no emissaries from Esquire and the Playboy club' and, by extension, no Medium Cool.[65] If these comments were intended as criticism, they carried a bitter irony in the sense that they echoed the film's key theme. The media did indeed have a 'script' – a standard story to which it returns time and again, often to the detriment of other important issues. Wexler had constantly asserted his own complicity in this script, turning the camera on himself – literally and figuratively – throughout.

Perhaps here lies the paradox of Medium Cool. Born out of the firestorm of events, assassinations, issues and transformations circa 1968, it was conceived as both a filmic document of the times and proponent of the idea that there *can be no filmic document of the times*, for the camera creates its own reality. With an investment in left-wing politics, a small crew and hand-held equipment, Medium Cool was rapidly shaped and reshaped in response to a year of upheavals. Some political content was scripted, other material simply shot as events transpired. Certain issues were emphasized and developed (racism, class relations and the convention protests), while others modified and/or curtailed (Eileen's political awakening, for example). Blazing a powerful trail throughout the narrative was Wexler's relentless critique of television and the media as purveyors of half-truths, illusion, perhaps even falsification. 'Jesus, I love to shoot film,' says Cassellis in a line bristling with manic glee. In its scattergun array of formal and stylistic experiments, its frantic juxtapositions, its vibrant interrogation (however incomplete) of politics and culture circa 1968, so too does Medium Cool gleefully capture the energies, pleasures and pains that come with 'protest' – whether that protest occurs on city streets or along Hollywood's corridors of power.

Notes

1   Christie Milliken, '1969: Movies and the Counterculture', in *American Cinema of the 1960s: Themes and Variations*, ed. Barry Keith Grant (New Brunswick, NJ: Rutgers

University Press, 2008), 217–38; Paul Monaco, *The Sixties: 1960–69* (Berkeley: University of California Press, 2001), 177; Jonathan Kirshner, *Hollywood's Last Golden Age: Politics, Society and the Seventies Film in America* (Ithaca, NY: Cornell University Press, 2012), 56.

2 Kirshner, *Hollywood's Last Golden Age*, 56.

3 Films that offered a similar focus include: *Zabriskie Point* (Michelangelo Antonioni, 1970), *The Strawberry Statement* (Stuart Hagman, 1969) and *Getting Straight* (Richard Rush, 1970). See Mark Shiel, 'Hollywood, the New Left, and *FTA*', in *'Un-American' Hollywood: Politics and Film in the Blacklist Era*, ed. Frank Krutnik, Peter Stanfield, Brian Neve and Steve Neale (New Brunswick, NJ: Rutgers University Press, 2007), 212.

4 'Medium Cool', *Boxoffice*, 28 July 1969, A11.

5 Yannis Tzioumakis, *American Independent Cinema: An Introduction* (Edinburgh: Edinburgh University Press, 2006), 170.

6 Paul Cronin, 'Midsummer Mavericks: *Medium Cool*', *Sight and Sound* (September 2001): 26.

7 Peter Bart, 'I Like It. I Want It. Let's Sow It Up', *New York Times*, 7 August 1966, D11.

8 Robert Evans, *The Kid Stays in the Picture: Success, Scandal, Sex, Tragedy, Infamy, and that's Just the First Chapter* (London: Faber and Faber, 2003), 110.

9 'Peter Bart, N.Y. Times, Evans Aide at Par', *Variety*, 21 December 1966, 4.

10 David A. Cook, *Lost Illusions: American Cinema in the Shadow of Watergate and Vietnam* (Berkeley: University of California Press, 2000), 3.

11 Cook, *Lost Illusions*, 133.

12 'Bob Evans Pays Chips-Service to "Writer as Star" at Paramount', *Variety*, 1 May 1968, 19.

13 Cook, *Lost Illusions*, 3.

14 Jerry Beigel, 'Wexler's Woes on First Pic', *Variety*, 11 December 1968, 7.

15 See, for example, 'Vote Merger of Jupiter and Oil Company', *Chicago Tribune*, 1 March 1962, 56.

16 David A. Cook, 'Auteur Cinema and the "Film Generation" in 1970s Hollywood', in *The New American Cinema*, ed. Jon Lewis (Durham, NC: Duke University Press, 1998), 11–37.

17 Peter Krämer, *The New Hollywood: From Bonnie and Clyde to Star Wars* (London: Wallflower, 2005), 73.

18 David Talbot and Barbara Zheutlin, *Creative Differences: Profiles of Hollywood Dissidents* (Boston: South End Press, 1978), 105–28.

19 Talbot and Zheutlin, *Creative Differences*, 106.

20 Ernest Callenbach and Albert Johnson, 'The Danger is Seduction: An Interview with Haskell Wexler', *Film Quarterly*, 21, no. 3 (Spring 1968): 6.

21 Callenbach and Johnson, 'The Danger', 7.

22 Tzioumakis, *American Independent Cinema*, 172–7.

23 Paul Cronin, *Look Out, Haskell, It's Real* (2001). Documentary available on *Medium Cool* Dual Edition Blu-ray/DVD (Eureka, 2015).

24 'Wexler to Produce, Direct Paramount's *Wilderness*', *Boxoffice*, 1 July 1968, K4.

25 Jack Couffer, *The Concrete Wilderness* (London: Sphere Books, 1972), 50.

26 Cronin, 'Midsummer Mavericks', 25.

27 Beigel, 'Wexler's Woes', 7.

28 Quoted in Guy Flatley, 'Chicago and Other Violences', *New York Times*, 7 September 1969, D19.

29 Lawrence Webb, *The Cinema of Urban Crisis: Seventies Film and the Reinvention of the City* (Amsterdam: Amsterdam University Press, 2014), 42.

30 Vincent J. Cannuto, *The Ungovernable City: John Lindsay and his Struggle to Save New York* (New York: Basic Books, 2001), xi and 22–3.

31 David Farber, *Chicago '68* (Chicago: University of Chicago Press, 1988), 117.

32 Webb, *The Cinema of Urban Crisis*, 1.

33 Cronin, *Look Out Haskell*.

34 Studs Terkel, *Division Street America* (New York: Pantheon, 1966).

35 Footage available in Cronin, *Look Out Haskell*.

36 David Farber, 'The Silent Majority and Talk About Revolution', in *The Sixties: From Memory to History*, ed. David Farber (Chapel Hill: The University of North Carolina Press, 1994), 291–316.

37 Cronin, *Look Out Haskell*.

38 Kirshner, *Hollywood's Last Golden Age*, 52.

39 Rick Perlstein, 'Who Owns the Sixties?', *Linguafranca*, 6, no. 4 (May/June 1996), http://linguafranca.mirror.theinfo.org/9605/sixties.html

40 Alice Echols, *Shaky Ground: The Sixties and Its Aftershocks* (New York: Columbia University Press, 2002), 63–9.

41 Farber, *Chicago*, 3.

42 Farber, *Chicago*, 60–1.

43 J. Hoberman, *The Dream Life: Movies, Media and the Mythology of the Sixties* (New York: The New Press, 2003), 213.

44 Jay Beck, *Designing Sound: Audiovisual Aesthetics in 1970s American Cinema* (New Brunswick, NJ: Rutgers University Press, 2016), 44.

45 Milliken, '1969', 223.

46 Kirshner, *Hollywood's Last Golden Age*, 58.

47 Beck, *Designing Sound*, 44–5

48 Penny W. Lewis, *Hardhats, Hippies, and Hawks: The Vietnam Antiwar Movement as Myth and Memory* (Ithaca, NY: Cornell University Press, 2013), 126.

49 Jakobi Williams, *From the Bullet to the Ballot: The Illinois Chapter of the Black Panther Party and Racial Coalition Politics in Chicago* (Chapel Hill: The University of North Carolina Press, 2013), 129–30.

50 Flatley, 'Chicago', D19.

51 Beck, *Designing Sound*, 46.

52 Roger Ebert, '*Medium Cool*', *Chicago Sun-Times*, 21 September 1969, http://www.rogerebert.com/reviews/medium-cool-1969

53 Roger Ebert, '*Medium Cool* on Multiple Levels', *Chicago Sun-Times*, 30 November 1969, http://www.rogerebert.com/rogers-journal/medium-cool-on-multiple-levels

54 Hollis Alpert, 'SR Goes to the Movies', *Saturday Review*, 6 September 1969, 43.

55 Charles Champlin, '"Medium" with a Message', *Los Angeles Times*, 21 September 1969, Calendar, 1, 22 and 26.

56 Gene Siskel, '*Medium Cool* Takes a Long Look at Chicago', *Chicago Tribune*, 19 September 1969, Section 2, 1; see also Penelope Gilliatt, 'The Current Cinema: Getting Warm', *The New Yorker*, 13 September 1969, 144; Robert Hatch, 'Films', *The Nation*, 29 September 1969, 326.

57 Siskel, '*Medium Cool*', 1.

58 Hatch, 'Films', 326. See also Monaco, *The Sixties*, 178.

59 Vincent Canby, 'Real Events of '68 Seen in *Medium Cool*', *New York Times*, 28 August 1969, http://www.nytimes.com/movie/review?res=9F05E4DF1031EE3BBC4051DF BE668382679EDE

60 Gilliatt, 'The Current Cinema', 143.

61 Gilliatt, 'The Current Cinema', 144.

62 See, for example, Canby.

63 Vincent Canby, 'Our Time: Arlo and Chicago', *New York Times*, 31 August 1969, D1, 35.

64 Andrew Sarris, 'Films', *Village Voice*, 28 August 1969, 37.

65 Sarris, 'Films', 37.

Chapter 7

FROM EXPLOITATION TO LEGITIMACY: *EASY RIDER* (1969) AND INDEPENDENT CINEMA'S JOURNEY INTO HOLLYWOOD

Yannis Tzioumakis

Among all the films associated with the Hollywood Renaissance, *Easy Rider* (Dennis Hopper, 1969) is arguably the title that has invited the most passionate writing by scholars and critics. Be it because it dealt with the counterculture head-on, because it became a runaway commercial success against the odds, because it assaulted many of the narrative and stylistic conventions associated with mainstream Hollywood cinema, because it featured a number of popular rock songs that have been perceived since as era-defining, or because of its ambiguous message ('we did it' versus 'we blew it'), the film has attracted huge critical attention,[1] including a very strong interest in its seemingly unconventional production history.

The latter found perhaps its perfect embodiment as a chapter in Peter Biskind's best-selling anecdotal history of the Hollywood Renaissance years, *Easy Riders, Raging Bulls: How the Sex-Drugs-and-Rock 'n' Roll Generation Saved Hollywood*, which borrowed part of its title from the film.[2] Written authoritatively and with an emphasis on the personal drama surrounding the above-the-line talent involved in the production of the film, Biskind (via Buck Henry) ends his chapter marvelling at how *Easy Rider* became the defining film of the era:

> [*Easy Rider*] was vindication, beating Hollywood at its own game, proof that you could get high, express yourself, and make money all at the same time. In a certain sense, as Buck Henry put it, *Easy Rider* was authorless, the handwriting of the counterculture. He says, 'Nobody knew who wrote it, nobody knew who directed it, nobody knew who edited it, Rip [Torn] was supposed to be in it, Jack [Nicholson] was in it instead, it looks like a couple of hundred outtakes from several other films all strung together with the soundtrack of the best of the '60s. But it opened up a path. Now the children of Dylan were in control.'[3]

Despite making for pleasurable reading, this and similar accounts have contributed substantially to mythologizing a film that became a classic almost immediately after its theatrical release in November 1969.[4] More important for the purposes of this chapter, they discuss production practices, business strategies and corporate conduct through a prism that disavows them as such and displaces them as the outcome of personal dramatic encounters, influenced by the consumption of recreational drugs and the impact of epochal philosophies and ideologies. As a result, the film's production history tends to be interpreted as exceptional and unconventional with such views inevitably finding their way into scholarly studies, which in their turn legitimize accounts that are often vague, incomplete and inaccurate.[5]

This chapter will demonstrate that the production of *Easy Rider* was not as exceptional as Biskind and other accounts have suggested. It was also not as 'independent' as a lot of studies have argued,[6] especially if one defines independence as production that is financed by and takes place away from the auspices of a major Hollywood studio. Instead, the chapter will argue, *Easy Rider* was 'independent' in a much broader sense. Just like the majority of film productions in American cinema at the time, it was produced physically by corporations other than the Hollywood studios but which stood in close proximity to them and benefitted routinely from their financial and other resources.[7] With Columbia Pictures acting as distributor, possibly as a financier too, *Easy Rider*'s proximity to Hollywood has been much closer than other studies and the film's own mythology have implied it to be.

This chapter, then, will examine the film's production history by looking behind the sex, the drugs, the rock 'n' roll and the drama. It will scrutinize existing accounts for inconsistencies and data that are open to challenge, while also drawing on lesser utilized oral histories and the trade press of the time with a view to construct a more robust account of the film's production than currently available. At the core of this historiographical project is an effort to locate the film's place in American cinema, a task that is fraught with problems given the film's straddling of exploitation and mainstream filmmaking.

Exploitation, independent and mainstream American cinema

In her insightful examination of Hollywood Renaissance production company par excellence BBS, Teresa Grimes speculates whether *Easy Rider* could have achieved its status as the period's most definitive film and one of its most commercially successful had it been distributed by American International Pictures (AIP), the company that was originally interested in distributing the film, and not Columbia Pictures. As she writes:

> With the distributing power of Columbia behind it, what could have been just another Corman-produced biker film made it through the

conventional distribution/exhibition channels to reach a mass audience. Whether *Easy Rider* would have been the massive success it was had it been made and distributed by AIP is of course questionable [...]. Certainly AIP could not have given it as much exposure and advertising as Columbia.[8]

Besides distribution and exhibition, a similar point can also be made about the film's production. While the film was eventually set up as an 'independent' production that was (partly) financed by Bert Schneider under the banner of Raybert Productions (co-established with Bob Rafelson before it evolved into BBS), *Easy Rider* originated as an in-house production for AIP with Roger Corman, one of the most established exploitation filmmakers, attached as producer. Having worked with both Peter Fonda and Dennis Hopper on AIP's *The Trip* (Roger Corman, 1967), for which Hopper had also performed second-unit director duties, and with Fonda a year earlier starring in the commercially successful biker film *The Wild Angels* (Roger Corman, 1966), both films financed, produced and distributed by AIP, *Easy Rider* seemed to be a natural next step for all parties involved.

However, by February 1968 any potential deal with AIP and Corman had collapsed and Fonda and Hopper had moved to different production arrangements. Peter Fonda and William Hayward's Pando Company was one of two production outfits that were credited as the film's producers, with Raybert Productions being the other one. Once again, then, and to paraphrase Grimes, it is questionable that *Easy Rider* would have looked and sounded the way it did had it been produced by ultra-efficient and speedy Roger Corman and its production had been financed and arranged by AIP, a company famous for starting the production process from an exploitable title and then moving to make a film that fitted that title.[9] It is also debatable if *Easy Rider* would have been called *Easy Rider* given AIP's panache for choosing imaginative titles that lend themselves easily to exploitation and advertising, with the company's releases in 1969 carrying titles such as *Paroxismus* (Jesús Franco), *Hell's Belles* (Maury Dexter) and *The Great Sex War* (Norman Foster).

Of course, it is not possible to ever know if *Easy Rider* could have been made in a similar way had it not been the 'independent' production it was or if it would have been as successful commercially had it been released by a low-end independent exploitation film distributor such as AIP. What is possible, however, is to explore what it meant for *Easy Rider* not to have been made under the auspices of an exploitation producer-distributor and, equally importantly, what it meant for it to have the distribution might of a major Hollywood studio such as Columbia Pictures behind it. What limitations would production under the AIP banner in the late 1960s have imposed on the film that its production structure under Raybert/BBS enabled it to avoid? And, equally, what advantages did distribution by Columbia give *Easy Rider* that distribution by AIP would never have been able to provide?

In asking these questions, and beyond its historiographical approach, the chapter seeks to scrutinize the film's celebrated status as an 'independent' production at the heart of Hollywood by highlighting specifically Columbia's role beyond advertising and distribution, paying particular attention to its role in clearing the rights for the songs that appear in the film, which gave *Easy Rider* one of the most recognizable elements of its identity as a film. With many existing histories of the film's production using the term 'independent' unproblematically while also not questioning fully the nature of the Hollywood major's involvement in the film, the chapter will complicate definitions of 'independence' as these were utilized to account for productions during the Hollywood Renaissance period in general and in the case of *Easy Rider* in particular.

Another 'Biker' film: Easy Rider at AIP

By the time Fonda and Hopper were negotiating a deal for *The Loners* (as *Easy Rider* was originally entitled) with AIP in late 1967/early 1968,[10] the exploitation film production-distribution company was experiencing a very successful period. Established in 1954 as American Releasing Corporation by Samuel Z. Arkoff and James Nicholson with an initial investment of a few thousand dollars and contribution from a network of small exhibitors that were having increasing difficulty in securing product after the collapse of the studio system and the majors' shift to fewer and more expensive films in the 1950s, the company quickly asserted itself in the low-end independent film market.[11]

With that market dominated increasingly by exploitation filmmaking practices following the end of a lengthy period of a stable B film production during the 1930s and 1940s that had allowed low-end independent film companies to carve a niche next to the dominant Hollywood majors, American International Pictures (as its name changed to in 1956) made its own mark, primarily by making films that exploited the enhanced status of young people in US public discourse. As Bill Osgerby put it, the company's early films 'pitted autonomous and sexually aggressive teenagers against conformist and inhibited authority figures',[12] which, among other things, ensured interest from an increasingly large youth audience that was not fully catered for by the main powers of the industry.

By the early 1960s AIP had shifted its emphasis on more wholesome representations of young people, exemplified by the beach party film series, while at the same time finding success with a diversified programme of releases, including the Edgar Alan Poe film cycle that was produced and directed by Roger Corman. But as the country's cultural climate became much more negative in the second half of the 1960s, AIP was quick to follow the signs of the time. One of the ways it stayed in tune with the *zeitgeist* was through the introduction of a biker film cycle that quickly became not only a staple for the company but for a host of other exploitation companies as well.[13] Managing to exploit public fascination with and fear of motorcycle gangs and their (often tenuous) links to the emerging counterculture, itself perceived as strongly connected to subcultural youth, biker films attracted substantial audiences.[14] Starting with *The Wild Angels* in 1966, which proved the company's most commercially successful film to that date, by the end of the decade AIP had released almost a dozen such pictures.[15]

It was at a time when this cycle was in full swing that Fonda and Hopper approached AIP with the idea for *The Loners*. Although accounts vary in terms of some of the details of how the deal was initiated and what exactly it would have entailed, certain facts about its terms and why they were not eventually accepted by the filmmakers can be safely assumed given that they are included in a large number of sources. However, my discussion will also highlight inconsistencies and contradictions and will try to address some of these through recourse to primary sources, including articles in the trade press and oral histories.

What most sources agree on is that the idea for the film started with Peter Fonda in September 1967 during a visit to Toronto to promote the Corman-directed and AIP-produced and distributed *The Trip*.[16] Upon looking at a publicity still of his earlier Corman/AIP film *The Wild Angels* with himself and co-star Bruce Dern on a motorbike, Fonda came up with the idea for a film about two 'drug-dealing bikers,'[17] though according to Lee Hill, the idea was more about two 'hip guys travelling across America on bikes'.[18] Fonda then contacted his co-star in *The Trip* Dennis Hopper asking him to do the film together, with the two actors also co-authoring the screenplay, Fonda producing and Hopper directing as a way of keeping the costs down.[19]

From this point onward, it is not clear how exactly the film ended up at AIP and the precise role Roger Corman played in the potential deal. According to Patrick McGilligan, once Hopper agreed to come on board he and Fonda together with writer Terry Southern developed a treatment for the film, pitched it unsuccessfully to various studios but found interest from Corman who suggested that they brought the project to AIP.[20] This account also implies that Corman's involvement would have been only as a producer although it refrains from stating the exact nature of his role. Hill's own account also implies Corman's participation but is even less precise about its nature.[21] John Berra, on the other hand, explicitly states that Fonda and Hopper approached Corman to bring the project to AIP but claims that Corman was not interested in the project, which led Fonda to seek alternative arrangements and approach Schneider and Rafelson.[22] Indeed, in Berra's account no meetings with the AIP executives are mentioned, with Berra implying that Corman was standing for AIP, even though he did not have a corporate relationship with the company.

Other sources elaborate on this issue but do not necessarily agree on the details. In his autobiography, Samuel Arkoff states that *Easy Rider* came to AIP in 1968 but seems to imply that it was Fonda and Hopper themselves who brought the project to his company. In this account, Corman's potential involvement was raised by Arkoff as he objected to Hopper's desire to direct and (co-)produce the film. Thinking that the film had the potential to be commercially successful but mostly not wanting to greenlight a film with a novice director who also had a bad reputation as a troublemaker, Arkoff recommended Corman as a producer and potentially as the film's director.[23] This account, however, is contradicted in Mark Thomas McGee's history of AIP in which he suggests that Fonda involved Corman from the very start, asking him to be the film's producer and to broker a deal with AIP. Corman thought that the pitch for the film had potential and therefore was all too happy to set up the meeting with Arkoff.[24] Corman himself verifies McGee's account in his own autobiography, stating that he made a deal with Fonda immediately to act as producer for the film, which he considered as a continuation of themes and images from *The Wild Angels* and *The Trip* while also supporting Hopper's pitch for the role of director having seen his second-unit work for *The Trip*.[25]

Beyond the nature of Corman's involvement in the film, there were other issues in setting up *Easy Rider* as an AIP production that neither have been explored in any detail nor always agreed upon by existing studies. One issue that sources agree on is that AIP was uneasy with Hopper as director from the start and that, after realizing that the project could not progress with another director, the only way AIP would greenlight the film would be to insert a clause in the deal giving the distributor the right to take over the picture and replace Hopper with a different director if he fell behind schedule.[26] Indeed, Corman's account suggests that the length of the period 'behind schedule' that would automatically trigger this clause was just three days,[27] which demonstrates the extreme limitations exploitation film companies were in a position to impose on filmmakers working for them. As Arkoff himself reportedly put it: 'You know how AIP works, Dennis. We have to keep things moving. We have to stay on schedule'.[28]

Although this issue has received by far the most attention when it comes to AIP's involvement in the film, I would like also to raise some other issues that have been mentioned only in passing and complicate not only the film's production history but also approaches to low-end exploitation filmmaking within a discourse of American independent cinema. For instance, McGilligan, who does not mention at all AIP's proposed clause of replacing the director in his own otherwise detailed account of the film's production, talks about AIP not liking the concept of 'heroes who sold death drugs'.[29] Arkoff, on the other hand, admits in his autobiography that he was 'concerned about the "down" ending of two bike riders being blasted from their motorcycles by Southern rednecks'.[30]

Both these issues, especially the latter, seem to contradict accounts of filmmaking by exploitation and more generally low-end independent companies that wanted directors to work with often substantial freedom, and films to be nothing more than functional stories that broadly fit with an exploitable title and the publicity plans of the companies behind them. Writing specifically about Corman's New World Pictures, which was established just a year after the release of *Easy Rider*, Jim Hillier argues:

> [F]reedom was inherent in the ways the films were produced. Expectations tended to be low for a number of reasons: the films would have no aspirations to critical acclaim (as a rule, they would not be press shown), the budgets were extremely low, and producers would generally be absent and more concerned with selling the product than with actually making it.[31]

Although Hillier suggests that such freedom also existed in other exploitation companies,[32] the above issues related to *Easy Rider* demonstrate that AIP might not have operated in such a manner. This is also supported by Blair Davis, who showed that despite starting from an exploitable concept and title, AIP had a robust pre-production process that involved scripting in particular ways and gave the company's producers the power to revise scripts, especially as part of cost-cutting exercises.[33] In this respect, despite instances where the company's films did not follow this process (especially with Roger Corman productions),[34] in the majority of its productions AIP seemed to have provided little, if any, freedom to its filmmakers. Indeed, by the late 1960s and just prior to the release of *Easy Rider*, even Corman had started having problems with AIP's strict adherence to its principles, which eventually prompted him to start New World Pictures in 1970.[35]

To return to *Easy Rider*, if anything, the above issues imply that Corman was essential for guaranteeing whatever creative freedom Fonda and Hopper were hoping to have working for AIP. This was especially so as Arkoff was reported in production meetings to have encouraged the filmmakers to continue developing their script by taking into consideration 'suggestions' that would help 'make [the film] an AIP project'.[36] Although none of the sources on the film's history outline what kind of suggestions these might have been, Osgerby's detailed discussion of the biker film genre is an excellent guide in terms of what Hopper and Fonda could have expected. With Osgerby describing *The Wild Angels* and the biker films that followed in its wake, especially those by AIP, as being characterized by 'an aesthetic of astonishment' that drew on exhibiting 'the lifestyle of the outlaw biker' as 'a spectacle of the sensational, the forbidden and the monstrous',[37] one can anticipate that *The Loners/Easy Rider* had every chance of becoming 'just another biker movie' under AIP's watch. This is despite the fact that, according to Arkoff, AIP was willing to invest $340,000, making it one of its prestige productions.[38]

With Fonda and Hopper refusing to accept AIP's terms, the filmmakers were ready to explore other options. The next section will look in detail at Hopper and Fonda's deal with Raybert, focusing especially on Columbia's role in the making of the film. However, I would like to finish this section with one final issue about the possibility of *Easy Rider* taking place at AIP and the ways in which it could have shaped the film that has received no attention in any sources I have consulted: the use of popular music as part of the narrative.

Although AIP was using popular music in its films routinely given its focus on the youth demographic, its cost-effective practices kept the company firmly away from utilizing established artists or hit songs. For instance, despite the presence of several rock songs and music in *The Wild Angels*, the soundtrack for the film was done by Mike Curb, a young musician and owner of small label Sidewalk Productions, with all the songs performed by a band contracted to Curb's label. Curb was also responsible for the soundtrack of *The Trip*, with another band signed to his label performing all the songs. He was involved in other AIP films as well, including *The Born Losers* (Tom Laughlin, 1967) and *The Wild Racers* (Daniel Haller, 1968), having arranged a contract that entailed the production of soundtrack albums for the company through his label. Following the success of a number of his soundtracks for AIP, Curb was poached by MGM in November 1969 to head the company's music division, MGM Records.[39]

As it is clear from this very brief account of AIP's arrangements for scoring its films in the late 1960s, it is very likely that *Easy Rider* would have been assigned to Curb for a musical score featuring minor artists contracted to his label. With Hopper and Fonda having initially commissioned the soundtrack for their film to Crosby, Stills and Nash, who had just recorded, though not released, their very successful eponymous first album, it is unlikely that this commission would have materialized if the deal with AIP had gone through. With the three artists of the band having been members of major bands of the time such as The Byrds (Crosby), Buffalo Springfield (Stills) and The Hollies (Nash) and therefore well-established musicians, it is clear that AIP's resources would not have been able to stretch sufficiently to afford them. And even though that commission was eventually cancelled, Fonda and Hopper decided to use instead contemporary songs by similarly established, if not better-known, artists and bands, including The Byrds, Jimi Hendrix, Steppenwolf and The Band, the film rights for which have been estimated to have cost in the region of $1 million (see next section).[40]

With the music of these bands and artists having become arguably the most recognizable element of the film, it is extremely important to understand who paid for it in order to be part of the film's narrative and of course a major source of ancillary profits. As my discussion in the next section will demonstrate, there could have only been one agent with the resources to cover a song rights clearance bill that was three times the film's production budget: a Hollywood major, in this case Columbia Pictures. As for AIP, despite coming close to producing and distributing a biker film that 'started with an image',[41] fitted perfectly with its main film cycle at that particular historical moment and seemed to be tuned in to the counterculture *zeitgeist*, in the end it opted to adhere to its exploitation filmmaking practices that came with no provision for granting creative freedom to filmmakers, rather than taking a risk with enabling a more 'independent' mode of filmmaking.

'Hardly a pickup': Easy Rider, *Raybert Productions and Columbia Pictures*

Following the collapse of any potential deal with AIP, Hopper and Fonda ended up bringing *Easy Rider* to independent film and television production company Raybert Productions. As I would like to focus in this section primarily on the nature of Columbia's role, I will not review the literature that discusses who initiated the sequence of events that brought the film to Schneider and Rafelson's company. This is also because, unlike the film's production 'pre-history' with AIP, this part of *Easy Rider's* production trajectory has been examined rigorously, with all accounts agreeing that it was Hopper and Fonda's network of relations with a number of actors, directors, producers, writers and technicians who shared their youth and countercultural ideas that brought them to Raybert at a very particular moment in time.

Instead, what I concentrate on, is how Columbia is represented in these accounts and, more importantly, when these accounts report its presence in the film's production process. This is a particularly pertinent question for determining the nature of the film's 'independence', especially given Bert Schneider's familial relationship to Columbia's top executives, its chairman and chief executive officer (as of 1968) Abe Schneider (Bert's father) and its head of production (as of 1968) Stanley Schneider (Bert's older brother).[42] As my discussion will demonstrate, questions emerge in terms of who financed the film fully and with what funds; whether the film was an independent production the distribution rights of which were bought as a negative pick up by Columbia; and whether it was Columbia that paid for the rights to the film's music.

One good starting point for this part of the story is provided by the trade press of the time, which, once the film was put officially in production by its producing partners Pando and Raybert, started reporting updates on its production status. In this respect, one can get a good steer as to when particular events in the film's production timeline appear to have taken place. The first mention of *Easy Rider* seems to have appeared in *Variety* on 21 February 1968, with the trade publication announcing the film's launch as filmmakers and crew were going to New Orleans to start the shoot at the Mardi Gras.[43] This is confirmed by Biskind's account who dates this trip on 23 February.[44]

Following a number of updates on the film's location shooting that situate it in a seven week period between mid-May and early July,[45] the next mention of the film appears on 31 July 1968 when *Variety* reported that *Easy Rider* was 'about to be bought by a major'.[46] This report, on the one hand, clearly points to the film's independent status in the six month period (February–July) since *Easy Rider's* first mention in the trade press and, on the other, allows for a period of approximately one month from the end of the shoot (estimated in early July) for the producers of the film to 'shop' for a distributor. It would be another two months until Columbia was identified formally by both *Variety* and the *Hollywood Reporter* as the film's distributor, with both papers reporting the news on 31 October 1968.[47] Although this sequence of events sounds both logical and convincing, there are a number of competing accounts, especially with regards to when Columbia started being involved.

To understand fully whether Columbia was part of the picture (pun intended) from the start or not, one needs to commence from the film's financing, another aspect of its production history where the evidence is not particularly clear. One thing key sources agree on is that Bert Schneider bankrolled the beginning of the production with a personal cheque, which, according to Biskind, was for $40,000, that allowed a small crew to go to New Orleans and shoot the Mardi Gras footage in February 1968.[48] However, the picture gets more complicated when it comes to accounting for the rest of the budget.

Several sources claim explicitly[49] or implicitly[50] that Bert Schneider supplied the rest of the production costs too (in the region of $300,000 or the equivalent of approximately $2 million adjusted for inflation in 2017) from his personal finances. Citing the great commercial success of *The Monkees* (1966–8) TV show, which Schneider and Rafelson produced through Raybert, such sources claim that it was the show's profits that enabled Schneider to finance the film in full, with McGilligan characterizing Raybert Productions as 'swimming in Monkees money' and underlining the irony that the profits of one of the company's 'lamest TV shows' financed 'the self-styled hippest movie of the decade'.[51]

Although the idea that a wealthy producer like Schneider who had embraced the ideals of the counterculture and who was part of the same circle as many of the above-the-line participants in *Easy Rider* underwrote personally the production costs of the film and gave complete creative freedom to novice filmmakers makes for a sensational story, the fact that most of the sources steer clear of making this point explicitly or providing evidence to support it is a good indication of the extent to which it is true. Providing $40,000 from personal finances as start-up money with the rest of the investment to be arranged is very different from also providing almost eight times that amount without any guarantee for a return, which would explain why sources are much more precise about the initial investment and where it came from than the rest of the finance. Furthermore, if the money came from Raybert and the profits of *The Monkees*, as McGilligan suggests, then it is rather strange that sources attribute the rest of the financing only to Schneider and not to Rafelson too, who is not credited as financier of the film anywhere, despite being the other half of Raybert Productions.

With these questions in mind, it is perhaps not surprising that the two most authoritative sources on the film's production history state clearly that Schneider had approached Columbia for a distribution deal via his family connections very early in the process. McGilligan claims that Schneider flew to New York immediately after the original finance deal (at some point in early February 1968) 'to get a distribution commitment from Columbia' via his father,[52] while Biskind's account dates the distribution deal a bit later in February 1968, during the time of the New Orleans shoot.[53] However, perhaps the most telling comment on this issue comes from Richard Kahn, Columbia's distribution and advertising executive at the time, who in an interview about the film conducted as part of the Academy of Motion Pictures Arts and Sciences Oral History Programme, refused to label *Easy Rider* an independent production that was only distributed by Columbia, stating instead that 'the boss's son did *Easy Rider*, it was hardly a pickup'.[54]

Such an arrangement does not mean that Fonda and Hopper did not have creative control or that the money came with strings attached in terms of how the film's aesthetic design or content should be handled. However, in the first instance and at the very least, it means that besides wanting to empower young filmmakers and making different films, Schneider (and Rafelson?), if they did provide all the finance from the profits of *The Monkees*, made first and foremost a very substantial investment for which they expected a return. Such an expected return upon which the film's finance was predicated would be tied to the understanding (for lack of a potentially more formal arrangement at this early stage in the film's production) that major Hollywood distributor Columbia Pictures would release the film. But given that the major's attachment to the film was unofficial until October 1968, this enabled the production to be perceived by the film community and the trade press as 'independent', and for some scholarly accounts as a point of origin for and the main ancestor of what later was identified as contemporary American independent cinema.[55]

However, taking the above contradictory accounts into consideration one cannot but question the extent of the film's independence or at the very least reconsider its status as a negative pickup by a Hollywood distributor. I would like to suggest that *Easy Rider's* arrangement with Raybert is reminiscent of a very specific definition of independent film production in the post-studio era that Tino Balio advanced in his studies of United Artists.[56] In these accounts, Balio conceived of independent production as a partnership between a Hollywood major and a production entity, whereby the major would provide production finance and grant the producer creative control over the picture and a share of the film's profits in return for global distribution rights.[57] Balio suggests that the distributor maintained control of the film through a list of approvals (especially in terms of script and talent participation) and requirements (such as the film's running time to be within commercial release standards).

Although at first sight *Easy Rider* does not seem to be close to this model, if one assumes that Columbia's unofficial presence from the start guaranteed Raybert's investment in the film, one can see an arrangement at work that is very similar to the one Balio advanced and which he considered independent only in name as 'it has always been dependent on the major industry players'.[58] Indeed, I would like to suggest that this independent production model can be detected in a number of events during the film's production that key sources attributed to dramatic conflicts within the context of a production in disarray rather than to a producer's action to keep the production in check in order to deliver a professional film to a major distributor.

For instance, mid-way through production Schneider is attributed with firing the film's director of cinematography Barry Feinstein, who had repeatedly clashed with Hopper, and replacing him with László Kovács, while also installing a new unit manager (Paul Lewis) to exercise tighter control over the production than the person he replaced.[59] Perhaps more importantly, Schneider intervened in the film's editing process in order to ensure that the film's duration would fall within the commercial exhibition standards, when according to various sources the first cut of the film after a lengthy period of experimentation with editing came to approximately four hours.[60] Under Schneider's authority Hopper took an enforced leave of absence which allowed the film's producers to oversee cutting the film down to 95 minutes through the collective work of a number of people led by editor Donn Cambern.[61] As Berra suggests, this re-editing 'made the film more palatable, more accessible to the mass market', arranged 'in a relatively conventional fashion and paced in line with audience expectations of narrative forms'.[62] In this respect, while all the above can certainly be seen as evidence of a production constantly endangered by the dramatic actions of its key participants within the context of a transitional period in the history of Hollywood cinema, they also fall within the remit of a producer's role in an effort to deliver a film of a professional standard to a Hollywood major so that they stand a chance for a return on their investment in the film, whether they were responsible for the whole sum or just part of it.

Easy Rider's production as an 'independent' film in the way Balio defines the label is arguably best illustrated by Columbia's role in ensuring that the filmmakers were able to use a list of contemporary hit songs as part of the film's soundtrack for significant portions of screen time. Given that the film's soundtrack has become its undisputed trademark, it is remarkable that key histories of the film's production have provided only the sketchiest of accounts of how that music came to be part of the film. This section of the chapter, then, will close with a brief discussion of this issue to demonstrate the utmost significance of Columbia in the film's success and to question further *Easy Rider*'s status as a different type of independent film production that took place outside Hollywood.

Some basic details about the film's soundtrack are well known. As I mentioned in the previous section, Fonda wanted an original score consisting of contemporary popular songs written and performed by newly formed super-group Crosby, Stills and Nash. With Schneider and Rafelson heavily involved in the music scene via The Monkees such a deal was easy to make. According to Biskind, when the band was approached they were ready to be involved with the film. However, Hopper sabotaged the deal and all discussions of the band doing the film's score came to a halt.[63]

At this point it is not clear who would cover the cost of that soundtrack. Crosby, Stills and Nash had a contract with Atlantic Records, a key music label that in 1967 was taken over by Warner Bros.–Seven Arts and therefore had become a subsidiary of a conglomerate.[64] And with all three band members already successful musicians, it was clear that the cost of such a project would have been considerable. Given the fact that the deal had been brokered by the Raybert executives it looks like Schneider and Rafelson would have been responsible for that bill, unless this would also be a cost passed on to Columbia once the film was submitted for distribution.

With Crosby, Stills and Nash out of the picture, the filmmakers opted to use contemporary hit songs rather than commission another original soundtrack. The key accounts of the film's production history provide no evidence for how such a decision materialized in financial terms. McGilligan provides brief details about how the songs were selected, claiming that once the film was edited down to 94 minutes and was accepted in that form by the main parties, the production team kept bringing records and were mixing scenes 'to the hippest songs of the time'. Once the list of songs to be included was finalized, the filmmakers invited the bands to see a rough cut of the film with the music and approve its use in it, with all the key artists (bar Bob Dylan) enthusiastically endorsing such use.[65] McGilligan's account stops there with no mention about the cost of having the tracks used in the film as well as on a tie-in album that would promote the film in a key ancillary market.

A different account but with key financial details emerged in *Moviemaker* magazine's interview with László Kovács in 2004, in which the film's cinematographer pointed to lead editor Donn Cambern as being responsible for the choice of songs in the film, the licensing of which cost approximately $1 million.[66] This contradicts other anecdotal accounts that cite Fonda as stating that the production team paid each artist or band whose song was heard in the film $1,000 in exchange for their permission.[67]

Once again, I would like to suggest, the idea that the song rights for *Easy Rider* cost $1,000 per track that was paid for by the filmmakers or the production team makes for an impressive and sensational headline that nonetheless goes against standard practices in the use of popular music in film production. First, authority to grant permission for the use of pre-recorded material in another medium, lies not with the artists but with the labels they have a contract with. This means that if the production team did indeed pay each artist $1,000, this was more a symbolic gesture rather than a fee that would enable the filmmakers to use their songs in a major motion picture.

Second, in such cases, the production company would have to deal not just with one permission to clear a song's rights but with several as in such cases it is normally three types of copyright that have to be cleared: the publishing right, the recording right and the performing right. In the simplest cases whereby a label that controls the contract with an artist is also the company that owns the publishing rights to the artist's songs, a film production company would have to pay to clear these rights, before also paying additionally to use a recording of the artist's song in a film, in what is called synchronization rights.[68]

Finally, there is also the case of the LP tie-in with the music from the film for which the producer would have had to pay the publisher an additional fee to be able to license the songs for the album as well as clear the recording rights for this medium unless the album producer decided to use different bands to cover the film's songs. 'The Weight' was performed in the film by The Band but after Dunhill-ABC, the label that produced the tie-in LP failed to clear the song's rights for the album, it was performed instead as a cover version by Smith (a band with a contract with Dunhill-ABC). All other songs heard in the film are performed on the soundtrack album in their original recording by the same artists. This is with the exception of the Dylan–McGuinn composed 'The Ballad of Easy Rider' and the Dylan-composed 'It's Alright Ma (I'm only Bleeding)' that Roger McGuinn recorded specifically for the film.[69]

All these details clearly suggest that there was a huge bill to be paid for the use of the songs in the film as well as on the LP tie-in. With contributors to the film such as Kovács estimating that bill in the region of $1 million ($6.8 million if adjusted for inflation in 2017), there could only have been one party with deep enough pockets to pay that bill, Columbia Pictures. In this respect, it is clear that the company did not only contribute to the success of the film as a distributor with its immense advertising and marketing resources and with opening the film in quality theatres in major markets in the US and internationally. Its contribution extended to being financier and production partner, and enabling the filmmakers to use the songs they wanted in the film. This reinforces the idea that *Easy Rider* was not the type of 'independent' production that it has been perceived to be but rather it was not dramatically different from the other types of 'independent' productions that dominated the American film industry in the post-war/post-studio era.

Conclusion: From exploitation to legitimacy, from the margins to the mainstream

Easy Rider is a film that tends to invite emotional responses, even when it comes to constructing its production history. Its unexpected incredible commercial success, its complete transcendence of its exploitation origins and the limitations of the biker film genre, its deep connection to the wave of counterculture that was sweeping the US at the time, have all invited responses that often border on the mythical. Within this context, academic and popular historians and critics have often interpreted events in different ways and have submitted accounts of the film's production that have been widely different and more often than not contradictory in terms of when particular events happened, why they happened and who was responsible for them.

One of the outcomes of this type of engagement with the film was a shift of emphasis away from the film's industrial history to a history of personal drama that, not surprisingly, played up sensational angles and lurid details that seem particularly believable at the height of the counterculture. At the same time, important issues and questions were marginalized, forgotten or simply not asked, which suggests that these accounts contribute to the telling of the film's production history in a particular way, while also influencing the manner in which certain academic studies understand and approach the film and the era that gave birth to it.

Looking behind the myth and the drama, this chapter has asked some of these questions and challenged some assumptions associated with the film's production, including the degree of its independence (both in its failed deal with AIP and in the nature of its relationship with its Hollywood major distributor). In the process, it demonstrated that *Easy Rider* was a more conventional production than is widely assumed, with many of the events surrounding its production reconsidered as routine operations by a production company with a deal to deliver to a major studio a professional film for the purposes of commercial distribution.

Note: I would like to thank Carys Damon and Mike Jones for their advice on the issue of song clearance and the kinds of rights involved in it.

Notes

1 Some of the key works on *Easy Rider* include: Barbara Klinger, 'The Road to Dystopia: Landscaping the Nation in Easy Rider', in *The Road Movie Book*, ed. Steve Cohan and Ina Rae Hark (London: BFI, 1997), 179–203; Lee Hill, *Easy Rider* (London: BFI Modern Classics, 1996); and Peter Lev, 'Hippie Generation', in *American Films of the 70s: Conflicting Visions* (Austin: University of Texas Press, 2000), 3–21.

2 Peter Biskind, *Easy Riders, Raging Bulls: How the Sex-Drugs-and-Rock 'n' Roll Generation Saved Hollywood* (New York: Bloomsbury, 1998), 52–80.

3 Biskind, *Easy Riders, Raging Bulls*, 75.

4 Similar accounts include: Patrick McGilligan, 'The Ballad of *Easy Rider* (Or, How to Make a Drug Classic)', *Los Angeles Magazine* (March 1994): 57–65, and to a certain extent Mark Thomas McGee, *Faster and Furiouser: The Revised and Fattened Fable of American International Pictures* (Jefferson, NC: McFarland, 1996), 257–9.

5 The chapter will engage with some of these histories, including John Berra, *Declarations of Independence: American Cinema and the Partiality of Independent Production* (Bristol: Intellect, 2008), 34–9; Teresa Grimes, 'BBS: Auspicious Beginnings, Open Endings', *Movie*, 31/32 (1986): 54–66; and Chris Hugo, '*Easy Rider* and Hollywood in the '70s', *Movie*, 31/32 (1986): 67–71. This is not to suggest that everything in these accounts is problematic but that they contain information that is open to debate and challenge.

6 See, for instance, Berra, *Declarations of Independence*, 34–9.

7 See, for instance, Tino Balio, 'When Is an Independent Producer Independent? The Case of United Artists after 1948', *Velvet Light Trap*, 22 (1986): 53–64.

8   Grimes, 'BBS', 57.

9   Blair Davis *The Battle for the Bs: 1950s Hollywood and the Rebirth of the Low-Budget Cinema* (New Brunswick, NJ: Rutgers University Press, 2012), 111.

10 Biskind, *Easy Riders, Raging Bulls*, 61.

11 Yannis Tzioumakis, *American Independent Cinema* (Edinburgh: Edinburgh University Press, 2017), 134–9.

12 Bill Osgerby, 'Sleazy Riders: Exploitation, "Otherness" and Transgression in the 1960s Biker Movie', *Journal of Popular Film and Television*, 31 no. 3 (2003): 100.

13 Mark Thomas McGee and R. J. Robertson, *The J.D. Films: Juvenile Delinquency in the Movies* (Jefferson, NC: McFarland, 1982), 125.

14 Osgerby, 'Sleazy Riders', 101.

15 Osgerby, 'Sleazy Riders', 104.

16 Biskind, *Easy Riders, Raging Bulls*, 42; Hill, *Easy Rider*, 11; McGilligan, 'The Ballad of *Easy Rider*', 57 and 59; Berra, *Declarations of Independence*, 34 (with the last rather improbably locating the visit in 1968, given that *Easy Rider*'s production under Pando and Raybert started on 21 February 1968 [Amy Archerd, 'Just for Variety', *Daily Variety*, 21 February 1968, 2).

17 McGilligan, 'The Ballad of *Easy Rider*', 57.

18 Hill, *Easy Rider*, 11.

19 Berra, *Declarations of Independence*, 35; McGilligan, 'The Ballad of *Easy Rider*', 59; Biskind, *Easy Riders, Raging Bulls*, 42.

20 McGilligan, 'The Ballad of *Easy Rider*', 59–60.

21 Hill, *Easy Rider*, 20.

22 Berra, *Declarations of Independence*, 36.

23 Sam Arkoff and Richard Trubo, *Flying through Hollywood by the Seat of My Pants: From the Man Who Brought You I Was A Teenage Werewolf and Muscle Beach Party* (New York: Birch Lane Press, 1992), 177.

24 McGee, *Faster and Furiouser*, 258–9.

25 Roger Corman and Jim Jerome, *How I Made A Hundred Movies and Never Lost A Dime* (New York: Da Capo Press, 1998), 156.

26 Corman and Jerome, *How I Made A Hundred Movies*, 156; Hill, *Easy Rider*, 20; McGee, *Faster and Furiouser*, 259; Arkoff and Trubo, *Flying through Hollywood*, 177; Osgerby, 'Sleazy Riders', 105.

27 Corman and Jerome, *How I Made A Hundred Movies*, 156.

28 Arkoff and Trubo, *Flying through Hollywood*, 177.

29 McGilligan, 'The Ballad of *Easy Rider*', 60.

30 Arkoff and Trubo, *Flying through Hollywood*, 177.

31 Jim Hillier, *The New Hollywood* (London: Studio Vista, 1994), 47.

32 Hillier, *The New Hollywood*, 46.

33 Davis, *The Battle for the Bs*, 115.

34 McGee and Robertson, *The J.D. Films*, 118.

35 Corman and Jerome, *How I Made A Hundred Movies*, 152–3.

36 Arkoff and Trubo, *Flying through Hollywood*, 177.

37 Osgerby, 'Sleazy Riders', 103.

38 Arkoff and Trubo, *Flying through Hollywood*, 177.

39 Tino Balio, *MGM* (London: Routledge, 2018), 237.

40 Frank Mastropolo, 'The Story of the Groundbreaking "Easy Rider" Soundtrack', *Ultimate Classic Rock*, 14 July 2014, http://ultimateclassicrock.com/easy-rider-soundtrack

41 Elaine M. Bapis, *American Film as Agent of Social Change, 1965–1975* (Jefferson, NC: McFarland, 2008), 78.

42 Suzan Ayscough, 'Ex Col Titan Dies', *Variety*, 23 April 1993, http://variety.com/1993/film/news/ex-col-titan-schneider-dies-106225/; David A. Cook, *Lost Illusions: American Cinema in the Shadow of Watergate and Vietnam 1970–1979* (Berkeley: University of California Press, 2000), 315.

43 Archerd, 'Just for Variety', 2.

44 Biskind, *Easy Riders, Raging Bulls*, 63.

45 'Sabrina Scharf for Peter Fonda Flick', *Hollywood Reporter*, 15 May 1968; 'Pandro [sic] Pic to Texas', *Variety*, 5 June 1968, 18; 'Film Production Chart', *Daily Variety*, 28 June 1968, 10; and 'Film Production Chart', *Daily Variety*, 28 June 1968, 10.

46 Amy Archerd, 'Just for Variety', *Daily Variety*, 31 July 1968, 2.

47 'Col Distributor Pete [sic] Fonda's Indie "Easy Rider"', *Hollywood Reporter*, 31 October 1968; 'Col Distributor of "Easy Rider"', *Daily Variety*, 31 October 1968, 3.

48 Biskind, *Easy Riders, Raging Bulls*, 62; McGilligan, 'The Ballad of *Easy Rider*', 60.

49 Berra, *Declarations of Independence*, 37; Linda Werba, 'It All Became So "Easy" After Peter Fonda Met Bert Schneider', *Daily Variety*, 5 November 1969, 12.

50 Hill, *Easy Rider*, 21; McGilligan, 'The Ballad of *Easy Rider*', 60.

51 McGilligan, 'The Ballad of *Easy Rider*', 60.

52 McGilligan, 'The Ballad of *Easy Rider*', 60.

53 Biskind, *Easy Riders, Raging Bulls*, 66.

54 Richard Kahn, *An Oral History with Richard Kahn* (Los Angeles: Academy of Motion Pictures Arts and Sciences, 2013), 413.

55 Berra, *Declarations of Independence*, 29 and 37.

56 Balio, 'When Is', 53–64; Tino Balio, *United Artists: The Company that Changed the Film Industry* (Madison: University of Wisconsin Press, 1987).

57 Balio, *United Artists*, 42.

58 Balio, 'When Is', 53.

59 McGilligan, 'The Ballad of *Easy Rider*', 61; Peter L. Winkler, *Dennis Hopper: The Wild Ride of a Hollywood Rebel* (London: The Robson Press, 2012).

60 Hill, *Easy Rider*, 26; McGilligan, 'The Ballad of *Easy Rider*', 64.

61 Berra, *Declarations of Independence*, 38; McGilligan, 'The Ballad of *Easy Rider*', 64; Donn Cambern, 'Untitled', *Los Angeles Times*, 22 August 1999.

62 Berra, *Declarations of Independence*, 39.

63 Biskind, *Easy Riders, Raging Bulls*, 72.

64 Paul Ackerman and Mike Gross 'Atlantic Sold in Big $$ Grab Era', *Billboard*, 28 October 1967, 1 and 8.

65 McGilligan, 'The Ballad of *Easy Rider*', 65.

66 Bob Fisher, '*Easy Rider*: 35 Years Later', *Moviemaker*, 23 June 2004, https://www.moviemaker.com/archives/moviemaking/directing/articles-directing/easy-rider-35-years-later-2921

67 Cited in Mastropolo, 'The Story of the Groundbreaking'.

68 Ann Harrison, *Music – The Business: The Essential Guide to the Law and the Deal*, 6th Edition (London: Virgin Books, 2014), 93 and 106.

69 William Ruhlmann, 'All Music Review: *Easy Rider*', All Music, no date, http://www.allmusic.com/album/easy-rider-mw0000049299

Chapter 8

HOLLYWOOD TRADE: *MIDNIGHT COWBOY* (1969) AND UNDERGROUND CINEMA

Gary Needham

'Today's trade is tomorrow's competition'

— John Rechy[1]

In 1960s gay slang, 'trade' was a term for a 'straight' male hustler who has sex with men for money rather than pleasure. His masculinity, his virility, that which he apparently possesses and defines him as a 'straight man', is something that has economic value and can be traded as a form of sexual labour. Because 'trade' is deemed 'work', sex simply and purely for money, it remains untainted by pleasure and desire because these would make it what it is, sex between men. In *Midnight Cowboy* (John Schlesinger, 1969), Texas boy Joe Buck (Jon Voight) thinks he also has something to trade, his virility packaged as a cowboy, that women in New York will be eager and willing to pay a decent number of bucks in exchange for an authentic experience with a southern stud. Contrary to his expectations, the only New Yorkers interested in his trade are the so-called 'tutti-fruttis' of New York's queer demi-monde.

Like Joe Buck's cowboy, *Midnight Cowboy* is 'Hollywood Trade', a commercial exchange with the hustler subject matter that occupied gay culture for most of the twentieth century.[2] Both Joe Buck and *Midnight Cowboy* register an already visible homosexual relationality and subculture of hustlers, queens, johns and trade from queer 'novels of urban alienation'.[3] *Midnight Cowboy* premiered at the end of May 1969, a month before the historic Stonewall riots at the end of June. As a Hollywood production, *Midnight Cowboy* is trading as a 'straight film' about the gay subject matter of sexual-outlaw culture from a director, as it is often told, who was open about his own homosexuality at the time of the film's production. *Midnight Cowboy* trades on the transgressive potential of gay sexual subculture but the film is uneasy about identifying a political position on the matter. *Midnight Cowboy* gestures towards a new type of 'liberated' Hollywood film whose very progressiveness is also dependent on a negotiation of its own repression and paranoia about its relations with homosexuality, the increasing visibility of gay men in the 1960s, and 'the network that it never directly depicts, the network that actively thwarts Joe's inattention for his costume'.[4]

For many audiences, *Midnight Cowboy* was their first, Hollywood's first, narrative of male hustling. The film exemplified a new openness about sexuality and it was easy to see the dual impact of the sexual revolution in the US and the growing influence of European cinema's own gnawing at masculinity and sexuality. The long march towards a new explicitness and maturity in post-war European cinema, coupled with the stylistic anti-classicism of the multiple realisms and New Waves of an auteur-driven art cinema, has been an often-assumed antecedent, if not *the* antecedent, of the Hollywood Renaissance. The break from both classicism and the Production Code's moral policing is often anchored in relation to the European cinema that precedes it. However, this by-now-standard historical account pays little heed to the economic necessity of Hollywood's industrial transformation and neglects to name one of Hollywood's other influences in the American underground cinema.

In the first instance, then, this chapter on *Midnight Cowboy* challenges the dominant narrative of European influence, examining instead the role of American underground cinema in shaping the Hollywood Renaissance in the mid- and late 1960s. More than any other film from the Renaissance canon, *Midnight Cowboy*'s subject matter appears to invoke the underground through the figure of the male hustler but also the staging of an ersatz 'underground party' *a la* Andy Warhol's Factory. As a matter of fact, as I discuss below, the film's production reached out to Warhol to assist with the 'party scene'. With the links between the Hollywood Renaissance and US underground cinema established, the chapter then moves to detail the influence of the underground cinema on *Midnight Cowboy* specifically and the Hollywood Renaissance more broadly. Such an examination draws on archival material relating to Warhol's response to the film, which, as the chapter will demonstrate, was negative. Indeed, Warhol's perception that *Midnight Cowboy* tried to co-opt underground cinema practices, to the extent that he felt hustled by Hollywood. The chapter will close with a discussion of *Andy Warhol's Flesh* (Paul Morrissey, 1968), a film Warhol put into production at the same time as *Midnight Cowboy* with a view of presenting a more explicit and 'authentic' representation of hustling.

As one of the key Hollywood Renaissance films along with *The Graduate* (Mike Nichols, 1967), *Bonnie and Clyde* (Arthur Penn, 1967) and *Easy Rider* (Dennis Hopper, 1969), one would not deny *Midnight Cowboy*'s progressiveness in cultural, political and aesthetic terms. An adaptation of James Leo Herlihy's 1965 novel, and thus a pre-sold property, *Midnight Cowboy* bravely evokes the ongoing 'search for America' that defined the 1960s through a crisis in both politics and masculinity. Michael Moon characterizes the film as follows:

Midnight Cowboy takes the boy out of the country (which can mean both the West and the 'whole country', the nation) by setting him down on the streets of New York, and then plays with the idea, frightening to many Americans of the time, that you can actually take the country (the supposedly inbred nationalism) out of the boy.[5]

The film's political unconscious is refracted through the hustler's body, his 'costume's performative fragility' and his encounter with the city and with other bodies and sexualities in an exchange system based on sex that, Kevin Floyd argues, assumes the status of a national allegory (see Figure 8.1).[6] The alliance between stylistic innovation, new modes of performance, new audience demographics and the change from the Production Code to the ratings system, rightly positions *Midnight Cowboy* as one of the truly ground-breaking, epoch-shifting Hollywood films of the period, alongside those mentioned above.

Radical in its approach to representation of masculinity and discourses of sexuality, notably released in the same year as the western *True Grit* (Henry Hathaway, 1969) for which John Wayne won an Oscar for Best Actor, *Midnight Cowboy* is a trailblazer in depicting men's relationships with each other in mainstream American cinema. Nominated for seven Academy Awards and winning Best Picture, Best Director and Best Adapted Screenplay, the only X-rated film to do so, *Midnight Cowboy* is rightfully canonical, a key film in the history of the Hollywood Renaissance and of American cinema more broadly.

The film brought issues of male sexuality, male intimacy, male trauma and male damage to the fore in ways that had never been examined in Hollywood with such explicitness and sympathy, interrogating the iconicity of the cowboy

Figure 8.1 Joe hustling. Copyright MGM.

as a symbol of American masculinity par excellence. *Midnight Cowboy* is one of
the films that reveal the seams in the fabric of an America that is direction-less,
crumbling, falling apart. The particularities of *Midnight Cowboy*'s trading
on the subculture of hustling, an unexplored area of male sexuality and
representation in Hollywood, as a way into its masculine secrets and the
aesthetic anti-classicism of such revelations, are politically radical, even though
they represent territory that is well-rehearsed thematically and stylistically in
the American underground cinema.

Indeed, the hustler and the cowboy are abundant in underground cinema
and literature[7] and the fruit of many cinematic fantasies by, among others,
Warhol, Kenneth Anger and Bob Mizer, gay male moviemakers interested in
outlaw sex, the outlaw figure of the hustler and new expressions of film language
in post-war America. The American underground remains written out of the
Hollywood Renaissance, despite several overt references to Andy Warhol,
underground cinema and The Factory milieu throughout *Midnight Cowboy*'s
narrative. Like Joe Buck being conned out of money by the brassier Cass (Sylvia
Miles, herself later cast in *Andy Warhol's Heat* [Paul Morrissey, 1972]), *Midnight
Cowboy* seemingly takes from underground cinema without duly paying its
debts. Andy Warhol himself was certainly not quiet on this matter. From his
hospital bed he rushed into production his new hustler movie, *Andy Warhol's
Flesh*, to show Hollywood how the underground does it and, no doubt, to
capitalize on the mainstream popularization of hustling that *Midnight Cowboy*
would possibly catalyse. In this respect, it is imperative to finish the chapter
with an examination of this film.

The axiom of European influence

In the fifty years that have passed, the divorcement of underground cinema
from the Hollywood Renaissance and the privileging of the influence of
European cinema on it are now axioms when it comes to critical practice and
its engagement with the films of the period. In making this statement I do not
mean to discount European cinema's role in shaping the Hollywood Renaissance.
Beyond any doubt, it constitutes an important line of self-evident inspiration,
especially as numerous strong European connections were grounded in
authentic statements from directors, editors and cinematographers who
admired the French and Italian cinema of the 1950s and 1960s, while at the
same time a large number of above-the-line talent involved in the Hollywood
films were themselves European in origin, including the British Schlesinger.
'I absolutely worshipped the ground De Sica walked on' recalls Schlesinger in
one interview.[8] (See also Chapter 9 in this volume).

However, the European influence axiom appears to have left little room in
accounts of the Hollywood Renaissance for its relationship to other strands of
American cinema with the exception of exploitation film.[9] The rhetoric of

European cinema as a factor in the newness of the Hollywood Renaissance dates to the original 1967 *Time* article on *Bonnie and Clyde* that Peter Krämer has highlighted as a significant anchoring:

> In *Time* magazine's exploration of the wider cultural context of the Hollywood Renaissance in 1967, artistic developments in European cinema came top of the list. *Time* referenced the French New Wave and a related movement in Czechoslovakia as well as Italian filmmakers Antonioni and Gillo Pontecorvo and the Pole Roman Polanski. Indeed, the script for *Bonnie and Clyde* had been first offered to leading French filmmakers François Truffaut and Jean-Luc Godard before the American Arthur Penn took over, and the major Hollywood studios were now offering contracts to European directors such as Antonioni and Polanski.[10]

The relationship between Hollywood and Europe from the first émigrés to post-war runaway productions is well-established culturally and industrially as both cinemas are at their basis commercial film industries and have long exchanged talent, resources, ideas and genres.[11] Despite the persistence of the label 'European art cinema', European cinema is not an artisanal cinema, it is still an *industry*, and in that sense Hollywood does indeed have more in common with European cinema on a commercial level than what might be assumed. On the other hand, there is a preference to refer to artists' films or moving-image arts rather than art films when defining the cinema of Andy Warhol and other experimental filmmakers. However, *Time* magazine's assertion of a European-influenced Hollywood as a period of Renaissance for American cinema overlooks their own coverage of Warhol and underground cinema a few years prior to the publication of the 1967 article.[12] There were numerous articles devoted to Warhol and the underground film phenomenon and he became the most frequently referenced name in the popular press reporting such as *Life* magazine's 'Report from Underground',[13] 'Avant-Garde Fun for the Family'[14] and *Newsweek*'s 'Underground in Hell', an account of *The Chelsea Girls* (1966), that describes underground cinema as a

> national expression of a class: the young American dropouts who call all others copouts, the generation turned on, in and under; that subspecies at once passive and hysterical, sagacious and silly; that cadre of bizarre haberdashers who make far-out threads to replace the emperor's new clothes.[15]

Is the counterculture audience associated with the Hollywood Renaissance already in place as the audience previously associated with underground films? The following year *Newsweek* was still reporting on the underground which it then was calling 'the new American cinema' and 'the American anti-establishment filmmaking movement'[16] and despite the overlap in terminology between the underground cinema and what would be called problematically the 'New Hollywood' (since the term would come to include both Hollywood Renaissance films and later 1970s blockbusters) within the space of a year, connections between them were surprisingly mute even though they shared the same imaginary countercultural audience. *Time* magazine has inadvertently set the standard by which most academic accounts of the historical period tend towards a European cinema default.

Thomas Elsaesser's landmark essay from 1975, 'The Pathos of Failure', consolidated this position in reducing the experimental techniques in the Hollywood Renaissance to a game of spotting where devices already appear in European cinema.[17] While it would be an ambitious endeavour to detail every instance in which his critical manoeuvre has become a given, it is worth briefly mentioning Paul Monaco's *The Sixties* as exemplary of simultaneously including and excluding underground cinema.[18] A rich historical overview of American cinema in the 1960s, especially attentive to innovation, the final chapter on the American avant-garde is positioned hermetically in that it has no bearing on, for example, the earlier chapters such as 'Landmark movies of the 1960s' which fail to include any non-commercial features such as *Empire* (Andy Warhol, 1964), *Scorpio Rising* (Kenneth Anger, 1963), or *Wavelength* (Michael Snow, 1967).

The few exceptions to all this are David James' *Allegories of Cinema: American Film in the Sixties*[19] and Jonathan Rosenbaum's 'New Hollywood and the Sixties Melting Pot'[20] both of which detail how aspects of underground cinema were appropriated, for example, the use of pop music in *Scorpio Rising* taken up later in *Easy Rider*. Dennis Hopper is something of a bridge between underground and Hollywood, having appeared as a youth in *Rebel Without a Cause* (Nicholas Ray, 1955) and then later in a very early Warhol film shot in Los Angeles called *Tarzan and Jane Regained, Sort Of* (Andy Warhol, 1963). Hopper's own *Easy Rider*, in which the graveyard trip is rumoured to have been filmed by Bruce Conner, rather than being part of László Kovács innovative cinematography, has been excoriated by David James, calling Hopper's film 'a 35mm ersatz underground film'[21] that liberally borrows underground 'filmic codes' but 'fails to assimilate' them, 'remains a pastiche' and is 'essentially an orthodox industrial product'.[22]

Midnight Cowboy's *underground party*

A good deal can be gleaned from *Midnight Cowboy*'s relationship with, and Hollywood's attitude to, underground cinema through a key sequence in the film, one that brought the film's production in direct contact with the underground milieu of Warhol's Factory and its denizens. Two-thirds through *Midnight Cowboy*, Joe and Ratso are sitting in a diner as two beatnik-type individuals appear, dressed head to toe in black with high-necked knits (that remains Hollywood code for beatniks and oddballs even to this day). One of them, a young man called Hansel (Gastone Rassilli), intrusively begins snapping Joe with his camera and the other, a filmmaker called Gretel, played by the actual Warhol superstar Viva, gives Joe a flyer. They do not exchange any words; these 'fruity wackos', aloof, just saunter away. The flyer, 'a come-on to a party', according to Joe, is illustrated with a pagan sex scene over a cauldron with the words 'join us at the gates of hell' scrawled in large letters. It is an invitation to a downtown party that will stand in for Andy Warhol's Factory, his people and the underground film scene (see Figure 8.2).

Joe and Ratso head to the party trawling through the wintery streets of New York and ascend into the tenement. Ratso falters on the stairs due to his increasingly ill health and Joe supports him in one of many tender moments between them. Once they reach their destination, Joe opens the door into another cultural and social milieu. Hansel and Gretel are there filming, one individual is holding a light, while another is sitting on top of a ladder holding a noose. People are dancing, many dressed oddly by normative standards. Some look wealthy in their pearls and furs, others are clad in black leather, while many obvious homosexuals swish about. After a scan of the crowded party scene Schlesinger cuts to point-of-view of what Gretel captures through her 16mm camera. Schlesinger's film presents her 'underground movie' as a frame-within-the-frame surrounded by an out-of-focus border that helps fill out the ratio of *Midnight Cowboy*'s own commercial 35mm framing. But it also draws a sharp contrast between the mock amateurishness of the underground, the diminished spectacle of its 16mm 'square' format and the apparent grandiose polish of the Hollywood film that contains it. 'They're all wackos', Ratso declares as well as pointing out 'Hansel's a fag' as the scene cuts to another Warhol superstar (Ultra Violet) cramming a slice of salami in her mouth.

Figure 8.2 Party flyer. Copyright MGM.

Midnight Cowboy flips back to the underground film which now appears to be a series of interviews with pretentious espousals such as 'death is like heroin'. One can spot some of the Warhol crowd as extras, like Taylor Mead, and the underground movie includes one of Warhol's acid-coloured Marilyn images in the background as if to reinforce the obvious point that this scene stands in for The Factory (see Figure 8.3). Joe eventually strikes up a conversation with one of the partygoers, Shirley (Brenda Vaccaro), her style closely modelled on Edie Sedgwick with trademark large droop earrings. Both now watch the projection of another underground film, this one a vaguely kinky black and white film, as Shirley passes Joe a joint. The music is a cacophony to register both the weirdness of the scene and to hint at The Velvet Underground, *contra* the rest of the John Barry soundtrack, and Joe's disorientation as he comes-on from the drugs. This is accompanied by several experimental dissolves that lead to another type of underground movie, a materialist film of abstract composition. The effect of this experimentation in *Midnight Cowboy* is to fold the formal register of underground cinema's codes into its own expression, not dissimilar to the way in which the graveyard trip appears in *Easy Rider*.

The borrowing or aping of this style, referred to by Parker Tyler as 'drugtime', one that imitates the temporality of being on drugs, helps to convey the disorientation of Joe and the spectator and simultaneously gestures towards the alterity of non-Hollywood cinemas.[23] What brings Joe and the spectator back to reality, back to *Midnight Cowboy*'s normative time of the film itself, is Ratso's pickpocketing the guests and ransacking the buffet. The editing flips back to being elliptical and rapid here as Ratso becomes increasingly paranoid and the scene shifts to a brief speeded-up sequence, before descending yet again into more experimental editing techniques and temporal disjuncture and a swerving peripatetic camera that tries to imitate the 'bad camerawork' style of Warhol's

Figure 8.3 Underground party. Copyright MGM.

The Chelsea Girls. The party sequence ends on the stairs where it began, visually equating the descent as the come-down from the party. Ratso is negotiating the cost of Joe's services with socialite Shirley, 'twenty bucks', which leads to another sexual encounter in which the value of Joe's masculinity and prowess are put to the test.

The party sequence attempts to provide both a snapshot of the Warhol Factory scene and a pastiche of underground film style. Through the success of *The Chelsea Girls*, Warhol was involved in providing not only inspiration for the sequence but also numerous extras drawn from The Factory. While *Midnight Cowboy* represents this as a druggy, pan-sexual, far-out setting to which neither Joe not Ratso truly belong, history has accounted for The Factory and the New York avant-garde as one of the most important intersections of artistic, cultural and social life in the 1960s.[24]

The underground filmmaker in the sequence (see Figure 8.4) was originally to be played by Warhol himself, but during *Midnight Cowboy*'s production Warhol was shot by Valerie Solanos. As Warhol recounts:

> While I was in hospital, Paul [Morrissey] gave me reports in the local filming of John Schlesinger's *Midnight Cowboy*. Before I was shot, they'd asked me to play the underground filmmaker in the big party scene, and I'd suggested Viva for the part instead. They liked the idea of that. And then John Schlesinger had asked Paul to make an 'underground movie' to be shown during the 'underground party' scene, so Paul went and filmed Ultra for that.[25]

There is no evidence as to whether the underground films that appear in the party sequence were shot by Morrissey, Schlesinger or someone else. From the glimpses that we get they do not correspond to anything Warhol or

Figure 8.4 Underground filmmaker. Copyright MGM.

Morrissey filmed around 1968/69 or at any other time, leading one to speculate that they were put together by the *Midnight Cowboy* production team.

Along with the request to appear in *Midnight Cowboy* the film's producers also provided Warhol with a desired list of underground extras to populate the party. Callie Angell noted from a cast list held by the Andy Warhol Foundation for the Visual Arts, that list 'gives some idea of how Hollywood imagines the New York underground in 1968'.[26] *Midnight Cowboy*'s request was itemized and revealing in its wording ('dike' rather than 'dyke'), as well as making some ludicrous assumptions about who the people of the underground were:

- '6 male hippies'
- '9 female hippies'
- '2 hustlers'
- '1 poetic fag'
- '1 bum'
- '2 drag queens'
- '2 dike ladies'
- '6 social types'
- '3 black leather boys'
- '1 Buddha type pot roller'
- '1 super star'
- '1 American Indian woman'
- '2 student activists'
- '1 nude (painted) in a coffin'
- '1 fag hag'
- '6 chic hippies and theatricals'
- '5 high fashion types'
- '2 black nationals'
- 'A Polynesian prince'
- 'The Warhol/Morrissey film group'

Despite such a brazen request that Warhol provide so many 'wackos', surprisingly, those who did turn up on the *Midnight Cowboy* set wishing to appear in the film were not included in the final cut while many of those who were included and are recognizable in the sequence, ended up not being credited. Paul Morrissey, flabbergasted, was updating the hospitalized Warhol on the treatment of the superstars. Warhol recounts what Morrissey told him on the phone while still in hospital:

> Hollywood's just gotten around to doing a movie about a 42nd Street male hustler, and we did ours in '65. And there are all *our* great New York people sitting on *their* set all day – Geraldine, Joe, Ondine, Pat Ast, Taylor, Candy, Jackie, Geri Miller, Patti D'Arbanville – and they never even get around to using them . . .[27]

The frustration that Morrissey expresses here to Warhol about their 'great New York people sitting on *their* set' reveals some of the inequities between underground and Hollywood cinema. The reduction of underground stars to mere extras in a Hollywood film, then not being used, and the central figure of *their* hustler holding together a plot, having already played out in *My Hustler* (Warhol, 1965), was simply too much for Warhol:

> I had the same jealous feeling thinking about *Midnight Cowboy* that I had when I saw *Hair* and realized that the people with money were taking the subject matter of the underground, counterculture life and giving it a good, slick, commercial treatment. [...] But now that Hollywood – and Broadway, too – was dealing with those same subjects, things were getting a little confused ... I realized that with both Hollywood and the underground making films about male hustlers – even though the two treatments couldn't have been more different – it took away a real drawing card from the underground, because people would much rather go see the treatment that *looked* better. [...] I kept feeling, 'they're moving into our territory'.[28]

For Warhol, thematically at least, Hollywood was appropriating elements of the underground that was at the very least frustrating given that underground cinema had been making films about 42nd Street hustlers several years before *Midnight Cowboy*. The party sequence is striking and it is likely that the Warhol connections would have been obvious to audiences at the time since Warhol and his entourage were regularly covered by the news, certainly in New York. Viva was appearing both in *Nude Restaurant* (Andy Warhol, 1967) and *Lonesome Cowboys* (Andy Warhol, 1968) which were still in circulation in the city throughout 1969. An articulate, erudite raconteur known for her ability to talk for long stretches of unedited time usually in the nude is used in *Midnight Cowboy*, as *The New York Times* succinctly puts it, as 'a "Village" zombie with none of the flair she exhibits in Andy Warhol's improvisations'.[29]

Nonetheless, the closest audiences might have come to The Factory is through its representations in Hollywood films.[30] *Variety's* review of *Midnight Cowboy* also made note of the party sequence:

> 'The Party' sequence will be much discussed. It is openly a burlesque Andy Warhol who, of course, is burlesque to start with. Here production becomes 'busy' with weirdo characters criss-crossed with psychedelic fades, jumps, jumbles and sound effects mixed with John Barry-supervised music. All of which seems typical of present-day cinematic preoccupation with orgy. Schlesinger has borrowed some of Warhol's 'stock company' players. But the orgy is grafted onto the story, principally as the obligatory scene for a slumming franchise.[31]

In framing the references to Warhol's underground as a quasi-orgiastic encounter with 'wackos', *Midnight Cowboy* not only mocks the avant-garde as an artists' cinema but appears to disavow the underground as a source upon which the Hollywood Renaissance draws. This is what irked Warhol so much. *Midnight Cowboy* is disparaging in its representation of the avant-garde culture in New York, yet it draws upon it for sensation, transgression and formal experimentation. The underground appears silly and pretentious and is reduced to some stock extras and a less than effective series of undefined pseudo 'underground movies' and editing tricks. This strategy appears to discount the very cinematic influences that lend shape to *Midnight Cowboy* and other films of the period. This is both a 'moving into our territory' as Warhol claims and a burying of the underground's thematic and formal influences. More than just a reference to *My Hustler*, the failure of Joe Buck to follow up on his sexual boastfulness with Shirley had also been staged by Warhol and Edie Sedgwick in the feature-length *Beauty No.2* (Andy Warhol, 1965), shown in New York in the latter half of 1965. While it is unlikely that Schlesinger had seen this film since its release took place between Schlesinger making his British films *Billy Liar* (1963) and *Darling* (1966), nonetheless it accounts for how much of the Hollywood Renaissance depends on or alludes to material already well-rehearsed in underground cinema.

'Moving into our territory': Warhol, Flesh *and* Midnight Cowboy

The staging of the party sequence, the hustler as a central protagonist, the use of experimental film style – *Midnight Cowboy* seems to commercialize elements of underground cinema that can be utilized by Hollywood in ways that allow for claims of a formally/thematically progressive cinema to emerge in an industrial, capitalized context. The appeal of the Hollywood Renaissance is often in its purported radical break from the classical tradition; such anti-classicism and personalized vision appears to transcend its industrial basis as a wholly commercial enterprise and instead align with countercultural politics.

While one might consider the Hollywood Renaissance as having experimental ambitions, the underground's own trajectory, for Warhol at least, was to move towards a commercial underground cinema. Warhol's frustration with *Midnight Cowboy* and 'mainstream' culture moving into their 'territory' was exacerbated by his own ambitions to continue making money from underground cinema. Following the success of *The Chelsea Girls* which was widely reviewed at a time when underground cinema was brought increasingly to the attention of filmgoers at large as well as readers of national papers and weekly magazines. To understand the production of Warhol's *Flesh* as a reaction to *Midnight Cowboy* and the presence of underground cinema in the wider film culture of the 1960s, it is useful to account for how important *The Chelsea Girls* was as the first underground film to be widely seen and make a substantial profit, and the most likely underground film to have influenced American film culture at the time.

The Chelsea Girls was in circulation in 1966 and 1967 and the development of its notoriety and critical reception as an underground sensation became part of its advertising campaign with a famous *Newsweek* quote referring to the film as 'The Iliad of the Underground'.[32] *The Chelsea Girls* was indicative of the potential ascent of underground cinema towards a lucrative independent film sector or at least something that could generate audience interest among a demographic that otherwise wouldn't have paid any heed to underground or avant-garde filmmaking. *The Chelsea Girls'* success pressed Warhol into making underground sexploitation films destined for theatrical exhibition to commercialize his own moviemaking at least through a proper production, distribution and exhibition chain.

The films to emerge from this 1967–8 filmmaking period in Warhol's movie career, *Bike Boy, Tub Girls, Nude Restaurant, I, a Man, Loves of Ondine* and *Lonesome Cowboys* were critically trashed by mainstream and trade press as just bad filmmaking, nearly all of them excoriated by *Variety*, and rejected by the avant-garde as crass commercial features with no artistic merit. Nonetheless, Warhol made these films as there was an assumed demand for more underground films in regular theatre chains. *The Chelsea Girls* suggested a moment at which those films might become both popular and commercially viable, and the press was keen to make sense of the popularity in this otherwise, true to its name, underground cinema.

The 13 February 1967 issue of *Newsweek* declares in its title 'Up from Underground', noting that 'head spinning offers for it have come to the money-starved Filmmakers Cooperative from the big distribution chains, such as United Artists and Twentieth-Century Fox, including one of $100,000 from Trans Lux Corp'[33]. In the opening of his article Jack Kroll goes on to describe the underground as follows:

> the American anti-establishment filmmaking movement, with its hock-shop cameras, surplus film stock and hole-in-corner cinematheques, has grown steadily in numbers, self-awareness, audacity and importance. It is now as significant as the more organized, recognized, and 'official' avant-garde movements in other arts, which are changing the face of culture in this country. And, with the unprecedented financial success of Andy Warhol's film 'The Chelsea Girls' (*Newsweek*, Nov. 14, 1966), the underground has at last surfaced and is moving into public consciousness with a vengeance.[34]

The article is both an explanation of the underground cinema and a cautionary note on what could be coming to American screens if the success of *The Chelsea Girls* was the beginning of a new trend. Regular audiences better be prepared:

moviegoers, used to the machine tooled technique of Hollywood, are in for some shocks. They will see badly exposed shots, pimply faces with no make-up, very odd faces with too much make-up, amateur actors, no actors, shots held for unchanging hours, shots held for 1/24th of a second, and sometimes no shots at all but a blank screen.[35]

Kroll's *Newsweek* article is knowledgeable in its account of underground cinema and audience preparation for what eventually did not arrive on American screens, a commercial underground cinema. It is also one of many popular opinion pieces and reports in weeklies and newspapers across the US on the new visibility and imagined consequences of underground cinema seemingly taking hold in mainstream American movie culture at the time. And while Kroll's article is rather generous in its account, most of the pieces tend towards mocking explanation and hyperbolic exposé of the underground, often expressed through perplexity, hostility or condemnation that underground cinema is 'daring to do what Hollywood won't. What the dream factories of Culver City won't produce.'[36] The writer of the article 'Underground Films: Art or Naughty Movies' opens his piece with the following:

> You won't see Rock Hudson or Doris Day in any of these pictures; you may not always see a clear image; the camera angles may be peculiar and the colors; if they have it, may not be the best; the actors aren't too professional and the sets are not what you would call DeMille. But what you will see in the new wave of Underground films you will never forget.[37]

Underground cinema is often unfairly compared to the polish of Hollywood but also the apparently good morality it presents in its films, still affected then by the waning Production Code ethos. One way to denounce the underground is to play up the lack of censorship, the nudity and the homosexuality, by associating the films not with art but with pornography. This seems to be underground cinema's treatment by gossipy film magazines like *Confidential* which were all too keen to exploit the gay aspects of underground cinema and provide lurid descriptions of scenes from Warhol movies where the stars are 'calling each other things like "worn-out slut", "dirty bitch", "faded faggot" and other epithets the average moviegoer never gets to hear'.[38] The June 1967 issue of *Confidential* asks 'are the underground movies dirty, dirtier, dirtiest? Millionaires, geniuses, nuts and pornographers are taking over the kooky film world'[39]; 'this is not tinsel and glitter Hollywood or even bold and brooding, *dolce* Ponti, European movie-making'.[40]

Yet, despite the sensational rhetoric with which *Confidential* characterizes underground cinema, more licentious than European cinema, connections with Hollywood are being noted in relation to its potential influence as the article notes towards the end that 'it obviously has something to say to Hollywood visitors like Elia Kazan, Sidney Lumet, and Arthur Penn who have shown a great deal of interest in this New Cinema'.[41] There is a suggestion in many of the articles that the underground will have an effect on Hollywood, with the emergence of the Hollywood Renaissance being in part a consequence of this. But as I argued, Hollywood embraces some of the gains made by the underground cinema while downplaying its influence, and the influence of openly gay filmmakers like Warhol, effectively bringing it to an end before it even set foot on the road to commercial viability. Warhol was right in assuming that audiences would still prefer to see a polished movie about a hustler than his talky, unedited, ostentatiously gay, black and white movie *My Hustler*. But, for a moment, before the Hollywood Renaissance took its shape, there was a possibility that underground cinema might, as *The Toledo Blade* put it, 'move upstairs'.[42]

The *Midnight Cowboy* reports that Warhol received while recuperating in hospital, that Hollywood was making its own hustler movie with some of his superstars as background scenery, coupled with the media context in which underground cinema's press coverage was of national interest, constitute the point of genesis of the Morrissey-directed Warhol-produced *Flesh*. *Flesh* was put into production and came out before *Midnight Cowboy* as a 'this is how we do it in the underground' response to the territorial hijacking of the cinematic hustler. Warhol took out a full page advert in the *Village Voice* on September 1968 announcing 'Andy Warhol Presents Joe Dallesandro in *Flesh* in Color playing at the New Andy Warhol Garrick Theatre, 152 Bleecker Street, Air Conditioned'.[43] The advert appeared eight months before *Midnight Cowboy's* premiere in May 1969 with an image of Joe Dallesandro from Warhol's *Lonesome Cowboys*.[44] *Flesh* was filmed over a number of weekends in the summer of 1968 at a cost of $4,000.[45] It would run consecutively in New York for seven months at the Garrick Theatre in Greenwich Village from September 1968.[46]

Flesh, the first Warhol film directed by Paul Morrissey, opens with an extended scene of Joe Dallesandro sleeping naked in bed face down with everything *a tergo* exposed to the audience (see Figure 8.5). Uninhibited in its representation of male frontal and rear nudity, a taboo Hollywood was still unable to transgress except for some glimpses and long shots in scenes from *Medium Cool* (Haskell Wexler, 1969) and *Drive, He Said* (Jack Nicholson, 1971), *Flesh* asserts its underground credentials through the liberties it takes in Morrissey's filming the male body in a sustained and intimate way that is mutually supported by Dallesandro's uninhibited display as the film's hustler protagonist.

Flesh is a barely sketched day-in-the-life-of story in which Joe's wife sends him out to hustle to pay for *her* girlfriend's (then illegal) abortion. Knowing that Joe is good trade she gets him out of bed by tying a ribbon around his penis which results in an authentic on-screen erection dealt with in a rather matter of fact manner. Erections and male nudity are not particularly special nor out of place in underground cinema but unavailable to Hollywood audiences. The rest of the running time is Joe's encounters with various homo, hetero and

Figure 8.5 *Flesh*. Copyright The Andy Warhol Museum, Pittsburgh, PA, a museum of Carnegie Institute.

transgender friends and tricks. Unlike *Midnight Cowboy*, none of these encounters in *Flesh* is problematic or traumatic since hustling and sexuality are at home in the underground whereas in Hollywood they constitute a remote and unfortunate métier for its male protagonist, they are treated with caution and reluctance, in the sense that they question the fixity of heterosexuality and reveal its fragile construction.

Midnight Cowboy may ask us how unfortunate it is for a man to prostitute himself to make his way in the world. To counter-balance this ideological burden on masculinity and heterosexuality, *Midnight Cowboy* repeatedly points out the 'faggot stuff', the 'tutti-fruttis', and that which is 'strictly for fags'. The fact that cowboy-attire as mere style rather than function, history or labour has currency as homosexual erotic fantasy is as much a revelation for Joe Buck as it is for, one assumes, the audience of *True Grit*. When Joe says, 'John Wayne. You gonna tell me he's a fag', *Midnight Cowboy* 'outs' post-war gay culture's cultural production and erotic fascination with cowboys but with considerable anxiety that also explains the consistent homophobic tone of the film and the representation of all its homosexuals as tragic and self-loathing.

Another example in the late 1960s that comments on this period of transition for the cowboy in American cinema and works hard to deeply contrast this homosexualization, and 'ins' rather than 'outs' the cowboy is *Coogan's Bluff* (Don Siegel, 1968) featuring Clint Eastwood as Arizona Sheriff Coogan who heads to countercultural New York to extradite a killer. Like Joe Buck, Eastwood's southern Coogan is out of place in late 1960s New York and, like *Midnight Cowboy*, *Coogan's Bluff* contains its own Hollywood fantasy of a countercultural party scene. Psychedelic, youth-oriented, a touch of lesbianism, with an underground movie playing, Siegel's camera swerves and loops to capture the odd angles, rapid cutting and arbitrarily intercut images in a softer version of 'drugtime'. The partygoers are dressed in kaftans, *Sgt. Pepper* get-ups, flower motifs and painted faces as befits the population of extras in these scenes. Coogan's limits are tested as he enters the club's pot-den and in some pre-emptive *Dirty Harry* (Don Siegel, 1971) justice, metes out violence to disrespectful hippies.

Midnight Cowboy's sexual irregularities are partly explained in the continuum of trauma that characterizes Joe Buck's flashbacks, told in an elliptical experimental black and white style, in which we assume he was raped along with his 'nymphomaniac' girlfriend. His childhood also includes a sexually active grandmother, absent parents, a Freudian psychodrama that renders Joe excessively paranoid in relation to his own masculinity and (we assume) latent homosexuality that often results in violence towards other men who show signs of sexual interest. Joe and Ratso's bond, and their shared intimacy and tragic domesticity, a theme that characterizes the film as progressive in the eyes of scholars like Moon,[47] is difficult to accept since it also depends on the characters' demonstrable homophobia and messed-up-ness. Hustling is fraught for Joe, it triggers his childhood traumas, when sex enters relations with other men and women. Even his heterosexual encounters are problematic despite the fact that he does not have the perspicuity of those he is servicing.

His first sexual exchange with a young gay man (Bob Balaban), rather than his imagined fantasy of wealthy, horny New York women, occurs in a cinema showing a science-fiction B-movie. It is significant that Joe's first gay hustle happens when he reaches his lowest point in New York; down and out, he is in a desperate state. Only then does he trade for those most interested in his cowboy package. The science-fiction film playing in the cinema is indicative of how out of this world and alien such an experience is for Joe; it needs to be coded by *Midnight Cowboy* as something akin to science fiction. Paradoxically, while homosexual sex, hustling and underground cinema are source material for *Midnight Cowboy* it is, like Joe's first blow-job from another man, alien, remote and demeaning. They represent experiences than can only end badly and for which a 1969 X-rating is most definitely required. Indeed, the film was originally given an R-rating but after consultation with a psychiatrist at Columbia University, the rating was changed to 'X'.[48] Homosexuality was still defined as a mental health disorder by the American Psychiatric Association, which, concerned with the film's 'homosexual frame of reference' and the 'adverse effect' on youth audiences, recommended an increase from an R to X rating.[49] As is often noted, *Midnight Cowboy* was the first and last X-rated Hollywood film to win an Academy Award but it would not be last film to win for the portrayal of tragic homosexuals.

Conclusion

Besides the now famous article on the Hollywood Renaissance in *Time* magazine, 1967 saw also the publication of Gregory Battcock's anthology *The New American Cinema*.[50] The volume presented itself as a paradigm shift in the definition of 'American cinema' through a politicized anti-Hollywood rhetoric that instead favoured the terms 'independence', 'art' and 'authorship'. Battcock assembled previously published work on underground cinema (by authors including Jonas Mekas and himself), experimental and avant-garde film (by Amos Vogel, P. Adams Sitney, Annette Michelson), independent cinema (Andrew Sarris), essays written by filmmakers (Gregory Markopoulos, Stan Brakhage, Stan VanDerBeek), as well as Susan Sontag. Battcock's anthology sought to establish a critical discourse and an alternative to Hollywood in challenging the studios as the sole definition of American cinema. Left-leaning and antagonistic towards Hollywood as materialistic, industrialized, commercialized, bland, the writing was all published between 1963 and 1966 in the era in which *Cleopatra* (Joseph L. Mankiewicz, 1963), *It's a Mad, Mad, Mad, Mad World* (Stanley Kramer, 1963), *Mary Poppins* (Louis Stevenson, 1964) and *Hawaii* (George Roy Hill, 1966) dominated the box-office while fractious internal politics and ideological confidence in the US was changing through civil rights, second wave feminism and the discontent with the war in Vietnam. What the authors in *The New American Cinema* could not foresee in their hopefulness was the end of underground cinema through its appropriation and re-contextualization in the Hollywood Renaissance. As Suárez writes in the year that followed:

> The momentum of the American underground was over by 1968. By then, the alliance of formal innovation, playful/satirical attitudes towards mass culture, and sexual, social, and political protest that converged in the underground had dissolved, but each of these components survived separately in other arenas of discourse.[51]

As usual, Warhol was prophetic on this matter. 'People would much rather go see the treatment that *looked* better'.[52] Instead, Warhol established *Inter/View* in 1969. Initially a film magazine it is still in circulation today as a fashion magazine. In the June 1976 issue, Warhol interviewed Dustin Hoffman at the time he was filming John Schlesinger's *Marathon Man* (1976). They didn't discuss *Midnight Cowboy*.

Notes

1   John Rechy, *City of Night* (New York: Grove Press, 1963), 129.
2   Barry Reay, *New York Hustlers: Masculinity and Sex in Modern America* (Manchester: Manchester University Press, 2010).

3 Richard Dyer, *Now You See It: Studies in Lesbian and Gay Film* (London: Routledge, 2002), 140.

4 Kevin Floyd, *The Reification of Desire: Towards a Queer Marxism* (Minneapolis: University of Minnesota Press, 2009), 175.

5 Michael Moon, *A Small Boy and Others: Imitation and Initiation in American Culture from Henry James to Andy Warhol* (Durham, NC: Duke University Press, 1998), 120.

6 Floyd, *The Reification of Desire,* 156.

7 *Another Country* (James Baldwin, 1962), *City of Night* (John Rechy, 1963) and *Last Exit to Brooklyn* (Hubert Selby, 1965), to name only a few.

8 Ian Buruma, *Conversations with John Schlesigner* (New York: Random House, 2006), 75.

9 See, for instance, Yannis Tzioumakis, *American Independent Cinema*, 2nd Edition (Edinburgh: Edinburgh University Press, 2017), 156, in which he discusses the Hollywood Renaissance as a marriage between independent cinema, exploitation strategies and arthouse techniques.

10 Peter Krämer, *The New Hollywood from Bonnie and Clyde to Star Wars* (London: Wallflower, 2006), 67.

11 Geoffrey Nowell-Smith and Steven Ricci (ed.), *Hollywood and Europe: Economics, Culture, and National Identity, 1945–95* (London: BFI, 1998); James Morrison, *Passport to Hollywood: Hollywood Film, European Directors* (Albany, NY: SUNY Press, 1998).

12 'Edie & Andy', *Time,* 27 August 1965, 65–7.

13 'Report from the Undergound', *Life,* 29 January 1965, 23.

14 Rosalind Constable, 'Avant-Garde Fun for the Family', *Life,* 23 April 1965, 71.

15 Joseph Morgenstern, 'Underground in Hell', *Newsweek,* 14 November 1966, 109.

16 Jack Kroll, 'Up from the Underground', *Newsweek,* 13 February 1967, 117.

17 Thomas Elsaesser, 'The Pathos of Failure: American Films in the 1970s', in *The Last Great American Picture Show,* ed. Thomas Elsaesser, Alexander Horwath and Noel King (Amsterdam: Amsterdam University Press, 2004), 279–92.

18 Paul Monaco, *The Sixties 1960–1969* (Berkeley: University of California Press, 2001).

19 David E. James, *Allegories of Cinema: American Film in the Sixties* (New Brunswick, NJ: Princeton University Press, 1989).

20 Jonathan Rosenbaum, 'New Hollywood and the Sixties Melting Pot', in *The Last Great American Picture Show,* ed. Thomas Elsaesser, Alexander Horwath and Noel King (Amsterdam: Amsterdam University Press, 2004), 131–52.

21 James, *Allegories of Cinema,* 14.

22 James, *Allegories of Cinema,* 16.

23 Tyler's concept of 'drugtime' is a temporality of underground cinema as 'the time of sublimated leisure: *all the time in the world'* and is a formal expression in underground cinema that is equated with a trip or a drug experience in which time is not experienced conventionally as real-time or teleological time. Parker Tyler, 'Dragtime and Drugtime; Or, Film a la Warhol', *Evergreen Review* 11, no. 46, (1967): 28–9, 87–8.

24 Sally Banes, *Greenwich Village 1963* (Durham, NC: Duke University Press, 1993); Caroline Jones, *Machine in the Studio: Constructing the Postwar American Artist* (Chicago: University of Chicago Press, 1996), 189–267; Steven Watson, *Factory*

Made: Warhol and the Sixties (New York: Pantheon Books, 2003); and Sarah Glennie and Emer McGarry (ed.), *The Eternal Now: Warhol and the Factory '63–'68* (Birmingham: Ikon, 2008).

25 Andy Warhol and Pat Hackett, *POPism: The Warhol Sixties* (New York: Harcourt Brace, 1980), 280.

26 Callie Angell, *The Films of Andy Warhol: Part II* (New York: Whitney Museum, 1994), 35.

27 Morrissey quoted in Warhol and Hackett, *POPism*, 281.

28 Warhol and Hackett, *POPism*, 280.

29 Vincent Canby, 'Midnight Cowboy', *New York Times*, 26 May 1969, http://www.nytimes.com/movie/review?res=EE05E7DF1730E56EBC4E51DFB3668382679EDE

30 Representations of The Factory still continues as Warhol's scene is proffered as source material for popular texts as diverse as *Men in Black 3* (Barry Sonnenfeld, 2012) and *Mad Men* (AMC, 2007–2015).

31 Robert Landry, 'Midnight Cowboy', *Variety*, 14 May 1969, http://variety.com/1969/film/reviews/midnight-cowboy-review-1200421996/

32 Kroll, 'Up from the Underground', 117.

33 Kroll, 'Up from the Underground', 117–19.

34 Kroll, 'Up from the Underground', 117.

35 Kroll, 'Up from the Underground', 117.

36 Douglas Arango, 'Underground Films: Art or Naughty Movies', *Movie TV Secrets*, June 1967, 29.

37 Arango, 'Underground Films', 29.

38 Bruce Normale, 'Coming: Homosexual Action Movies', *Confidential*, February 1968, 13.

39 Christine Jaegger, 'Are the Underground Movies Dirty, Dirtier, Dirtiest?', *Confidential*, June 1967, 34.

40 Jaegger, 'Are the Underground Movies Dirty', 43.

41 Jaegger, 'Are the Underground Movies Dirty', 44.

42 Bob Thomas, 'Underground Movie Fad: Cellar Cinema Moves Upstairs', *The Toledo Blade*, 7 January 1968, 3.

43 The advert appears on page 55 of the *Village Voice*, 26 September 1968.

44 Warhol didn't release films chronologically so *Flesh* would be exhibited at the same time as a number of other Warhol productions from the 1967/68 period including *Bike Boy, Nude Restaurant, I, a Man, Lonesome Cowboys, Blue Movie, Loves of Ondine, Imitation of Christ* and *Tub Girls*. *Flesh* would be the longest in circulation and unlike most of the other 'sexploitation film' was distributed outside the US.

45 Victor Bockris, *Warhol: The Biography* (Cambridge: Da Capo Press, 1997), 309.

46 Copy from newspaper ad in *Village Voice*, 13 March 1969.

47 Moon, *A Small Boy and Others*, 117–32.

48 Tino Balio, *United Artists: The Company Built by the Stars Volume 2: 1951–1978* (Madison: University of Wisconsin Press, 1987), 293.

49 Balio, *United Artists*, 293.

50 Gregory Battcock (ed.), *The New American Cinema: A Critical Anthology* (New York: Dutton & Co., 1967).

51 Juan A. Suárez, *Bike Boys, Drag Queens, and Super Stars: Avant-Garde, Mass Culture, and Gay Identities in Underground Cinema* (Bloomington: Indiana University Press, 1996), 260.

52 Warhol and Hackett, *POPism*, 280.

Chapter 9

ZABRISKIE POINT (1970), MICHELANGELO ANTONIONI AND EUROPEAN DIRECTORS IN HOLLYWOOD

Melis Behlil

Among the films covered in this volume, Italian auteur Michelangelo Antonioni's *Zabriskie Point* both fits a norm and constitutes an anomaly. Its narrative of rebellious young people in love (or at least making love) and trying to make sense of the world is familiar from many of the other Hollywood Renaissance films, so is its non-traditional style that defies Classical Hollywood conventions. But it is also the only film in this volume that is directed by a European bona-fide 'art cinema' director; although both the British John Schlesinger (*Midnight Cowboy*) and Canadian-born Sidney J. Furie (*Lady Sings the Blues*) were part of the British realist movement in the early 1960s, the UK film industry has long been inextricably tied to Hollywood studios. And perhaps most interestingly, *Zabriskie Point* is the only massive flop among the thirteen films discussed in this volume. Not only was it panned universally by critics,[1] but it also grossed only $900,000 on an estimated budget of $7 million.[2]

Hollywood has always had a close relationship with filmmakers from Europe. Even before the famed 1930s and 1940s 'émigré' generation of directors like Billy Wilder and Fritz Lang, numerous pioneers of 1920s European cinema, including Friedrich Wilhelm Murnau, Paul Leni and Victor Sjöstörm had been lured to work in the US for major studios. After the Second World War, the studios faced a number of challenges and the westward flow of talent diminished somewhat until the mid-1970s, with a few exceptions. By that time, Hollywood had undergone major changes. The studios had experienced a major recession in the 1969–71 period, while the abolition of the Production Code and the introduction of the ratings system in 1968 ushered in a period of uncertainty and experimentation. Around the same time, universities in the US started opening film departments. These would be instrumental in cultivating the next generation of American filmmakers, who were raised as cinephiles with a fondness for the post-war European art cinema.

It was then that some of the European filmmakers who had made their mark on world cinema in the late 1950s and 1960s started collaborating with Hollywood studios, but shooting their films in Europe. In 1966 François Truffaut directed *Fahrenheit 451* for Universal in the UK. The same year and in the same country, Michelangelo Antonioni made *Blow-Up* for Metro-Goldwyn-Mayer, a project developed by the famed Italian producer Carlo Ponti. Shot in swinging London, *Blow-Up* would be considered to be a part of the 'New Cinema' that inspired the Hollywood Renaissance according to the seminal *Time* cover story.[3] The film became a commercial success, the first in a three-picture deal for Antonioni with MGM. The other two films, *Zabriskie Point* and *The Passenger* (1975), did not do as well at the box office. Antonioni, not surprisingly, never became a mainstream Hollywood director and he continued his work in Europe. This, however, did not deter other renowned figures of European art cinema such as Ken Russell from Britain, Ingmar Bergman from Sweden, Louis Malle from France and Wim Wenders from Germany from working on Hollywood projects in the 1970s. They replicated the pattern of the 1920s, when bringing in directors from Europe had been a source of prestige for the studios. The partnerships in these cases, though, often ended quickly.

This chapter takes Antonioni's *Zabriskie Point* as its point of departure to discuss European directors in Hollywood. Their presence and influence were particularly important for the Hollywood Renaissance, considering that the Nouvelle Vague directly inspired *Bonnie and Clyde* (Arthur Penn, 1967). According to the *Time* article that gave the movement its name, the scriptwriters of the film, Robert Benton and David Newman 'began thinking about the movie [. . .] after mulling over the films of François Truffaut'.[4] When they approached Truffaut and were turned down, Jean-Luc Godard was their next choice; he agreed to do it, but eventually stepped out because of delays in production. It is useful to remember that of course both Truffaut's and Godard's cinema had been very much shaped by their love for the films of Hollywood's Classical era.

Like Truffaut and Godard, Antonioni was one of the inspirations for a decidedly new style of cinema adopted in Hollywood during this period. But at the same time, *Zabriskie Point* echoes some of the earlier Hollywood Renaissance films discussed in this volume, such as *Bonnie and Clyde* and *Easy Rider* (Dennis Hopper, 1969).[5] Thus, this chapter considers *Zabriskie Point* within a back-and-forth series of influences, but also positions Antonioni within the tradition of transferred European talent that Hollywood has long espoused. First, I briefly review the emigration patterns of earlier European filmmakers in Hollywood, dating back to the rise of the studios. This is a chance to show that the idea of employing European creative artists to garner prestige has been a part of the studio mentality from almost the very beginning. Then I examine the impact of Antonioni's *Blow-Up* as an example of a quintessential European art film exerting influence on the Hollywood Renaissance, which is particularly significant considering that it was the enormous success of that film which allowed the director to receive free rein once he arrived in the US to shoot

Zabriskie Point. I then focus on *Zabriskie Point*, exploring its narrative as well as its narration, concentrating on its kinship with other films of the Hollywood Renaissance. I conclude with an investigation of the negative reception of the film, which calls for a comparison with earlier as well as later European arthouse directors who have failed within the studio system.

European directors in Hollywood

Already in 1908, in the earliest days of the American film industry, when production was still concentrated on the East Coast of the US, the idea of 'importing' directing talent from Europe was proposed by an executive of the Edison Manufacturing Company.[6] Their search for a competent stage director in Paris was abortive, but it does demonstrate the beginning of a pattern. In the immediately following years, a number of French filmmakers including Alice Guy, her husband Herbert Blaché and Maurice Tourneur arrived on the East Coast to explore the American market for large French companies. Once the film industry moved to the West Coast, and the French film industry lost its importance after the First World War, Weimar Germany became the place where American producers primarily looked for new talent. In the 1920s, Germany had the largest film industry in Europe, the only one that could possibly challenge Hollywood. High-level executives from the American studios travelled to Europe for what Fritz Lang termed 'trophy-hunting'.[7] These hunts served two purposes: first, to make American pictures more popular worldwide and, second, to diminish Germany's role in the global film market. But except for Ernst Lubitsch and Michael Curtiz (Mihaly Kertész), the imported European filmmakers could not deliver the box-office success expected of them. These included Murnau and Leni, who both passed away at a young age in the US. Alexander Korda and Lothar Mendes went to the UK, while Ludwig Berger and Ewald André Dupont returned to Germany. Around the same time, Victor Sjöström (Seastrom) and Mauritz Stiller, who were among the 'founders' of Scandinavian cinema, were invited to work for the studios, but they also did not sustain Hollywood careers.

The apparent failure of these filmmakers is often ascribed to the opposing Hollywood and European styles of filmmaking. Invited to Hollywood on the strength of the films they had made in Europe, these directors were expected to remain European and be 'exotic', but at the same time to adapt to the norms and expectations of the American studios. Their motivation for going to Hollywood was largely economic and professional. Having been lured by higher budgets, more advanced technology and larger audiences,[8] and not being forced away from their homelands for political reasons, they were free to go home and continue their careers there, as some of them did. Others were not as lucky, particularly Murnau, who died in a car crash shortly before returning to Germany and became the romantic and sad example of a European artist who was destroyed by the Hollywood studio system. The Russian directors who emigrated to Hollywood in the same decade, such as Richard Boleslawski, Fyodor Otsep and Dimitri Buchovetski, soon adapted to Hollywood, occasionally even modifying the classically tragic endings of their films to happy ones. Unlike the Germans and the Swedes, they no longer could go back home, which had now become the USSR.

Following the Nazi party's seizure of power in Germany in 1933, the second large wave of European directors arrived in Hollywood. Billy Wilder, an iconic figure among these directors on account of his Jewish roots, early appearance and subsequent success, was one of the first to arrive via France in 1933. But it is important to keep in mind that although these directors left Germany and Austria (and in later years France and the Netherlands) for political reasons and to flee the war, quite a few of them probably would have made the transition to Hollywood even if the political climate had been different. Fred Zinnemann, who is often seen as a member of this group, arrived in the US as early as 1929 in order to find work as a cameraman.[9] When Fritz Lang signed his deal with David O. Selznick in 1934, there were other producers interested in him.[10] Otto Preminger was working in Viennese theatre when he was invited to work in Hollywood by Joseph Schenk in 1935.[11] Even Anatole Litvak, who had a particularly tumultuous life as a political refugee leaving Russia for Germany in the 1920s, and Germany for France in the 1930s, moved to the US upon being offered a four-year contract by Warner Bros. after the success of his hit *Mayerling* (1936).[12]

There were many more arrivals from Europe during the war, such as Robert Siodmak, Wilhelm Thiele and Douglas Sirk from Germany, and Max Ophuls, Jean Renoir, René Clair and Julien Duvivier from France. Many of the directors who had arrived in the US before and during the war subsequently remained there.[13] From the end of the war until the Hollywood Renaissance, however, there are only a few European filmmakers who went to work in Hollywood. David Lean and Carol Reed from Britain shot their Hollywood-backed films on location around the world without fully relocating to the US. Opportunities provided by British studios and the internationalization of film production during these decades resulted in a number of American directors preferring Europe as their shooting location instead. Early instances of runaway productions included films by émigré directors such as Wilder, Preminger and Zinnemann. Some of these directors had a great impact on European film culture, influencing authors of *Cahiers du cinéma* and ultimately, the Nouvelle Vague.

In the 1960s, as in the 1950s, Europeans who worked for Hollywood studios were largely British. Members of the social realist movement, Tony Richardson and Karel Reisz, were followed by John Boorman and Schlesinger.[14] This is a direct result of the close relations Britain has had with Hollywood. In 1966, 75 per cent of production financing in Britain came from Hollywood companies, and this went up to 90 per cent the following year.[15] British directors are often overlooked in the narratives of Europeans in Hollywood because of this embeddedness. But the strong presence of Hollywood studios in the UK also enabled Truffaut and Antonioni to work with the studios without relocating to the US in the 1960s, a practice that would continue in the following decades. In fact, with runaway productions becoming more and more commonplace, later continental European directors such as Paul Verhoeven and Uli Edel also shot their Hollywood debuts in Europe.[16]

Also in the 1960s, another transformation began in Hollywood that would change the structure of the industry. The studios, which used to be stand-alone units, faced financial challenges that forced them to be absorbed into larger corporations, mostly unrelated to cinema or even cultural industries. Throughout the 1960s, Universal was purchased by the Music Corporation of America, Paramount Pictures by Gulf + Western, Warner Bros. by Seven Arts and later by Kinney National Services, United Artists by the Transamerica Corporation and MGM by financier Kirk Kerkorian.[17] Over the next two decades, through a series of mergers and acquisitions, all studios ended up becoming parts of large multinational corporations like Sony and News Corp. As Hollywood evolved from being the shorthand for the American film industry into a global or multinational film culture,[18] the number of Europeans working in Hollywood rose enormously, joined by Asian and Latin American directors. Antonioni, however, had his American experience at a time when European art cinema still held its weight in the US market, Hollywood was still an 'American' cinema, and Europeans scarcely ventured out to the wild West.

Before Zabriskie Point

Michelangelo Antonioni started his cinematic career as a screenwriter and assistant director during the period of Italian Neorealism. His own films, from *Cronica di un amore* (1950) on and especially throughout the 1960s, broke with the neorealist tradition, in that they focused on individuals from the middle and upper classes and espoused a very formalist style that employed deep focus photography, long shots and long takes that made it virtually impossible to form a close relationship with the films' characters. Starting with *L'avventura* (1960), which was famously booed at Cannes but won a Jury Prize and was hailed as a masterpiece by the year's end, his films made Antonioni one of the leading figures of European art cinema, both in Europe and in the US. Martin Scorsese discusses *L'avventura, La notte* (1961) and *L'eclisse* (1962) as filmgoing experiences that 'haunted and inspired' him in his documentary on Italian cinema, *Il mio viaggio in Italia* (1999).

Following the success of his first colour film, *Il deserto rosso* (1964), Antonioni opened himself to international markets.[19] He was offered a three-picture deal by Carlo Ponti. These films would be shot in English and distributed by MGM, then headed by Robert O'Brien. The deal coincided with *Doctor*

Zhivago's (David Lean, 1965) massive success,[20] a project Ponti had brought to O'Brien. Ponti's pitch for *Doctor Zhivago* had been accepted by MGM on the condition that he secured David Lean as the director of the epic film; O'Brien was known to be 'one of the few studio bosses who inspired loyalty in his directors; he trusted [your] judgment', according to Stanley Kubrick.[21] This was at a time when MGM was having financial difficulties, and its only choice was to gamble, often on talent.[22]

The first of the three films in the Ponti-Antonioni-MGM deal was *Blow-Up*, based on a novel by Julio Cortázar and shot in London. Made for less than $2 million, the film was released in 1966 not only in arthouse theatres in the US but in first-run theatres, becoming the first European import to compete openly with Hollywood fare on American screens.[23] Antonioni had reportedly been given complete control over the production, over subject, script, actors and editing,[24] although other sources state that MGM held the rights to final cut, but acceded to Antonioni's wishes.[25] The *Time* article that gave the Hollywood Renaissance its name a year later states: 'The New Cinema has been displayed on US screens recently with astonishing variety and virtuosity. Michelangelo Antonioni parodied the modish artsiness of fashion photography to help create the swinging London mood of *Blow-Up*.' The article continues with comments on *The Battle of Algiers* (1967) by 'Italy's Gillo Pontecorvo', practically establishing Antonioni as a pan-European auteur without a nationality.[26]

Blow-Up became one of the defining films of the 1960s, of the mod sensibility, of cinematic self-reflexivity and of a freedom that was just reaching Hollywood. The direct influence of the film on the young generation of American filmmakers can be observed both in Francis Ford Coppola's *The Conversation* (1974) and in Brian De Palma's *Blow Out* (1981), which are aural variations on *Blow-Up*'s gradual visual discovery (see also Chapter 13 in this volume). *Blow-Up* was released without a Production Code Seal of Approval and was 'Condemned' by the Catholic Legion of Decency.[27] The lack of approval by the PCA and the Legion did not prevent it from becoming a massive box-office hit (perhaps it even helped it), earning $20 million by the end of the decade.

Zabriskie Point *and the Hollywood Renaissance*

It was on the heels of *Blow-Up*'s phenomenal critical and commercial success in 1967 that Antonioni started working on his first fully American movie. During the long preparation process, he travelled across America and chose Death Valley as his favourite spot, particularly Zabriskie Point, named after Christian B. Zabriskie, the man who had mined borax from this lunar-looking landscape in the early twentieth century. During his travels, Antonioni also read a newspaper article about a young man who was killed while trying to return a stolen plane, which would become the backbone of the film's narrative.[28]

His other experiences, as these were outlined in an article on the making of the film, included meeting with various radical groups, being tear-gassed at the Democratic National Convention, witnessing the devastation of Watts, attending rock concerts and love-ins, and smoking 'a little pot'.[29]

At this point, Antonioni became the reincarnation of the 1920s' imported European talents. It was no longer necessary for studio heads to scour Europe, as films by directors like Antonioni were already available in the US, and the transfer was facilitated by more European talent, in this case an Italian producer. The most significant difference with that generation, however, was that Antonioni was given completely free rein over his project. This was partially due to his popularity on college campuses in the wake of Blow-Up, and it can also be ascribed to MGM's interest in capturing the booming youth market that was both a reason for and a result of the 'New Cinema'.

Although MGM was once the most established and possibly the most conservative of the studios with the famous claim to have 'more stars than in heaven', in the late 1960s it was going through numerous financial calamities. By giving complete freedom to Antonioni, the studio was hoping to gain credibility with the coveted youth segment. It was a strategy that had already worked with Blow-Up. The advertising for Zabriskie Point, both at the pre-production stage and upon release, highlighted Antonioni himself and not the two unknown, non-professional leads that the director had sought out among thousands of candidates.[30]

MGM had three different presidents during the period Antonioni made and released Zabriskie Point. In 1969, O'Brien was replaced by Louis (Bo) Polk, a Harvard MBA. Polk was a corporate type with no experience in the movies, but the fact that he credited Blow-Up for making him interested in cinema may have helped Antonioni protect his freedom on the project. It was later reported that Polk asked Antonioni to remove the famous love-in scene, otherwise known as 'the orgy scene', where about three hundred extras (and numerous crew members) rolled around clothed and naked in the sand in groups of two, three or more (see Figure 9.1).[31] However, this report is based on James T. Aubrey's comments, the MGM president who replaced Polk within almost a year, and is contradicted by other accounts. For instance, Beverly Walker, who was brought in from New York to manage the film's public relations campaign after the spread of rumours that Antonioni had made an anti-American movie, refutes it. She also claims that Aubrey, who was nicknamed 'the Smiling Cobra' at MGM, changed the song accompanying the closing credits without Antonioni's consent, and added 'So Young', sung by Roy Orbison and written by Aubrey's protégé, Mike Curb.[32] Indeed, reports of the film's production are rife with conflicting anecdotes and stories, which may have played a part in the final denunciation of Zabriskie Point by audiences, critics and even some of the cast and crew. As a matter of fact, some of the reported disputes among the crew during production could be seen as a struggle between different styles of filmmaking: European and American, but also New Hollywood (reflected in

Figure 9.1 The orgy scene. Copyright Warner Home Video.

the films of the Hollywood Renaissance) and Old (represented by the classical mode of production within the studio system).

Antonioni may have been working for MGM in the US, but the way he operated remained 'diametrically opposed to the way things are done in that enormous bureaucratic machine known as Hollywood'.[33] He had problems with union regulations and found union members he was forced to work with too inflexible. For some of the crew, he was able to hire younger people. His first assistant Bob Rubin was twenty-seven, and the executive producer Harrison Starr was in his mid-thirties and not Hollywood-oriented, which was the main reason he was chosen.[34] But because he was allegedly unable to get enough 'young people used to shooting in the modern way', he brought along several craftsmen from Italy, people he was accustomed to working with.[35] However, this would prove to be somewhat disruptive as the American union members resented the presence of foreigners on the set and this created considerable tension. They did not speak each other's language, figuratively and literally. Also, due to union regulations, which required a 'stand-by' for non-members working on a film, each Italian was doubled by a union member, hence doubling the cost.

The script was a collaborative effort, credited to Antonioni, Sam Shepard, Tonino Guerra, Clare Peploe and Fred Gardner. The initial ideas came from Antonioni, and he worked on them with Guerra, but Guerra had to go back to Italy since he could not speak English and Antonioni felt that he had to write the dialogue in English.[36] Sam Shepard, who was twenty-four at the time and worked in Off-Broadway theatre,[37] was brought in to write the first draft of the script with Antonioni. While on the set, Clare Peploe also became involved with the script. Antonioni's translator during the making of *Blow-Up*, Peploe was his companion at the time, and a major influence on his work.[38] She would later work on *1900* (1976) and marry its director, Bernardo Bertolucci. Her younger brother, Mark Peploe, is credited with the original story for Antonioni's next film, *The Passenger*. The last name on the scriptwriting credits was Fred Gardner, a Berkeley-based political organizer and journalist. The reason Antonioni chose

Gardner was that he was deeply involved with the student groups active at Berkeley at the time, a connection that was thought to give Antonioni access and credibility.[39]

Zabriskie Point's opening credits are laid over somewhat disorienting close-ups of young people. Pink Floyd's 'Heart Beat, Pig Meat', which contains barely comprehensible sound bites from television and radio, plays in the background. The location is a classroom, where a heated political discussion is going on. In contrast to much of the rest of the film, the scene is almost shot in the style of cinema vérité. Some of the participants are actual members of the Black Panthers, brought to the production through the liaison of Fred Gardner.[40] These scenes and all others that use a college as their background were shot on location at Contra Costa College in Marin County.

The film tells the story of two young people, Mark and Daria. Mark, played by Mark Frachette, who was a carpenter and a member of the Boston-based Fort Hill cult, is among the students in the opening scene. He leaves the room, declaring that he is 'willing to die, but not of boredom'. From here until roughly the halfway point of the film, the narrative crosscuts between Mark and Daria. Mark drives around Los Angeles, goes to the police station to bail out his activist roommate, purchases a gun, is mistakenly accused of murdering a policeman whose death he witnesses, and finally steals a small private airplane. Daria is portrayed by Daria Halprin, a Berkeley student from a respected San Francisco family, whom Antonioni discovered upon seeing her in a documentary on the counterculture. Daria initially works as a temp at a real estate firm, but only 'when she needs the bread'. There she attracts the attention of tycoon Lee Allen (Rod Taylor), who hires her as a secretary. Allen owns the Sunny Dunes Land Development Company, which is developing desert holiday homes. The two are supposed to go to Phoenix together, but Daria leaves early in the morning by car and drives off to find a friend in the desert somewhere that is supposed to be a 'fantastic place for meditation'. She never does find her friend, but instead finds the 'emotionally disturbed' children she works with, who harass and humiliate her.

Getting away from the dusty little 'ghost town', Daria and Mark's paths cross for the first time. She is in her car, he is flying the plane he stole, and they have a *North by Northwest*-style encounter. Eventually, when the plane has run out of gas and landed, they get together to look for gas. They talk about a variety of mostly trivial issues, and ultimately find themselves at Zabriskie Point, where they make love in the sand, surrounded by the hundreds of people mentioned above. This is presumably a dream sequence, set inside Daria's head. Even though it came to be known as the orgy scene, the sequence contains no graphic sex, and in most of its earlier parts, the participants are seen engaging in a playful, animalistic ritual resembling a dance.

Daria and Mark paint the plane in bright, playful colours and shapes and go (or fly) their separate ways. Upon landing, Mark is fatally shot by the police. Daria hears about the incident on her car radio, but continues to drive, initially seemingly unfazed. She arrives at Allen's mansion on top of a rocky hill in

Phoenix. Unnoticed by the slightly older and apparently affluent women relaxing by the swimming pool, she weeps and drenches herself in the waterfall built below the house. Allen is busy closing a deal but notices her when he takes a break from negotiations and directs her to her room downstairs. Instead, Daria leaves the house and drives a short distance away. When she turns back to look at the house, it goes up in a spectacular explosion, which is repeated numerous times from various angles, followed by images of household objects blowing up and burning, presumably another dream sequence. Daria walks back to her car, gets in, and drives off into the sunset.

The narrative of the film clearly is inspired by the ongoing youth movement, which was at its peak when shooting began in California in the summer of 1968. Like in several other films of the era, the main characters are young rebels, who are not even sure they want to rebel but just want to live their own lives. In this sense, the closest and most obvious affinity *Zabriskie Point* has with another Hollywood Renaissance classic is with *Bonnie and Clyde*. It also shares elements with Mike Nichols' *The Graduate* (1967) with its disillusioned young protagonist, while *Easy Rider* also comes to mind with its finger on the pulse of the counterculture and its protagonists travelling across the desert. Incidentally, Daria Halprin later married (and then divorced) *Easy Rider* director Dennis Hopper. Finally, one could also argue that the film's preoccupation with the desert and water came back in a neo-noir style in *Chinatown* (1974), made by another European director, Roman Polanski. And as with Bonnie, Clyde, the three protagonists of *Easy Rider* and *Chinatown*'s Evelyn, *Zabriskie Point*'s Mark also comes to a gruesome end at the hands of the 'establishment', making the connection among these films even stronger.

But the narrative alone is not sufficient to describe *Zabriskie Point*. Antonioni's authorial presence draws attention to many scenes that do not directly forward the story. Much of the film, especially in the first half, is devoted to images of advertising and brash commercialism. As Mark drives through the city, the camera focuses on enormous billboards in the background. The bright colours and striking graphics seem to force the audience to be alert at every step, even if the messages on the billboards do not directly interfere with the narrative of the film. The advertising video prepared for the Sunny Dunes Estate is presented in its entirety, its garish colours and even more excessive commercialism almost foreshadowing David Lynch's uncanny vision of Small Town USA. David Fresko discusses *Zabriskie Point* in terms of the confrontation between New Left politics and the inherent commercialism of making a Hollywood studio film, calling Los Angeles a 'dystopian site of plastic signification', and the desert a 'symbol of nothingness'.[41] Daria's encounters with commercialism and her passage through the nothingness of the desert culminate in her fantasy of blowing up everything that stands for the capitalist order that she initially tried to sidestep, through working only 'when she need[ed] the bread'. Among the images of burning and destroyed icons of this order is a loaf of Wonder Bread (see Figure 9.2).

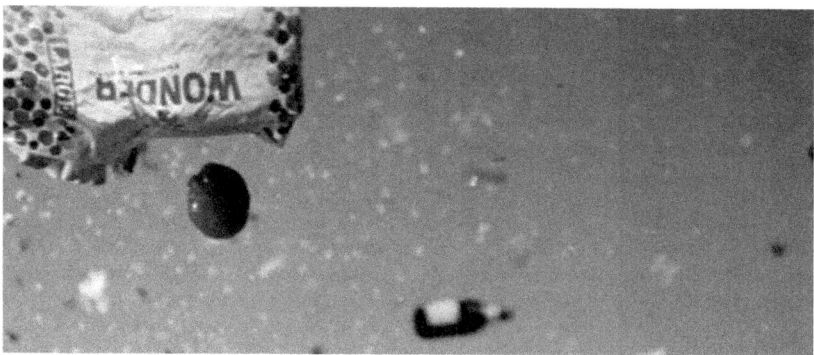

Figure 9.2 The flying Wonder Bread. Copyright Warner Home Video.

In his examination of the advertising images presented in the film, as well as the film's advertising, Christopher Sieving draws attention to the use of Pop Art. This art movement, often embracing images from advertising and pop culture, is reflected in *Zabriskie Point*'s giant billboards. The characters seem to be dissolving into the advertisements; this is especially true for Mark due to his good looks and 'depthless, affectless acting style'.[42] Murray Pomerance also analyses these sequences, pointing out parallels between Alfio Contini's cinematography and works by the era's leading photographers such as Walker Evans and Lee Friedlander.[43] This almost abstract quality of both the earlier urban sequences and the lunar landscapes of Death Valley carries on Antonioni's austere formalist style from his European films, combining it with the commercial imagery of the late capitalist United States.

Additionally, *Zabriskie Point* is close to other Hollywood Renaissance films through its use of music. Antonioni had already worked with contemporary music in *Blow-Up*, for which Herbie Hancock composed, conducted and played the score. For *Zabriskie Point*, Antonioni wanted to work only with Pink Floyd, but the final soundtrack includes other musicians such as The Grateful Dead, Patti Page and The Youngbloods. The use of a 'lyric interlude', with a song written specifically for a film and often set to a montage, had already become a staple of the Hollywood Renaissance style with *The Graduate* being a key example,[44] but Antonioni did express his doubts about using rock music, which was intrinsically tied up with big business.[45] Indeed, the soundtrack album was released by MGM Records immediately following the opening of the film (the song 'So Young', allegedly added by Aubrey, was not on the album).[46]

After Zabriskie Point

When *Zabriskie Point* was finally released in February 1970, it opened to devastating criticism ultimately landing in a book on 'the fifty worst films of all time' in 1978.[47] In one of his interviews at the beginning of the production, Antonioni spoke of an 'opposite approach to life itself, a refusal to accept embalmed ideas and clichés, affectation and imitation' when comparing his style to that of Hollywood.[48] The general critical consensus charged the film with doing exactly the opposite; the film was seen as clichéd, and that was one of the least scathing adjectives used.[49] Usual champions of Antonioni's work tried to explain 'what went wrong' with this disaster of a film. In addition to the negative response of reviewers, the student movement and social groups represented in the film also resented their portrayals. As Walker points out, the expectations were extremely high, not only MGM's, but also 'those of students and radicals across the United States, cinema aesthetes, and Antonioni himself'.[50]

Angelo Restivo categorizes the negative discourses that surrounded the film's reception under three 'usual suspect' headings: that a brilliant auteur could not navigate the waters of a foreign culture, or that a perfectionist director used to tight budgets 'fell prey to a misguided perfectionism' when given free rein, or that a visionary filmmaker charged himself with making a definitive statement about a culture, epoch, or memory.[51] None of these really explain the harshness of people's responses, including some of the cast and crew. Fred Gardner disassociated himself from the film, and Frachette and Halprin, living together at the time, attacked it.[52] The time frame within which the film was made witnessed exceptionally quick changes in American culture. The youth movement and the liberalism of the 1960s, which were still prevalent when Antonioni was shooting, had subsided significantly by the time he finished editing, a year and a half later. Lyndon B. Johnson's presidency was over, replaced by the conservative government of Richard Nixon. Not only was Antonioni a foreigner looking at and reflecting on the fabric of American society, but he did so when that society was changing by the day. He did defend himself by saying that he was not trying to 'explain' the country, but 'just trying to feel something about America, to gain some intuition', but it was too late.[53]

Antonioni's attempt to reconcile the opposing Hollywood and European styles of filmmaking failed, much like the earlier efforts of the filmmakers of the 1920s. *Zabriskie Point* was ultimately re-evaluated and found by some critics to be ahead of its time.[54] The free rein Antonioni was given during the production of his MGM films was unprecedented and not replicated for other émigré directors. In the 1970s, there were others such as Roger Vadim, who was widely popular in France and moved to Hollywood in 1971, but never quite reached the same level of popularity as with his French films. Vadim, however, never had the same arthouse clout as Antonioni. Also in the early 1970s, a new generation of political émigrés from Eastern Europe emerged as important filmmakers, including Milos Forman, Ivan Passer and Roman Polanski. Of these three, only Forman could establish himself as a major Hollywood director. Polanski had to flee the US, and Passer's films never found any significant commercial success.

Throughout the 1980s, and to the present, the number of European and other foreign filmmakers in Hollywood increased significantly. But many of them transitioned from making Hollywood-style mainstream films or genre pictures in their own countries to doing similar work for Hollywood studios, in many cases not even physically relocating to the US.[55] These directors were expected to know that they did not have any real say in their projects, and some of them have had so much interference from studio executives in particular films that they took their strife to the media as in the case of Jose Padilha's work on the reboot of the *RoboCop* franchise.

The few arthouse directors that followed Antonioni and that I mentioned earlier such as Russell, Bergman, Malle and Wenders either went back to working in their homelands, or followed up their American films with international co-productions. But they were never given the absolute free rein that Antonioni had been given; his was a special case. It was a time of change when the studios still dared to take risks, and he was a leviathan filmmaker who defined European art cinema at the time. Much like the specific circumstances that brought about the Hollywood Renaissance, his involvement in *Zabriskie Point* was the product of a combination of elements which we are not likely to encounter again.

From its narrative inspired by real events to its choice of location, from the commercial imagery it brandishes to the soundtrack provided by young, cutting-edge American and British musicians, *Zabriskie Point* clearly demonstrates late 1960s American cultural influence on Antonioni. And besides its textual kinship with other important Hollywood Renaissance examples, Antonioni himself has made a number of references to the film's and his own affinities with contemporary American cinema. Specifically, he mentions underground cinema without indicating any specific directors or artists, but also names *Easy Rider* as a 'sincere film' that is 'skillful but genuine'.[56] Similarly, he acknowledges particularly Coppola's and Steven Spielberg's work, but also refers to Scorsese, Robert Altman, Kubrick, Penn and Bob Rafelson as important American filmmakers.[57] This demonstrates the extent to which they were all part of the same era, which underlines the ways in which European and American filmmakers of the time were influencing each other, as I mentioned at the beginning of this chapter. It is clear then that the Hollywood Renaissance was not simply a European art cinema influenced American film phenomenon, but a more complex configuration that involved American filmmakers affecting the work of even the most venerable of the European art cinema masters.

Notes

1   The film now has a 67 per cent positive rating on rottentomatoes.com, but all of these reviews come from after 2000.
2   IMDb http://www.imdb.com/title/tt0066601/business

3   Stefan Kanfer, 'The Shock of Freedom in Films', *Time*, 8 December 1967, http://www.time.com/time/magazine/article/0,9171,844256,00.html

4   Kanfer, 'The Shock of Freedom in Films'.

5   *Easy Rider* premiered at Cannes in May 1969, which was around the same time as the shooting wrapped for *Zabriskie Point*. Nonetheless, one can see a shared *zeitgeist* among the two films.

6   Charles Musser, *Before the Nickelodeon: Edwin S. Porter and the Edison Manufacturing Company* (Berkeley: University of California Press, 1991), 447.

7   John Russell Taylor, *Strangers in Paradise: The Hollywood Émigrés, 1933–1950* (London: Faber and Faber, 1983), 57.

8   For a discussion of the motives behind the emigration during this era, see Thomas Elsaesser, 'Ethnicity, Authenticity, and Exile: A Counterfeit Trade?', in *Home, Exile, Homeland: Film, Media and the Politics of Place*, ed. Hamid Naficy (London and New York: Routledge, 1999), 97–123.

9   Robert Keser, 'Fred Zinnemann', *Senses of Cinema*, no. 31 (2004), http://sensesofcinema.com/2004/great-directors/zinnemann/

10 Taylor, *Strangers in Paradise*, 59.

11 Gene D. Phillips, *Exiles in Hollywood: Major European Film Directors in America* (Bethlehem, PA: Lehigh University Press, 1998), 102.

12 Taylor, *Strangers in Paradise*, 69.

13 The main exceptions were French directors. For a more detailed account, see Janet Bergstrom, 'Émigrés or Exiles? The French Directors' Return from Hollywood', in *Hollywood & Europe: Economics, Culture, National Identity 1946–95*, ed. Geoffrey Nowell-Smith and Steven Ricci (London: British Film Institute, 1998), 86–103.

14 Ian Scott, *From Pinewood to Hollywood: British Filmmakers in American Cinema, 1910–1969* (Basington: Palgrave Macmillan, 2010).

15 Robert Murphy, *Sixties British Cinema* (London: BFI, 1992), 258.

16 I have previously written in detail about European (and other) émigrés in Hollywood. See Melis Behlil, *Hollywood Is Everywhere: Global Directors in the Blockbuster Era* (Amsterdam: Amsterdam University Press, 2016), 72.

17 For a concise overview of this period, see Drew Casper, *Hollywood Film 1963–1976: Years of Revolution and Reaction* (Oxford: Wiley-Blackwell, 2011), 31–4.

18 Frederick Wasser, 'Is Hollywood America? The Transnationalization of the American Film Industry', *Critical Studies in Mass Communication* 12, no. 4 (1995): 423–37.

19 James Brown, 'Michelangelo Antonioni', *Senses of Cinema*, no. 20 (2002), http://sensesofcinema.com/2002/great-directors/antonioni/

20 According to boxofficemojo.com, *Doctor Zhivago* is still number eight among top domestic grossers adjusted for ticket price inflation; http://www.boxofficemojo.com/alltime/adjusted.htm

21 Before being replaced, O'Brien also oversaw Kubrick's *2001: A Space Odyssey* (1968). See Gene D. Phillips, *Beyond the Epic: The Life and Films of David Lean* (Lexington: University Press of Kentucky, 2006), 325.

22 Tom Paulus, 'Walsh's Movers and Boorman's Walker', *cinea*, 29 June 2012, https://cinea.be/walshs-movers-and-boormans-walker

23 Murray Pomerance, *Michelangelo Red Antonioni Blue: Eight Reflections on Cinema* (Berkeley: University of California Press, 2011), 237.

24 Alexis More, 'Antonioni in the American Wilderness', *Chicago Tribune Magazine*, 31 May 1970, 24.

25 Pomerance, *Michelangelo Red Antonioni Blue*, 249.

26 Kanfer, 'The Shock of Freedom in Films'.

27 Leonard J. Leff and Jerold Simmons, *The Dame in the Kimono: Hollywood, Censorship, and the Production Code* (Lexington: University Press of Kentucky, 2001), 273.

28 Frank P. Tomasulo, 'Life is Inconclusive: A Conversation with Michelangelo Antonioni', in *Michelangelo Antonioni: Interviews*, ed. Bert Cardullo (Jackson: University Press of Mississippi, 2008), 165.

29 Beverly Walker, 'Michelangelo and the Leviathan: The Making of *Zabriskie Point*', *Film Comment* 28, no. 5 (1992): 37.

30 Christopher Sieving, 'The Man Can't Bust Our Movies: Buying and Selling the Counterculture with *Zabriskie Point* (1970)', *The Sixties* 9, no. 2 (2016): 222.

31 Louise B. Sweeney, 'Zabriskie Lives!', *Show* (Ferbruary 1970): 42.

32 Walker, 'Michelangelo and the Leviathan', 49.

33 Bert Cardullo, 'Film is Life: An Interview with Michelangelo Antonioni', in *Michelangelo Antonioni: Interviews*, ed. Bert Cardullo (Jackson: University Press of Mississippi, 2008), 149.

34 Walker, 'Michelangelo and the Leviathan', 37.

35 Marsha Kinder, '*Zabriskie Point*', *Sight and Sound* 38, no. 1 (1968): 30.

36 Kinder, '*Zabriskie Point*', 28.

37 More, 'Antonioni in the American Wilderness', 24.

38 Walker, 'Michelangelo and the Leviathan', 39.

39 Kinder, '*Zabriskie Point*', 27.

40 Walker, 'Michelangelo and the Leviathan', 47.

41 David Fresko 'Magical Mystery Tours: Godard and Antonioni in America', in *The Global Sixties in Sound and Vision*, ed. Timothy Scott Brown and Andrew Lison (New York: Palgrave Macmillan, 2014), 46, 48.

42 Sieving, 'The Man Can't Bust Our Movies', 229.

43 Pomerance, *Michelangelo Red Antonioni Blue*, 190.

44 Angelo Restivo 'Revisiting *Zabriskie Point*', in *Antonioni: Centenary Essays*, ed. Laura Rascaroli and John David Rhodes (London: Palgrave Macmillan, 2011), 94.

45 Cardullo, 'Film is Life', 141.

46 David Fricke, '*Zabriskie Point*', http://www.phinnweb.org/links/cinema/directors/antonioni/zabriskie/

47 Harry Medved and Randy Dreyfuss, *The Fifty Worst Films of All Time (And How They Got That Way)* (New York: Popular Library, 1978).

48 Cardullo, 'Film Is Life', 149.

49 Guy Flatley, 'Antonioni Defends *Zabriskie Point*: "I Love This Country"', *The New York Times*, 22 February 1970.

50 Walker, 'Michelangelo and the Leviathan', 48.

51 Restivo, 'Revisiting *Zabriskie Point*', 82.

52 Walker, 'Michelangelo and the Leviathan', 49.

53 Flatley, 'Antonioni Defends *Zabriskie Point*'.

54 Restivo, 'Revisiting *Zabriskie Point*', 87.

55 Behlil, *Hollywood Is Everywhere*, 65.

56 Michele Mancini, Alessandro Cappablanca, Ciriaco Tiso and Jobst Grapow, 'The World Is Outside The Window', in *The Architecture Of Vision: Writings & Interviews*

On Cinema, ed. Carlo di Carlo, Giorgio Tinazzi and Marga Cottino-Jones (New York: Marsilio, 1996), 178.

57 See Sophie Lannes and Philippe Meyer, 'Identification of a Filmmaker', and Ugo Rubeo, 'A Constant Renewal', both in *The Architecture Of Vision: Writings & Interviews On Cinema*, ed. Carlo di Carlo, Giorgio Tinazzi and Marga Cottino-Jones (New York: Marsilio, 1996), 252, 324.

Chapter 10

BECOMING HAL ASHBY: INTERSECTIONAL POLITICS, THE HOLLYWOOD RENAISSANCE AND *HAROLD AND MAUDE* (1971)

Philip Drake

As a number of writers have outlined, the late 1960s and early 1970s were a period that saw the rise of the director as a recognized auteur within industry and critical discourse, and the creation of a Hollywood cinema seeking not only aesthetic but political credibility, whilst gradually re-establishing its commerciality.[1] The period saw the end of the Production Code and its replacement in 1968 with a ratings system that permitted – subject to rating – swearing, nudity and extra-marital sex to be shown on screen, as well as the explicit treatment of controversial topics. These shifts, bringing new aesthetic and thematic paradigms, can be seen as part of renewed claims to cultural and political legitimacy on the part of the industry, as well as a response to the restructuring and changing ownership of the film studios, and reconfiguration of cinemas towards a youth audience. Such shifts in social views and the influence of 1960s counterculture movements found their expression both in the re-evaluation of established critical canons and in an interest in new forms of filmmaking and film criticism. By the end of the 1960s both filmmaker and critic occupied new cultural ground, with films (and music) critically celebrated as articulating the American experience in new, sometimes profound, ways, and a body of films seen as epitomizing a 'Hollywood Renaissance'.

Such changes were taking place against (and reacting to) a backdrop of significant social change and upheaval in the 1960s. Complex and multifaceted, these included disparate but often connected social movements and events such as the historic civil rights marches that led to the Civil Rights Act of 1964, the so-called Summer of Love of 1967, rock music and the Woodstock and Altamont Festivals of 1969, the related rise of the Hippie and more politicized Yippie movements, anti-war protests against US military action in Vietnam, the use of drugs, and the sexual revolution in part enabled by the availability of birth control methods, finally legalized for unmarried couples in 1972. The assassination of Democrat US President John F. Kennedy in 1963, disillusionment with his successor Lyndon B. Johnson, and his replacement in 1969 by the eventually discredited Republican Richard Nixon, all provide an important political backdrop to films of the period, along with reverberations from the assassinations of both civil rights campaigner Martin Luther King, Jr and Senator and presidential candidate Robert F. Kennedy in 1968.

Industrial changes were also significant in this period. The acquisition of Paramount Pictures in 1966 by Charles Bluhdorn's Gulf + Western, and the hiring of producer Robert Evans as Paramount's Head of Production, alongside industry journalist Peter Bart, signalled a significant departure from the old order represented by moguls such as Adolph Zukor. A string of commercial and critical successes under Evans and Bart, which included Hollywood Renaissance films such as *Rosemary's Baby* (Roman Polanski, 1968), *The Godfather* (Francis Ford Coppola, 1972) and *Chinatown* (Roman Polanski, 1974), seemed, by the mid-1970s, to have demonstrated that the risk in working with unproven talent had been vindicated. Similarly, United Artists' 1967 purchase by Transamerica Corporation consolidated their earlier strategy of working with independent production companies and producers to garner critical success, from which they had won five Best Picture Academy Awards during the 1960s, with a further six Best Picture nominations. Independent producers such as The Mirisch Brothers, Joseph E. Levine and Stanley Kramer worked closely with the Hollywood studios to co-produce films, many of which transgressed traditional boundaries in their treatment of social issues.

Whilst writers on the Hollywood Renaissance commonly give credit to 1967's *The Graduate* (Mike Nichols) and *Bonnie and Clyde* (Arthur Penn) as pivotal films that marked a shift to a new kind of Hollywood cinema, the same year also yielded ground-breaking films such as Stanley Kramer's *Guess Who's Coming to Dinner?* and Norman Jewison's *In the Heat of the Night,* the latter topping that year's list of Academy Awards, and both starring black actor Sidney Poitier in films dealing explicitly with interracial relationships. The exclusion of the latter films from consideration from the critical canon of the Hollywood Renaissance, and their frequent dismissal as 'social conscience films', raises key questions around film historiography, and processes of inclusion in, and exclusion from, canonical works and movements.

During the 1960s, editor Hal Ashby had built up an impressive track record, editing five of the films directed by Norman Jewison and winning an Academy Award as editor for *In the Heat of the Night.* Unlike the 1960s film-school graduates that made up a proportion of the Hollywood Renaissance directors, Ashby – like other directors including Arthur Penn, Robert Altman, Mike Nichols and Roman Polanski – had already spent many years building experience in the industry. He was born in 1929 and trained and served time both in the classical Hollywood studio system, working as an editor with directors including William Wyler and George Stevens, and outside Hollywood (and the United States) with directors such as Tony Richardson and Norman

Jewison. By the time of his directorial debut, *The Landlord* (1970), Ashby was over forty and had already amassed a lengthy list of credits. Over the next decade, Ashby went on to become one of the most commercially and critically successful Hollywood film directors of the 1970s. Yet until recently, Ashby's films have received scant scholarly attention. He remains one of the least conspicuous of the cluster of filmmakers associated with the period, a neglect partly due to his premature death in 1988 and partly due to his problematic fit with the discourse of the Hollywood Renaissance.

As I noted in an earlier work,[2] pioneering studies of the Hollywood Renaissance such as Robin Wood's *Hollywood from Vietnam to Reagan* and Michael Ryan and Douglas Kellner's *Camera Politica* barely give Ashby a mention,[3] and in his *Biographical Dictionary of Film*, David Thomson witheringly called Ashby 'a sad casualty who depended on strong collaborators'.[4] Diane Jacobs' early book *Hollywood Renaissance* is an exception to this,[5] although other scholars did not develop her treatment of Ashby until thirty years after its publication.

Critical interest, such as it is, has also focused primarily on six of Ashby's first seven feature films made in the 1970s: *Harold and Maude* (1971), *The Last Detail* (1973), *Shampoo* (1976), *Bound for Glory* (1977), *Coming Home* (1978) and *Being There* (1979). In Peter Biskind's popular and influential book *Easy Riders, Raging Bulls* Ashby is positioned as an outsider, a maverick who lost his father when young to suicide, and in turn became a father figure to younger 'movie-brat' filmmakers, and nurtured the talent in others.[6] Ashby appears throughout Biskind's account as a symbol of idealistic, sometimes uncompromising and conflicting countercultural values, married and divorced twice before the age of twenty-one, at the same time both a gentle hippie and intransigent idealist, a talented filmmaker who fell out with the studios, eventually suffering damage to his reputation from which he did not recover before his premature death, aged just fifty-nine.

Ashby's career, his films and his approach to direction therefore make it difficult for critics to locate him within an auteur mode of filmmaking, and auteur was indeed a label Ashby himself rejected. As revealed in interviews at the time, Ashby refused to take sole credit for the production of his films. In one interview he stated: 'The great thing about film is, it really is communal. It really is the communal art, and you don't lose anything—all you do is gain. Your film just gains and gains. The more input you get, the better it is.'[7] Ashby's films confused auteur critics of the period, with no obvious constant theme, style, genre or setting, and ranging widely from dark comedies to war films, buddy movies to biopics. Ashby's films are varied, collaborative and too whimsical and quirky in tone to easily fit the narrative of male anti-heroes that structures dominant histories of the Hollywood Renaissance. Furthermore, the various legal battles and disputes with producers and studios over creative control across Ashby's career resulted in his final three projects being taken out of his hands prior to completion, further tarnishing his reputation as an auteur.[8]

My earlier research on Ashby explored issues of creative control and conflict at this later point of his career, and in this I argued for the need to consider the competing discourses around contractual texts and creative control. This drew on revisionist archival history, informed by New Cinema History scholarly approaches.[9] Such research attempts to reconstruct history through a reconsideration of historical contexts, production, distribution and exhibition histories and accounts of film reception.

When I first viewed Ashby's archive at the Margaret Herrick Library at the Academy of Motion Picture Arts and Sciences scarcely over a decade ago, there was a paucity of published academic work on the filmmaker, a surprise considering he had directed so many critically acclaimed American films of the 1970s. Since then a modest number of academic articles and books have explored his work, sometimes using materials from the archive, including Nick Dawson's biography and useful collection of interviews,[10] Christopher Beach's analysis of his films[11] and Aaron Hunter's recent book which explores claims of authorship around Ashby's films, drawing on the work on C. Paul Sellors to examine how Ashby's practice can function as a critique of dominant conceptualizations of authorship.[12] Hunter argues that 'Ashby, by rejecting the auteur mantel [sic], effectively both barred himself from attaining any significant power during the era and marginalized himself within scholarly consideration of the era [. . .] [however] his own role in authoring the films can still be detected.'[13]

For Hunter, Ashby's lack of visibility in scholarship on the Hollywood Renaissance is part of the problematic myth of the Hollywood auteur. In his analysis, he offers details of Ashby's multiple collaborations with writers, editors, producers and musicians, arguing that Ashby epitomized collaborative authorship, working repeatedly and collaboratively with a range of notable creative talent (for instance renowned cinematographers Gordon Willis and Haskell Wexler). Hunter's study, however, is also concerned with historical recuperation. Whilst not wishing to reclaim Ashby as an auteur, Hunter is nonetheless convinced of his important place in American film history. Similarly, Dawson's biography of Ashby presents a biographical narrative from his traumatic early life in Ogden, Utah to his battle with cancer and early death, creating a narrative of pathos, whilst arguing for Ashby's place in cinema history.

I wish here to avoid either a biographical account of Ashby, or a consideration of his work through the lens of auteur theory. As I discussed in my earlier work, Ashby's frequent fights with studio executives over creative control – a trend that occurred throughout his career – raises important questions over an 'auteurist' reading of his films. Incidents from his later work, such as when he was fired from the production of *8 Million Ways to Die* (1986) or when *Looking to Get Out* (1982) was re-edited for release, demonstrate the contingency of creative control (and therefore authorship), and the reputational damage that such battles exacted.

In my approach, I draw on John Caughie's useful essay on the value of authorship as a discursive formation.[14] Caughie argues that using the concept of 'director-centred criticism' helps to avoid the pitfalls of auteur theory, in particular the intentional fallacy that it promotes. I also prefer to adopt a 'director-centred criticism' perspective in this chapter, given that such an approach understands authorship as a *performative* function of both critical and industry discourse, playing a significant role in reifying what are complex industrial and collaborative processes. In the rest of this chapter I wish to explore a number of aspects of Hal Ashby's early films, focusing primarily on *Harold and Maude,* in order to consider his relationship to the so-called Hollywood Renaissance, suggesting that the reasons his films fit awkwardly with dominant historical accounts not only demonstrate a gap in studies of the period but, perhaps more importantly, question the progressive political basis on which a 'renaissance' can be claimed.

I also need to present a point of clarification: by referring to 'Ashby's films' I do not claim that Ashby was the sole author, nor indeed does this necessarily indicate that he was the most significant individual in terms of creative input. Indeed, as my earlier work makes clear, the contingency of creative control, the importance of collaborators, the relative power of the personnel involved and the contracts that they negotiate, all place limits on authorship. As I will argue, Ashby's early films, including *Harold and Maude,* stylistically, tonally and politically challenge what has become a hegemonic discourse of the Hollywood Renaissance, with its tendency to privilege narratives of white male narcissism, consigning other kinds of films to be forgotten. The films that I discuss here are not unique in this, as the lack of significant accounts of marginalized black and women filmmakers of the period also attests (see also Chapter 11 in this volume). Looking at Ashby's early films, I shall argue that they are linked by a strong humanist connection to social issues, often questioning inequalities of race and ethnicity, class and age, and provoking – through the use of humour and satire – acute observations about social divisions, inequality and the place of individualism within a society requiring conformism.

Intersectional politics and the Hollywood Renaissance

In 1989, law professor Kimberlé Crenshaw wrote a short but highly influential article on 'intersectionality'.[15] From a legal perspective, the concept describes intersecting social identities and related systems of oppression, domination or discrimination. Crenshaw was particularly concerned with intersections of race and gender; however, scholars have deployed the concept for different kinds of multidimensional analysis of overlapping social categories. In considering the inequalities faced by black women, cultural theorist Angela Davis has argued that we need to develop a more complex understanding of how class intersects with gender and race.[16] Such intersectional issues of gender, class, race and age are often explored and performed in Ashby's early films. Before looking in detail at Ashby's second film as director, *Harold and Maude*, with its intergenerational love story, I will turn to Ashby's first, often overlooked film as director, *The Landlord*, a film that can be seen as significant in its approach to political issues and collaborative filmmaking.

The Landlord, produced by The Mirisch Company and released by United Artists, was based on a 1966 novel by black female author Kristin Hunter, adapted by black American writer/director Bill Gunn. It was made just a year after Dr Martin Luther King's assassination, and following the Civil Rights Act of 1968 that outlawed discrimination in housing, expanding on the landmark 1964 Civil Rights Act. *The Landlord* offers an early and prescient examination of gentrification, race and class, with a narrative focused on inner-city gentrification in Park Slope, Brooklyn and the displacement of black Americans, and presenting a commentary on white privilege, liberalism and interracial relationships. As Academy Award winning editor of *In the Heat of the Night*, a multi-award-winning film that explored race relations, Ashby had previously worked closely with Norman Jewison, editing five of his films. Jewison offered to produce *The Landlord* with Ashby directing, securing a sizeable $2 million budget from the Mirisch Company (although the film eventually went $450,000 over budget).[17] Mirisch had also produced *In the Heat of the Night* and although the company had concerns about Ashby's status as a first-time director, they were convinced when Jewison offered to produce the film.

The plot of the film is straightforward: Elgar Enders (Beau Bridges) is a 29-year-old white man who decides to leave his parents' home, and buys a tenanted apartment building in the black ghetto of Park Slope, Brooklyn. He plans to evict all the occupants and construct a luxury home for himself. However, once he ventures into the building, he meets the low-income black residents (including Pearl Bailey as Marge) who dwell there, and likes them, repairing the building but also, rebelling against his family's wishes, becoming romantically linked to two black women, one of whom is mixed-race and sometimes also passes as white. As a satire on inequality, the film presents an aesthetic that is at times almost documentary in feel, yet this is offset by quirky comedic performances and an offbeat use of style, editing and use of sound. The scene where Elgar announces 'I think I love a girl who is a negro' is followed by his mother's reaction and a brief momentary cutaway to an African village, in order to underline her prejudice, yet also her attempts to appear liberal-minded, commenting, when taken to task by him on her attitudes to black people, 'Didn't we all go together to see *Guess Who's Coming to Dinner?*'

Throughout *The Landlord* formal and stylistic experimentation mixes with black comedy and social satire. A party scene with Elgar and his black tenants provides perhaps the most powerful social commentary when a character exclaims: 'You whiteys scream about miscegenation, and you done watered down every race you ever hated!' The irony of the scene – Elgar is in a relationship with a black woman when he also sleeps with another (one of the tenants) – and its biting commentary on gentrification, demonstrate the intersectional politics at play, allowing cross-cutting issues of class, gender and race to be explored throughout the film. The film's deployment of offbeat humour frequently offers an acute and important, but not didactic, commentary about inclusive and communal social values.

Despite dealing with significant social issues of the time, *The Landlord* was not a box-office success. It grossed approximately $1.5 million, proving a disappointment against its almost $2.5 million production budget.[18] Reviews of the film were generally positive, although the film's marketing was mishandled by United Artists who attempted to advertise the title as a sex comedy with the tagline 'Watch the Landlord Get His', and – on the poster – a picture of a finger pointing towards two doorbells designed to look like female breasts. Nonetheless the lack of attention given to the film since its release and its absence from most discussions of the period raises questions about how film history can also contribute to an erasure of consideration of intersectional politics. Seen now, the film offers a strong critique of gentrification and a complex exploration of intersectional issues of the period.

I now turn to consider Ashby's 1971 second directorial feature, *Harold and Maude*, an intergenerational black comedy. As I will argue, this film exemplifies an approach to filmmaking that foregrounds questions of intersectional politics and deploys an eclectic style, mixing different emotional tones and registers, provoking questions around conformism, class and age. Yet despite its ostensibly radical premise, the film sits uneasily within the Hollywood Renaissance canon and contributed to Ashby's marginalization in studies of the cinema of the period. However, as I also demonstrate, *Harold and Maude* eventually acquired a strong cult film status that helped it become canonized retrospectively, further complicating questions of authorship and the extent to which such frames adequately determine our understanding of film history.

The cult intersectional politics of Harold and Maude

Just as with the contentious representation of miscegenation in *The Landlord*, the characters Harold and Maude, played by Bud Cort and Ruth Gordon respectively, tackle the potentially taboo subject of a romantic and sexual relationship between a 19-year-old man and a 79-year-old woman. In addition, the film includes the staging of Harold's fake suicides and Maude's eccentricity, exuberance and non-conformity. It was made for Paramount, after Peter Bart and Robert Evans championed it. Budgeted for $1.285 million – a more realistic target to recoup compared to his previous film – the costs of *Harold and Maude* also went over budget. In particular, the addition of fourteen extra weeks for editing raised costs to just over $1.6 million, $315,000 over the original budget when finalized in October 1971, causing Ashby some difficulties with Evans.[19] A deal memo dated 26 May 1970 summarized the original finances, with

Paramount paying $100,000 for the screenplay by Colin Higgins plus his services as screenwriter, and bringing in Howard Jaffe and Mildred Lewis as co-producers, eventually adding – at Ashby's request – Charles Mulvehill, formerly Head of Production at Mirisch, as an additional producer.

Initially down to direct, recent UCLA graduate Higgins was given an advance of $7,500 to shoot three scenes. That footage, however, was deemed unsatisfactory by the studio, which nonetheless gave him a co-producer credit and net profit participation contract.[20] Both the producing team and the director, then, were relatively inexperienced and without a major hit, demonstrating Evans and Bart's willingness to take a risk on, at this point, relatively unproven talent.

As with *The Landlord*, Ashby did not find working on the film easy. In an emotional letter to Evans, dated 1 December 1970, Ashby expresses his frustration, threatening to quit the film: 'it seems that Paramount has either disappointed or failed me just once too often, and the stress of my coping with the whole damn thing has indeed taken its toll.'[21] In the letter Ashby details the studio's interference, which included preventing him from hiring Gordon Willis as his preferred director of photography (who, due to the studio's delay, had committed to filming *The Godfather*), and its quibbling over the budget and locations. Nonetheless Ashby did continue directing the film, albeit with a number of disagreements with the studio over various areas, as I detail below.

The film is focused on Harold, a wealthy 19-year-old man obsessed with death, who stages his own fake suicides and who drives a hearse, and Maude, a 79-year-old eccentric woman who meets Harold through their shared hobby of attending the funerals of strangers. During carefully staged 'suicides' in front of his mother (Vivian Pickles), we learn that, rather than communicate or understand him, she aims to find him a wife or get him to join the military. Maude befriends Harold through her eccentric hobbies, including taking trees from the streets and returning them to nature, and an infectiously rebellious yet positive attitude to life. The characters spend time together, opening up to each other about life issues, and growing close.

Much of the comedy of the film comes from the warmth of their relationship – Maude's vivaciousness and love of life slowly brings out Harold's own joy, and they become lovers despite their large age difference. Having announced they will marry, to the consternation and disgust of Harold's mother, his psychiatrist and his priest, Harold prepares a celebration for Maude's 80th birthday, only then learning she had decided to end her life that day. Taken to multiple hospitals after a deliberate overdose, Maude dies. In the final sequence, we see Harold's car – a sports-car converted into hearse – plunging off a cliff, but after the crash the film reveals Harold standing at the top, playing on his banjo – a gift from Maude – the affirmative song she taught him: Cat Stevens' 'If You Want to Sing Out, Sing Out'.

As should be clear from the description above, the film is highly quirky in its use of black humour and comedy, and bold in its depiction of an intergenerational romantic relationship between a young man and an elderly woman. The mix of tones in the film is unusual, with Harold's morbid staging of convincing suicides contrasting with the exuberant escapades of Maude. The humour in flouting the authority of various institutional figures (notably the police and military) makes them appear ridiculous and diminished, and the eccentricity of Maude's world – living in a quirky railway carriage – offers a stark contrast to the muted brown palette of Harold's wealthy family home.

It is significant that it is Maude, a 79-year-old woman, who epitomizes the anti-authoritarian free spirit of the film, rather than the young male protagonist. Maude also recalls her early life, alluding to her time in Vienna, thinking she would marry a soldier, before a later scene reveals a number tattooed on her arm, confirming her as a survivor of the Holocaust, bringing a darker element to what was a romantic scene. Such switching between pathos, introspection and comedy is quirky and unusual, and often signalled through stylistic markers, for instance in the different colour palettes of the two homes, the use of short cutaway shots, the montage sequences and use of Cat Stevens' songs to narrate the moods of the characters. One of the trailers for the film offers a number of scenes cut from the final version that highlight further the film's concern with intersectional politics, for instance, a scene at the Emeryville mudflats where driftwood letters spell out 'Fuck War', as well as the trailer's unambiguous 'Harold And Maude Say: Get Together Regardless of Your Age, Race, Creed, Color or National Origin' message.

The scene where Harold and Maude, after a day together, decide to consummate their relationship is an example of both creative compromise and invention – remarkable as according to accounts of the film's production, Ashby was asked by Robert Evans to remove the sex scene.[22] With Paramount having

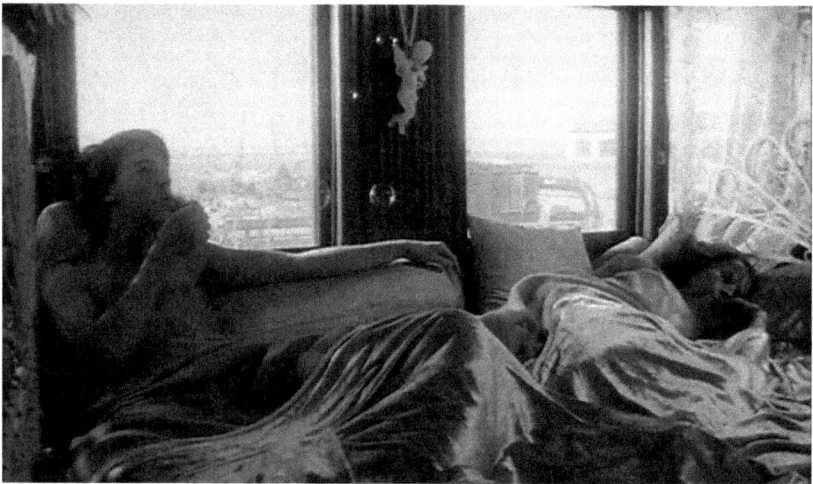

Figure 10.1 Taboo breaking and intergenerational sex. Copyright Paramount.

insisted that the sex itself must be unseen, the film instead shows Harold and Maude lying in bed with Maude still sleeping and Harold lying next to her (see Figure 10.1). Intercut with fireworks, Harold smiles and blows bubbles whilst the Cat Stevens' song 'I Can See the Light' starts to play.

Despite the absence of the depiction of sex, the level of intimacy between the two characters was (and remains) taboo breaking in its presentation of intergenerational relationships. The film acknowledges this by following the scene with direct addresses straight to camera by three characters who express their disgust: Harold's Uncle Victor (a military General), Harold's psychiatrist and a priest who – during a slow zoom in on his face – grotesquely contorts his face to express to the camera his revulsion: 'The thought of your young body co-mingling with the withered flesh, sagging breasts and flabby buttocks makes me want to vomit.' Each of the characters has behind them a reinforcing authority figure in a picture frame in their office: for the General, President Richard Nixon (whom he salutes with his mechanical arm), for the psychiatrist, Sigmund Freud and, for the priest, a religious authority figure (See Figures 10.2a–c). The breaking of the fourth wall through direct address in this way is highly unusual in Hollywood cinema (although the opening scene of *The Landlord* features a similar direct address to camera) and brings the spectator into the narrative through this mode of the actor's performance. The zoom in on the priest during his monologue in particular, emphasizes, through the use of heightened, caricatured performance, the grotesque nature of imposing such moralizing judgements on the two protagonists. Hence the film asserts an intersectional critique of social conventions of age and gender through its clear ridiculing of these representatives of moral authority.

(a)

(b)

(c)

Figures 10.2a–c *Harold and Maude's* caricatured figures of moral authority. Copyright Paramount.

The politics of the film also appeal to countercultural values, particularly those of a youth audience, through forms of comedic knowingness. The realistic nature of the suicide scenes is juxtaposed with their comedic inventiveness: self-immolation, committing hara-kiri, Harold chopping off his hand: all witnessed impassively by his mother and shocking various visitors. The scene where Harold, having scared off another suitor organized by his mother, turns

Figure 10.3 Harold looks at the camera. Copyright Paramount.

and briefly looks directly at the camera is evidence of this – Harold deliberately breaks the fourth wall to acknowledge the audience, a Brechtian device that brings an intertextual knowingness to the scene, momentarily disrupting the realist narrative frame to point out the absurdity of the situation (see Figure 10.3).

Released by Paramount just before Christmas 1971, *Harold and Maude*'s critical reception was mixed; whilst it garnered many positive reviews some were vitriolic. *Variety*'s review notoriously stated 'Harold and Maude has all the fun and gaiety of a burning orphanage. Ruth Gordon heads the cast as an offensive eccentric who becomes a beacon in the life of a self-destructive rich boy, played by Bud Cort. Together they attend funerals and indulge in specious philosophizing.'[23] *New York Times* critic Vincent Canby's review stated that Ruth Gordon and Bud Cort's performances were 'so aggressive, so creepy and off-putting that Harold and Maude [were] obviously made for each other' and that 'Mr. Cort's baby face and teenage build look grotesque alongside Miss Gordon's tiny, weazened frame'.[24] In essence, such critiques mirrored the moral authority characters I have just described within the film, with reviewers clearly uncomfortable with its radical take on intergenerational relationships.

Despite their concern over the consummation scene, Robert Evans and Peter Bart at Paramount had not expected such a negative critical reaction. Before the film's release, audience previews were carried out that recorded scores of 177 for 'excellent', 112 for 'good', 23 for 'fair' and 13 for 'poor'.[25] In addition, the publicity department at Paramount planned a number of elaborate campaigns that underlined the quirky intergenerational politics of the film. Alongside interviews given by the stars and director, the studio's plan – perhaps not entirely grasping the social critique of conformism in the film – included potential promotional ideas such as creating ice sculptures in local parks, local flower show tie-ins, radio/television show discussions on the theme of 'You needn't grow old', and a local newspaper essay contest on the most humorous reply to 'How I Stay Young', as well as activities such as senior citizens arts festivals and local tree plantings. In their plan they also noted that 'generally the off-beat nature of the property has the college and undergrounds anxious to see the film'.[26]

Cynthia Baron and Mark Bernard present an interesting analysis of *Harold and Maude* in relation to the politics of age and gender.[27] Noting that the film is an anomaly in the casting of an elderly female actor as a lead, they suggest that the era's new permissiveness, whilst allowing such representations, generally tended to rely on 'sex-goddesses expanding the moral boundaries art and exploitation cinema could cross'.[28] They argue, drawing on Robert Sklar,[29] that the critic Manny Farber was significant in the film's eventual success, stating that 'his essays led a younger generation of cult connoisseurs to prize Gordon's performance in *Harold and Maude*'.[30] Quoting Sklar, who argues that Farber advocated a 'resistant cult taste for more obscure and less clearly commodified cultural objects',[31] Baron and Bernard's article notes, for instance, that on 19 May 1972 the *Daily Journal* in Fergus Falls, Minnesota urged readers to see the film.[32] Yet the film only gradually built its audience and became a slow-burning cult success after being re-released twice in the cinema during the 1970s. As Danny Peary confirms, the film eventually became a 'cause célèbre among college-age moviegoers throughout the United States and Canada, breaking longevity records in cities like Detroit, Montreal, and most memorably, Minneapolis, where residents actually picketed the Westgate Theater trying to get the management to replace the picture after a consecutive three-year run'.[33]

This kind of slow-burn success, built on repeated circulation and engagement with a college-age audience, is characteristic of cult films. Many cult films achieved their cultural status through regular and repeated screenings at independent cinemas, often late at night – the so-called 'midnight movies'.[34] Such films – sometimes shown by student film societies – were often socially transgressive, appealing to a youth audience that was sympathetic to the politics of the counterculture. The intergenerational relationship between Harold and Maude, its rejection of traditional social views and flouting of authority, were all important factors in establishing it as a cult film. In an interview, when asked why the film was a cult success, Ashby commented:

> I think it's probably due to a number of things, the first being the kind of black humor that's in the film. I also think that a lot of it has to do with what Ruth Gordon says about life and love in the film. That's the impression I get with the feedback. It's not that she said such profound things in the film, as it is maybe the way she said them. And the spirit of the film makes people laugh. They have a good time with it.[35]

Harold and Maude's enthusiastic adoption by audiences as a cult film, after its initial box-office failure and mixed critical reception, is interesting in relation to the politics of the Hollywood Renaissance. The 'cultification' of *Harold and Maude* presents a contradiction. Whilst the film certainly breaks taboos, its cultification through the 1970s and 1980s also familiarizes the difficult elements, contains the transgressive politics that shocked at the time, and potentially draws attention away from the film's radical intersectional critique. At the same time, the process of becoming a cult film arguably denies Ashby a place in the auteur pantheon of the Hollywood Renaissance: after all, the meanings of cult films belong as much to their audiences as to their filmmakers. The film – perhaps fitting Ashby's own emphasis on collaborative authorship – becomes less determined or framed by the director's personal vision or signature and more a form of communal experience, a sharing of values with and by an audience. A selection of fan mail – in Ashby's papers – illustrates how the film connected intensely with many of its viewers who wished to defend it against its detractors.[36]

It is impossible to discuss *Harold and Maude*, its intersectional politics and its rise to cult status, without discussing its music by Cat Stevens (now Yusuf Islam). The songs often function intertextually, commenting on the mental or emotional state of the characters, or to make a political point – as, for instance, in the scene where a very long zoom out on a cemetery takes place alongside the song 'Where Do the Children Play?', offering a critique of American militarism.

Two signature songs were especially written by Stevens for the film – 'Don't Be Shy' and 'If You Want to Sing Out, Sing Out'. Both songs have a close connection to the content of the film and the two lead characters, commenting on the intersectional nature of their relationship and their eccentricities. The first song accompanies the opening scene. In this scene, Harold (whose face is mainly out of shot), walks slowly down the stairs, then puts a record on; the music is 'Don't Be Shy'. Not only is the song therefore diegetic, it has been chosen by the character to accompany the actions that follow; Harold is 'soundtracking' his own life. The use of the song in this way connects Cat Stevens' music and lyrics directly with the main character's self-expression. The lyrics of the songs work closely with the content of the film, commenting on Harold's character:

Don't be shy, just let your feelings roll on by
Don't wear fear or nobody will know you're there
Just lift your head, and let your feelings out instead
And don't be shy, just let your feelings roll on by.

The other signature song written especially for the film, 'If You Want to Sing Out, Sing Out', is similarly 'chosen' by Maude, but more significantly, it is she who sings and performs the song first. This is during Harold's third visit to her home. She performs it somewhat sloppily, singing out of tune, but with uninhibited joy and brio, encouraging Harold to join in (which he does quietly and shyly). She plays the song in full – her performance is not cut short, condensed or faded out – and as she starts to dance it is comically revealed to have been a pianola automatically playing the notes, another quirky element that adds to the film's cult appeal. It is significant that the studio-recorded version with Cat Stevens' vocals is not heard until much later in the film, after the song's signature status has already been established for Maude and her connection with Harold. The song lyrics are:

> If you want to sing out, sing out.
> Well, if you want to sing out, sing out
> And if you want to be free, be free
> 'Cause there's a million things to be

This song in particular became emblematic for the film and its treatment of personal politics, appearing three times, including the closing scene with Harold, and expressing the countercultural 'live free' philosophy espoused by the film as well as an embrace of the intergenerational bond between the two characters. Both songs played a key role in establishing both the film's cult status and its countercultural appeal. Jamie Sexton, in an examination of cult film and music, notes how film soundtracks 'become enhanced within cult communities',[37] and both the cult status of *Harold and Maude* and the intersectional critique it offers are closely entwined with Cat Stevens' songs.

Oddly, despite the importance of Stevens' songs to the film, a soundtrack of the film was not released until decades later, in spite of his huge success as an artist in the 1970s. Although there was an agreed soundtrack contract between Stevens and the studio, neither song was released until 1984 on any format, contributing to the cult 'rare' nature of the film. The scarcity of the soundtrack songs arguably contributed to the repeated viewing of the film, thus reinforcing its cult status. The cinema was, during the 1970s, the only place where these songs could be heard.[38] Indeed, the two songs maintained their scarcity value; even today, despite the film's reputation, there is no readily available soundtrack: an album was released in 2007 only as a special edition of 2,500 copies, becoming an instantly collectable object reselling for over $600 a copy.[39] Yet the impact of Cat Stevens' songs was not just their place in helping the film acquire cult status, they also position the film's intersectional politics, and its advocacy of free-spirited liberalism: they not only narrate the film, but – as with the actors' performances – reinforce its political message.

Eventually, after multiple re-releases and pioneering the midnight movies exhibition circuit, *Harold and Maude* became not only a cult film but profitable (unlike *The Landlord*). In a memo following an audit of the film's revenues in 1981, the film was recorded to have produced total gross receipts of approximately $6,000,000.[40] The film's slow edging towards profitability mirrors its gradual acquisition of cultural status, and subsequently the film has been released on multiple formats, and in 2012 – emblematic of its status in the canon of cinephile films – was granted a Criterion Collection special collectors release.

This shows the limits of the film auteur model; as I have indicated above, the film was collaborative in production. Ashby's insistence on crediting the contributions of the writer Colin Higgins, cinematographer John Alonzo, musician Cat Stevens and main actors, Ruth Gordon and Bud Cort, is at odds with the Hollywood Renaissance emphasis on the director as sole author. Equally, as the fan letters and cultification of the film show, the meanings of the film and its place in a canon also lie in its reception: whilst *Harold and Maude* was not a success on its initial release, in the following decade it built a dedicated audience following and garnered both critical and commercial success. This points to the contingency of film history – where reputations can rise and fall over time – and the need for scholars to provide diachronic, revisionist accounts of the Hollywood Renaissance period.

Conclusion

In this chapter I have examined how the early films of Hal Ashby engage with intersectional politics. In *The Landlord*, cultural questions of race, class, gentrification and urban displacement are explored, and in *Harold and Maude* intersectional issues of social alienation, gender and age are placed front and centre. In my analysis, I have suggested that the overall exclusion of Ashby's films from dominant narratives of the Hollywood Renaissance has been due partly to their unusual mix of subjects, variations of tone, quirky aesthetics and hippie sensibility, but partly also due to their engagement with and exploration of intersectional politics and countercultural values. These films explore age, gender and race in ways notably different from those addressed by other Hollywood Renaissance filmmakers of the period. Ashby's early films explore social and political issues through a worldview touched by both radical politics and liberal humanism.

Although his type of authorship did not fit the paradigm of the 'movie-brat', and he rejected the auteur label and emphasized the importance of collaboration, I argue that this does not account fully for Ashby's absence from the majority of histories of the Hollywood Renaissance. The use of comedy in *The Landlord* and *Harold and Maude* does not fit canonical accounts of the Hollywood Renaissance, it troubles them: the films are too odd, too bold and too challenging to fit the dominant narrative. Indeed, the use of comedy in Ashby's early films challenges the tacit rules of the Hollywood Renaissance by avoiding a narcissistic focus on the male anti-hero.[41]

One final question that might be posed is what elevated *Harold and Maude* but not *The Landlord* to cult status? In part, I suggest, it is the anti-authoritarian spirit of the former, with Harold and Maude targeting clear authority figures –

the military trying to enlist Harold, the psychiatrist trying to normalize him, the priest offering condemnation – that a college audience can easily align with, or – in Ashby's earlier words – 'have a good time with'. In contrast, *The Landlord* offers a more uncomfortable, rather less palatable truth for audiences: showing that systemic racism and class privilege are intertwined. The elevation of *Harold and Maude* to cult film status, however, also brings potential risks: celebration of the cult object reduces its sense of unfamiliarity, potentially depoliticizing the radical intersectional politics it seeks to explore.

If film history is a process – of remembering, recuperating but also forgetting – then it is also a process of privileging certain forms of knowledge and frames of understanding, over others. Remembering Hal Ashby, and understanding his collaborative filmmaking and humanist vision, questions academic and critical preoccupation with auteur theory and the hegemonic, even reified, narratives of the Hollywood Renaissance. I have argued that such narratives have marginalized or ignored films such as *The Landlord* and *Harold and Maude* that demonstrate important engagements with social issues: of interracial relationships, of age and gender, of social class and the intersectional politics that cut across them. These films present us with an inclusive, life-affirming approach to society and social cohesion, despite their black comedy. In doing so they offer – to revise Robert Kolker's words – a cinema of humanism and community, rather than of loneliness and isolation.[42]

Note: I would like to express my thanks to Nessa Johnston for her insightful comments on the use of music in the films.

Notes

1   For overviews see Geoff King, *New Hollywood Cinema: An Introduction* (London: I.B. Tauris, 2002) and Peter Krämer, *The New Hollywood: From Bonnie and Clyde to Star Wars* (London: Wallflower Press, 2005).

2   Philip Drake, 'Reputational Capital, Creative Conflict and Hollywood Independence: The Case of Hal Ashby', in *American Independent Cinema: Indie, Indiewood and Beyond*, (ed.) Geoff King, Claire Molloy and Yannis Tzioumakis (London: Routledge, 2012), 140–52.

3   Robin Wood, *Hollywood from Vietnam to Reagan* (New York: Columbia University Press, 1986); Michael Ryan and Douglas Kellner, *Camera Politica: The Politics and Ideology of Contemporary Hollywood Film* (Bloomington and Indianapolis: Indiana University Press, 1988).

4   David Thomson, *A New Biographical Dictionary of Film*, 4th edition (London: Little, Brown, 2002), 34.

5   Diane Jacobs, *Hollywood Renaissance* (New York: A. S. Barnes, 1977).

6   Peter Biskind, *Easy Riders, Raging Bulls: How the Sex-Drugs-and Rock 'n' Roll Generation Changed Hollywood* (New York: Simon & Schuster, 1998).

7   Ashby, quoted in Nick Dawson, *Being Hal Ashby: Life of a Hollywood Rebel* (Lexington: University Press of Kentucky, 2009), 101.

8   Drake, 'Reputational Capital', 138.

9   These include Richard Maltby, Daniel Biltereyst and Philippe Meers (ed.),
    Explorations in New Cinema History: Approaches and Case Studies (London:
    Routledge, 2011) and James Chapman, Mark Glancy and Sue Harper (ed.) *The New
    Film History* (Basingstoke: Palgrave Macmillan, 2007), building on the pioneering
    work of Robert C. Allen and Douglas Gomery, *Film History: Theory and Practice*
    (New York: McGraw-Hill, 1985).

10 Dawson, *Being Hal Ashby* and Nick Dawson, *Hal Ashby: Interviews*, (Jackson:
    University Press of Mississippi, 2010).

11 Christopher Beach, *The Films of Hal Ashby* (Detroit: Wayne State University Press,
    2009).

12 Aaron Hunter, *Authoring Hal Ashby: The Myth of the New Hollywood Auteur* (New
    York: Bloomsbury Academic, 2016).

13 Hunter, *Authoring Hal Ashby*, 3.

14 John Caughie, 'Authors and Auteurs: The Uses of Theory', in *The SAGE Handbook
    of Film Studies*, ed. James Donald and Michael Renov (London: SAGE, 2008),
    408–23.

15 Kimberle Crenshaw, 'Demarginalizing the Intersection of Race and Sex: A Black
    Feminist Critique of Antidiscrimination Doctrine, Feminist Theory and Antiracist
    Politics', *University of Chicago Legal Forum* (1989): 139–67.

16 Angela Davis, *Women, Race & Class* (New York: Random House, 1981).

17 F377 *The Landlord* – budgets, Hal Ashby papers, Margaret Herrick Library,
    Academy of Motion Picture Arts and Sciences (hereafter MHL AMPAS).

18 Dawson, *Being Hal Ashby*, 118.

19 F295 *Harold and Maude* – costs, Hal Ashby papers, MHL AMPAS.

20 F315 *Harold and Maude* – Lewis-Higgins, Hal Ashby papers, MHL AMPAS.

21 F289 *Harold and Maude* – correspondence, Hal Ashby papers, MHL AMPAS.

22 Hunter, *Authoring Hal Ashby*, 31.

23 'Harold and Maude', *Variety*, 7 December 1971.

24 Vincent Canby, 'Harold and Maude', *The New York Times*, 21 December 1971.

25 Paramount Production Records – *Harold and Maude*.

26 Paramount Production Records, *Harold and Maude* – publicity.

27 Cynthia Baron and Mark Bernard, 'Cult Connoisseurship and American Female
    Stars in the Sixties: Valuing a Few Withered Tits in the Midst of a "Mammary
    Renaissance"', in *Cult Film Stardom: Offbeat Attractions and Processes of
    Cultification*, ed. Kate Egan and Sarah Thomas (Basingstoke: Palgrave, 2013),
    259–75.

28 Baron and Bernard, 'Cult Connoisseurship', 260.

29 Robert Sklar, 'In Memoriam: Manny Farber, 1917–2008', *Cinema Journal*, 48, no. 3
    (Spring 2009): 66–9.

30 Baron and Bernard, 'Cult Connoisseurship', 261.

31 Sklar, 'In Memoriam', 15, 16.

32 'Everybody's Talking about "Harold and Maude"', *Daily Journal* (Fergus Falls,
    Minnesota), 19 May 1972, 5.

33 Danny Peary, *Cult Movies: The Classics, the Sleepers, the Weird, and the Wonderful*
    (New York: Dell, 1981), 135.

34 Gregory A. Waller, 'Midnight Movies, 1980–1985: A Market Study', in *The Cult Film Experience: Beyond All Reason*, ed. J. P. Tellotte (Austin, TX: University of Texas Press, 1991), 167–86.

35 Ashby quoted in Ralph Appelbaum, 'Positive Thinking: Hal Ashby in an Interview with Ralph Appelbaum', *Films and Filming*, 24, no. 10 (July 1978), http://www.halashby.co.uk/page5.html#FILMS AND FILMING

36 F303 *Harold and Maude* – fan mail, Hal Ashby papers, MHL AMPAS. A selection of the fan mail illustrates how the film connected strongly with its audience. One viewer wrote to Ashby, enclosing their letter to the editor of the *Saturday Weekender* taking it to task for their poor review. Another handwritten letter (4 January 1972) states that it is 'the best movie I have ever seen', having 'seen it 8 times'. Another letter (no date) expresses surprise that the film had such a limited run which elicited a reply by producer Chuck Mulvehill on 17 February 1972: 'Mr Ashby and I are both as upset as you with regard to the handling of "Harold and Maude"'.

37 Jamie Sexton, 'Creeping Decay: Cult Soundtracks, Residual Media, and Digital Technologies', *New Review of Film and Television Studies*, 13, no. 1 (2015): 12.

38 Cat Stevens' deal was originally $10,000 for his services plus 25 per cent of the publisher's share of mechanical income from licensing, with Island Records (and A&M) having the right to use a single released on an album. At this stage, according to the contract notes, it was planned to release a single four weeks prior to the film's opening (on A&M in US and Island Records in UK). However, though Stevens was paid $40,000 for the soundtrack, an album or single was not released with these two songs (F295 *Harold and Maude* – costs, Hal Ashby papers, MHL AMPAS).

39 Oliver Lyttelton, 'The Films Of Hal Ashby: A Retrospective', *Indiewire*, 6 May 2011, http://www.indiewire.com/2011/05/the-films-of-hal-ashby-a-retrospective-118773/

40 F314 *Harold and Maude* – Legal, Hal Ashby papers, MHL AMPAS. This included $200,000 to be recouped before payment of deferments. Ashby was due payments of $65,000 fixed and $35,000 deferred plus 10 per cent of the net profits. In a later audit dispute with the studio, Ashby claimed that he and the producers had not been paid their deferments or profits, claiming that $150,000 was owed to them. The studio was unable to locate information covering $537,769 of distribution expenses and did not include HBO television revenue (recorded as $100,000 by June 1979). By 4 May 1981 a reply from Paramount stated 'everyone seems to think that the film is now operating in the black' and in an agreement made on 14 February 1984 between Hal Ashby and Paramount Pictures a settlement was made with $233,283 added to the net profits, of which Mildred Lewis and Colin Higgins (as producers) received $93,313 and Ashby $23,328.

41 Thomas Elsaesser 'The Pathos of Failure', *Monogram* 6 (1975): 13–19.

42 Robert Phillip Kolker, *A Cinema of Loneliness: Penn, Kubrick, Coppola, Scorsese, Altman* (New York and Oxford: Oxford University Press, 1980).

Chapter 11

A MATTER OF RACE AND GENDER: *LADY SINGS THE BLUES* (1972) AND THE HOLLYWOOD RENAISSANCE CANON

Charlene Regester

When the lynching of an African American is vividly reconstructed onscreen, the sexual exploitation of a young black female adolescent is implied and the drug addiction of a jazz artist is convincingly recreated, we are introduced to *Lady Sings the Blues* (Sidney J. Furie, 1972), a film that emerged during the Hollywood Renaissance of the late 1960s and early 1970s. This has been widely perceived as an era characterized by a level of freedom rarely explored in American film and known for introducing a dramatic transformation in existing film industry standards. Considering that the industry had previously neglected to provide candid representations of African American life, it was only in the context of this renaissance that it was possible to produce such pictures as *Lady Sings the Blues*, based on the life of African American jazz artist Billie Holiday (who was born in 1915 and died in 1959) as recreated in her similarly titled 1956 autobiography (co-authored with *New York Post* writer William Dufty). The film can be regarded as groundbreaking since it demonstrated that pictures featuring black life onscreen could appeal to mainstream audiences, a belief Hollywood had historically denied.

The production of *Lady Sings the Blues*, film scholar Gary Storhoff affirms, succeeded as a crossover film in that it attracted the 'sympathies' of white and black audiences for commercial purposes.[1] As a crossover vehicle, he insists, the film specifically 'depicts experiences unique to African Americans, but it does so by immersing those experiences within a narrative structure that affirms white, middle-class sensibilities and values'.[2] The film was unique to the Hollywood Renaissance not only because it developed cross-racial appeal but also because it foregrounded an African American female jazz artist which was a rarity for Hollywood. Furthermore, the production also employed a number of talented (above- and below-the-line) black workers, which broke with Hollywood tradition and aimed to reflect the politically inspired black American culture associated with the late 1960s and early 1970s when African Americans sought to have their voices heard and their presence acknowledged.

Although the film achieved critical and commercial success, *Lady Sings the Blues* has been rarely, if at all, featured in histories and critical examinations of the Hollywood Renaissance, an issue that more broadly reflects the fact that such histories and examinations have tended to marginalize films representing the African American experience with one or two notable exceptions, such as *Sweet Sweetback's Baadasssss Song* (Melvin van Peebles, 1971). This chapter aims to redress this absence by considering *Lady Sings the Blues* as part of developments associated with the Hollywood Renaissance. Commencing from the film's rather uneasy position between the critically esteemed Hollywood Renaissance and black exploitation filmmaking, the chapter examines the film's long and complicated production history, before discussing its main themes and reception among academic scholars and popular critics.

Lady Sings the Blues: *Between the Hollywood Renaissance and black exploitation*

In many ways, *Lady Sings the Blues* is at odds with the Hollywood Renaissance canon. First and foremost, the film features black protagonists onscreen at a time when their presence was still limited. Second, it was produced by an African American producer, Berry Gordy, founder of Motown Records, who was so committed to the project that he invested approximately $2 million of his own money.[3] Third, it caters both to a black and a mainstream audience, which separates it from the era's black exploitation films that targeted primarily the former demographic even though these films may have appealed to others. Fourth, it contains an impressive array of black talent including actors (Diana Ross, Billy Dee Williams, Richard Pryor, Virginia Capers, Jester Hairston, Lynn Hamilton, Jayne Kennedy – uncredited, Harry Caesar, Paulene Myers, Scatman Crothers), technicians (Charles Washburn – assistant director, Ernest Robinson – stunts, Louis McKay [Holiday's former spouse] – technical advisor) and musical composers (Oliver Nelson, who abandoned the project due to his disappointment with the script).[4] Finally, the film creates a (black) soundtrack using musicians who actually worked with Holiday such as Harry 'Sweets' Edison (trumpeter), Red Holloway (bassist) and John Collins (guitarist),[5] aiming to provide as rich and authentic an experience to audiences as possible.

It is clear then that *Lady Sings the Blues* mirrors the Hollywood Renaissance in its innovativeness, ability to cross traditional boundaries and introduction of experimental approaches to producing pictures in ways Hollywood previously ignored, neglected or failed to attempt. This is perhaps best encapsulated in the casting of singer/recording artist Diana Ross as Holiday, untested as an actress in a big studio production, but also in the film's frank representation of issues such as drug addiction which would not have been possible a mere five years earlier, before the ratings system was instituted in 1968 and provided Hollywood with the freedom to make films for a variety of audience demographics. As Hollywood challenged its traditional practices with the film's production, the filmmakers found an opportunity to introduce a complicated story which reflected the complex artist whose life it represented.

In addition to the strong affinities *Lady Sings the Blues* has with the Hollywood Renaissance, the film also is strongly associated with the black exploitation era which emerged concomitantly in the late 1960s and crystalized in the first half of the 1970s. Films emerging from the black exploitation period, according to Mark Reid, corresponded 'to the black community's increasing rejection of nonviolent protest' and represented the 'desires of the African-American audience (to be more visibly seen) and their lived experiences (to be more visibly reconstructed onscreen)'.[6] While *Lady Sings the Blues* was not deliberately designed to oppose non-violence as a form of resistance, it nonetheless did indirectly appropriate the African American experience through Holiday's politicization as her politically inspired music reverberated with the racial politics unique to the 1930s, 1940s and 1950s. Moreover, black exploitation films, according to Novotny Lawrence, depict a 'black hero or heroine' and feature a range of black supporting characters, an attribute *Lady Sings the Blues* clearly shares with them. These films also frequently include 'contemporary rhythm-and-blues soundtracks that match the filmic images in theme and content', another characteristic *Lady Sings the Blues* shares with black exploitation titles.[7] As Ed Guerrero argues, many of these black-centred revolutionary films grew out of the 'rising political and social consciousness of black people', not surprisingly also creating 'a large black audience thirsting to see their full humanity depicted on the commercial cinema screen'.[8] These pictures were deliberately designed to satiate the appetite of audiences who craved such multidimensional representations with 'black-focused themes and narratives',[9] another element they share with *Lady Sings the Blues*.

As Hollywood responded to this rising black consciousness by making a large number of films, Guerrero claims that in the aftermath of the black exploitation era the industry 'developed more subtle and masked forms of devaluing' blacks onscreen. When black exploitation films were no longer profitable, Hollywood resorted to 'openly stereotypical modes of representation'.[10] In his estimation, in order for Hollywood to retain its black audience, it started 'produc[ing] more "crossover" films and focus[ing] on the careers of a few isolated black celebrities who fit into the traditional, white-dominated "star system"'.[11] Certainly *Lady Sings the Blues* is a crossover film, especially as the film focuses on the representation of black stardom and exploits both Holiday's and Ross's star status to ensure that *Lady Sings the Blues* will have crossover appeal. Treading a thin line between Hollywood Renaissance and black exploitation filmmaking makes *Lady Sings the Blues* a particularly interesting example of representing the black experience, all the more so given its sixteen-year production history and Holiday's complex relationship with the American cinema industry.

Old Hollywood to Hollywood Renaissance: Making Lady Sings the Blues

With the publication of Holiday's 1956 autobiography it was well understood that the singer was interested in having her story depicted onscreen since it was designed 'to make some money' and she desired to 'possibly sell it to the movies'.[12] Yet, Holiday had reservations about the project, especially given her previously alienating experience with Hollywood when she was cast in the demeaning role of a maid in *New Orleans* (Arthur Lubin, 1947). Having made an earlier uncredited appearance in 'mob scenes in a picture with Paul Robeson'[13] – a picture that may have been *The Emperor Jones* (Dudley Murphy, 1933)[14] – Holiday was later recruited for a 'real part' in Duke Ellington's movie-short *Symphony in Black: A Rhapsody of Negro Life* (Fred Waller, 1935)[15], a film she describes as 'a musical, with a little story to it, and it gave me a chance to sing a song—a real weird and pretty blues number'.[16]

While these early screen appearances suggested a potentially promising movie career, her casting as a maid in *New Orleans* left her with a bad taste. The film allegedly was an outgrowth of an earlier production Orson Welles (who had established a relationship with Holiday) developed; it was called *The Story of Jazz* and was to be part of an anthology (*It's All True*) on jazz but was never completed. However, this idea later became the nucleus for *New Orleans*,[17] a film which focuses on white opera singer Miralee Smith (Dorothy Patrick) who travels to New Orleans with her mother to cultivate her career – a career which is interrupted when she develops an attraction to gambler Nick Duquesne (Arturo de Cordova), halted when she gravitates to jazz and ragtime music with her black maid Endie (Billie Holiday) and stalled when she becomes mesmerized with New Orleans music dives where Louis (Satchmo) Armstrong (along with his band) plays.

In her subservient role as maid to white opera singer Miralee, Holiday/Endie is provided with opportunities to showcase her voice and talent. While in a nightclub, she is invited by trumpeter Louis Armstrong to sing 'Do You Know What It Means to Miss New Orleans', and later she sings 'Farewell to Storyville' (with the nightclub audience singing the song's refrain). Later in the film when the story relocates her and Armstrong to Chicago, she sings 'The Blues are Brewin', which represents her final film appearance.[18] Even though Holiday was granted some opportunities to sing onscreen, she disliked immensely her casting as a maid and, not surprisingly, became extremely apprehensive about working in another Hollywood picture. As a result, after *New Orleans* she appeared only in the movie-shorts *Frankie 'Sugar Chile' Robinson, Billie Holiday, Count Basie and His Sextet* (Will Cowan, 1950) and *The Sound of Jazz* (Jack

Smight, 1957),[19] both productions where she played herself (a performer) and was not required to act.

But these minimal roles did not fulfil her desire to have her own story depicted onscreen and when discussions surfaced regarding a film adaptation of her autobiography, Holiday realized that she was 'too old' by industry standards to play herself and feared she would be grossly distorted when the picture was made. Acknowledging her inability to depict herself, Holiday desired to produce the film's soundtrack with a younger actress who would be cast as herself. Plans were proposed to record songs for the picture's soundtrack in France, 'but it all fell through when the Algerian crisis forced the French government to close all the concert halls'.[20] Although the soundtrack was never produced, several actresses were considered for the coveted role, including black actress Dorothy Dandridge (the first black actress nominated for a best actress Academy Award for *Carmen Jones* [Otto Preminger, 1954]).[21] While Holiday lent her tacit approval to Dandridge, she was less approving of white actress Ava Gardner – an actress who played the mulatto role in *Show Boat* (George Sidney, 1951), a part denied to black actress Lena Horne, Holiday's confidante.[22] Other white actresses considered for the prominent Holiday role included Lana Turner (an avid Holiday fan[23]) whom Holiday viewed with some degree of affection but this did not necessarily mean she endorsed her as the picture's lead.

The project, however, did not gain momentum until film producer Lester Cowan submitted a letter to Holiday and Louis McKay (Holiday's second spouse) proposing that she 'could make "honest movies about people who stay brown all year round" if [she] wrote off the South, made up the gross from Europe, and raised capital to make the film from exhibitors in the North, who would then show the film no matter how controversial it turned out to be'.[24] Cowan's wife Ann Ronell (a songwriter) developed the initial script entitled *The Trial of Billie Holiday*,[25] while Cowan 'optioned' the biography 'as a United Artists project' for Dandridge with proposed director Anthony Mann (director of *The Glenn Miller Story* in 1954).[26] According to press reports, United Artists 'advanced money' for the film and the Puerto Rican government agreed to 'fund [the] construction' of sets required for the picture's production in that region.[27] But this film version never materialized. Cowan then moved to replace Dandridge as the film's lead, proposing instead black actress Diahann Carroll but, again, he was unsuccessful in getting the film into production. Other reports, however, suggest that as early as 1959 producer Philip A. Waxman established a verbal agreement with Dandridge for the picture to be co-produced with Albert Zugsmith, who 'bought the option' to the book.[28] Unfortunately, this venture too became another failed attempt, even though additional reports claim both Dandridge and Carroll were being considered for two different Holiday films.[29] Cowan, insistent on filming Holiday's life, later proposed another script entitled *Blue New York* which Dufty and Ronell co-wrote. White French actress Jeanne Moreau was considered for the lead due to her performance in *Eva* (Joseph Losey, 1962)[30] but, like the other attempts, this one did not materialize either.

Representing another unsuccessful effort to produce Holiday's story, in 1965 black actor and producer Ossie Davis proposed *The Billie Holiday Story*. Despite developing the property for three years (a *Variety* report in 1971 claimed Davis had a film package in place which included himself as producer, Millard Lampell as screenwriter, John Berry as director and black actress Diana Sands as the film's lead[31]), the film never made it into production. Davis worked with the production company Third World Cinema and recruited John Hammond to serve as musical director (Hammond was hired to produce a soundtrack using Columbia's original recordings of Holiday's songs).[32] But as Davis' project failed, in 1968 Joe Glaser, Holiday's former agent, 'obtained the rights to [her] [...] life story based on the book'[33] with the intent of adapting it to the screen himself. However, Glaser's Associated Book Corporation which represented Holiday's estate struggled with producer David Susskind over the film rights – a struggle that ultimately led to another thwarted attempt to produce a Holiday picture.

One year later, Jay Weston, a publicity agent for Paul Anka, Cinerama and the Newport Jazz Festival, who had been interested in the project as early as 1964, renewed his interest and secured the film rights from McKay and Glaser.[34] Previously, Weston had successfully produced *For Love of Ivy* (Daniel Mann, 1968), a romantic film which featured black actors Sidney Poitier and Abbey Lincoln. Based on her performance in that film, Lincoln was considered for the revived Holiday picture but she declined the offer which led to Diahann Carroll being reconsidered for the role.[35] When the production company Cinema Center Films relinquished its support of this revived project,[36] Weston approached Canadian screenwriter Terence McCloy to write a script which impressed filmmaker Sidney J. Furie who approached Paramount for the production of the picture. At Furie's suggestion, several black actresses were considered for the lead, including Carroll, Cicely Tyson (cast in *A Man Called Adam* [Leo Penn, 1966], and later nominated for a best actress Academy Award for *Sounder* [Martin Ritt, 1972]), Lola Falana (*The Liberation of L.B. Jones* [William Wyler, 1970])[37] and Diana Ross (lead singer with the Supremes and Motown recording artist).

Ultimately, Berry Gordy, Jr, who signed on with the project, made the final decision regarding the film's lead. Initially, he was reluctant to accept Furie's casting proposition which included Ross as the lead since he believed she lacked acting experience but he reconsidered her when he learned she could be nominated for an Academy Award. Entertaining the possibility that this could be a vehicle for Ross that would help her to ascend from pop singer to international superstar (and increase Motown's visibility globally), Gordy agreed to Furie's casting preference.[38] In July 1971, the announcement that Ross was the film's lead encountered considerable opposition, particularly from those who either remembered Holiday or were enamoured with the former jazz singer.[39] According to Daniel Kremer, Furie's biographer, 'Most everyone's initial reaction to the announcement was one of doubt, if not pure trepidation.'[40] Many critics were concerned the film would fail to accurately reflect Holiday's life and believed Ross was inappropriate for portraying the singer. Among those who opposed Ross were Louis McKay, Leonard Feather (jazz pianist, promoter) and Roger Ebert (film critic).[41] Specifically, Ebert charged that while Ross had the potential to be convincing as Holiday and he knew she could sing, he 'couldn't imagine [her] [...] reaching the emotional highs and lows of one of the more extreme public lives of our time.'[42] Affirming his doubts, film historian Donald Bogle expounds:

> Nobody was quite prepared for this screen version of jazz singer Billie Holiday's life. In fact, a number of people were ready to dismiss the film right off the bat as simply a fraud and a travesty. From the moment it had been announced that pop singer [...] Ross would portray Holiday, most thought her all wrong for the role. Where Lady Day had been all stillness and quiet fire [...] Ross was a razzle-dazzle extrovert, a skinny, high-strung live wire who never seemed to stop moving. Then, too, it was feared the movie would whitewash Holiday's drug experiences and her series of love affairs and marriages.[43]

Farah Jasmine Griffin also located opposition to Ross's casting as being related to her lack of acting experience and perceived inability to effectively reproduce Holiday's music so as to convey the black suffering infused in Holiday's songs, especially as 'Ross had never listened to Holiday's recordings' prior to her involvement with the picture.[44]

Ignoring these concerns, with Gordy's commitment to the project and a script rewritten by Gordy's creative assistant Suzanne de Passe and Chris Clark (both of whom had been involved in the development process from the start), it was clear that the film would be made. The revised script was submitted to Paramount, which approved the project, secured financing, and hired Louis McKay as technical consultant. While Ross was hired as the film's main star, her romantic partner remained undecided until two black male actors, Paul Winfield and Billy Dee Williams auditioned for the part. Based on their performance, Gordy detected a chemistry between Ross and Williams during their auditions and decided on him. Furthermore, Gordy believed Williams personified a black version of white romantic screen idol Clark Gable, and this propelled his decision.[45] Later in the process, black comedian Richard Pryor joined the cast (as Piano Man) and he was so impressive, his role was expanded to accommodate his magnetic screen persona.[46]

With the cast assembled, the picture's production began but tensions escalated between white director Furie (who quit twice) and black producer Gordy. According to Kremer, 'Furie told Gordy that he wanted his input but [...] the film had to have only "one boss on the set."'[47] As these differences were resolved, the film exceeded the $2 million budget Paramount provided, and in order to complete the project and exert some degree of control, Gordy invested his own money and doubled the film's budget.[48]

At the film's completion and with Gordy's promotion, *Lady Sings the Blues* became one of the highest grossing films of 1972, received five Academy Award nominations (including one for Ross in the Best Actress category) while the film's soundtrack became the fastest selling album in Motown's history. Moreover, the picture won an NAACP Image Award as the year's best picture and received the Martin Luther King, Jr. Award for cinematic excellence. Even as late as the 1990s *Ebony* magazine characterized *Lady Sings the Blues* as one of the top black films of all time.[49] Considering the picture's commercial and promotional success, it is necessary to examine the film's plot and focus on some of the key issues and themes advanced, and thus to explore its relationship with the Hollywood Renaissance in more detail.

Lady Sings the Blues: *Gender, stardom and race*

The film opens when Holiday is fingerprinted, photographed and escorted to a prison by cell guards who struggle to hold her upright as her uncontrollable body shrieks from their gripping hands while she attempts to retain some level of consciousness in her drug-induced state. She is carried to a padded cell where she is locked in solitary confinement and collapses to the floor while jerking her head back and forth; she screams and cries out as the overhead shot provides spectators with a glimpse of this dispossessed woman wearing a straitjacket, an image in stark contrast to the sultry, seductive beauty Holiday (the real person) radiated onstage. The film then cuts to a young Holiday as an adolescent in the late 1920s who is fascinated with music but confined to domestic labour when she prepares to clean a brothel. Observing the young woman, an older gentleman waves money in the air for sexual favours but the brothel's madame (Isabelle Sanford) deters his request. The audience realizes that Holiday's narrative unfolds through a series of flashbacks as scenes from the later stages of her life when she faces drug addiction (in the late 1940s) are contrasted with her early years (in the 1920s) when as an adolescent she resides with relatives. The young Holiday (the character) disillusioned with domestic work and subjected to sexual assault, flees this environment to reunite with her mother who works as a domestic. But determined to reject life as a domestic or a prostitute, Holiday is intent on building her singing career. Her initial attempt at establishing this career is deterred when she auditions as a dancer and is flatly rejected but when the piano player salvages her audition and commands her to sing for the club owner, Holiday impresses with her singing talent and is hired on the spot. During the audition, Holiday detects the club owner reviewing a playbill featuring white actress Billie Dove and this compels her to suddenly adopt the stage name Billie (Holiday).

Overcoming her insecurities as a singer and refusing to pick up tips with her skirt, she meets romantic idol Louis McKay (Billie Dee Williams) who introduces her to more sophisticated venues for developing her talent and who later becomes her booking agent, protector, confidante and lover. As Holiday gains notoriety as a singer her first night club employer celebrates her one-year anniversary; here she is introduced to the white Reg Hangley Band (loosely based on Artie Shaw's band) who she later joins (1938). Touring the South with this white band Holiday faces some of the most segregated practices characteristic of the region; she witnesses a lynching which leads her to popularize the song 'Strange Fruit'. Enduring this exhausting tour, she is introduced to morphine which leads to her later addiction. As her addiction escalates, her relationship with McKay declines. In one scene she hides in a bathroom against his wishes and nearly assaults him with a razor as he attempts to halt her from engaging in another fix. In another scene, Holiday collapses onstage and during intermission she receives a phone call announcing her mother's death but she is so inebriated that she is barely able to verbally articulate the news and seems slow to react emotionally, yet the piano man embodies the emotionalism she should possess.

Recognizing her deterioration, Holiday admits herself to rehab when McKay visits and proposes marriage but her temporary happiness is disrupted when two narcotics detectives arrest her. Following her return from incarceration, she is denied a license to perform in New York and McKay attempts to revive her career; he arranges for her to perform in Los Angeles but the weakened Holiday, along with her piano man, returns to indulging in drugs. McKay rescues Holiday from a drug deal gone bad and returns her to New York to prepare her for her premiere concert at Carnegie Hall (1956, three years prior to her 1959 death). Holiday's life story is narrated through a number of newspaper clippings which are flashed on the screen and unfold through her music, music that frequently coincided with her experiences evinced in songs such as, 'God Bless the Child', 'I Cried for You', 'Them There Eyes' and 'Lover Man', among others.

One of the more apparent themes which surfaces in the dramatization is how the black male figure assumes a dominant position, often sidelining the female protagonist. In *Lady Sings the Blues*, we as spectators no longer 'gaze/look' at Holiday as the object of desire but instead 'gaze/look' at Williams who becomes the object of desire as he seems 'too good to be true'. He is well mannered, groomed and dressed in his capacity as lover, manager and agent for Holiday as he protects her from herself. He intervenes when she is overcome with addiction, he provides a home for her when needed, he protects her from music industry predators, he shields her from imposing photographers and news reporters and he comforts her at her lowest points. With these attributes, he is to be admired and may be even more admired than Holiday who has tremendous talent but whose vulnerabilities destabilize her star stature. In de-centering the black female figure in her own narrative at the expense of positioning the black male as the object of desire, *Lady Sings the Blues* is in line with Hollywood Renaissance films which are well known for privileging male perspectives and filtering narrative events through male viewpoints.

At the same time, Holiday is constructed as a star and her stardom becomes most apparent in the costumes she displays throughout the film. As she gains notoriety as an artist her costumes become more sophisticated. For example, when she auditions in a yellow belted dress with a matching hat and gloves, she not only wins her first public opportunity to sing before audiences but garners the attention of McKay. On another occasion, when Holiday is invited to perform for a radio show where only white entertainers are allowed and she is deliberately rejected in the studio, her alienation is compensated for when spectators view her star-like power which is expressed in her tailored blue suit with a matching hat trimmed in mink. Her attire suggests that while the racial politics denied her access, she is still very much a star and therefore a powerful woman in her own right. Throughout the film as she performs onstage, she wears elegant gowns often accompanied with white gardenias in her hair, a further hint at her signature style and star status. Later in her career, when she ventures to the West Coast she is seen on the beach wearing a turban, scarf and fox fur, another unmistakable indication of the stardom she has achieved. Through her costumes Holiday claims the star status she earned and reflects the star status which the film intends to convey, despite the fact that her central position in the narrative and her position as an object of desire are often destabilized, as I mentioned earlier. In this respect, *Lady Sings the Blues*, like several other films of the era, seems to embrace contradictory impulses.

While many doubted that rhythm-and-blues singer Diana Ross had the ability to execute Holiday's story, this pop artist succeeds on some level but this is certainly not to deny that Ross physically did not resemble Holiday since Ross was darker in complexion, slimmer in size and more girlish in her demeanour in comparison to Holiday who was lighter in complexion, larger in size and much more mature in her demeanour. Despite these physical differences between the two women, the film managed to compensate for their differences even in their singing styles. Ross, a pop artist, successfully interprets Holiday's music and re-introduces the music to another generation of fans. She makes the music meaningful through the songs which reverberate with the personal struggles Holiday faced in her own life. Further, Ross manages to convey how Holiday was a race woman articulated through her music which speaks to the racial politics of an earlier era yet resonated with the political consciousness associated with the black exploitation period, making Holiday's music even more relevant and palatable to a different generation. Holiday's music foregrounded in the film is designed to not only capture her spirit and convey what she contributed to the music industry, but also to demonstrate how she used music to bridge the racial divide that existed not only in 1950s segregated America but permeated an integrated (though racially polarized) 1970s America. The fact that this political project is achieved through the onscreen reconstruction of a black woman's life is certainly radical and underscores even more the film's kinship to the Hollywood Renaissance as such stories were rarely considered worthy of production in Hollywood cinema before that time. Not surprisingly, when the picture was released, it invited an abundance of divergent opinions from scholars and critics.

Lady Sings the Blues: *Scholarly and critical reception*

Commercially successful and the recipient of numerous awards, *Lady Sings the Blues* received very mixed reviews, with the negative ones often focusing on the film's inability to capture the essence of Holiday and the ways she represented a very particular black experience. The writer James Baldwin asserts: 'The film that has been made is impeccably put together, with an irreproachable professional polish, and has one or two nice moments. It has absolutely nothing to do with Billie, or with jazz, or any other kind of music, or the risks of an artist, or American life, or black life [...]. The script is as empty as a banana peel, and as treacherous.'[50] But then Baldwin shifts from directing his comments toward the film to criticizing the cinema industry for its misuse of African American actors. He asserts, 'They [the actors] might have been treated with more respect by the country to which they gave so much' and sarcastically notes, 'but, then, we had to send telegrams to the mayor of New York City, asking him to call off the cops who surrounded Billie's bedside – looking for heroin in her ice cream – and let the Lady die in peace.'[51] Baldwin makes the point that black actors were not only marginalized onscreen but were marginalized offscreen as was the case with Holiday when attempts were made to arrest her while she was hospitalized prior to her death.[52] Regarding the film actors, Baldwin posits:

> For, indeed, the most exasperating aspects of *Lady Sings the Blues*, for me, is that the three principals – [Ross, Williams and Pryor] – are, clearly, ready, willing, and able to stretch out and go a distance not permitted by the film. And, even within this straitjacket, they manage marvelous moments, and a truth which is not in the script is sometimes glimpsed through them. Diana Ross, clearly, respected Billie too much to try to imitate her.[53]

In comparison, film scholar Maureen Turim, casting aspersions on *Lady Sings the Blues*, suggests that the film 'cheats us of a real remembrance of or education about the singer's life and instead hands us a formula.'[54] Regarding Ross's depiction of Holiday, Turim emphatically declares, 'the modern star plays the dead artist; the dead artist remains dead, but the modern star gains a new life.'[55] According to Turim, 'the danger behind this substitution of a Hollywood image for reality is obvious; it leads to a false sense of history and therefore a false political perspective.'[56] From Turim's perspective, 'By far the most serious fault of the film is its refusal to present Billie Holiday as a serious artist, which I contend was done for three reasons – because she was black, because she was a woman and because it preferred to wallow in a voyeuristic and simplistically moralistic view of her struggle with dope addiction.'[57] Turim concludes, 'What we don't have [with the film], because Hollywood didn't find it convenient, is a real understanding of this woman as an artist or a real historical picture of the racism that she faced,'[58] a position other critics articulate as well. According to Turim, 'the final product is shamefully didactic and apologetic – presenting jazz for the white man not in black terms but whitewashed and made legitimate by white participation'.[59]

As scholars have admonished the film for its distorted representation of Holiday and inability to capture the authentic Holiday, film reviewers revealed a range of responses that extend from extolling the film's strengths to illuminating its weaknesses. *Variety* observed, 'Individual opinions about *Lady Sings the Blues* may vary markedly, depending on a person's age, knowledge of jazz tradition and feeling for it, and how one wishes to regard the late Billie Holiday as both a force and a victim of her times.'[60] In terms of the film's strengths, Bogle admitted, 'There had never been [...] a black movie like it.'[61] Bogle further emphasized the picture's strengths when he insightfully noted that for once 'we see a black couple meet, court, fight, make up, fight again, and are more cautious about commitment,'[62] an attribute seldom seen on screen when it came to black life. Given that black romance historically had rarely been presented in this manner, the film succeeded in conveying to audiences that blacks were no longer dehumanized through avoiding 'more authentic' visual representations of romantic encounters.

Bogle, like a number of popular film reviewers, focused substantially on Ross's strengths in her Holiday characterization. For example, he observed, Ross 'performs with such a surprising mixture of confidence, vulnerability, and open-faced charm that you can't help liking and rooting for her'.[63] In a similar vein, *New York Times* critic Vincent Canby noted, 'Most important, [Ross's] singing of the more than a dozen songs once sung by Miss Holiday is a talented, very intelligent singer's homage to a jazz style of a sophistication never since matched by anyone.'[64] Paralleling Canby, Margaret Devoe was impressed with Ross's portrayal and unequivocally declared, 'The only bright point to the movie is [...] Ross [...]. And she doesn't save the portrayal of Billie Holiday but she does prove that there is quite a bit more to [the actress] than the sequin-bedecked, bouffant-hairdoed image projected [...] as lead singer of the *Supremes*.'[65] Affirming Ross's contribution, Holiday's biographer John Szwed insisted, 'Ross was certainly not bad in her performance, and if anything, she was almost too good – too beautiful, too charming, too full of energy and playfulness to be Billie Holiday.'[66] Szwed's comments, however, should be viewed with caution since others attested to Holiday's beauty, charm and wit. Laudatory of Ross's ability to re-enact Holiday, *New York Times*'s Caryn James opined, 'Though [Ross's] performance captured Holiday's toughness and vulnerability, it also created an effect resembling double exposure, with one singer layered over another. On screen, the audience was clearly meant to recognize Holiday with her trademark gardenia and blues, but the face and voice just as clearly belonged to Diana Ross.'[67]

However, not all critics applauded Ross. For instance, a reviewer for the Baltimore-based *Afro-American* wrote, 'Like most beginning actors, Miss Ross mimics. And while I sympathize with her mimicking, I am untouched, unmoved, and unconvinced. I even wonder if Miss Ross should be grateful for this opportunity to have a public acting lesson.'[68] In his estimation, 'the choice of a fine singer without any acting experience to portray a complex human being who happens to be a singer is itself a typical Nothingness decision.'[69] *Los Angeles Times* critic Charles Champlin admitted that, while 'in some of the songs she [...] reproduces, with startling fidelity, that wistful, plaintive, wounded child quietness which made Billie Holiday heartbreaking to hear', in others 'she misses [...] something of the rhythmic and melodic freedom which made Holiday a true jazz singer'.[70] Articulating a similar sentiment, *New Yorker* magazine's Pauline Kael insisted, 'There's no pain in [...] Ross's voice, and none of that lazy, sullen sexiness that was a form of effrontery and a turn-on.'[71]

These critics and others accused the film of neglecting the racial ostracism that Holiday endured in her own life. Among those who elaborated on the film's inauthentic representations, Bogle candidly revealed:

> Although there is a melodramatically jolting Southern sequence with the Klan, there are few of the nondramatic everyday humiliations and tensions that gnawed at and eroded Holiday's spirit: the times when she was told not to mix or mingle with the whites who came to hear her perform; the occasions when she had to use the back entrances of the clubs or take freight elevators so as to not offend white patrons; the times club managers and owners complained that her singing style was too slow and moody, not fast or peppy enough.[72]

These racial offences are avoided in the film, according to Bogle, and shield spectators not only from the harsh realities of race during segregation but the experiences of a black woman attempting to cultivate her talent in an unequal and uneven world. Similarly, the Baltimore *Afro-American* reviewer was critical of the film's inability to capture Holiday's persona and relates, 'It is the portrayal of complex human conditions without assigning any rank of importance to them and without any meaningful explanation of the causes and effects of the conditions. It emphasizes spectacle rather than thought.'[73] Kael posited that the film 'fails to do justice to the musical life of which Billie Holiday was a part', and faltered in its inability to '[show] what made her a star, much less, what made her an artist'.[74] Moreover, Kael characterized the film as 'Factually [...] a fraud' even while proclaiming it delivers 'emotionally',[75] yet in her opinion it still 'avoids the complexity of the race issues in [Holiday's] life, making her strictly a victim'.[76]

As it is clear from these reviews, *Lady Sings the Blues*, despite its strong affinities with the Hollywood Renaissance, was largely perceived by critics as lacking some of the key elements that came to characterize its most important films. At a time when the spirit of the counterculture could be detected in films with anti-heroes who were questioning America and filmmakers who would experiment with narrative, style and genre, *Lady Sings the Blues* was seen to be rather superficial in these respects, despite its effort to provide a black perspective and to destabilize the spectators' relationship with narrative roles and viewing positions. It is not surprising then that it has not been considered a key film in the Hollywood Renaissance canon.

Conclusion

Lady Sings the Blues received a mixed reception from both scholars and film reviewers yet the film did succeed on many levels – it conveyed Holiday's story, became a commercial success and won a number of awards. Emerging during the later years of the Hollywood Renaissance, an era that witnessed a new level of freedom in the cinema industry and became known for its innovativeness in filmmaking techniques, but also an era that coincided with black exploitation films and privileged the articulation of male perspectives in Hollywood storytelling, *Lady Sings the Blues* was a deeply contradictory filmic statement. Sharing elements with both black exploitation and Hollywood Renaissance filmmaking, telling the story of a black woman while also highlighting the pleasures of looking at a black man, oscillating between privileging narrative and emphasizing stardom, reconciling jazz with pop, Billie Holiday with Diana Ross, the conservative 1950s with the progressive 1970s, it is not surprising that *Lady Sings the Blues* fits awkwardly with the canon of the films that constitute the object of study in this collection. On the other hand, it is important for studies of the Hollywood Renaissance to start questioning its canon and the extent to which it privileges particular types of film while excluding others. Besides providing a unique opportunity to explore the intersection of race and gender and in spite of Diana Ross's arguable engagement in her own mythmaking, *Lady Sings the Blues* established a renewed appeal for Holiday, re-introduced Holiday to a later generation of viewers previously unfamiliar with the singer's musical genius and fostered the continuing legacy of this complex performer in a film that would not have been possible before the years of the Hollywood Renaissance.

Notes

1   Gary Storhoff, '"Strange Fruit": *Lady Sings the Blues* as a Crossover Film', *Journal of Popular Film and Television* 30, no. 2 (2002): 105.

2 Storhoff, "'Strange Fruit'", 112.

3 Daniel Kremer, *Sidney J. Furie: Life and Films* (Lexington: University of Kentucky Press, 2015), 166. According to Kremer, Berry Gordy embarked on test screenings of the film during production to ensure the picture's appeal and improve its production quality. He even edited portions of the film and was instrumental in producing the picture's soundtrack.

4 Donald Clarke, *Billie Holiday: Wishing on the Moon* [Original book title *Wishing on the Moon: The Life and Times of Billie Holiday*] (Cambridge: Da Capo Press, 2002), 450–1 and Internet Movie Database www.imdb.com/title/tt0068828/fullcredits.

5 'Lady Sings the Blues', *American Film Institute* (AFI) *Catalog*, http://www.afi.com/members/catalog

6 Mark A. Reid, *Redefining Black Film* (Berkeley: University of California Press, 1993), 70.

7 Novotny Lawrence, *Blaxploitation Films of the 1970s: Blackness and Genre* (New York: Routledge, 2008), 19, 20.

8 Ed Guerrero, *Framing Blackness: The African American Image in Film* (Philadelphia, PA: Temple University Press, 1993), 69.

9 Guerrero, *Framing Blackness*, 70.

10 Guerrero, *Framing Blackness*, 70.

11 Guerrero, *Framing Blackness*, 71.

12 Clarke, *Billie Holiday*, 395.

13 Billie Holiday with William Dufty, *Lady Sings the Blues* (London: Barrie & Jenkins, 1956), 52.

14 Clarke, *Billie Holiday*, 83.

15 Holiday with Dufty, *Lady Sings the Blues*, 52; and Larry Richards, *African American Films Through 1959: A Comprehensive, Illustrated Filmography* (Jefferson, NC: McFarland, 1998), 169.

16 Holiday with Dufty, *Lady Sings the Blues*, 52.

17 John Szwed, *Billie Holiday: The Musician and the Myth* (New York: Viking, 2015), 56–9.

18 *New Orleans* (1947), http://www.imdb.com/title/tt0039655/soundtrack. Soundtrack credits for *New Orleans* indicate that Holiday sings 'Endie' and Louis Armstrong plays the song when his band tours Paris and he is reunited with Miralee. In the version screened, Holiday's version of the song may have been deleted.

19 Richards, *African American Films*, 165 and 159.

20 Clarke, *Billie Holiday*, 420.

21 Clarke, *Billie Holiday*, 400.

22 Clarke, *Billie Holiday*, 400.

23 Holiday with Dufty, *Lady Sings the Blues*, 102; Szwed, *Billie Holiday*, 65.

24 Clarke, *Billie Holiday*, 402.

25 Szwed, *Billie Holiday*, 64.

26 Kremer, *Sidney J. Furie*, 152–3.

27 Szwed, *Billie Holiday*, 65.

28 Kremer, *Sidney J. Furie*, 153; 'Lady Sings the Blues', *AFI Catalog*.

29 Szwed, *Billie Holiday*, 67.

30 Szwed, *Billie Holiday*, 66.

31 'Lady Sings the Blues', *AFI Catalog*.

32 Szwed, *Billie Holiday*, 67. Davis even intimated that he and his production team would conduct research on Holiday's early years in Baltimore, rather than rely on Holiday's autobiography, which suggests that he probably did not own the rights to Holiday's biography.

33 'Lady Sings the Blues', *AFI Catalog*.

34 Kremer, *Sidney J. Furie*, 153; 'Lady Sings the Blues', *AFI Catalog*.

35 Szwed, *Billie Holiday*, 68.

36 Kremer, *Sidney J. Furie*, 154.

37 Kremer, *Sidney J. Furie*, 154–5.

38 Kremer, *Sidney J. Furie*, 155–6; Farah Jasmine Griffin, *If You Can't Be Free, Be a Mystery* (New York: The Free Press, 2001), 59.

39 Kremer, *Sidney J. Furie*, 156; Farah Jasmine Griffin, *If You Can't Be Free*, 59.

40 Kremer, *Sidney J. Furie*, 156.

41 Kremer, *Sidney J. Furie*, 157.

42 Roger Ebert, 'Lady Sings the Blues Movie Review', 1 January 1972, http://www. rogerebert.com/reviews/lady-sings-the-blues-1972.

43 Donald Bogle, *Blacks in American Films and Television: An Encyclopedia* (New York: Garland, 1988), 126.

44 Griffin, *If You Can't Be Free*, 59.

45 Kremer, *Sidney J. Furie*, 159–60.

46 Kremer, *Sidney J. Furie*, 160.

47 Kremer, *Sidney J. Furie*, 161.

48 J. Randy Taraborrelli, *Diana Ross: An Unauthorized Biography* (New York: Citadel Press, 2007), 258.

49 'To Honor the Star: Lady Sings the Blues', *Chicago Defender* (Daily Edition), 15 March 1973, 15; 'Lady Sings the Blues', *AFI Catalog*; 'Lady Sings the Blues Is Fastest Selling Album in Motown's History', *Pittsburgh Courier*, 30 December 1972, 19; 'Lady Sings the Blues Wins NAACP Image Award', *Atlanta Daily World*, 23 November 1972, 3; 'Top Black Films of All Times', *Ebony* 54, no. 1 (November 1998), 154; 'Lady Sings the Blues is Biggest Hit', *Chicago Daily Defender*, 14 December 1972, 17.

50 James Baldwin, *The Price of the Ticket: Collected Nonfiction, 1948–1985* (New York: St. Martin's/Marek Press, 1985), 620.

51 Baldwin, *The Price of the Ticket*, 621.

52 Clarke, *Wishing on the Moon*, 438.

53 Baldwin, *The Price of the Ticket*, 622–3.

54 Maureen Turim, 'Lady Sings the Blues', *Velvet Light Trap* 8 (Spring 1973), 34.

55 Turim, 'Lady Sings the Blues', 35.

56 Turim, 'Lady Sings the Blues', 35.

57 Turim, 'Lady Sings the Blues', 35.

58 Turim, 'Lady Sings the Blues', 36.

59 Turim, 'Lady Sings the Blues', 37.

60 'Lady Sings the Blues', *Variety Movie Reviews*, 1 January 1972, 57.

61 Bogle, *Blacks in American Films and Television*, 128.

62 Bogle, *Blacks in American Films and Television*, 128.

63 Bogle, *Blacks in American Films and Television*, 128.

64 Vincent Canby, 'Screen: Billie Holiday: Lady Sings the Blues Stars Diana Ross', *New York Times*, 19 October 1972, http://www.nytimes.com/movie/review?res=9B07E5D A113DEF34BC4152DFB6678389669EDE&mcubz=1.

65 Margaret Devoe, 'Paying Back Debts: Billie Holiday', *Off Our Backs* 3, no. 5 (January 1973): 14.

66 Szwed, *Billie Holiday*, 71.

67 Caryn James, 'Film View: Movie Biography Mustn't Tamper with Pop Icons', *New York Times*, 3 September 1989, H11.

68 'Movie Review: *Lady Sings the Blues*', *Baltimore Afro-American*, 18 November 1972, 11.

69 'Movie Review: *Lady Sings the Blues*', 11.

70 Charles Champlin, 'Movie Review: Two Ladies Who Sing the Blues', *Los Angeles Times*, 25 October 1972, E1.

71 Pauline Kael, 'The Current Cinema: Pop Versus Jazz', *New Yorker*, November 4, 1972, 157.

72 Bogle, *Blacks in American Films and Television*, 127.

73 'Movie Review: '*Lady Sings the Blues*', 11.

74 Kael, 'The Current Cinema: Pop Versus Jazz', 152.

75 Kael, 'The Current Cinema: Pop Versus Jazz', 152.

76 Kael, 'The Current Cinema: Pop Versus Jazz', 154.

Chapter 12

DE NIRO AND SCORSESE: DIRECTOR-ACTOR COLLABORATION IN *MEAN STREETS* (1973) AND THE HOLLYWOOD RENAISSANCE

R. Colin Tait

There is no doubt that Martin Scorsese is one of the quintessential American filmmakers. Forged in – and contributing to – the crucible of the Hollywood Renaissance, Scorsese's films *Mean Streets* (1973), *Alice Doesn't Live Here Anymore* (1974), *Taxi Driver* (1976) and *New York, New York* (1977) remain some of the most distinctive works of the 1970s, and have established the filmmaker within the pantheon of great American directors. All but one of these films starred Scorsese's comrade-in-arms and key collaborator Robert De Niro, who is mostly omitted from this larger history. Scorsese is one of the key filmmakers in Robert Kolker's study of 1970s filmmaking *Cinema of Loneliness*[1] and Peter Biskind's popular and sordid account of the 1970s, *Easy Riders, Raging Bulls*.[2] Moreover, Scorsese talks regularly about his own place in cinema, appearing in multiple volumes such as *Scorsese on Scorsese*[3] and in myriad documentaries. He not only presents himself as one of the survivors of an otherwise messy decade, but as one of the foremost authorities of film.

Although it is inarguable that Scorsese remains the template of *the* American auteur, he did not become this archetype alone. In fact, as he admits, his success in the 1970s came from his able collaborators who helped him to shape, hone and refine his auteur signature, if not his craft. These early contributors include editors Marcia Lucas (*Taxi Driver*, *New York, New York*), screenwriters Mardik Martin (*Mean Streets*) and Paul Schrader (*Taxi Driver*), and cinematographer Michael Chapman (*Taxi Driver*, *The Last Waltz*, 1978, *American Boy: A Profile of Steven Prince*, 1978), among many others. Most importantly, his collaborators include a trio of actors, all of whom worked with him in different phases of his career in multiple films: Robert De Niro, Daniel Day-Lewis and Leonardo di Caprio.

Among all of these partners, De Niro stands the tallest. However, in the ensuing decades between the 1970s and today, De Niro's reputation as a creative and intellectual force in filmmaking has receded, while Scorsese's has grown.

Certainly, the actor's career today, not to mention his less critic-friendly movies such as *Meet the Parents* (Jay Roach, 2000) and *Dirty Grandpa* (Dan Mazer, 2016), have contributed to this fall from the canon of great actors. Biographer Shawn Levy describes the 'present-day' De Niro in the following way: 'thirty years later it can be hard sometimes to see De Niro's early glories through what had become the muddle of his later career'.[4] Levy notes that the actor in the twenty-first century 'erased much of the goodwill – and, indeed the awe – accrued by the younger De Niro'.[5] As Scorsese's auteur status ascended, so has De Niro's reputation as an esteemed actor and creator declined.

Within the contexts of De Niro's declining reputation and his omission from the auteur-driven histories of the Hollywood Renaissance, this chapter will redress the balance by examining the actor's contribution to Scorsese's films, paying particular attention to their first film together, *Mean Streets*. This examination, however, will not locate De Niro's contribution in isolation but instead will seek to (re)attach it to Scorsese's contribution, in the form of a 'creative pair'.

However one looks at De Niro's career, his best performances are found in Scorsese's Hollywood Renaissance and early post-Renaissance films, from *Mean Streets* to *Taxi Driver*, to *New York, New York, Raging Bull* (1980) and *The King of Comedy* (1982). Taken together these titles represent some of the most important films of the Hollywood Renaissance and beyond. They urge us to revisit Scorsese's films with an eye not only to understanding how Scorsese made them, but how De Niro functioned as an equal partner within them. Using archival documents found in Robert De Niro's own script notes and associated papers related to *Mean Streets*, I read along the 'archival grain'[6] to find substantial traces of De Niro within these films that extend beyond his performance, to describe how the Scorsese-De Niro early partnership began with this film and how it subsequently evolved.

Along the way, I use Joshua Wolf Shenk's book *Powers of Two* to establish how De Niro and Scorsese constitute one of film history's most significant creative duos, comparable to other famous pairs whose last names indicate their closeness.[7] Shenk proposes that these collaborative works result in art that is greater than either artist can create individually, and that the film medium is one of the best places to explore how such collaboration takes place. One major site of this process is the practice of improvisation, which I explore throughout this essay.

Following George Kouvaros' study of John Cassavetes, *Where Does it Happen: John Cassavetes and Cinema at the Breaking Point*,[8] I establish that both Scorsese and De Niro were greatly influenced by the era in which they were making films. For Scorsese, this means that he emulated the collaborative/improvisatory model he admired in Cassavetes' work. How he was going to achieve this effect was another story. When De Niro entered the production of *Mean Streets*, he was well-seasoned in the practice of working scenes in rehearsal via the acting exercise of improvisation. A student of Stella Adler,

De Niro's technique was grounded in script analysis which he learned in Adler's class. At the same time, his early film work with Brian De Palma, in such films as *Greetings* (1968), *The Wedding Party* (1969) and *Hi Mom!* (1970), almost entirely liberated De Niro from needing a script, leaving him free to engage in a synthesis of flexible, on-screen and in-character exploration, as well as teaching him how his characters dictate action in a film.[9] When De Niro and Scorsese finally met, each possessed the skills that they needed to complement the other's artistic practices, especially at this early point in their careers. It is fair to say that each individual within the duo grew significantly with each film in their Hollywood Renaissance streak and beyond, reaching their peak with *Raging Bull* – a high watermark for American cinema, if not for film history.

In writing the history of the partnership and collaboration between De Niro and Scorsese, with particular emphasis on their first film and the help of De Niro's own documents related to it, this chapter aims to re-insert the actor as a major creative force in the films that he helped make. Putting aside the inevitable comparisons to star and auteur studies for the moment, utilizing this archival material allows scholars to directly locate De Niro's individual contributions to the film that extend beyond creating his performance – from alterations to the script and rewriting scenes via improvisation to his intensive character work and even his choice of Johnny Boy's iconic hat, haircut and costumes.

Harvey Keitel is certainly *Mean Streets*'s protagonist, yet De Niro's Johnny Boy gradually overshadows Keitel's Charlie, simply by way of out-acting his scene partner. Though Johnny Boy was a supporting role, De Niro received star billing in the film, which ultimately led to his being cast in *The Godfather II* (Francis Ford Coppola, 1974) in the following year. While it is impossible to pinpoint whether this greater emphasis was a result of De Niro's 'quality' as an actor, it is clear, via the script pages, that De Niro not only argued for more screen time, but also urged Scorsese to make structural changes to the script that made his character and his arc much stronger than Scorsese as director and co-screenwriter originally had intended.[10] The next section discusses how specifically De Niro influenced the production of *Mean Streets*. First, however, I outline the ways in which Scorsese and De Niro can be approached as a creative pair.

De Niro, Scorsese and the 'Powers of Two'

Although Scorsese retains the aura of the lone, solitary genius, fighting against the system in the Hollywood Renaissance years and beyond, the reality is that he could not have done this without De Niro, nor could De Niro have ascended to the heights he did without a willing partner like Scorsese. Shenk provides an excellent framework to consider how this creative pair became an autonomous, interdependent artistic team.

Using the example of one of the greatest music duos, John Lennon and Paul McCartney, Shenk outlines not only how they came to write some of the most memorable songs of the twentieth century, but also how neither figure quite achieved the same heights outside of their partnership. Applying this template to De Niro and Scorsese provides a useful comparison to consider how this partnership functioned. Shenk refers to Lennon and McCartney's songs as co-owned.[11] Likewise, I suggest that the De Niro-Scorsese films, especially the ones they made during the 1970s, are not the product of a single auteurist sensibility, but are 'co-owned' by this creative pair. Scorsese's own description of his working relationship with De Niro resembles Shenk's description of 'homophily' – where the partners cement their friendship based first on their 'love of the same', then beginning a necessary progression through the three key stages of 'presence, confidence and trust'.[12]

In Scorsese's early interviews about *Mean Streets,* 'trust' and 'intimacy' are terms that the director uses to describe his relationship with De Niro: 'We feel many things the same way. We understand each other perfectly. We don't need words to work together. The communication between us is like a form of sign-language.'[13] Levy interprets this relationship as a 'subverbal understanding of one another'.[14] Elsewhere, Scorsese states that working with 'Bobby' is like being 'as close as Siamese twins emotionally', and that they were 'tied together for the good and the bad – for everything', although there are qualities of the relationship that they themselves 'cannot explain'.

Reluctant to describe any part of his process, De Niro stated that there is 'a connection [with Scorsese] but it's hard for me to define'.[15] Elsewhere, De Niro resisted the claim that he is Scorsese's 'alter ego':

> Sometimes I say, 'Look, I'm gonna do this,' and somehow he knows that's right to do, to make that choice. Marty is very good at picking up on things. He gives people more latitude to come up with ideas, because he's not afraid to experiment with things or accept ideas from other people. And even if they seem a little off-the-wall, sometimes an idea that's so out in left field is actually more appropriate than you would imagine. And he's able to see that and orchestrate it in the scene—maybe bring it down a notch if it's too much but still keep the basic idea intact. We have a kind of shorthand understanding about a lot of things. It's a lot more complicated than 'alter ego.'[16]

That Scorsese is so talkative while De Niro is taciturn does not mean that one partner is more intellectual about the process of filmmaking. Rather it means that one of Scorsese's greatest strengths within the early partnership was sharpening De Niro's talents for the big screen. Likewise, De Niro translated the shorthand that he and Scorsese had and interpreted it on screen. Often it is workshopped together in private meetings before shooting scenes. From there, De Niro brings choices to his performance and gives the director options, as he did in *Mean Streets* and later in their collaborative partnership.

Scorsese 'found a perfect actor for the work he wanted to do' and De Niro 'had found a director who was willing to work with him in a way that felt familiar and comfortable, who accepted his groping process, his incessant questioning of details, his need to make every bit of work intimate in order to allow his energy to flow fully'.[17] De Niro's trust in Scorsese elevated his acting game *and* Scorsese's direction. What makes a De Niro-Scorsese film great is the fusion of confidence, trust and faith in the other person's abilities.[18]

Shenk outlines six stages about how creative pairs operate and the various phases of their output: i) Meeting; ii) Confluence; iii) Dialectics; iv) Distance; v) The Infinite Game; and vi) Interruption.[19] In this chapter, I focus on the first three stages which Shenk defines as follows:

I.   *Meeting.* Looking at the earliest encounter of individuals who will form a pair, the conditions and characteristics that engender chemistry or electricity – unusual similarities coinciding with unusual differences – become clear.

II. *Confluence.* Over time, two individuals move beyond mere interest and excitement in each other – they truly become a pair by surrendering elements of their singular selves to form what psychologists call a 'joint identity'.

III. *Dialectics.* In the heart of their creative work, pairs thrive on distinct and enmeshed roles, taking up positions in archetypal combinations that point to the essential place of dichotomy in the creative process.[20]

Specifically, I examine how stages one and two came together, aiming to demonstrate how they were synthesized in stage three, with *Mean Streets* as a case study.[21] Given the amount of attention dedicated to Scorsese's practice my emphasis here is primarily on De Niro's role and the extent to which his approach to his craft and his labour found a perfect recipient in Scorsese and his own approach to work.

Besides utilizing Shenk's approach to creative pairs I also borrow from Aaron Hunter and his work on another director, Scorsese's contemporary Hal Ashby. Hunter's assessment of Ashby's collaborative filmmaking practice actively works against the auteur myth that has underlined many histories of the Hollywood Renaissance (see also Chapter 10). He states that 'a typical Ashby film is noticeable for the ways in which it bears the marks of its multiple authors',[22] an argument that is also applicable to Scorsese's work. Like Ashby, Scorsese utilizes the 'collaborative approach to film practice, one which resulted in a recognizable form of multiple authorship' in order to potentially 'expand current conceptions of New Hollywood and its canon rather than simply replicating existing ones'.[23] Hunter's ideas enable the identification of both De Niro and Scorsese as primary authors of their films, while also leaving room to consider the contributions of others. Re-viewing *Mean Streets* in this particular way allows for the possibility of acknowledging Scorsese's directorial contributions, while also facilitating a more complete understanding of other agents' work, and De Niro's in particular. It is now time to examine how Shenk's first three stages in the formation of creative pairs can be detected in the Scorsese-De Niro collaboration.

I. Meeting

For stage one, we can see how the odd coincidence of De Niro and Scorsese meeting at a party led to their initial collaboration in *Mean Streets*. Descriptions of their encounter by Scorsese indicate that there was a creative spark from the very beginning. As Levy puts it, 'from such a humble instance of kismet came the decades-long relationship between the great director Martin Scorsese and his greatest asset and alter ego, Robert De Niro'.[24] After realizing that they had seen each other in various places growing up near New York City's 14th Street, and that they had friends in common, the pair moved into a gentle ease of talking to one another – which was not something that De Niro was known for. According to Julia Cameron, Scorsese's second wife, the director and actor were soon engrossed in conversation. Cameron stated that 'De Niro found in Martin the one person who would talk for fifteen minutes on the way a character would tie a knot.' She had also 'seen them go at it for ten hours virtually non-stop'.[25]

New York City proves an important 'Magnet Place', for the pair's mutual interests and their meeting.[26] Though they lived mere blocks apart, they could not have had more different backgrounds. The story of Scorsese's upbringing – a frail child, watching the criminal activities of Little Italy's mean streets – is told in many places, not least of which is documented in the opening sequence in one of Scorsese's most famous films, *GoodFellas* (1990). De Niro's, however, is less-well-known. Though the pair lived on opposite sides of 14th Street – Scorsese in Little Italy and De Niro in Greenwich Village – the differences between the neighbourhoods dictated very different childhoods. Scorsese was immersed in the Italian-American milieu, complete with the crime, excessive masculinity, Catholicism and distinctive cultural identity that defined his working-class neighbourhood. He channelled this into his *Mean Streets* screenplay with New York University friend and collaborator Mardik Martin.

De Niro was the child of two Modernist painters, Virginia Admiral and Robert De Niro Sr. According to John Baxter, the De Niro-Admiral apartment was an exciting place to live, resembling a French salon,[27] as was the multi-ethnic neighbourhood that the De Niros inhabited. De Niro's parents were opposites in this regard as well. De Niro Sr was the son of Italian immigrants whose homosexuality and obsession with his painting led to heartbreak throughout his life.[28] Admiral was from Oregon, dabbled in Communism at Berkeley and later became a painter, then a typist, then a writer.[29] Her status as a woman and mother underscored and undermined her brilliance and determination to finance 'Bobby's' childhood. The elder Robert's self-destructive tendencies meant that the couple divorced soon after they were married.[30]

'Bobby Milk' – as De Niro was called on account of his pale skin – was encouraged to follow his artistic and intellectual pursuits and inclinations early, enrolling first in German émigré dramatist's Erwin Piscator's school of drama at an early age at the nearby New School and observing the diversity of people and ideas in his Greenwich Village home. In and out of various schools, and eventually a high school dropout, De Niro's upbringing – divorced parents, experiential rather than traditionally intellectual, quietly observant rather than verbose – contrasted with Scorsese's traditional Italian-Catholic upbringing. However, both were pedigreed in different ways. De Niro studied with Stella Adler and eventually with Lee Strasberg, and Scorsese in one of the first film classes at New York University's formative programs with Haig Manoogian, to whom he would later dedicate *Raging Bull*. While it is generally assumed that De Niro resembles the Italian characters that he became identified with, the 'real' De Niro's cultural make-up is multi-layered, much like the actor himself.

These details feed into Shenk's first category, 'Meeting'.[31] As the actor and director both describe, they had seen each other around the neighbourhood and knew the same people. They were introduced by a mutual friend, Brian De Palma, who had directed De Niro in three movies, *The Wedding Party*, *Greetings* and *Hi Mom!* and had helped him adapt his improvisatory character work from the stage to the big screen. This initial meeting led the director and actor to expose each other to their similarities, and also the differences that would define the dialectics of their creative partnership as described in Shenk's Stage 3.

II. Confluence and III. Dialectics

After Scorsese pitched *Mean Streets* to him, De Niro expressed his desire to play the lead role. Eventually, the actor was convinced that Johnny Boy was the character to whom he could best apply his skills, resulting in the confluence of their mutual interests. For Scorsese, De Niro possessed the extensive experience with the improvisatory practices that the director wanted to utilize for his new film effort. In Scorsese, De Niro saw a figure that he could talk to and who understood what he was trying to bring to life on screen. While De Niro was on-set, Scorsese employed open stagings of scenes, letting the actor unleash the explosive performances that came to characterize his work in the Hollywood Renaissance films and beyond, while in other scenes Scorsese employed longer and longer takes, running the camera for extended periods as he followed De Niro's improvisatory experiments. Thus, the dialectical signature of the pairing began to be established as it would continue into the later part of the decade.

De Niro's notes are instructive, not only for the creation of his *Mean Streets* character, but also for the material *labour* he put into this role and the ways in which it shaped the production of the film more broadly. Considering Shenk's 'dialectics' category, De Niro's writing reveals the work on his character, and also how he and Scorsese expanded the role and in the process modified the film itself. Paraphrasing Shenk, De Niro's acting multiplied by Scorsese's direction equals cinematic gold. These notes reveal how his technique and craftsmanship were able to evolve, while simultaneously demonstrating how Scorsese's filmmaking became more complicated once he began collaborating with the actor. Of course, it is impossible to describe exactly the electric quality surrounding their work. However, approaching that work through the prism of Shenk's initial three categories will provide strong insights into that elusive quality (see Figure 12.1).

Returning to De Niro's role in the film's creation, it is instructive to look at his films before *Mean Streets* to trace how he translated the lessons he learned from Stella Adler into his own orthodoxy for his film career. The first way that De Niro contributed to *Mean Streets* was through his intensive research – a practice that began as a student of Adler's script analysis class, and which he applied to his period work as a Depression-era robber in Roger Corman's *Bloody Mama* (1970). These techniques became more pronounced with his performance as Bruce Pearson in *Bang the Drum Slowly* (John D. Hancock, 1973), where De Niro played a baseball player who is dying of a terminal illness. Though released in the same year, *Bang the Drum Slowly* was shot before *Mean Streets* and De Niro had spent much of the previous year first preparing for that role, then shooting on the set. Cast in the role of a baseball player, De Niro started learning the sport from scratch, taught himself to be a back-catcher and spent time in a small Georgia town, recording conversations with locals, and modelling his behaviour after the people he observed there.[32]

Figure 12.1 De Niro's labour affected Scorsese's approach to filmmaking and vice versa. *Mean Streets.* Copyright Warner Bros.

Similarly, for *Mean Streets*, the De Niro Papers reveal, the actor spent a long period outside of his Greenwich Village neighbourhood, observing the residents of Little Italy, and finding models for his characterization of Johnny Boy. In this sense, one can see how the actor embodied Shenk's category of 'confluence'. His often exhaustive research made his character come close to the ideal Scorsese had in mind when it came to the portrayal of Johnny Boy, given the filmmaker's upbringing in Little Italy and the actor's background outside it. On the other hand, for Scorsese, it meant that he found an actor that he could absolutely trust in materializing his very specific vision on screen.[33]

De Niro's notes during this research period reveal the stages of his work as he moved from his notebooks to his script, and eventually to his performance. One of the first ways that one knows De Niro spent time in Little Italy is in an early note, where the actor outlines his mission to 'find out how I'm really different from [how] they are'.[34] In the same document, De Niro chronicled common expressions and mannerisms, such as the expression 'Madonna mia!' followed up by the note to not 'overdo it cause *they* don't',[35] and the practice of crossing himself when he passes by a church, or polishing his shoes on his pants.[36]

De Niro also added flourishes to his character's dialogue, noting that 'I say "you know," and "but" a lot'.[37] While this detail seems insignificant, one can see how this vernacular speech made its way into the script in De Niro's dialogue, reflecting the actor's commitment to verisimilitude. Elsewhere, De Niro asks 'what time period' the movie takes place in, demonstrating a commitment to historical accuracy that became more pronounced in the actor's work later in his career.[38] De Niro questioned the relationships of his character with his friends in the film, writing, 'What's my feeling and attitude toward Charlie, Jimmy, Michael, Tony + everyone' noting that he wants to '[h]ave it when enter[ing] each scene'.[39]

A hallmark of all of De Niro's scripts, the actor wrote lists of questions for his director. One document/note, entitled 'Notes for Marty', has more than twenty-four bullet points, questioning what season the film takes place in and other specific points within the script. One assumes from questions like 'Why am I the way I am (+ don't appreciate Charlie's help) when I catch them together ... p. 90 [in the script]' produced later conversations between the director and the actor as did points regarding the order of shooting, which was very important to the actor. De Niro's central question for Scorsese is summed up in one of his notes, where he asks, simply 'Can I be arrogant?' – arguably the central trait in Johnny Boy's character. Finally, since the movie is based on biographical details from Scorsese's life, De Niro asks questions like, 'have you ever seen anybody get shot?'[40]

The second way we can trace De Niro's labour in the film's development is via his costume work. Although costume choice is usually the domain of the production designer, De Niro's selection of props and outfits are not only proof of these elements being crucial to his creation of a character, but also of a blurring of the lines between the role that De Niro was hired for (acting) and other roles in the production process. De Niro does not simply see himself as a 'mere' actor, but as someone who contributes uncredited labour to other departments as well. In *Mean Streets* this labour extends to story and screenwriting via improvisation and costume work, whereas by the time *Raging Bull* was made, De Niro's labour includes costume, screenwriting, producing and casting. While this is a thread that is rarely addressed in relation to acting, De Niro's careful selection of his wardrobe – including Johnny Boy's iconic hat – constitutes concrete choices which expand his character beyond Mardik Martin's and Scorsese's script. That De Niro kept all of his costumes from all of his movies, and the fact that he agreed to the donation of his papers on the condition that the archive could prioritize care of *these* artefacts, indicates that costume work is as important and valid a means of understanding the actor's process as any other.

In De Niro's audition he wore the iconic hat that would define his portrayal of Johnny Boy (see Figure 12.2). According to Levy,

> De Niro went to discuss the role with Scorsese and, as ever, came prepared with props – in this case a small brimmed fedora. Little did he know when he selected it from his closet that it would be the thing that nailed it for him. 'I had never seen Bobby act when I cast him in *Mean Streets*,' Scorsese remembered. 'We just talked. He was wearing a hat and tilted it a certain way, saying that he thought the character would wear it that way, and I hired him' (As he put it later, 'When I saw him in that crazy hat, I knew he'd be perfect').[41]

Figure 12.2 Johnny Boy's iconic hat was brought in by De Niro himself. *Mean Streets.* Copyright Warner Bros.

So, while it may seem counterintuitive to concentrate on De Niro's costume choices within the film, elements of building his performance on screen can be identified – from his audition for *Mean Streets* and in increasing degrees within the collaborative partnership. Moreover, the fact that his labour in the film's pre-production made it to the screen as part of his overall performance offers more proof that the pair were moving away from singular artistic personalities towards a joint identity.

Notes regarding De Niro's choices, found in the *Mean Streets* shooting script, are concrete examples of what can be considered the actor's supplemental 'writing' within the production. In particular, a note entitled 'Costume list' reveals substantial contributions of De Niro regarding Johnny Boy's dress and what it ultimately means for the actor. That De Niro was allowed to include these details indicates a substantial amount of trust on the part of the director and demonstrates that the collaboration between De Niro and Scorsese went beyond the normal boundaries between the categories of actor and director, especially within the context of American cinema that had been historically characterized by a clear division of labour.

The note begins with 'Clothes' and 'what to get'. In this list, De Niro has noted to get a 'handkerchief', a 'knit shirt', a 'three quarter jacket' and a 'St. Christopher Medal' which were presumably based on his observations of the neighbourhood. De Niro also had planned his scouting mission, indicated in his note to 'Walk around Westside + see styles', including '[s]hoes, hair, clothes, etc.'[42] The goal, it seems, was to '[l]ook at clothes' in particular stores in Little Italy, so that he can observe fashion trends on the Westside in order 'to see how styles are'.[43] To produce an idea of authenticity, De Niro sought out '[m]ainly guys in neighborhood'.[44]

Johnny Boy's hairstyle is also extremely important to the actor, reappearing in notes to Scorsese related to the time period, in addition to getting a 'Haircut (after decide with Marty)'. Additionally, he asked the director whether 'Is it now. Cause if now hair styles could be different. More mod esp. for me also for youth esp. other guys are not into much.'[45] While this list may seem trivial, these details reveal De Niro's commitment to authenticity for his character.

De Niro's elaboration of Johnny Boy's backstory is another aspect of this labour, as revealed in a page pertaining to his character's debts. This document was entitled, 'What I Owe' and has actual calculations of Johnny's debts, how much money he makes at his job, and finally what remains to be paid to his friends.[46] For example, De Niro worked out the specific details of who his character owes money to, and how much the totals are. Though it is not *directly* indicated in the script, De Niro has inferred that, 'I owe Mickey 3,000, about. I ain't paid him for 8 months. Started as $500.00 loan.' He also writes that 'I owe Tony [the bartender] about $80. He charges us a dollar a shot plus puts it on our tab.' Since debt is such a huge issue for his character, De Niro has also counted the gap between what and when he gets paid, and how these issues relate:

I get paid on Tuesday for the Mon thru Fri. before. I work on the truck down at St. Johnsbury on Spring Street. I don't like it. I don't go there anymore. I get 4 dollars an hour. After taxes $110.00 about. Moreover, someone, presumably Charlie 'went thru a lot to get me on the trucks.'[47]

This last area opens up space for De Niro's biggest additions to *Mean Streets*, where the actor added formal changes to his shooting script and nuance to his character in his collaboration with Scorsese and his co-star Harvey Keitel. As I will demonstrate in the next section, De Niro's contributions included his work via improvisation. While it is impossible to tell precisely how improvisation operated within the film, and who contributed what, the actor's records reveal, at the very least, how he prepared for particular scenes and the lines *he* brought to the set to experiment with in his scenes with Keitel.

The best example can be found in the 'Joey Clams' scene – as inspired a work of improvisation as anything in cinema. It is here that De Niro best *enhances* Scorsese's and Martin's original script, adding his improvisatory skill to Scorsese's filmmaking practice. In these moments, we can best see the fusion of the director's and the actor's work, where it is impossible to tell who is doing what on screen. As indicated previously, the fusion of De Niro's style and Scorsese's approach amounts to a dialectical synthesis, and the movie produces electricity when De Niro is on screen, and sags when he is not. Thus, when De Niro's unique acting style and presence meet Scorsese's distinctive auteur vision, the synthesis of these elements results in the 'genius' that is usually attributed to Scorsese but is actually due to the combination of this creative pair.

Improvisation in film: The 'Joey Clams' scene

In 1980 Virginia Wright Wexman questioned the lack of writing on acting and collaboration between actors and directors in cinema. Entitling her pioneering essay 'The Rhetoric of Cinematic Improvisation', she asks the reasons for these omissions:

Yet the contributions of actors are also an important part of cinema, now more than ever before when the collaboration of actors, writers and directors has been emphasized by recent films that stress improvisation. What the directors who work in collaboration with actors seem to be striving for is the sense of discovery that comes from the unexpected and predictable in human behavior. If we think of art as a means of giving form to life, improvisation can be looked at as one way of adding to our sense of the liveliness of art, a means of avoiding the sterility that results from rote recitations of abstract conventional forms. [...] Though many films make extensive use of improvisation, it is usually difficult, if not impossible, to obtain accurate documentation about precisely when and how the improvisation occurs.[48]

Assessing De Niro's improvisatory contribution with documentation from the De Niro Papers offers a partial solution to this problem. Comparing De Niro's scripts to Scorsese's and Mardik Martin's shooting drafts (also found in the *Mean Streets* file at the archive) allows us to assess the changes occurring between the writing and shooting phases. De Niro's notes indicate that his improvisatory practice is not 'spontaneous'. Rather, he worked out scenes on paper, then in rehearsal before coming to the set, suggesting that there is 'writing' taking place on his end of the production, a practice that has expanded in his later work with Scorsese.

Scorsese has spoken specifically about the nature of improvisation in the scriptwriting and rehearsal process in *Mean Streets*. According to the filmmaker:

> For *Mean Streets*, we rehearsed for ten days, untangling the web of relationships between the four male characters and Teresa. I gave them the impression that they could invent anything they liked. When they were relaxed, they were happy to add humor to their dialogue [...]. Improvisation didn't mean we departed from the script. We couldn't allow ourselves to do that.[49]

Improvisation was used throughout the film and the rehearsal process, so comparing the shooting script to De Niro's notes reveals the changes taking place between development and rehearsal and the actual shooting. De Niro's notes on the back of his script pages are indicative of these changes. The script was not rewritten into updated drafts, suggesting that De Niro had the freedom to contribute significantly through improvisation as the shooting continued.

As these notes are undated, determining precisely what occurred during shooting is not possible. Maybe De Niro copied down ideas discovered in the rehearsal process and these then made their way into the script. However, these notes indicate that De Niro contributed something significant to the fabric of the film. They reflect that De Niro came up with variations of certain lines in advance, complicating ideas about improvisation and spontaneity on film. These parenthetical notes are the best indications of his contributions to the film that start from creating his performance and extend to 'writing' the story.

Because Scorsese was a novice to improvisation, whereas De Niro was well schooled in it, my conclusion is that improvisation is the intangible category where De Niro and Scorsese combined their talents. According to Scorsese, by the time of *New York, New York*, the improvisation and shooting stages were abbreviated and ultimately fused, to the point of rehearsing 'as we filmed', and 'film[ing] as we rehearsed'.[50] Since Scorsese has not only noted the influence of Cassavetes on his own filmmaking, but made *Mean Streets* on Cassavetes' strong encouragement and with his support, it is important to take a brief detour and consider the nature of Cassavetes' practice, particularly as this provides a framework to understand how improvisation works in cinema.[51]

George Kouvaros' book on John Cassavetes' filmmaking processes is useful here, as it provides a detailed examination of the actor-filmmaker's reliance on seasoned actors, rehearsals, character backstories and improvisation to create on-screen spontaneity. Kouvaros describes acting in Cassavetes' films as 'creating', with 'the performer's mannerisms, gestures, and vocal range construct[ing] a history of relationships that is multifaceted yet bound to a singular space of corporeal expression'.[52] Applying this to De Niro, it is possible to write a history of his own collaborations by way of the differences between the actor's mannerisms, gestures and vocal performances, measured *against* the script – making way for understanding De Niro's interpretation of his characters in great detail.

One major obstacle in the process of writing such a history is that documents pertaining to rehearsals are almost impossible to find. Nevertheless, considering how rehearsals help to shape relationships (such as Johnny Boy's and Michael's) on screen, can demonstrate how the actors' labour remains important. Writing specifically about *Shadows* (John Cassavetes, 1959), Kouvaros states that it was based on a 'series of dramatic improvisations, supervised by Cassavetes' where the 'actors were encouraged to develop their characters and relationships in the weeks of rehearsal prior to filming'.[53] Since this was also the practice in De Palma's early movies, where actors improvised together in rehearsal and then the script was written from audio recordings of these sessions,[54] I see De Niro as the missing link that bridges Cassavetes, De Palma and Scorsese.

As De Niro was versed in this practice, he brought these skills to Scorsese's set and helped to incorporate this new working method into the films he has directed. This is particularly true of the scenes with De Niro, where the actor distinguishes himself from the rest of the cast with his vibrant dialogue, some of which he has clearly rewritten in tandem with Scorsese. Once again, one can see these episodes less as the efforts of two individual players, and more as 'jam-sessions' where each musician adds their best ideas to the final product.

I have argued in this chapter and in my earlier work that De Niro's script notes are important sources where one can trace the exact nature of his labour in a film production. While in my previous work I provide an analysis of these notes, here I would like to go further by focusing solely on the actor's labour within the production, citing moments where De Niro contributed physically to the production process.[55] Or, to put it differently, I provide a very brief example of De Niro's 'history of relationships' in *Mean Streets* as this relates to a particular scene by comparing the creation of this history by De Niro during the development and rehearsal periods of the film with the script and its materialization on screen. The best evidence for this is found in the 'Joey Clams' scene, for which De Niro is arguably the primary author. His fusion with Scorsese is at such a high level that the director is simply recording the scene and Harvey Keitel is keeping up.

Robert Kolker wrote that the scene, if not *Mean Streets* as a whole, is less about plot and more about dialogue. He states: '*Mean Streets* is not about what motivates Charlie and Johnny Boy [...] but about how they see, how Charlie perceives his world and Johnny Boy reacts to it.'[56] In his view, the film's dialogue is as important as what the viewer sees, as it is rooted in the particulars of 'New York working-class usage, profoundly obscene and charged with movement.'[57] For him, the 'Joey Clams' scene holds the key not only to understanding how the film works, but how Johnny Boy's telling of his story in the scene 'serves to create the character who tells it'.[58] As I have put it elsewhere:

> On its face, the scene is deceptively simple: several minutes of two friends joking with each other about the serious issue of Johnny's debt. Underlying this humorous exchange is Charlie's concern for his friend, and the characterization of Johnny as someone who makes excuses for his behavior, amusing others with his irresponsibility. The scene also establishes the major conflicts within the film, foreshadowing its outcome and exposing Johnny as a chaotic force that will ultimately prove to be Charlie's cross to bear.[59]

Combining this passage with Wexman's ideas about improvisation, the collaborative aspects of filmmaking as highlighted by Hunter's and Kouvaros' approaches to film analysis, along with the details included in De Niro's notes, one can safely make the argument that the ownership of Johnny Boy in this scene is in De Niro's court. He has written and drafted this dialogue in multiple stages, both during his own scratched brainstorms and via earlier notes that he submitted to Scorsese. The evidence, then, reveals De Niro's investment in his character, a level of investment that transcends current understandings of acting, agency and collaboration. De Niro make his mark on a character 'who makes himself from moment to moment' and also, as Kolker put it, 'speaks himself into being'.[60]

De Niro's notes about the scene suggest that Johnny Boy's seemingly spontaneous dialogue was actually authored by De Niro and is also the final version of the on screen monologue:

> You know what happened to me, you know what happened to me
> Tried to avoid? Jimmy Sparks. He caught near my building
> I didn't pay $100
> He always right across the street. Had to give him $60, had to give some to my
>   mother + I had 25 for rest of week.
> [. . .] what happened I went to Heather Street just before, got into a
> game + some punk kid, I shot I wanna kill him
> after coming out bing bing bing
> Frankie Clams I owed him 1300 for 8 months
> I'm gonna payaaaa! What are you worried about?[61]

For a character who lives, as Kolker remarks, via his dialogue, we can clearly see the origins of the scene already existing for De Niro in his preparatory work, which eventually made its way into the film.

De Niro's labour and the way it informs his relationship with Scorsese in the creative process is not only evident in the comic banter of the 'Joey Clams' scene. It also can be detected in later, formal changes in the script that the actor requested from Scorsese, and which the director agreed to. One such request came in the form of a brief note that De Niro recorded and, one can assume, gave to Scorsese. It read: 'Should be more of me, one scene, added. I can make it work but people will want to know <u>why</u> I'm crying + want to see <u>more</u> of me. I'm telling you. I know <u>from experience</u>.'[62]

Conclusion: 'De Niro's Method' in the Hollywood Renaissance

De Niro's performance as Johnny Boy is indicative of something new in terms of acting, labour and collaboration. This is even more true concerning the burgeoning relationship between De Niro and Scorsese, as each figure allowed the other to expand within their respective crafts, leaving space for experimentation that harkened back to the earliest phases of the Hollywood Renaissance, and allowing both to carry this torch into the next decade. With their collaboration emerging clearly through events that correspond to stages one and two in Shenk's creative pairs schema/model, *Mean Streets* became the film in which this collaboration moved to the next level, that is, it achieved a dialectical synthesis. Such a synthesis was best embodied through the ways in which De Niro's improvisatory practices became enmeshed in Scorsese's approach to filmmaking while the latter was realized in the best possible way because of the impact of the actor's technique and labour.

While it is certain that other actors before and after this era possessed a great deal of power within their own collaborative relationships with their respective directors, there is a particular alchemy in the De Niro-Scorsese films of the 1970s and early 1980s, which not only seems remarkable, but entirely unique. No doubt, the context of the Hollywood Renaissance with its emphasis on experimentation, stylistic and narrative innovation and generic openness has played a role in creating the conditions that enabled the introduction of working methods which broke with established traditions and paved the way for new approaches and practices, including collaborative efforts determined by creative pairs. Indeed, more work is needed in placing such developments in more detail within industrial, institutional and economic contexts in the period in question.

As I have argued throughout this chapter, the actor's relationship with his director brought out new aspects in his craft that complemented what the director wanted to do, and vice versa. In other words, De Niro's performances, improvisatory collaboration and script suggestions were perfectly calibrated to the visual and audio language that Scorsese was pioneering as he chronicled the mean streets of Little Italy that he knew so well. Furthermore, this movie was only the first step in a growing creative partnership that came to define some of the most distinctive films, not only within the 1970s, but in all of American cinema.

Notes

1 Robert Phillip Kolker, *A Cinema of Loneliness: Penn, Kubrick, Coppola, Scorsese, Altman* (Oxford: Oxford University Press, 1980).
2 Peter Biskind, *Easy Riders, Raging Bulls: How the Sex 'n' Drugs 'n' Rock 'n' Roll Generation Saved Hollywood* (London: Bloomsbury, 2007).
3 Michael Henry Wilson, *Scorsese on Scorsese* (Paris: *Cahiers du cinema*, 2011).
4 Shawn Levy, *De Niro: A Life* (New York: Crown, 2014), 6.
5 Levy, *De Niro*, 6.
6 Ann Laura Stoller, *Along the Archival Grain: Thinking Through Colonial Ontologies* (Princeton, NJ: Princeton University Press, 2008).
7 Joshua Wolf Shenk, *Powers of Two: Finding the Essence of Innovation in Creative Pairs* (New York: Houghton Mifflin Harcourt, 2015).
8 George Kouvaros, *Where Does it Happen?: John Cassavetes and Cinema at the Breaking Point* (Minneapolis, MN: University of Minnesota Press, 2004).
9 R. Colin Tait, *Robert De Niro's Method: Acting, Authorship and Agency in the New Hollywood (1967–1981),* Doctoral thesis (Austin: University of Texas at Austin, 2013).
10 R. Colin Tait, 'When Marty Met Bobby: Collaborative Authorship in *Mean Streets* and *Taxi Driver*', in *A Companion to Martin Scorsese*, ed. A. Baker (Malden, MA: John Wiley and Sons, 2015), 292–311.
11 Shenk, *Powers of Two*, 27.
12 Shenk, *Powers of Two*, 30.
13 Scorsese, quoted in Wilson, *Scorsese on Scorsese*, 51.
14 Levy, *De Niro*, 119.
15 De Niro, quoted in Levy, *De Niro*, 199.
16 De Niro, quoted in Andrew J. Rausch, *The Collaborations of Martin Scorsese and Robert De Niro* (Lanham, MD: The Scarecrow Press, 2010), i.
17 Levy, *De Niro*, 119.
18 Shenk, *Powers of Two*, 35.
19 Shenk, *Powers of Two*, xxv
20 Shenk, *Powers of Two*, xxv
21 For a similar examination of the De Niro-Scorsese collaboration in later films see R. Colin Tait, 'Robert De Niro's *Raging Bull*: A History of the Performance and the Performance of History', *The Canadian Journal of Film Studies*, 20, issue 1 (Spring 2011): 20–40.
22 Aaron Hunter, *Authoring Hal Ashby: The Myth of the New Hollywood Auteur* (New York: Bloomsbury Academic, 2016), 1.
23 Hunter, *Authoring Hal Ashby*, 3–4.
24 Levy, *De Niro*, 105.
25 Cameron, quoted in John Baxter, *De Niro: A Biography* (London: HarperCollins, 2003), 96.
26 The term 'Magnet Place' is from Shenk, *Powers of Two*, 8–9, and connotes how figures are drawn to one another in significant geographical spaces, such as New York City, Paris or Hollywood.

27 Baxter, *De Niro*, 31–2.
28 Baxter, *De Niro*, 9–15.
29 Baxter, *De Niro*, 9–10.
30 Baxter, *De Niro*, 18.
31 Baxter, *De Niro*, 95.
32 Tait, *Robert De Niro's Method*, 116–49.
33 Kolker, *A Cinema of Loneliness*, 190.
34 Robert De Niro, 'Character Notes for *Mean Streets*', 1973, Folder 93.10 *Mean Streets* Screenplay (*Mean Streets*, by Scorsese & Martin) with RDN Notes throughout, The Robert De Niro Papers (RDNP), The Harry Ransom Center, University of Texas at Austin.
35 De Niro, 'Character Notes for *Mean Streets*', De Niro's emphasis.
36 De Niro, 'Character Notes for *Mean Streets*'.
37 De Niro, 'Character Notes for *Mean Streets*'.
38 De Niro, 'Character Notes for *Mean Streets*'.
39 De Niro, 'Character Notes for *Mean Streets*'.
40 De Niro, 'Character Notes for *Mean Streets*'.
41 Scorsese, quoted in Levy, *De Niro*, 119.
42 De Niro, 'Character Notes for *Mean Streets*'.
43 De Niro, 'Character Notes for *Mean Streets*'.
44 De Niro, 'Character Notes for *Mean Streets*'.
45 De Niro, 'Character Notes for *Mean Streets*'. Underlining in the original.
46 De Niro, 'What I [Johnny] Owe[s]'. 1973, Folder 93.10 *Mean Streets* Screenplay (*Mean Streets*, by Scorsese & Martin) with RDN Notes throughout, RDNP.
47 De Niro, 'Character Notes for *Mean Streets*'.
48 Virginia Wright Wexman, 'The Rhetoric of Cinematic Improvisation', *Cinema Journal*, 20, no. 1, (1980): 29.
49 Scorsese, quoted in Wilson, *Scorsese on Scorsese*, 39.
50 Scorsese, quoted in Wilson, *Scorsese on Scorsese*, 73.
51 Martin Scorsese, '*Mean Streets*' in *Conversations with Scorsese*, ed. Richard Schickel (New York: Alfred A. Knopf, 2011), 97.
52 Kouvaros, *Where Does it Happen*, xiii.
53 Kouvaros, *Where Does it Happen*, 5.
54 Baxter, *De Niro*, 46–7.
55 Tait, 'When Marty Met Bobby'.
56 Kolker, *A Cinema of Loneliness*, 190.
57 Kolker, *A Cinema of Loneliness*, 190.
58 Kolker, *A Cinema of Loneliness*, 190.
59 Tait, 'When Marty Met Bobby', 299.
60 Kolker, *A Cinema of Loneliness*, 147.
61 De Niro, 'What I [Johnny] Owe[s]'
62 De Niro, 'Note to Marty' in Character Notes for *Mean Streets* (1973c). Folder 93.10 *Mean Streets* Screenplay (*Mean Streets*, by Scorsese & Martin) with RDN Notes throughout, RDNP. Underlining in the original.

Chapter 13

COPPOLA'S *THE CONVERSATION* (1974) AND WALTER MURCH'S SOUND WORLDS

Frederick Wasser

The Conversation (Francis Ford Coppola, 1974) was a late entry in the Hollywood Renaissance love affair with the European art film. Francis Ford Coppola wrote the original screenplay for the movie in 1967, under the deep influence of Michelangelo Antonioni's *Blow-Up* (1966). He would finally direct it seven years later. Such a long gestation period gives us the opportunity to examine how Antonioni's metaphysical musings metamorphosed in 1970s Hollywood.

Coppola was 'Papa Bear' to the movie-brat cohort of directors who emerged even as the renaissance receded. His own career straddled the tensions between personal 'authentic' filmmaking and generating huge profitable audiences for big budget movies that the studios wanted. His moment was the mid-1970s when he managed to successfully mentor the breakthrough career of George Lucas, keep the San Francisco studio of Zoetrope alive, negotiate the epic demands of two *Godfather* movies, take a break with the personal filmmaking of *The Conversation* and complete *Apocalypse Now* a few years later in 1979. After that his various projects declined, Zoetrope went bankrupt and Lucas largely went his own way. *The Conversation* endures as a movie where art film, movie-brats and indifferent Hollywood executives came together at the same time.

My thesis is that in the aftermath of *The Conversation* the importance of sound is solidified for a new generation of filmmakers. First of all, the storyline of *Blow-Up* was transformed by Coppola who uses a sound recordist as the central protagonist instead of the original photographer. While this was a story transformation, there was also an important formal innovation. Coppola and his sound designer Walter Murch exploited the plasticity of sound, moving away from codes of photorealism, in order to entice the audience into the subjective experience of the character. Murch had already created worlds of sound that loosened the connection between sound and image in his work with Lucas. This loosening built upon avant-garde notions of sound in film. After

The Conversation, Murch went further in creating his award-winning sound montages for *Apocalypse Now*. At the same time Lucas and Steven Spielberg were enhancing the sound structures of their big budget movies. Thus the low budget *The Conversation* re-imagining the metaphysics of *Blow-Up* and other art films, inspired the sound aesthetic of big budget Hollywood.

I will examine the three-way relationship between Coppola, Lucas and Walter Murch. Murch had been classmates with Lucas in film school and they worked together on the student production *Electronic Labyrinth: THX 1138 4EB* in 1967. This was remade as a studio feature, entitled *THX 1138*, and released in 1971. Murch worked on the remake as well as doing the sound and the picture editing on Lucas' second Hollywood financed film *American Graffiti* (1973). He then became involved with Coppola and also Fred Zinnemann. Therefore, Lucas was unable to get him back for his *Star Wars* production in 1977. Murch's career after *The Conversation* and *Apocalypse Now* involved a brief stint as a director and continuing high profile assignments as an editor.

In order to understand the importance of sound innovations in the period of *The Conversation*, this essay will examine the genesis of the movie and summarize its storyline. This summary leads to considerations of how to classify the film in its time period. It is not quite a paranoid film, nor a San Francisco crime thriller, although it uses elements of both. Coppola actually gives the audience a prescient reference to the emerging electronic ethos of the Bay area. Describing this leads to a consideration of his own view of the movie as a character study which brings the analysis back to the issue of how *The Conversation* differs from *Blow-Up*. At this point it is important to discuss theories of sound both in general society and its use in films. This discussion will help us understand what Lucas and Murch were trying to do in *THX* and how the disappointing reception of that movie led to modifications in Murch's subsequent approach in *American Graffiti* and *The Conversation*. These modifications solidify their influence after the breakthrough successes of *Star Wars* and *Apocalypse Now*. The conclusion is that the Lucas/Murch/Coppola use of sound is contrary to classical Hollywood's understanding of photorealism and lays the groundwork for the digital feature film.

The genesis of The Conversation

After completing his script for *The Conversation*, Coppola tried to raise production financing but his contacts were not interested. In the meantime, he had won an Academy award for the single-authored screenplay *Patton* (Franklin J. Schaffner, 1970). He alternated between the two registers of self-expression and pleasing the audience, having directed the high budget *Finian's Rainbow* (1968) and the low budget *The Rain People* (1969). Already he had established a pattern of impressing major studios such as Warner Bros. and Paramount enough to win jobs and resources and yet rebelling against the Hollywood mainstream and seeking independence by going on location and setting up American Zoetrope with production and post production facilities in San Francisco. But by June 1970, the Warner executives financing Coppola's studio were repelled by the minimal bleakness of Zoetrope's first production – *THX 1138*. They demanded repayment of Warner's loan to Zoetrope.[1]

In the midst of this setback, Coppola took the assignment to direct *The Godfather* (1972) for Paramount. He was able to get several key people who shared his encounter with foreign cinema onto his large crew. For example, Dean Tavoularis became *The Godfather*'s production designer, soon after working for Antonioni on *Zabriskie Point* (1970). Coppola was able to use the tremendous success of the gangster epic to again demand financing for his shelved script *The Conversation*. Paramount was eager to agree in order to get him to direct *The Godfather II*. Coppola used the money to revive Zoetrope and to further development on several films (such as *Apocalypse Now*) but *The Conversation* was the only fully completed production in this period.

He recruited Tavoularis as a designer along with Murch as the supervising editor. Murch was finishing his work on *American Graffiti*. Haskell Wexler started shooting *The Conversation*, but was replaced by Bill Butler as cinematographer. Thus, Coppola's crew was moving between film as art and film as big business as much as he was. They were young enough to have first experienced the foreign films in their pre-career idealism. For all their world cinema bravado, they were also skilled Californian craftspeople. They may not have served long apprenticeships on studio lots but they had absorbed the lessons of Hollywood from their childhood on. American filmmaking peer standards remained their primary focus even as they borrowed from the Nouvelle Vague and the Italians. 1973–4 coincided with key moves by two other young directors. George Lucas had launched *American Graffiti* largely inspired by Federico Fellini's *I vitelloni* (1953). Steven Spielberg was still under the new wave influence with the stylistic and narrative excesses of *The Sugarland Express* which he completed in 1974.[2] In both cases the directors subsequently turned to the American mainstream. Coppola's *The Conversation* belonged to the same moment and already was a hybrid between personal expression and the more typical American commitment to linear narrative.

The story

The movie begins with a long crane and zoom shot above San Francisco Union Square's lunchtime crowd, moving down as the opening credits roll. The camera follows a mime who imitates random passers-by in the square. There are musicians playing on the right side of the screen and the sound is a mélange of street noises, music, the odd wows and flutters and other unexplained sound effects that defy labelling. These sounds may be a sort of feedback. One can hear such oddities when identical tracks are played at the same time.

The mime trips into the space of the protagonist Harry Caul (Gene Hackman) standing with the lunchtime crowd. There is a cut to a street-level view of Harry avoiding the mime while the camera picks up other people in the square. The viewer starts noticing a recurring couple, a young woman Ann (Cindy Williams) and an equally young man Mark (Frederic Forrest) both in office attire, walking and talking together. Other shots establish that men are recording sound; one wears an earphone, while another is on a rooftop, with a unidirectional microphone mounted on a tripod. Harry approaches a parked van. Stan (John Cazale) is inside, and he lets Harry in. Inside the van, the strange sounds are explained since we are now hearing three different audio feeds from the various recorders and the resulting interference and other buzzes. Harry Caul is running a surveillance operation and the young couple are the object of the surveillance.

The next day, Harry and Stan are together in a loft/studio at their work benches full of electronic and audio devices. Harry lines up the various audio tapes and starts mixing and filtering them in order to make the 'conversation' audible. In a subsequent scene he calls his client from a phone booth out in the street to set up the delivery of the mixed tapes. But when he arrives at an office in a skyscraper, the client, 'the Director' (Robert Duvall), is not there. Harry finally decides not to give the tapes to the director's assistant Martin Stett (Harrison Ford). After a tussle, he leaves the office. On the way out he notices both the man and the woman who were the object of the taping in the building. While he avoids Mark, he inadvertently gets on the same elevator as Ann. However, neither one seems to notice Harry. He goes back to his loft to analyse the tapes further and eventually filters out the music to uncover a key piece of the conversation when Mark says to Ann: 'He'd kill us if he got the chance.'

Harry's backstory is established through various scenes at a surveillance convention and at a party of associates. He is well known for being able to surreptitiously record where there is no access. However one of his legal recordings for a prosecuting attorney resulted in a brutal beheading of an entire family. The audience learns that Harry feels guilty for the results of his bugging.

Meredith (Elizabeth MacRae) meets Harry at the convention and seduces him back in his own loft/work space. His post-coital dream is that he is warning Ann about the client who commissioned the surveillance. When he awakes he discovers that Meredith has left with the tapes. He then gets a call to come and get his money from 'the Director'. He goes to the office building and collects his money but receives no answer from 'the Director' about what is going to happen to the couple. He sees a photograph suggesting that Ann is married to his client.

Harry decides to go to the hotel rendezvous mentioned in the surveillance. He books a room next to the one mentioned and installs a listening device by punching a thin hole in the wall between the two rooms. But he panics when he hears sounds of a violent struggle. He crawls into bed while turning on the television to drown out the sounds from next door. He falls asleep and when he awakes he works up the courage to break into the other room. There is nothing out of place until he flushes the toilet and a horrifying amount of blood comes flowing out.

The next day at a public event, Harry witnesses Ann making a statement about taking over the company. There is a headline declaring that 'the Director' died in an accident. There is an image of 'the Director' cornering Ann in the hotel room and then another one of Mark coming up from behind to knife 'the Director'. Harry goes home to take a phone call telling him that 'we are listening'. It seems to be the voice of Stett. Harry tears apart his apartment looking for a bug. He gives up finally after committing the sacrilege of breaking his statuette of the Virgin to look inside. The movie ends with the defeated Harry Caul playing his saxophone amidst the ruins.

The Conversation's *setting*

Although the conception and production of the movie pre-dated the Watergate break in, its release in April 1974 came nine months after it was revealed that Nixon had been secretly recording all the meetings in the Oval Office of the White House. Everyone could read into the film at the time the national politics of paranoia. *The Conversation*'s parallel with the illegal recordings of the Republican administration became part of the word of mouth marketing campaign. Coppola's own technical expert was called to Washington to examine the missing eighteen minutes on a Nixon tape.[3] The movie made a respectable profit based on its timeliness as a political thriller, although Paramount gave it a minimal marketing campaign. For everyone involved it was a success.

Is the movie a political thriller? *The Parallax View* (Alan J. Pakula, 1974) and *Three Days of the Condor* (Sidney Pollack, 1975) are more direct in their implication of a malevolent government. In contrast, Coppola's only reference to the government is that Harry had worked for a New York prosecutor and that his crew includes a former policeman. In this regard it is intriguing that the movie is set in San Francisco. Hollywood had identified that city in the audience's mind with cop stories ranging from the movies *Bullitt* (Peter Yates, 1968) and *Dirty Harry* (Don Siegel, 1971) to contemporary TV series such as *Ironside* (NBC, 1967–75) and *Streets of San Francisco* (ABC, 1972–7).

This was Coppola's first film to feature his adopted home city. But he did not use the location to depict Frisco detectives, the 1960s music scene or the counterculture that was fast fading. Instead, he was prescient about the emergence of a new economy in the Bay area. In 1974, its industrial base was not as monolithically driven by software as it is today, but there was already a powerful emerging electronic economy. Silicon Valley (geographically just to the south of San Francisco) had taken shape with advances in electronics that were an outgrowth of government research. Within a decade it was to change the world with the spearheading of personal computing in the 1980s. But already for San Franciscans everything was new, everything was to be reinvented.

Coppola was living that dream himself, reinventing filmmaking several hours north of Los Angeles. The focus was just as much on new ways of making movies as on new types of stories. In 1968 at the same time Lucas was introducing Murch to Coppola, Coppola was buying one hundred thousand dollars of equipment to facilitate lightweight location shooting and portable editing studios. By the end of 1969 he opened American Zoetrope with the help of Lucas, Murch and many others.[4] He had overextended Zoetrope because of his fascination with new editing equipment from Germany and other developments in post-production technology. Aspects of that technological fascination were incorporated into the script for *The Conversation*.

Harry is an information entrepreneur, working in a repurposed loft space probably once used for manufacturing, and is now part of the emerging electronic cottage industry. His and his associates' thinking about electronics is halfway to digital thinking. While Harry has the discipline for the new economy, Coppola is astute enough to expose a certain electronic 'autism'. It is a marker of a certain kind of Californian worship of technology to have only peripheral concern with the human consequences of using new technologies and new disciplines. The technologists notoriously have little interest in the social collective.[5] Famously, Harry tells Saul that he is not interested in what the subjects are saying, only in recording it cleanly. Just as insidiously Harry denies Stan's request to learn his techniques. These are the corrosive effects of a 'California' ideology that rewards the individual hoarding of 'objective' knowledge.[6]

While Coppola was using new technology to plot his own liberation from Hollywood studios and their crafts unions, his visuals represent the technologies of surveillance as sinister. There is the introductory montage that features a microphone positioned as a sniper's rifle. There are the percussive sounds of tapes being wound back and forth. There is Harry Caul crawling into unsavoury spaces to place his microphone. There is the artwork for the 'one sheet' poster for the film, which uses a graphic of a tape recorder and a head shot of Harry wearing a head set. Its tagline – 'So far, three people are dead because of him' – suggests a dystopian science thriller. Yet Coppola successfully resists reducing the movie to a technological nightmare.

Sources for The Conversation

The Conversation consistently parallels Antonioni's *Blow-Up*, which is itself inspired by Julio Cortázar 1959 short story about an expatriate photographer entitled *Las babas del diablo* (*The Devil's Drool*). In the nineteenth century photography was initially considered as a form of translating nature into 'sun pictures'. But then the French government declared photography to be an art in

1862 precisely because the image was controlled by the creator. Inspired by this legal foray into philosophy, Cortázar story questions the uses and status of photography. In the story Cortázar uses photography to play with the relation between a creator (photographer) and the 'real'. The storyteller's identity is tentative even though it is his story. Sometimes he tells it using first person 'I', sometimes he tells it about Roberto Michel in the third person. Michel's paying job is translating, his passion is photography. He is taking a break from his desk job to photograph in the streets of Paris. His camera may or may not have aborted the seduction of a teenage boy. The written narrative meanders through several endings.

Antonioni, following Cortázar, also wants us to be unsure of photography or of other mimetic arts. He wants to show the lack of control of the artist. He transposes the Parisian story to England and the marketing campaign took full advantage of the fact that the movie was set in 'swinging London'. He necessarily has to reify Cortázar impressionistic writing by filming actual actors actually doing things. Nonetheless, the filmmaker keeps the writer's interest in the flimsiness of creation. The more Antonioni's photographer, Thomas (David Hemmings), investigates the photographs the more no one knows him. His conversation with his neighbour's wife (Sarah Miles) is at utter cross purposes about the corpse in the park that he thinks he has photographed. He cannot get anyone to go back with him to search for the corpse.

Antonioni attacks the stable perspective of photography on its own terms. Thomas has photographed something that he does not see. After he becomes suspicious, he blows up the photographs in order to uncover an image that he cannot interpret. He returns to the scene to find a murdered body in the park that may have been the image that he could not interpret in the blow up. But upon his second return to the park, the body is gone. The audience anticipates that Thomas will tackle the question of convincing others that the body was there. But the director defeats this anticipation. Instead, he photographically removes Thomas himself in the final fade out of the movie.

Antonioni knows to disguise his metaphysics in the appearance of a narrative film. The metaphysics dominate narrative logic and the elusive state of the photographic becomes another sign that God has abandoned our world. Dennis Turner writes of *Blow-Up*: 'The characters on the screen have begun to see things we cannot see, and have begun to disappear before our eyes. In this way the problem of the visible is deliberately thrust out onto the spectating audience, as in the "art film," and not sealed off inside the text, as in the genre film of detection.'[7]

The comparable American films of this time never attempted this. Robert Kolker notices how *The Conversation* 'Americanizes' (i.e. ignores) the ontological problem of Cortázar and Antonioni: 'But Antonioni is not as concerned with developing a moral focus through his photographer as he is in managing a perceptual gamesmanship in which the cinematic photographic image of the world becomes a locus of existential dread. Coppola, much more in the tradition of American films, attempts to locate an individual angst, a localized suffering which, in this instance, may reflect a larger cultural situation.'[8]

The Conversation is not philosophy, it is not a thriller; it is a character study. Coppola has a profound understanding of what Antonioni was trying to do. But his scenario has subtle yet decisive differences from Antonioni's disintegration of the photographer's existence. A character study does not question its own reality status. Accordingly, Coppola changes Thomas' disintegration into Harry's guilt and alienation. He speaks of another inspiration coming from Herman Hesse's 1927 novel *Steppenwolf* and its portrayal of extreme mental isolation. The point is that Harry Caul still has an integrated personality at the end of the story. He is, perhaps, on the road to a new beginning. The ambiguity of the real world has led to Harry fingering the wrong victim. But this mistake is not an annihilation of his soul or even an irredeemable sin. Indeed, this time it is the client and not Harry who is responsible for the events that destroyed the client.

The audience sees and hears nothing except through the eyes and ears of Harry Caul. The camera is either on him or seeing what he is seeing. What he is seeing is easily separated into two categories: objective and subjective. The distinction between the two is well marked with standard cues. Coppola uses heavy fog and eerie sounds to code the dream sequence when Harry warns Ann. Again the editing uses suggestive subjectivity when he panics at the hotel. There is an image of 'the Director' cornering Ann. There is also an unexplained shot of a bloody handprint on the plastic sheet. It comes from Harry's imagination. The images of the murder of 'the Director' are logically deduced by Harry. This is confirmed by the order of the shots. He does not imagine the dead body of 'the Director' until he knows objectively that Ann and Mark are still alive.

It is interesting that Cortázar plot was used yet again (albeit without a recognizable trace) in an American mainstream movie. This is *Blow Out* (1981), starring John Travolta and directed by Brian De Palma. De Palma follows Coppola in having no interest in photography but uses sound as the thing that must be interpreted correctly to yield the key clue to an assassination. While *Blow Out* is not a character study and lacks the ambition of *The Conversation*, the coincidence of the two movies shifting to sound as the sense that must be deciphered is another sign of how the Americans were changing Antonioni's image of constantly blowing up a photograph in the false hope of finding the real. The American shift to sound is the shift from metaphysics to emotion. The omnipresence of sound engages the audience in a different manner than the single point perspective of photorealism. Sound does not ask the same question about its relationship to a profilmic reality that photography does. Therefore Coppola is side stepping Cortazar/Antonioni's philosophical musing when he relocates the clues that drive the story from Thomas' blow ups to Harry's sound surveillance. The image is supposed to be self-explanatory while sound is dependent on interpretation. This becomes its role in 'the genre film of detection'.

Sound theory

The Conversation is a landmark in the new prestige of movie sound. The elevation of sound resonates with other concurrent cultural movements. We should remember that the leading media theorist of the 1960s was Marshall McLuhan. McLuhan postulated a shift in Western people's balance of senses in response to television and new media. Walter Ong and others followed McLuhan to speak of a de-emphasis on literacy and the rise of 'secondary orality' in contemporary societies.[9] This phrase means that, while the original oral culture was prior to the invention of writing, a second oral culture was emerging in the electronic age, with a corresponding decline in print culture.

Orality studies bring out profound differences between sight and sound. Ong notes that oral cultures had to deal with the ephemeral nature of sound and had to increase the agnostic nature of sound, in other words the emotions, in order to make oral messages more memorable. Sheila Nayar uses such oral theorizing to analyse Hindi popular films made between 1950 and 2000 since their primary audiences are people more attuned to the oral than to the written: 'In the Bollywood universe, sound is generally aggrandized, exaggerated expression is favored, and the value of the visual is conditioned less by cinematography than by a collectively agreed-on ascendancy of the voice that inhabits the image.'[10] She notices among other things a structure based on repetitions, recycling and formulas and a tone that favours inflated violence, amplified characters and settings.[11] This is a specific instance of Ong's association of orality with agonistic storytelling.

The American film industry has doubled down on this path of 'inflated violence, amplified characters and settings' since the 1970s. While *The Conversation* is still prior to this shift, it is germane to the argument that Lucas, Murch and Coppola will all go on to work on big budget action adventure in the late 1970s. Their work helped establish action adventure, comic book heroes and fantasies as pre-eminent genres. Not enough research has been done to establish why the audience turned this way. Secondary orality theorists would find it suggestive that 1970s American film audiences were losing the habit of *reading* magazines and newspapers. Others might attribute it to the globalization of audiences and the need to attract young adults of many different cultures. As global films aim to overcome linguistic barriers, they use the emotionality of music and sound effects to make an immediate appeal to many different sensibilities.

Inspired by art films, Lucas, Murch and Coppola undid sound's dependency on the image. They were interested in disassociating sound from image in order to make it co-equal. Disassociation has been a ploy of an intellectual approach to filmmaking since Sergei Eisenstein and others first started thinking about the use of synchronized sound on film in the 1930s.[12] The Soviets were interested in using autonomous sound as another element to be juxtaposed in a montage that would ask the audience to reflect on the meaning that emerges from the different elements. In other writings, Eisenstein muses about the plasticity of sound versus the resistance of the visual: 'The shot, considered as material for the purpose of composition, is more resistant than granite. This resistance is specific to it. The shot's tendency toward complete factual immutability is rooted in its nature.'[13] He contrasts this with the compliance of sound tones: 'the immutable fragment of actual reality in these cases is narrower and more neutral in meaning, and therefore more flexible in combination, so that when they are put together they lose all visible signs of being combined, appearing as one organic unit. A chord, or even three successive notes, seems to be an organic unit.'[14]

At the earliest stages of their careers, Lucas and Murch became enchanted with the experimental uses of sound. Walter Murch said: 'When George [Lucas] saw *21-87* (dir. Arthur Lipsett, 1963), a light bulb went off. One of the things we really wanted to do in *THX* was to make a film where the sound and the picture were free floating. Occasionally they would link up in a literal way, but there would be long sections where the two would wander off and it would stretch the audience's mind to figure out the connection.'[15]

THX 1138 is a science fiction depiction of an all-controlling society *a la* Aldous Huxley and George Orwell. It was filmed entirely in minimally decorated interiors, such as the not yet completed tunnels of the Bay Area Rapid Transit (BART) system. In such moviemaking audio backgrounds become particularly important. The visual void was partially compensated by dimensional sounds that immersed movie goers into the environment. Murch and his crew sought out sounds that defy pinpointing, that come from everywhere. This was the creation of a multidimensional world.

But *THX* was a bridge too far. I have already mentioned that Warner executives were very angry with Lucas and his producer Coppola when they screened the movie before its release. The studio gave it a poorly financed release and the movie correspondingly did little box office. For his next project, Lucas chose to ignore his instinct for fantasy and went on to develop *America Graffiti* based on his own teenage experiences in small town California. Universal decided to produce it with Lucas directing.

It is the interwoven stories of four recent high school graduating boys circulating in and out of each other's lives over the course of a day and night in the summer of 1962. They cruise in cars, listening to music and pursuing or abandoning girls. Despite this conscious turn to location realism, the sound has greater autonomy and goes beyond the usual classical Hollywood function of sound merely confirming the reality of the image. Murch, acting again as sound designer, got to give the various spaces of the town and surrounding areas various sound signatures. He differentiated between pristine non-diegetic music cues and 'worldized' music coming out of car radios, mixed with engine noise and backgrounds. He even had the songs bounce from car to car.[16] Thus he foregrounded sound as a separate dimension from the image. In short, he created a world.

As Murch was finishing *Graffiti* he started to work on *The Conversation*. Similar to his collaboration with Lucas, Murch and Coppola gave sound autonomy without going so far as to totally disassociate it from the image. This was not a collapse into classical Hollywood's subordination of sound to image, even though it was an evolution away from the disassociations of the art film. The point can be clarified by looking at the difference between two scenes, the first from the end of *Blow-Up* and the second from a scene in the first-third of *The Conversation*.

Antonioni had used certain sounds to construct his own metaphysical montage. In particular, he used it to establish the declining presence of the real in *Blow-Up*. When Thomas goes to the park to take photographs, there is a heavy wind rustle through the trees. When he is back in his studio re-photographing the park shots, the wind rustle comes back shifting the realism effect from the studio to the park even though the scene is firmly set in the studio. Again at the end Thomas watches in the park as a group of mimes mimic a tennis game without either rackets or a ball. The two on the court swing their arms as if they are holding rackets and are volleying between them and everyone watches as if a ball is going back and forth. The imaginary game is entirely visual until there is a final close up of Thomas. His eyes are moving as if again watching the back and forth of a tennis volley. With each back and forth there is the distinct sound of a ball hit on the sound track. The sound falsely confirms the reality of a non-existent game. In the next and final shot of the movie, the image of Thomas himself is erased from the background of the lawn which remains as end credit comes up.

It should be noted that Antonioni uses the sound of the ball only over the close up of Thomas. The sound never has profilmic status. In contrast, Murch and Coppola eventually reveal and justify the source of all the sounds in *The Conversation*. There are many initially disassociated sounds but through repetition they become re-associated with the events that created these sounds. The squawks that mystify the opening shot of Union Square are eventually associated with the feedback of overlapping microphones and even later the sound of tape moving backwards over the playback head on a tape recorder.

There is one almost Antonioni-type sound moment. This is a disintegrating event which comes 33 minutes into the movie, when Harry Caul is on the elevator with Ann. She does not see him. None of the previous elevator passengers have noticed him. In his isolation, the elevator sound becomes stronger. There is an almost metaphysical breakdown on the elevator. Murch takes the movement of the elevator to introduce a heavy vortex-like wind mixing with an ascending whine that finally cross fades with the sound of spinning. One might be reminded of the free-floating aural cues of *THX*. But then the film dissolves through to spinning reels on a magnetic tape recorder. When the image catches up with the sound the melodramatic realism of the Hollywood character study is restored. We now see Harry re-engaged and back at work searching for something on the tape. This search will uncover the line 'He'd kill us if he gets the chance' which becomes an important plot point.

It is when Harry suspects murder is in the air that he starts to become re-engaged with the world. In contrast to *Blow-Up*, Harry interacts more and more with people who are frustrating his investigation. Coppola never questions the illusion of the real in the image; each image makes sense as the narrative unfolds. Coppola and Murch keep repeating images and sounds until they finally reveal their clue-like meaning. For example, the line and the corresponding image of 'He'd kill us if he gets the chance' is repeated at least four more times. Murch uses different takes of the same line at different points in the movie and argues (in his DVD commentary) that there is a shift in emphasis from 'He'd *kill* us if he gets the chance' to 'He'd kill *us* if he gets the chance' by the time the line is played for the final time. He chooses this shift in order to signify the couple's decision to kill the director rather than be passive victims.

The disintegrating sound on the elevator does not have the same status as the tennis ball hits at the end of *Blow-Up* although both might be ascribed to the subjective minds of the on screen characters. Antonioni is ending the movie on the next shot reducing the photographic image to a phantasm. This is because he is concerned with the image and only uses the sound to undermine the reality status of the image. Neither Coppola nor Murch are interested in undermining the image. Murch, in particular, is promoting sound as a co-equal dimension with the image. Perhaps in the days of *THX*, he was interested in disassociated sound as a formal experiment, but now he along with his directors is stumbling onto the dimensional power of sound to create 'worlds' in audiences' imaginations.

After the three filmmakers suffered the disappointment of *THX* and the success of *American Graffiti* and *The Conversation*, they went on to fully implement dimensional sound designs in the more fantastic worlds of *Star Wars* (science fiction) and *Apocalypse Now* (a real war experienced as if it was a hallucination). What they had improvised in their experiment with disassociated sound was the visceral power of sound. They were a generation inspired by Kubrick's *2001: A Space Odyssey* (1968).[17] They learned from *2001* to give the audience a visceral immersion into the filmic world, which is quite different from character identification, catharsis and interest in the moral resolution of a realistic narrative. This filmmaking motivation becomes widespread after the multi-hundred-million-dollar successes of *Star Wars* and Spielberg's *Close Encounters of the Third Kind*, both released in 1977 and, two years later, *Apocalypse Now*. *American Graffiti* and *The Conversation* taught them how to make sound an important part of this audience immersion without the alienation of the free-floating sounds of *THX* or the metaphysics of *Blow-Up*.

Murch and sound worlds

The interest in immersion and sound 'worlds' also separates them from another non-classical contemporary approach to sound associated with the films of

John Cassavetes, Arthur Penn and Robert Altman. These directors insisted on natural sound even to the point of obscuring the audience's ability to hear the dialogue.[18] They allowed extremes of loud and soft sound juxtapositions and overlapping dialogue to muddy the aural sphere, in order to valorize authenticity.

Authentic sound does not interest Murch. In the decades that followed the success of *The Conversation* and *Apocalypse Now*, Murch writes about the lessons he learned from sound editing. He pens the introduction to Michel Chion's book *Audio-Vision*. Chion works with ideas of disassociation when he considers that sound can be separated from what causes it. He labels this 'acousmatic'[19] and Murch goes even further to applaud that 'it might have been otherwise – the human mind could have demanded absolute obedience to "the truth" – but [...] we are lucky that it didn't: the possibility of reassociation of image and sound is the fundamental stone upon which the rest of the edifice of film sound is built'.[20]

It is of key importance that he uses the word 'reassociation'. He is alluding but not quite subscribing to Eisenstein's montage of sound. He wants to maintain the classical Hollywood continuities but with a more dimensional use of sound. The audience's willingness to meld even unidentified (acousmatic) sound with the image that they are seeing is called 'synchresis' by Chion.[21] The sound editors were increasingly placing 'sound sweeteners' to heighten the emotion of a particular event. Even when the sound sweeteners did not originate in the image, the audience easily accepted them as part of the image. An earlier famous example was when Steven Spielberg placed an animal roar in the midst of a truck cascading down a cliff in *Duel* (1971). The audiences already were conditioned to use sound to confirm what they saw. Sound designers could build on this disposition to create entire emotional environments through sound with only the slightest visual cues of the movie.

Murch's excited claim that the human mind makes few 'truth' demands on sound (except in the case of spoken dialogue which must match lip movements) reveals his interest in its emotionality. He writes that triggering an emotion is twice as important as telling a story in determining how to edit a narrative film.[22] This emotional emphasis was exemplified by Coppola and Murch's collaboration on *Apocalypse Now*. The film was structured around Joseph Conrad's 1899 novella *Heart of Darkness* and emphasized atmospherics over narrative action. Murch layered in various sounds of Vietnam and war in order to create emotional worlds within a world. For example, the movie's opening scene directly borrows from the elevator scene in *The Conversation*, when the sounds of helicopter blades and a ceiling fan are melded together to immerse the audience into the psyche of the main character Capt. Willard (Martin Sheen).

Again the *Apocalypse Now* work was done in San Francisco, far away from the Hollywood sound editors who had been trained to use sound only to service the narrative. This created a new cohort that eventually pursued their professions in Los Angeles working on the many action adventure films that became the predominant genre of the 1980s.[23] Their influence spread, even as Coppola slipped away from a leadership position in the 1980s. Following Murch, other sound designers have made similar statements against sound realism. Gary Rydstrom suggested that sound based on replicating reality is flawed and demands that filmmakers 'use sound in less realistic ways'. Randy Thom told his interviewer: 'Movies are not about depicting reality [...] movies are [...] saying something more interesting about what's really true than you could possibly say if things were real.'[24] Under Murch's direct and indirect guidance, a generation of editors learned to bring in many sounds in order to give the designer choices during the mix of sounds and to add more dimensionality.

The difference from photorealism

The desire to create sound worlds may be contrasted with classical Hollywood's approach to realism of sound. Studio Hollywood was largely determined by the melodramatic realism codes of the nineteenth century which presumed the world to already exist, independent of its representation. American filmmaking turned towards location shooting after the 1940s. This was a more committed version of photorealism that wanted to use the camera and microphone as objective recording tools. The film theorists André Bazin and Siegfried Kracauer championed realism and other naturalistic cinematic strategies for this reason. They argued that all cinema relies on photorealism. Although a neutral objectivity is theoretically impossible, photorealism gains great aesthetic power from the presumption that a pre-filmic reality resists the artist who then wrestles with the image to shape the story. The struggle itself promotes a certain kind of creative honesty from the artist.

For both studio and location shoots, sound realism was subordinate to photorealism and its chief functions were to convey the dialogue and confirm the reality of the image placed in front of the camera. The Hollywood dialogue is placed front and centre with the occasional minimal attempt at perspective for extreme long shots.[25] But when Coppola went from making a film about sound in *The Conversation* to making a film using acousmatic and other formal properties of sound in *Apocalypse Now* in conjunction with Lucas using innovative sounds to fill out the dimensions of his fantasy in *Star Wars*, this was a shift away from the earlier Hollywood functions of sound.

This shift facilitated the newly popular genres of science fiction, action/ adventure and, in general, the emotional worlds of high concept. At this point sound took on new importance precisely because it was more malleable and synthetic. The ability to combine sounds with less regard for the 'truth' of their indexical connection to the visual enhanced the audience's experiences of the dimensionality of these fantastic and emotional 'worlds'. This, in turn, led to developing the digital technology of enhancing the camera image. Since many of the same people who increased the use of sound in the 1970s were pushing digital imagery, prominently George Lucas, we are not surprised that the aesthetic of sound influenced the development of digital imagery software. Synchresis not only applied to sound but to digital enhanced images as this technology was adopted in the late 1980s and early 1990s. Adding sounds as sweeteners was soon translated into digital enhancements sweetening the image. For instance, Stephen Prince describes a kind of stop motion technique in *Avatar* (James Cameron, 2009): 'Facial Performance Replacement [FPR] sessions enabled the actors to come back after scenes were shot and redo elements of their performance, akin to what is routinely accomplished with sound during an ADR [automatic dialog replacement] session.'[26]

Julie Turnock makes an interesting argument that the increase in the use and sophistication of special effects was an evolution of 'auteurist' filmmaking. Even if we accept her thesis, we should think about the resonance between special effects and the sound aesthetic. Special effects creation largely rejects the photorealism of pre-existing objects in a natural order. It necessarily recombines objects that the audience accepts as actual. Turnock sums it up as 'a new style of photorealism that struck viewers as *both* fantastic and strikingly realistic' (also see Chapter 5).[27] I perhaps differ from her willingness to continue to use the term 'photorealism' given the anti-real mix of fantasy and 'realism' although I accept that the audience believes in the 'actuality' of the fantasy. I embrace her thesis in part since it directs our attention to how sound helps facilitate this combination of the fantastic and the real that supports contemporary filmmaking.

Conclusion

Direct influence on sound mixing practices is not as important to the Lucas/ Murch/Coppola legacy as their development of a new sound aesthetic. This is an aesthetic that assumes the audience wants an enhancement of the fully dimensional cinematic experience even at the expense of the authenticity of photorealism. It was a consistent yet unstated attitude of a new generation. We should remember that Kracauer and Bazin linked photorealism to a democratic culture. Sound as a replacement for photorealism coincides with a reduced interest in the challenging themes of the 1960s. The blockbuster audiences wanted the thrill of the movie experience and turned their back on using movies to explore the world 'as-is'. *The Conversation* (along with *American Graffiti*) from this perspective was a transitional film that took Lucas/Murch/Coppola away from the experimentalism of disassociated sound of *THX* in order to make the influential move to the design of sound as a co-equal dimension of the movie experience.

Notes

1   Michael Rubin, *Droidmaker: George Lucas and the Digital Revolution* (Gainesville, FL: Triad Publishing, 2005), 38.

2   Warren Buckland, *Directed by Steven Spielberg: Poetics of the Contemporary Hollywood Blockbuster* (New York: Continuum Press, 2006), 84.
3   Robert Thomas, 'Hal Lipset, Private Detective with a Difference, Dies at 78', *New York Times*, 12 December 1997, B14.
4   Rubin, *Droidmaker*, 28–36.
5   Fred Turner, *From Counterculture to Cyberculture: Stewart Brand, The Whole Earth Network, and the Rise of Digital Utopianism* (Chicago: University of Chicago Press, 2006).
6   Richard Barbrook and Andy Cameron, 'The Californian Ideology', *Science as Culture* 6, no. 1 (1996), 44–72; and Steven Levy, *Hackers: Heroes of the Computer Revolution* (Garden City, NY: Anchor Press/Doubleday, 1984).
7   Dennis Turner, 'The Subject of *The Conversation*', *Cinema Journal* 24, no. 4 (Summer 1985): 11.
8   Robert Phillip Kolker, *A Cinema of Loneliness: Penn, Kubrick, Coppola, Scorsese, Altman* (New York: Oxford University Press, 1980), 198.
9   I do not think McLuhan actually uses the term but his remarks throughout *Understanding Media: The Extensions of Man* (New York: McGraw-Hill, 1964) build the basis for secondary orality. Walter J. Ong actually defines it in his book *Orality and Literacy: The Technologizing of the World* (New York: Routledge, 2002), 132–4.
10 Sheila Nayar, *Cinematically Speaking: The Orality-Literacy Paradigm for Visual Narrative* (New Jersey: Hampton Press, 2010), 31.
11 Nayar, *Cinematically Speaking*, 75.
12 See, for example, Sergei Eisenstein, Vsevolod Pudovkin and Grigori Alexandrov, 'Statement on Sound', in *The Film Factory: Russian and Soviet Cinema in Documents, 1896–1939*, ed. Richard Taylor and Ian Christie (Cambridge, MA: Harvard University Press, 1988), 234–5.
13 Sergei Eisenstein, *Film Form: Essays in Film Theory* (New York: Harcourt Brace and World Inc., 1934/1949), 5.
14 Eisenstein, *Film Form*, 4.
15 Rubin, *Droidmaker*, 35.
16 Stephen Keane, 'Walter Murch and Ben Burtt: The Sound Designer as Composer', in *Sound and Music in Film and Visual Media: An Overview*, ed. Graeme Harper (New York: Continuum Press, 2009), 456.
17 William Whittington, *Sound Design and Science Fiction* (Austin, TX: University of Texas Press, 2007), 7.
18 Jay Beck, *Designing Sound: Audiovisual Aesthetics in 1970s American Cinema* (New Brunswick, NJ: Rutgers University Press, 2016), 31–3.
19 Michel Chion, *Audio-Vision: Sound on Screen* (New York: Columbia University Press, 1994), 71.
20 Walter Murch, 'Introduction' in Michel Chion, *Audio-Vision: Sound on Screen* (New York: Columbia University Press, 1994), xix.
21 Chion, *Audio-Vision*, 63–4.
22 Walter Murch, *In the Blink of an Eye: A Perspective on Film Editing*, 2nd edition (Beverly Hills, CA: Silman-James Press, 2001), 18.
23 James Borgardt, Cliff Latimer, Jerry Ross, Tracy Smith and Karen Wilson are some of Murch's sound editors and assistants known personally to me.
24 Mike Alleyne, 'Sound Technology', in Harper, *Sound and Music*, 36–8.

25 James Lastra, *Sound Technology and the American Cinema: Perception, Representation, Modernity* (New York: Columbia University Press, 2000), 139.
26 Stephen Prince, *Digital Visual Effects in Cinema: The Seduction of Reality* (New Brunswick, NJ: Rutgers University Press, 2012), 135.
27 Julie A. Turnock, *Plastic Reality: Special Effects, Technology and the Emergence of 1970s Blockbuster Aesthetics* (New York: Columbia University Press, 2015), 122.

INDEX